Also by G. Scott Thomas

Sports
Cooperstown at the Crossroads
A Brand New Ballgame
The Best (and Worst) of Baseball's Modern Era
Leveling the Field

History
Presidential Election Record Book 2020
Counting the Votes
A New World to Be Won
Advice From the Presidents
The United States of Suburbia
The Pursuit of the White House

Demographics
Dreamtowns
Micropolitan America
The Rating Guide to Life in America's Fifty States
Where to Make Money
The Rating Guide to Life in America's Small Cities

BASEBALL'S BEST (AND WORST) 2023 YEARBOOK

BASEBALL'S BEST (AND WORST) 2023 YEARBOOK

G. Scott Thomas

NIAWANDA BOOKS

Baseball's Best (and Worst) 2023 Yearbook

Copyright © 2023 by G. Scott Thomas

All rights reserved. No part of this book may be reproduced, distributed, or transmitted in any form or by any means, including photocopying, recording, or other electronic or mechanical methods, without the prior written permission of the publisher, except in the case of brief quotations embodied in critical reviews and certain other noncommercial uses permitted by copyright law. For permission requests, write the publisher at the address below.

Niawanda Books
949 Delaware Road
Buffalo, NY 14223

Printed in the United States of America

First Edition
10 9 8 7 6 5 4 3 2 1

CONTENTS

Part 1: 2022 and 2023

The Stats 13

2022: Team Ratings 29

2022: Best Performances 53

2022: Worst Performances 77

2023: Predictions 99

Part 2: Team Profiles

Key to the Profiles 109

Arizona Diamondbacks 117

Atlanta Braves 127

Baltimore Orioles 137

Boston Red Sox 147

Chicago Cubs 157

Chicago White Sox 167

Cincinnati Reds 177

Cleveland Guardians 187

Colorado Rockies 197

Detroit Tigers 207

Houston Astros	217
Kansas City Royals	227
Los Angeles Angels	237
Los Angeles Dodgers	247
Miami Marlins	257
Milwaukee Brewers	267
Minnesota Twins	277
New York Mets	287
New York Yankees	297
Oakland Athletics	307
Philadelphia Phillies	317
Pittsburgh Pirates	327
St. Louis Cardinals	337
San Diego Padres	347
San Francisco Giants	357
Seattle Mariners	367
Tampa Bay Rays	377
Texas Rangers	387
Toronto Blue Jays	397
Washington Nationals	407

BASEBALL'S BEST (AND WORST) 2023 YEARBOOK

Part 1
2022 AND 2023

THE STATS

Doug Melvin put it best. "You can't win the game without moving the pieces on the board," said the former general manager of the Milwaukee Brewers and Texas Rangers. "It's all about capturing bases."

Melvin was voicing a concept that players, executives, and fans have understood since the sport's earliest days. The name of the game, after all, is *base*ball.

I've always found it strange that statisticians don't tally up the bases that batters reach and pitchers allow. They keep tabs on almost everything else—pitches, at-bats, innings pitched, runs, hits, errors, strikeouts, walks, and on and on. But not bases.

The only exception—and a partial one at that—is total bases, the collective stat for bases reached through singles, doubles, triples, and home runs. TB is accurate as far as it goes, yet it's a misnomer in the final analysis, since it ignores walks, hit batters, stolen bases, and other productive outcomes.

Several proposals have been advanced in recent decades to address this shortcoming, though their creators never seem to follow through. Their base-related ideas tend to sink without a trace.

I joined the parade in 2016, unveiling a pair of new statistics, BPO (bases per out) and BV (base value), in *The Best (and Worst) of Baseball's Modern Era*, a book about the period after 1960. That, in turn, led to *Baseball's Best (and Worst)*, an online newsletter that cites the same stats with regularity.

Which brings us to this book. I generate a wealth of data for my two weekly installments on the web, though only a small fraction of that material can ever be used. I calculate BPO for every batter in both leagues, for example, just so I can cite the very best (and worst) figures in an upcoming story. There's no room for the rest.

A book isn't saddled with the same limitations. *Baseball's Best (and Worst) 2023 Yearbook* contains all the necessary space for a wide range of statistics from the 2022 season, including BPO, BV, and several others that you won't find anywhere else. It also features a unique (though certainly not foolproof) system to predict 2023's standings.

If you're fascinated by statistics—and what baseball fan isn't?—the next 400 pages should fit your interests.

Counting the Bases

WE'VE REACHED THE POINT where we need to focus on mathematics for a few minutes. Why? Because the opening chapter is really the best place to explain the formulas that generate the stats that populate this book.

Our first building block is the simplest formula of all. It's a straightforward equation that adds six different factors to determine a player's number of bases:

$$B = TB + BB + HBP + SB + SH + SF$$

The formula starts with total bases, of course, but my aim is to go further, encompassing the other ways that a player can get on base or achieve an extra base for his team. That's why I've added walks, hit batters, stolen bases, sacrifice hits, and sacrifice flies. Every proposed formula that I've seen includes TB and BB. The remaining components vary in popularity, but I consider them all to be sensible and essential, so I've included them here.

Let's put the formula into action, comparing the 2022 stats for a couple of stars with different skills. Anthony Rizzo is a first baseman who flashed power last season for the New York Yankees (32 home runs), though his batting average was unimpressive (.224). Carlos Correa, a shortstop for the Minnesota Twins, didn't hit as many homers (22), but his average was much more respectable (.291). We'll calculate their base counts on the next page:

$$B = TB + BB + HBP + SB + SH + SF$$

$$\text{Rizzo} = 223 + 58 + 23 + 6 + 0 + 2 = 312$$

$$\text{Correa} = 244 + 61 + 3 + 0 + 0 + 4 = 312$$

It's a dead heat. Correa rapped 48 more hits than Rizzo (152 vs. 104), propelling him to a higher TB count (244 vs. 223). Correa also posted slight leads in walks and sacrifice flies, but Rizzo had a decisive edge in getting hit by pitches (23 vs. three) and a surprising advantage in stolen bases. The final result: 312 bases for each.

That's interesting as far as it goes, though it doesn't tell the whole story. Correa played six more games and made 42 more plate appearances than Rizzo in 2022. There are a couple of ways to statistically eliminate this disparity in playing time. We could divide bases by appearances, much as we divide hits by at-bats to determine a batting average. The other method—the one I've chosen—is to calculate a ratio between bases and outs.

That raises the obvious need to tally a batter's outs:

$$O = AB - H + CS + GDP + SH + SF$$

I begin by subtracting hits from at-bats, yielding the number of outs the batter made while swinging away. This figure will probably include a few occasions when he reached base because of a fielder's error. He ideally would have been out in those instances, so that's how he'll be credited. The same principle applies to batting averages.

I add the times when the player was caught stealing, created an additional out by hitting into a double play, laid down a sacrifice bunt, or rapped a sacrifice fly. The latter two factors are included in both of the formulas that I've described, since they involve the trade of an out for a base.

Back to our examples from 2022:

$$O = AB - H + CS + GDP + SH + SF$$

$$\text{Rizzo} = 465 - 104 + 5 + 13 + 0 + 2 = 381$$

$$\text{Correa} = 522 - 152 + 1 + 18 + 0 + 4 = 393$$

Correa's extra playing time translated into a larger number of outs, 393 vs. Rizzo's 381. We're now able to determine each batter's ratio of bases per out (BPO), using simple division:

$$BPO = B / O$$

$$\text{Rizzo} = 312 / 381 = .819$$

$$\text{Correa} = 312 / 393 = .794$$

Anthony Rizzo reached .819 bases for every out that he made in 2022, putting him slightly ahead of Carlos Correa's ratio of .794 bases per out. Correa's batting average may have been far better—67 points superior—but our BPO matchup makes it clear that Rizzo was a bit more productive at the plate last season.

A Second View

THE RIZZO/CORREA CASE may seem to be closed, but it isn't. A second stat—base value (BV)—offers another perspective.

It can be quickly and easily explained. BV is defined as the difference between the number of bases a player actually attained in a given season and the number he might have been expected to reach.

The latter element—the expected total of bases—is calculated by multiplying a batter's outs by the average BPO for all big leaguers in the same season. (The average for 2022 was .660. To be more precise: .660083.) The resulting product is the number of bases that a typical player would have attained with the same amount of playing time. This total is then subtracted from the given batter's real number of bases, and the answer is rounded to the nearest whole number:

$$BV = B - (O \cdot \text{MajorBPO})$$

$$\text{Rizzo} = 312 - (381 \cdot .660083) = 60.51 = 61$$

$$\text{Correa} = 312 - (393 \cdot .660083) = 52.59 = 53$$

Rizzo and Correa exceeded the major-league BPO of .660, which is why their base values are positive numbers. Both reached more bases than the typical player would have attained under the same circumstances. But Rizzo again had a slight edge, surpassing expectations by 61 bases, eight better than Correa.

Four Strengths

I HAVE NO QUIBBLE with sabermetricians. I've said frequently that I find their work to be stimulating. I'm fascinated by the thinking behind WAR and wRC+ and BABIP and UZR and the other measures they have devised. There is no denying that they have had a strong, positive impact on the game of baseball.

But I'm also aware that some sabermetricians disapprove of base/out averages such as BPO and BV. Brandon Heipp advanced their key objections in a 2008 article in *The Hardball Times:* "First, the idea of a base-to-out or PA ratio appeals to a lot of baseball observers, but inevitably fails to gain traction in the sabermetric community and, second, there is absolutely no need for any more metrics of this family to be 'invented.'"

I disagree. BPO and BV, as I see it, have four strengths. Let me summarize them.

1. They're easy to calculate and understand.

Take a player's number of bases. Divide it by his number of outs. That's his BPO. Couldn't be easier. The formula for BV is equally straightforward.

And there's no doubt about what these numbers mean. Bases per out—the name is self-explanatory.

Compare it to OPS, the sport's current darling. Its benign abbreviation hides a clunky name—on-base-plus-slugging—and an illogical formula. OPS is calculated by adding a player's on-base percentage and slugging average, a dubious concept at best. The two components of OPS have wildly different ceilings (1.000 for OBP and 4.000 for SA), so it makes no sense to assign equal weight to both. They also have different denominators (the sum of AB, BB, HBP and SF for OBP, only AB for SA), and any sixth grader knows that you can't add fractions unless their denominators are the same.

A batting average of .300 means that a batter gets three hits in every 10 at-bats. A BPO of .700 equals seven-tenths of a base per out. But what does an OPS of .800 mean? Absolutely nothing. It doesn't translate to anything.

2. They measure all aspects of a batter's performance.

Scouts refer to the perfect prospect as a five-tool player. This ideal athlete is somebody who can hit for average, hit for power, run the bases with skill and speed, throw accurately, and field his position well.

Most baseball statistics measure only one of these characteristics. Among the obvious examples are hits, batting average, home runs, slugging percentage, and stolen bases. But BPO and BV encompass all three batting tools. Every hit or stolen base increases a batter's number of bases, with homers and other extra base hits providing the biggest boost.

I acknowledge the importance of the latter two of the five tools. Throwing and fielding aren't always given the emphasis they deserve, an oversight that might be rectified as sabermetricians continue to devise better ways to quantify their impact. But it's a simple fact that we judge non-pitchers primarily by their ability at the plate. Ty Cobb, Babe Ruth, and Ted Williams aren't in the Hall of Fame because of their ability to hit the cutoff man. Harmon Killebrew and Frank Thomas didn't join them in Cooperstown because they were dazzling infielders. The dominant skills of these all-time greats—and almost all present-day batters—are best expressed by BPO and BV.

3. They apply equally to batters and pitchers.

The same BPO and BV formulas that we use for batters can also be used for pitchers. Just keep one important point in mind: The scale of excellence is reversed. A batter wants to drive his BPO as high as possible and his BV deep into positive territory. A pitcher wants to head in the opposite direction, getting his BPO as low as he can and his BV into negative digits.

That makes sense. A pitcher's job, after all, is to keep runners off the basepaths. The lower his BPO and BV, the better his performance.

Seven pitchers started at least nine games for the Atlanta Braves in 2022. The table atop the next page gives their statistics for the year (encompassing starts and relief appearances), ranked according to earned run average:

Pitcher	G	GS	IP	B	O	BPO	BV	ERA
Max Fried	30	30	185.1	265	560	.473	-105	2.48
Spencer Strider	31	20	131.2	180	398	.452	-83	2.67
Bryce Elder	10	9	54.0	101	163	.620	-7	3.17
Kyle Wright	30	30	180.1	304	546	.557	-56	3.19
Charlie Morton	31	31	172.0	361	514	.702	22	4.34
Ian Anderson	22	22	111.2	239	335	.713	18	5.00
Jake Odorizzi	10	10	46.1	114	140	.814	22	5.24

Note how nicely BPO tracks with ERA—not perfectly, but very closely. Max Fried posted the best ERA among Atlanta's starters, with Spencer Strider a close runner-up. They flipped places in the BPO column: Strider first and Fried second. Jake Odorizzi ranked last in both categories.

This table also demonstrates the separate importance of base value. Strider's BPO was lower, but Fried shouldered a heavier workload, almost 54 innings more. Fried's total contribution was greater, which is why he finished the season with a better BV (minus-105 vs. Strider's minus-83). Three Atlanta starters surrendered more bases than the major-league average. The worst base values were plus-22 for Odorizzi and Charlie Morton.

We're accustomed to single-duty stats—BA for batters, ERA for pitchers—so the switch-hitting role for BPO and BV is a bit unusual. But it's also remarkably convenient to be able to measure all players against the same benchmark.

4. They're closely linked to the odds of victory.

Perhaps the greatest strength of base-related stats is their tight correlation with winning. And winning, need we say, is what baseball is all about.

I crunched the numbers for all 112,821 major-league games between 1961 and 2014, searching for the best predictors of team success. I reported my findings in 2016, and the results were so emphatic that I see no need to update them.

My first focus was on 11 counting statistics—eight for batting, two for pitching, and one for fielding. I compared the better team in each category with the team that won the game. ("Better" means exactly what you think it does—more bases and hits by batters, fewer walks by pitchers, fewer errors in the field, and so on.)

The best predictor, of course, was runs. The team that scored the most runs won every single game. Quite the coincidence, don't you think?

Bases finished second on the list. The winning team accumulated more bases than the losing squad in 81.8 percent of all games. No other counting stat topped 77 percent as a predictor, and most were below 65 percent. Four of them, including home runs, actually dropped beneath the 50-50 line in terms of predictive value:

Counting Stat	Winning Team Better (W)	Losing Team Better (L)	Both Teams Same (S)	W%	L%	S%
R (bat)	112,821	0	0	100.0%	0.0%	0.0%
B (bat)	92,249	16,020	4,552	81.8%	14.2%	4.0%
TB (bat)	86,630	20,217	5,974	76.8%	17.9%	5.3%
H (bat)	80,244	22,168	10,409	71.1%	19.6%	9.2%
XH (bat)	71,171	21,803	19,847	63.1%	19.3%	17.6%
BB (pitch)	63,236	33,271	16,314	56.0%	29.5%	14.5%
SO (pitch)	57,107	43,014	12,700	50.6%	38.1%	11.3%
HR (bat)	53,775	19,668	39,378	47.7%	17.4%	34.9%
E (field)	45,526	25,744	41,551	40.4%	22.8%	36.8%
LOB (bat)	44,840	55,344	12,637	39.7%	49.1%	11.2%
SB (bat)	41,487	23,108	48,226	36.8%	20.5%	42.7%

My next move was to compute averages for both teams in each game, once again comparing the statistical results with the final outcome. Every average was solely for the game in question. If a team got 11 hits in 37 at-bats, for example, its BA for the game was .297. There were eight sets of averages in all—five for batters, two for pitchers, one for fielders.

Earned run average topped the rankings. The team with the lowest ERA won 93.7 percent of the 112,821 games. No big shock there.

A base-related stat again was the runner-up, as the team with the better BPO emerged victorious 86.1 percent of the time. All other averages trailed in importance, even the venerated OPS, which connected with 84.9 percent of the winners. Check out the chart on the next page:

Average	Winning Team Better (W)	Losing Team Better (L)	Both Teams Same (S)	W%	L%	S%
ERA (pitch)	105,726	3,609	3,486	93.7%	3.2%	3.1%
BPO (hit)	97,152	14,715	954	86.1%	13.0%	0.8%
OPS (hit)	95,789	17,014	18	84.9%	15.1%	0.0%
SA (hit)	91,888	20,072	861	81.4%	17.8%	0.8%
WHIP (pitch)	91,480	17,593	3,748	81.1%	15.6%	3.3%
OBP (hit)	91,350	20,183	1,288	81.0%	17.9%	1.1%
BA (hit)	89,091	22,229	1,501	79.0%	19.7%	1.3%
FLD% (field)	54,149	30,307	28,365	48.0%	26.9%	25.1%

We've always lacked a simple all-purpose stat that simultaneously measures the run-generating ability of batters and run-prevention skills of pitchers. It's true that sabermetricians have devised complex systems to serve this purpose, such as linear weights and wRC+. These advanced metrics are logically and cleverly constructed, and they yield plausible results. But they fall short of the first strength I mentioned a few pages ago. They are not easy to calculate and understand. So, despite their many attributes, they are unlikely to gain wide circulation.

I have been pushing BPO and BV since 2016 as the logical candidates to fill this void. They're the tools that will be used throughout this book to identify 2022's best and worst teams and individual performances.

Three More Items

THREE HOUSEKEEPING DETAILS REQUIRE our attention before this chapter runs its course.

An important acknowledgment first. I dredged information for *Baseball's Best (and Worst) 2023 Yearbook* from several reputable sources, including newspapers, books, and websites. But the most important source—by far—was Baseball Reference, the amazing online compendium of statistics for every player, every manager, every team, and every season in big-league history. Baseball Reference doesn't offer the stats that I've originated—BPO, BV, and the like—but it did provide the raw data that I used to calculate them. It truly is the sport's statistical oracle.

It should also be noted that this book contains other unique statistics, many of which follow the BPO/BV model. I'll explain them when the time comes, rather than extending this chapter unnecessarily.

The final matter involves abbreviations. You're a baseball fan, so I'm sure you're familiar with the game's standard abbreviations. I've included them in the following list anyway, along with citations for new statistics that are introduced in this book and a few terms that require elaboration.

2B: Doubles.

3B: Triples.

AB: At-bats.

Attendance: Home attendance for a season.

Att:W: Attendance-win ratio. It's the quotient of a team's home attendance divided by its seasonal total of wins.

B: Bases. It's the sum of total bases (bases reached by hits), walks, hit batters, stolen bases, sacrifice hits, and sacrifice flies.

BA: Batting average.

BB: Walks.

BBV: Walk value. It's the difference between (1) the actual number of walks a batter obtained and the number he might have been expected to get, or (2) the actual number of walks that a pitcher allowed and the number he might have been expected to yield. (See BV.)

BP: Balls in play. It's the number of at-bats that did not result in strikeouts.

BPO: Bases per out. It's the quotient of bases divided by outs.

BPO-R: Bases per out allowed by a relief pitcher.

BPO-S: Bases per out allowed by a starting pitcher.

BPV: Ball in play value. It's the difference between (1) the actual number of balls in play that a batter hit and the number he might have been expected to hit, or (2) the actual number of balls in play that a pitcher yielded and the number he might have been expected to allow. (See BV.)

BR: Baserunners.

BV: Base value. This formula determines the difference between (1) the actual number of bases that a batter reached and the number he might have been expected to attain, or (2) the actual number of bases that a pitcher allowed and the number he might have been expected to yield. The expectation is calculated by multiplying the average BPO for all major-leaguers by the number of outs made by a given batter or induced by a given pitcher. BV is often followed by the bracketed clarification of "[bat]" or "[pitch]." Similar stats in this book, all carrying titles that end with the word value, are calculated in similar fashion.

CM: Closest matches. These are the teams from the free-agency period (1976-2020) that most closely resembled a current club. Matches are determined by comparing team scores for past and current clubs over periods of three years. (See TS. A club from 1980, for example, would be scored from 1978 through 1980. A current team would be scored from 2020 through 2022.) TS comparisons are weighted on a 3-2-1 basis, assigning the heaviest weight to the most recent seasons.

CS: Times caught stealing.

CT: Contact rate. It's calculated in two steps: (1) subtracting strikeouts from at-bats, (2) dividing that number by at-bats.

Div: Division.

E: Errors.

ER: Earned runs.

ERA: Earned run average.

ERA-R: Earned run average for a relief pitcher.

ERA-S: Earned run average for a starting pitcher.

ERV: Earned run value. It's the difference between the actual number of earned runs a pitcher allowed and the number he might have been expected to yield. (See BV.)

EY: Batting eye rate. It's calculated in three steps: (1) subtracting intentional walks from total walks, (2) subtracting intentional walks from plate appearances, (3) dividing the number from Step 1 by the number from Step 2.

FLD%: Fielding percentage. It's calculated in three steps: (1) adding putouts and assists, (2) adding putouts, assists, and errors, (3) dividing the number from Step 1 by the number from Step 2.

FSI: Fan support index. It's calculated this way: (1) dividing a team's attendance-win ratio (Att:W) by the average ratio for all major-league teams in the same season, (2) multiplying the result by 100.

G: Games.

GDP: Times grounded into double plays.

GR: Games relieved.

GS: Games started.

GShr: Game share. It's the percentage of a team's total games that fit into a specific category.

H: Hits.

HBP: Times hit by a pitch, also known as hit batters or hit batsmen.

HR: Home runs.

IBB: Intentional walks.

IP: Innings pitched.

ISO: Isolated power average. It's calculated in two steps: (1) adding a batter's extra bases, with one for each double, two for each triple, and three for each home run, (2) dividing that number by his at-bats. The same stat can be calculated for the extra bases yielded by pitchers.

L: Losses.

LC: Number of league championships.

Lg: League.

LOB: Runners left on base.

MajorBPO: Average bases per out for all major leaguers in a given season. ("Major" serves a similar purpose as a prefix before any stat.)

ME%: The percentage of clubs in the Modern Era (1961-2022) that a given team outranked in team score. (See TS.) Team scores are calculated to allow direct comparisons of clubs from different years. A total of 1,656 big-league teams competed in the era's 62 seasons.

MLB: Major League Baseball.

Next: The season immediately following a designated three-year period in a list of closest matches.

O: Outs. It's calculated in two steps: (1) subtracting hits from at-bats, (2) adding the number from Step 1 to the sum of double plays, caught stealings, sacrifice hits, and sacrifice flies.

OBP: On-base percentage. It's calculated in three steps: (1) adding hits, walks, and hit batters, (2) adding at-bats, walks, hit batters, and sacrifice flies, (3) dividing the number from Step 1 by the number from Step 2.

OBV: Overall base value. It's calculated by subtracting pitching base value from batting base value. Why subtraction? A positive BV is a batter's target, while a negative BV is a pitcher's goal. Subtracting a negative number converts it into a positive numeral. A positive OBV is the aim for any team or player.

OPS: On-base-plus-slugging. It's the sum of on-base percentage and slugging average.

PA: Plate appearances.

PA-IBB: Plate appearances minus intentional walks.

Pct.: Winning percentage.

Post: Postseason results, with P for any team that reached the playoffs, LP for any team that won its league title, and WLP for any team that won the World Series.

PQ: Number of teams qualifying for the playoffs.

R: Runs scored.

R/G: Runs scored per game.

RA: Runs allowed.

RA/G: Runs allowed per game.

Rating: A five-star system that denotes performances as excellent (★★★★★), above average (★★★★), average (★★★), below average (★★), or poor (★).

RBI: Runs batted in.

SA: Slugging average. It's the quotient of total bases divided by at-bats. (See TB.)

SB: Stolen bases.

SC: Scoring. It's calculated in two steps: (1) adding runs and runs batted in, (2) subtracting home runs from that number. Sabermetricians will hate this stat. They will say—correctly—that it doesn't give credit to everybody who helps to produce a run. Consider this example involving the New York Yankees: DJ LeMahieu gets hit by a pitch, Aaron Judge doubles him to third base, and Anthony Rizzo drives in the run with a weak infield squib. Both LeMahieu and Rizzo get credit in the SC column, while Judge, the man who made the key hit, gets nothing. That's unfortunate, but there are parallels in most sports. Football, basketball, and hockey statisticians tally touchdowns, baskets, and goals respectively, without concern for the lineman who makes a key block, the forward who zips an effective outlet pass, or the goalie who triggers a breakaway.

SCV: Scoring value. It's the difference between the scoring total (SC) a batter attained and the total he might have been expected to get. (See BV.)

SE: Scoring efficiency rate. It's the quotient of scoring (SC) divided by plate appearances.

SF: Sacrifice flies.

SH: Sacrifice hits.

SO: Strikeouts.

SV: Saves.

TB: Total bases. It's the confusing name for a stat that counts only the bases reached by hits. (Not the same thing as the earlier entry for B.)

Top Match: The team from the free-agency period (1976-2020) that most closely resembled a current club.

TS: Team score. It's the measure of the relative excellence of a given team in a given season, as expressed on a 100-point scale. The formula gives equal weight to four factors: winning percentage, the differential between runs scored and allowed per game, the differential between BPO produced and BPO allowed, and postseason success. The score for each of the first three factors is based on a comparison of the team's number and the respective category's leaguewide average and standard deviation for that year. The fourth category gives 25 points to any World Series champion and 20 points to any league champion that lost the World Series. Any other team receives a bonus from 0 to 15 points, based on its regular-season record. The four category scores are added to yield the team score. The formula effectively equalizes a club's TS, making it an excellent indicator of a team's relative strength—and allowing direct comparisons of clubs from different years.

UBB: Unintentional walks. It's the result when intentional walks are subtracted from the total number of walks.

W: Wins.

WHIP: Walks and hits allowed per inning pitched.

WS: Number of World Series championships.

WShr: Win share. It's the percentage of a team's total wins that fit into a specific category.

XB: Extra bases. It's the total number of bases reached by hits, excluding first base. A double is worth one extra base, a triple two, and a home run three.

XH: Extra base hits. It's the sum of doubles, triples, and home runs. Not the bases reached, just the number of such hits.

XV: Extra base value. It's the difference between (1) the actual number of extra bases a batter reached and the number he might have been expected to attain, or (2) the actual number of extra bases that a pitcher yielded and the number he might have been expected to allow. (See BV.)

2022: TEAM RATINGS

THE HOUSTON ASTROS WERE the best team in the major leagues in 2022.

That certainly shouldn't come as a shock. We all watched the Astros pile up 106 victories in the regular season, run away with the American League West by a 16-game margin, and sweep to a world championship by winning all but two of their 13 playoff games. Everybody was aware that they were a dominant force.

But I base my assertion on three different sets of data that are addressed in this chapter:

- Houston finished 2022 with a team score of 87.893 points, nearly nine points better than the runner-up Los Angeles Dodgers. It was the 10th-best TS recorded by any club in the Modern Era, which dates back to 1961.
- The Astros employed the stingiest staff in the majors last season, surrendering 475 fewer bases than the big-league average. They ranked first among the 30 clubs in base value for pitchers, earning the ultimate honor of five stars on this book's evaluation scale.
- Houston also received five-star ratings for another pair of key indicators: overall base value and base value for batters. Only three of the remaining 29 teams—the Dodgers, Atlanta Braves, and New York Yankees—received the full complement of five stars for OBV, BV [bat], and BV [pitch].

There's a lot to explain. Let me start with team score.

If you browsed through the abbreviation section in the previous chapter, you encountered a lengthy entry for TS. It explained that team score is a measure of the relative excellence of a given team in a given season, as expressed on a 100-point scale. The formula gives equal weight to four factors: winning percentage, the differential between runs scored and allowed per game, the differential between BPO produced and BPO allowed, and postseason success.

I'm not going to delve too heavily into the mechanics. Suffice it to say that I used basic statistical tools—standard deviations and z-scores—to determine each club's team score. The TS formula compares each team's numbers to the norms for its league in a given season, effectively equalizing scores across time. That allows us to make direct comparisons of clubs from different years. The 1990 Toronto Blue Jays, 2003 Philadelphia Phillies, and 2016 Seattle Mariners all finished with 86-76 records, but we can say with confidence that the Jays (TS of 60.794) were considerably better than the Phils (55.176) or M's (52.729).

The five-star ratings are something different. I generated 11 separate values for each club, highlighting various aspects of its 2022 performance. Each value was calculated in a similar fashion to BV, a process that was explained in the previous chapter. And each has a similar intent, indicating whether the team produced/allowed more or less of a particular stat than the big-average average.

A team's rating in a given category was based on its relative position in the standings. I used z-scores, which won't (and shouldn't) matter to most readers. If you care, the following table shows the ranges I chose:

Z-Score Range	Performance Level	Rating
0.90 or higher	Excellent	★★★★★
0.25 to 0.89	Above average	★★★★
-0.24 to 0.24	Average	★★★
-0.89 to -0.25	Below average	★★
-0.90 or lower	Poor	★

My system resulted in a fairly even distribution of ratings. No more than seven teams—and no fewer than five—reached the top level in any category. The average list featured 6.18 five-star and 6.00 one-star ratings. The most common score was right in the middle, with an average of 6.55 clubs at the three-star level.

The last set of rankings in this chapter has nothing to do with on-field performance. It measures the level of fan support for each club, based on a comparison of win-loss record and home attendance. I'll explain further when we get there.

The Categories

THE FINAL PORTION OF this chapter presents 2022's team ratings in a series of 13 top-to-bottom tables. Let's hit the highlights before you flip ahead a few pages and dive into the numbers.

Standings

Four teams won more than 100 games during 2022's regular season, and all four ranked among the top 15 percent of the Modern Era's 1,656 big-league clubs, spanning the period from 1961 through 2022.

The Astros, as we've already seen, posted the year's highest team score, 87.893 on the 100-point scale. The other franchises to reach triple digits in the victory column were the Dodgers (111 wins, second in TS at 78.998), Braves (101, fourth at 66.029), and New York Mets (101, fifth at 63.991). Sandwiched in their midst were the 99-win Yankees, whose team score of 72.714 ranked third for the year.

Houston's 2022 score was the 10th-best for the entire 62-year period, outperforming 99.5 percent of the era's other 1,655 teams. These were the percentiles (designated as ME% in the corresponding table) for the remainder of the year's top five: the Dodgers at 96.9 percent, Yankees at 93.1 percent, Braves at 87.8 percent, and Mets at 85.0 percent.

The National League champion Philadelphia Phillies finished sixth in the year's TS standings with a score of 63.652 points. The Phils notched only 87 wins in the regular season, barely squeaking into the NL's final playoff spot before catching fire in the playoffs.

At the opposite end of the scale were four 2022 clubs that played worse than at least 90 percent of all Modern Era teams: the Pittsburgh Pirates (with an ME% of 10.0 percent), Kansas City Royals (9.6 percent), Washington Nationals (4.5 percent), and Oakland Athletics (4.0 percent).

Overall Performance

The Dodgers outpointed the Astros—and every other team—in one key measure of team achievement in 2022. Their overall base value (OBV) of 904 was by far the best in the majors.

OBV combines a club's separate base values for batters and pitchers, resulting in an effective measure of overall performance.

But it's not a simple merger. You'll recall that batters aim for a positive BV, while pitchers strive for a negative number. If we were to combine the marks for a strong team like the Dodgers, the two values would essentially cancel each other out, yielding an OBV in the vicinity of zero.

That's why the sign in front of the BV for pitchers is reversed when OBV is calculated. Negative becomes positive, and vice versa. We achieve this effect with a simple subtraction:

OBV = BV [bat] − BV [pitch]

Dodgers = 441 − (−463) = 904

Subtracting a negative number, as any middle schooler can tell you, is the same as adding its positive value. The Dodgers' hitters topped the majors in 2022 with their BV [bat] of 441. Their pitchers finished second to Houston with a BV [pitch] of minus-463. The formula essentially tells us to add 441 and 463, yielding an outstanding OBV of 904.

The higher its overall base value, the higher the combined potency of a club's base production and prevention. Joining the Dodgers with five-star ratings in this category were the Astros (OBV of 679), Yankees (674), Braves (538), and Mets (376).

Here's how the formula works for a team that's weak in both aspects of the game, such as the Washington Nationals:

OBV = BV [bat] − BV [pitch]

Nationals = (−161) − 486 = (−647)

The Nats were underwater on both sides of the equation. Their batters fell 161 bases below expectations, while their pitchers surrendered 486 bases more than average. The result was the worst OBV in 2022: minus-647.

The big-league average is always zero for any of the value calculations in this chapter, whether for OBV, BV, or the related stats that will be unveiled below. A positive number for OBV or any of the five batting values is, by definition, better than the norm for all 30 clubs. The same is true for a negative number for any of the five pitching values. This simple rule of thumb, in combination with the five-star ratings, allows you to make a quick assessment of each team's strengths and weaknesses.

Base Production

The previous chapter offered a detailed explanation of bases per out (BPO), the comprehensive stat that encompasses a batter's abilities to hit for average, hit for power, and reach base in any way possible.

The big-league average for BPO, in turn, is a factor in determining a club's base value for batters. Let me restate the formula, followed by the calculations for the best and worst performers in 2022:

$$BV\ [bat] = B - (\ O \cdot MajorBPO\ )$$

$$Dodgers = 3{,}258 - (\ 4{,}267 \cdot .660083\ ) = 441.43 = 441$$

$$Tigers = 2{,}398 - (\ 4{,}324 \cdot .660083\ ) = (-456.20) = (-456)$$

Our previous discussion of OBV noted that the Dodgers topped the BV [bat] standings with a value of 441, which means they reached 441 more bases than the typical club would have accumulated under the same circumstances. The Detroit Tigers, on the other hand, finished last. Their batters fell 456 bases short of the big-league average for 2022.

Run Production

Other sports keep track of individual scoring. Football tallies the points that each player scores by touchdowns and placekicks. Basketball adds baskets and free throws. Hockey does the same thing with goals and assists.

But not baseball. This books tries to redress the balance by adding runs scored and runs batted in, then subtracting home runs, since an HR counts in both the R and RBI columns. The result is a player's scoring total, abbreviated as SC.

This category calculates the scoring total for each club as a whole, and then converts it to a scoring value (SCV). The two-step approach is identical to the one described for BPO and BV in the previous chapter.

The first move is to determine a ratio, known in this case as the scoring efficiency rate (SE). It relates SC to a team's number of plate appearances. Underneath the formula are calculations for the Dodgers and Athletics. Los Angeles finished 2022 with 847 runs, 812 RBIs, and 212 homers, yielding an SC total of 1,447. The corresponding figures for Oakland were 568 runs, 537 RBIs, and 137 homers, resulting in an SC of 968:

SE = SC / PA

Dodgers = 1,447 / 6,247 = .232

Athletics = 968 / 5,863 = .165

We then use the major-league SE of .194950 to determine each club's scoring value. You'll notice that the SCV formula bears a strong resemblance to its BV forerunner. Here it is, along with the calculations for Los Angeles and Oakland:

SCV = SC - (PA • MajorSE)

Dodgers = 1,447 – (6,247 • .194950) = 229.15 = 229

Athletics = 968 – (5,863 • .194950) = (-174.99) = (-175)

The Dodgers, as you might have guessed, topped the majors in run production, while the A's finished last. The SCV for Los Angeles was 229 above the big-league average for 2022, while the value for Oakland was deficient by 175.

I went to this length with the mathematics for SE and SCV to demonstrate the common traits of all value calculations, highlighting their similarities to the BPO and BV formulas. The point has now been sufficiently made. Subsequent summaries in this chapter will be more direct and much briefer. If you want details about a particular formula, flip back to the appropriate listing in the abbreviations section of the first chapter.

Power Hitting

The Atlanta Braves accumulated 1,049 extra bases through hits in 2022. That total doesn't include any trips to first base—no singles and no initial bases touched on doubles, triples, and home runs.

The important word in this category is the adjective *extra*. A batter is credited with one XB for each double, two for each triple, and three for each homer.

The resulting value, XV, is an ideal indicator of power production. It tells us that Atlanta's total of extra bases was 211 higher than expected, the best performance by any club in this category. Six other teams were awarded five stars for power: the Dodgers (XV of 182), Yankees (178), Astros (129), Milwaukee Brewers (118), and Phillies (92).

Six clubs, on the other hand, suffered severe power shortages, as indicated by their one-star ratings. The Tigers finished dead last with an XV of minus-199.

Contact Hitting

No 2022 team was better than the Guardians at putting the bat on the ball. Cleveland led the majors in balls in play (4,436), contact rate (.798), and ball in play value, abbreviated as BPV (plus-266).

Contact rate (CT) is defined as the percentage of at-bats that don't culminate in strikeouts. Cleveland's CT of .798 translated to a strikeout rate of 20.2 percent. The typical big-league team posted a CT of .750 last season, indicating that its batters struck out in a quarter of all at-bats.

Hitters for the Guardians suffered 266 fewer strikeouts than average, which means they put 266 more balls in play. Hence their BPV.

Six other clubs finished with values higher than 130. All received five-star ratings. The Los Angeles Angels were the worst team for contact hitting, as reflected in their unhappy BPV of minus-185.

Batting Eye

Batting eye rate (EY) is calculated by tallying the unintentional walks a hitter draws, then dividing that figure by his number of plate appearances minus all intentional walks. EY serves as a strong indicator of a batter's knowledge of the strike zone and his ability to work pitchers for walks.

Three clubs rose to the top of this category in 2022. The New York Yankees and Seattle Mariners tied for the EY lead at .095, well above the big-league average of .079. And the Los Angeles Dodgers drew the most unintentional walks, 585, one more than the Yanks did.

New York eked out a narrow win in the value calculations for this category. Batters for the Yankees drew 98 walks more than expected, taking first place in walk value (BBV). The Mariners (BBV of 96) and Dodgers (92) were close behind.

The Chicago White Sox seemed to have the worst comprehension of the strike zone. Their batters posted an anemic BBV of minus-105.

Base Prevention

The ratio of bases per out (BPO) is an ideal measure of a batter's skill, and it's an equally effective gauge of a pitcher's performance. The only difference, of course, is that a hitter aims for the highest BPO, while a pitcher wants to drive his number as low as possible.

No club was more effective in the latter pursuit than the Astros. Houston's pitchers surrendered just .551 bases per out in 2022, the lowest (and best) ratio for any club.

Last season's big-league average BPO, as we already know, was .660. If Houston's pitchers had matched that norm, they would have yielded 2,871 bases. They actually allowed only 2,396, which gave them a BV [pitch] of minus-475, also the best in the majors.

The Dodgers were close behind at minus-463. Four other staffs earned five stars on the rating scale for base prevention: the Yankees (BV of minus-370), Atlanta Braves (minus-264), Tampa Bay Rays (minus-231), and Cleveland Guardians (minus-222).

At the opposite end of the standings were three teams that surrendered at least 425 bases more than average: the Cincinnati Reds, Colorado Rockies, and Washington Nationals. The latter finished at the very bottom with an astronomical BV of plus-486.

Run Prevention

Perhaps a more precise title for this category would be *earned* run prevention. It compares the number of earned runs a team allowed and the big-league average for the same span of innings pitched.

The Dodgers were the stingiest in that regard in 2022. Their earned run average of 2.80 was the lowest in the majors. The Astros, at 2.90, had the only other mark under 3.30. The ERA for all pitchers in both leagues was 3.96.

A typical staff would have allowed 639 runs across the plate during the 1,451.1 innings that the Dodgers spent in the field. But Los Angeles kept its total down to 451, pegging its earned run value (ERV) at minus-188. The Astros came next at minus-171, followed by the other four clubs that previously received five stars for base prevention.

Washington and Colorado were the only teams to soar as high as 5.00 in ERA, and also the only ones with earned run values above plus-150. The Rockies were the very worst at plus-175.

Power Prevention

We've already sung the praises of Houston's pitchers. They were unexcelled at base prevention in 2022 and a close runner-up in run prevention.

Here's another of their strengths. They were unusually good at keeping the ball inside the fences. The Astros gave up 134 homers last season—second-fewest to San Francisco's 132—and they were easily the best at dampening opponents' power. Batters reached only 638 extra bases against Houston. Every other club allowed at least 694. (Keep in mind that each double translates to one extra base, each triple to two, and each home run to three.)

The resulting extra base value (XV) for Houston was minus-168. The Braves finished second at minus-130.

The unfortunate Nationals again brought up the rear. Washington surrendered 1,029 extra bases in 2022, giving it an XV of plus-189.

Strikeout Pitching

The New York Mets were blessed with a fireballing staff in 2022. Eight of their pitchers worked at least 50 innings and averaged at least nine strikeouts per complete game, led by a pair of former Cy Young Award winners, Jacob deGrom (14.3 SO per nine innings) and Max Scherzer (10.7 SO per nine).

So it's no surprise to find at Mets at the top of the rankings for strikeout pitching, as determined by ball in play value, BPV [pitch].

Opponents made contact at a rate of .711 against the Mets last season, well under the big-league norm of .750. The number of balls in play allowed by New York's pitchers was 215 below average, as indicated by the club's BPV of minus-215, the best for any staff. Atlanta (minus-203) and Houston (minus-202) were nearly as good.

The Colorado Rockies definitely lacked a strikeout punch in 2022. They ranked worst in the majors in three related stats: the highest number of balls in play allowed (4,382), the highest contact rate (.787), and the highest BPV (plus-203).

Control Pitching

Tampa Bay's pitchers kept the ball in or close to the strike zone in 2022. That doesn't mean they struck out opposing hitters at a high rate—the Rays earned only three stars for strikeout pitching—but it does mean that they exhibited exceptional control.

No team issued fewer unintentional walks in 2022 than Tampa Bay's 369, no club allowed a smaller batting eye rate (EY) than the Rays' .062, and none had a lower (and hence better) walk value than Tampa Bay's minus-99.

The two runners-up, the Dodgers and Toronto Blue Jays, finished well off the pace with identical BBV [pitch] scores of minus-69. The Cincinnati Reds brought up the rear at plus-100, which means they issued precisely 100 more unintentional walks than the major-league average.

Fan Support Index

Let's head into the grandstands for the final set of ratings. The fan support index (FSI) tracks the annual relationship between a team's attendance and its victory total. It separates the baseball hotbeds from the places that can either take the sport or leave it.

FSI is calculated in these steps:

• A team's home attendance for a given season is divided by its number of victories, both home and road, yielding an Att:W ratio that is rounded to the nearest whole number.

- The team's Att:W is divided by the rounded big-league Att:W for the same season. The latter was 26,567 for 2022, based on total attendance of 64,556,678 for 2,430 games.
- The result is multiplied by 100.

Here's the formula, along with a couple of extreme examples that show FSI in action:

FSI = 100 • ((Attendance / W) / MajorAtt:W)

Rockies = 100 • (2,597,428 / 68) / 26,567 = 143.8

Rays = 100 • (1,128,127 / 86) / 26,567 = 49.4

FSI, as you can see, is designed to quantify a franchise's relative level of fan enthusiasm. A score of 100 indicates support that is commensurate with a team's quality on the field. A higher number suggests unusual box-office strength, as in Colorado, where a 68-win team still managed to draw nearly 2.6 million fans in 2022. A two-digit FSI (yes, that's you, Tampa Bay) is a sign of lethargy.

The largest attendance doesn't automatically bring the FSI crown for a given season. The key is to draw bigger crowds than a team's win-loss record might lead you to expect. Colorado indeed finished first in 2022's fan support standings, while Tampa Bay tied for last place with Oakland.

The 2022 Ratings

Standings (2022)

Rank	Team	Division	W	L	Pct.	Post	TS	ME%
1	Houston Astros	AL West	106	56	.654	WLP	87.893	99.5%
2	Los Angeles Dodgers	NL West	111	51	.685	P	78.998	96.9%
3	New York Yankees	AL East	99	63	.611	P	72.714	93.1%
4	Atlanta Braves	NL East	101	61	.623	P	66.029	87.8%
5	New York Mets	NL East	101	61	.623	P	63.991	85.0%
6	Philadelphia Phillies	NL East	87	75	.537	LP	63.652	84.7%
7	St. Louis Cardinals	NL Central	93	69	.574	P	59.061	76.9%
8	Toronto Blue Jays	AL East	92	70	.568	P	58.043	75.5%
9	Cleveland Guardians	AL Central	92	70	.568	P	56.219	72.3%
10	Seattle Mariners	AL West	90	72	.556	P	54.850	68.3%
11	San Diego Padres	NL West	89	73	.549	P	51.860	62.2%
12	Tampa Bay Rays	AL East	86	76	.531	P	51.731	61.8%
13	Milwaukee Brewers	NL Central	86	76	.531		51.203	60.1%
14	San Francisco Giants	NL West	81	81	.500		47.298	52.3%
15	Baltimore Orioles	AL East	83	79	.512		45.422	48.9%
16	Minnesota Twins	AL Central	78	84	.481		44.243	46.5%
17	Chicago White Sox	AL Central	81	81	.500		42.539	43.1%
18	Arizona Diamondbacks	NL West	74	88	.457		39.806	36.9%
19	Boston Red Sox	AL East	78	84	.481		39.805	36.8%
20	Los Angeles Angels	AL West	73	89	.451		38.838	34.7%
21	Chicago Cubs	NL Central	74	88	.457		38.643	34.5%
22	Texas Rangers	AL West	68	94	.420		34.910	26.9%
23	Miami Marlins	NL East	69	93	.426		34.066	26.0%
24	Colorado Rockies	NL West	68	94	.420		29.455	17.9%
25	Detroit Tigers	AL Central	66	96	.407		25.392	10.6%
26	Cincinnati Reds	NL Central	62	100	.383		25.242	10.2%
27	Pittsburgh Pirates	NL Central	62	100	.383		25.094	10.0%
28	Kansas City Royals	AL Central	65	97	.401		24.678	9.6%
29	Washington Nationals	NL East	55	107	.340		19.213	4.5%
30	Oakland Athletics	AL West	60	102	.370		18.351	4.0%

Overall Performance (2022): OBV

Rank	Team	OBV	Rating	W-L	BV [bat]	BV [pitch]
1	Los Angeles Dodgers	904	★★★★★	111-51	441	-463
2	Houston Astros	679	★★★★★	106-56	204	-475
3	New York Yankees	674	★★★★★	99-63	304	-370
4	Atlanta Braves	538	★★★★★	101-61	274	-264
5	New York Mets	376	★★★★★	101-61	187	-189
6	St. Louis Cardinals	360	★★★★	93-69	235	-125
7	Philadelphia Phillies	244	★★★★	87-75	168	-76
8	Toronto Blue Jays	239	★★★★	92-70	218	-21
9	Milwaukee Brewers	199	★★★★	86-76	149	-50
10	Cleveland Guardians	191	★★★★	92-70	-31	-222
11	Seattle Mariners	160	★★★★	90-72	53	-107
12	Tampa Bay Rays	133	★★★★	86-76	-98	-231
13	San Francisco Giants	103	★★★★	81-81	43	-60
14	San Diego Padres	98	★★★	89-73	-18	-116
15	Minnesota Twins	6	★★★	78-84	13	7
16	Los Angeles Angels	-36	★★★	73-89	-112	-76
17	Baltimore Orioles	-43	★★★	83-79	-29	14
18	Chicago White Sox	-135	★★	81-81	-139	-4
19	Arizona Diamondbacks	-138	★★	74-88	-19	119
20	Chicago Cubs	-153	★★	74-88	-20	133
20	Texas Rangers	-153	★★	68-94	-20	133
22	Boston Red Sox	-156	★★	78-84	68	224
23	Miami Marlins	-319	★★	69-93	-238	81
24	Kansas City Royals	-434	★	65-97	-104	330
25	Detroit Tigers	-467	★	66-96	-456	11
26	Colorado Rockies	-481	★	68-94	-53	428
27	Pittsburgh Pirates	-484	★	62-100	-244	240
28	Cincinnati Reds	-627	★	62-100	-202	425
29	Oakland Athletics	-629	★	60-102	-412	217
30	Washington Nationals	-647	★	55-107	-161	486

Base Production (2022): BV [bat]

Rank	Team	BV [bat]	Rating	B	O	BPO
1	Los Angeles Dodgers	441	★★★★★	3,258	4,267	.764
2	New York Yankees	304	★★★★★	3,158	4,323	.731
3	Atlanta Braves	274	★★★★★	3,103	4,286	.724
4	St. Louis Cardinals	235	★★★★★	3,071	4,297	.715
5	Toronto Blue Jays	218	★★★★★	3,058	4,303	.711
6	Houston Astros	204	★★★★★	3,015	4,259	.708
7	New York Mets	187	★★★★★	3,009	4,275	.704
8	Philadelphia Phillies	168	★★★★	3,005	4,298	.699
9	Milwaukee Brewers	149	★★★★	3,014	4,341	.694
10	Boston Red Sox	68	★★★★	2,923	4,325	.676
11	Seattle Mariners	53	★★★★	2,917	4,339	.672
12	San Francisco Giants	43	★★★	2,891	4,315	.670
13	Minnesota Twins	13	★★★	2,869	4,326	.663
14	San Diego Padres	-18	★★★	2,840	4,330	.656
15	Arizona Diamondbacks	-19	★★★	2,837	4,326	.656
16	Chicago Cubs	-20	★★★	2,854	4,354	.655
16	Texas Rangers	-20	★★★	2,845	4,341	.655
18	Baltimore Orioles	-29	★★★	2,828	4,329	.653
19	Cleveland Guardians	-31	★★★	2,850	4,364	.653
20	Colorado Rockies	-53	★★	2,812	4,341	.648
21	Tampa Bay Rays	-98	★★	2,731	4,286	.637
22	Kansas City Royals	-104	★★	2,740	4,309	.636
23	Los Angeles Angels	-112	★★	2,746	4,330	.634
24	Chicago White Sox	-139	★★	2,742	4,364	.628
25	Washington Nationals	-161	★★	2,685	4,311	.623
26	Cincinnati Reds	-202	★	2,650	4,321	.613
27	Miami Marlins	-238	★	2,629	4,343	.605
28	Pittsburgh Pirates	-244	★	2,610	4,324	.604
29	Oakland Athletics	-412	★	2,462	4,354	.565
30	Detroit Tigers	-456	★	2,398	4,324	.555

Run Production (2022): SCV [bat]

Rank	Team	SCV [bat]	Rating	PA	SC	SE
1	Los Angeles Dodgers	229	★★★★★	6,247	1,447	.232
2	New York Mets	132	★★★★★	6,176	1,336	.216
3	Toronto Blue Jays	130	★★★★★	6,158	1,331	.216
4	New York Yankees	114	★★★★★	6,172	1,317	.213
5	Atlanta Braves	113	★★★★★	6,082	1,299	.214
6	St. Louis Cardinals	112	★★★★★	6,165	1,314	.213
7	Boston Red Sox	86	★★★★	6,144	1,284	.209
8	Philadelphia Phillies	76	★★★★	6,077	1,261	.208
9	Houston Astros	58	★★★★	6,054	1,238	.204
10	Cleveland Guardians	32	★★★★	6,163	1,233	.200
11	San Diego Padres	30	★★★★	6,175	1,234	.200
12	Colorado Rockies	28	★★★★	6,105	1,218	.200
13	San Francisco Giants	23	★★★	6,117	1,216	.199
14	Milwaukee Brewers	16	★★★	6,122	1,209	.197
15	Arizona Diamondbacks	12	★★★	6,027	1,187	.197
16	Texas Rangers	4	★★★	6,029	1,179	.196
17	Chicago White Sox	-3	★★★	6,123	1,191	.195
18	Minnesota Twins	-6	★★★	6,113	1,186	.194
19	Tampa Bay Rays	-10	★★★	6,008	1,161	.193
20	Seattle Mariners	-36	★★	6,117	1,157	.189
21	Baltimore Orioles	-37	★★	6,049	1,142	.189
22	Cincinnati Reds	-55	★★	5,978	1,110	.186
23	Kansas City Royals	-57	★★	6,010	1,115	.186
24	Chicago Cubs	-66	★★	6,072	1,118	.184
25	Washington Nationals	-123	★	5,998	1,046	.174
26	Los Angeles Angels	-132	★	5,977	1,033	.173
27	Miami Marlins	-164	★	5,949	996	.167
28	Pittsburgh Pirates	-165	★	5,912	988	.167
29	Detroit Tigers	-167	★	5,870	977	.166
30	Oakland Athletics	-175	★	5,863	968	.165

Power Hitting (2022): XV [bat]

Rank	Team	XV [bat]	Rating	AB	XB	ISO
1	Atlanta Braves	211	★★★★★	5,509	1,049	.190
2	Los Angeles Dodgers	182	★★★★★	5,526	1,023	.185
3	New York Yankees	178	★★★★★	5,422	1,003	.185
4	Houston Astros	129	★★★★★	5,409	952	.176
5	Milwaukee Brewers	118	★★★★★	5,417	942	.174
6	Philadelphia Phillies	92	★★★★★	5,496	928	.169
7	St. Louis Cardinals	87	★★★★	5,496	923	.168
8	Toronto Blue Jays	86	★★★★	5,555	931	.168
9	Seattle Mariners	40	★★★★	5,375	858	.160
10	Los Angeles Angels	26	★★★★	5,423	851	.157
11	Texas Rangers	24	★★★	5,478	858	.157
12	San Francisco Giants	21	★★★	5,392	841	.156
13	Arizona Diamondbacks	15	★★★	5,351	829	.155
14	Baltimore Orioles	12	★★★	5,429	838	.154
15	Minnesota Twins	6	★★★	5,476	839	.153
16	New York Mets	4	★★★	5,489	839	.153
17	Boston Red Sox	-2	★★★	5,539	841	.152
18	Chicago Cubs	-21	★★★	5,425	804	.148
19	Colorado Rockies	-48	★★	5,540	795	.144
20	Pittsburgh Pirates	-58	★★	5,331	753	.141
21	San Diego Padres	-61	★★	5,468	771	.141
22	Tampa Bay Rays	-76	★★	5,412	747	.138
23	Cincinnati Reds	-80	★★	5,380	739	.137
24	Kansas City Royals	-90	★★	5,437	737	.136
25	Miami Marlins	-101	★	5,395	720	.133
26	Chicago White Sox	-117	★	5,611	737	.131
27	Oakland Athletics	-119	★	5,314	690	.130
28	Washington Nationals	-127	★	5,434	700	.129
29	Cleveland Guardians	-130	★	5,558	716	.129
30	Detroit Tigers	-199	★	5,378	619	.115

Contact Hitting (2022): BPV [bat]

Rank	Team	BPV [bat]	Rating	AB	BP	CT
1	Cleveland Guardians	266	★★★★★	5,558	4,436	.798
2	Houston Astros	171	★★★★★	5,409	4,230	.782
3	New York Mets	153	★★★★★	5,489	4,272	.778
4	St. Louis Cardinals	146	★★★★★	5,496	4,270	.777
5	Toronto Blue Jays	145	★★★★★	5,555	4,313	.776
6	Washington Nationals	136	★★★★★	5,434	4,213	.775
7	Chicago White Sox	132	★★★★★	5,611	4,342	.774
8	Kansas City Royals	70	★★★★	5,437	4,150	.763
9	Colorado Rockies	53	★★★★	5,540	4,210	.760
10	San Diego Padres	38	★★★★	5,468	4,141	.757
11	Minnesota Twins	14	★★★	5,476	4,123	.753
12	Boston Red Sox	10	★★★	5,539	4,166	.752
13	Philadelphia Phillies	9	★★★	5,496	4,133	.752
14	Los Angeles Dodgers	6	★★★	5,526	4,152	.751
15	Arizona Diamondbacks	-5	★★★	5,351	4,010	.749
16	Baltimore Orioles	-35	★★	5,429	4,039	.744
17	New York Yankees	-37	★★	5,422	4,031	.743
18	Tampa Bay Rays	-44	★★	5,412	4,017	.742
19	Seattle Mariners	-55	★★	5,375	3,978	.740
20	Oakland Athletics	-62	★★	5,314	3,925	.739
21	Detroit Tigers	-70	★★	5,378	3,965	.737
22	Texas Rangers	-78	★★	5,478	4,032	.736
23	Miami Marlins	-82	★★	5,395	3,966	.735
24	Cincinnati Reds	-87	★★	5,380	3,950	.734
25	Chicago Cubs	-94	★★	5,425	3,977	.733
26	Milwaukee Brewers	-112	★	5,417	3,953	.730
27	San Francisco Giants	-116	★	5,392	3,930	.729
28	Atlanta Braves	-123	★	5,509	4,011	.728
29	Pittsburgh Pirates	-166	★	5,331	3,834	.719
30	Los Angeles Angels	-185	★	5,423	3,884	.716

Batting Eye (2022): BBV [bat]

Rank	Team	BBV [bat]	Rating	PA-IBB	UBB	EY
1	New York Yankees	98	★★★★★	6,136	584	.095
2	Seattle Mariners	96	★★★★★	6,100	579	.095
3	Los Angeles Dodgers	92	★★★★★	6,225	585	.094
4	San Francisco Giants	74	★★★★★	6,103	557	.091
5	Milwaukee Brewers	69	★★★★★	6,097	552	.091
6	San Diego Padres	63	★★★★★	6,151	550	.089
7	Arizona Diamondbacks	41	★★★★	6,013	517	.086
8	St. Louis Cardinals	39	★★★★	6,154	526	.085
9	Houston Astros	32	★★★★	6,036	510	.084
10	Minnesota Twins	24	★★★★	6,102	507	.083
11	Tampa Bay Rays	12	★★★	5,995	487	.081
12	Chicago Cubs	11	★★★	6,056	491	.081
13	Toronto Blue Jays	0	★★★	6,145	487	.079
14	New York Mets	-2	★★★	6,151	485	.079
15	Pittsburgh Pirates	-5	★★★	5,898	462	.078
16	Baltimore Orioles	-12	★★★	6,039	466	.077
17	Philadelphia Phillies	-17	★★	6,062	463	.076
18	Kansas City Royals	-22	★★	6,003	453	.075
19	Atlanta Braves	-24	★★	6,069	457	.075
20	Cincinnati Reds	-27	★★	5,972	446	.075
21	Boston Red Sox	-30	★★	6,121	455	.074
22	Texas Rangers	-32	★★	6,017	444	.074
23	Oakland Athletics	-38	★★	5,856	426	.073
24	Colorado Rockies	-40	★★	6,095	443	.073
25	Miami Marlins	-41	★★	5,943	430	.072
26	Washington Nationals	-44	★★	5,986	430	.072
27	Los Angeles Angels	-50	★	5,949	421	.071
28	Cleveland Guardians	-71	★	6,127	414	.068
29	Detroit Tigers	-92	★	5,862	372	.063
30	Chicago White Sox	-105	★	6,114	379	.062

Base Prevention (2022): BV [pitch]

Rank	Team	BV [pitch]	Rating	B	O	BPO
1	Houston Astros	-475	★★★★★	2,396	4,350	.551
2	Los Angeles Dodgers	-463	★★★★★	2,434	4,389	.555
3	New York Yankees	-370	★★★★★	2,509	4,361	.575
4	Atlanta Braves	-264	★★★★★	2,617	4,365	.600
5	Tampa Bay Rays	-231	★★★★★	2,632	4,337	.607
6	Cleveland Guardians	-222	★★★★★	2,670	4,381	.609
7	New York Mets	-189	★★★★	2,661	4,317	.616
8	St. Louis Cardinals	-125	★★★★	2,716	4,304	.631
9	San Diego Padres	-116	★★★★	2,751	4,344	.633
10	Seattle Mariners	-107	★★★★	2,758	4,340	.635
11	Los Angeles Angels	-76	★★★★	2,788	4,339	.643
11	Philadelphia Phillies	-76	★★★★	2,754	4,288	.642
13	San Francisco Giants	-60	★★★	2,784	4,309	.646
14	Milwaukee Brewers	-50	★★★	2,824	4,354	.649
15	Toronto Blue Jays	-21	★★★	2,833	4,323	.655
16	Chicago White Sox	-4	★★★	2,871	4,355	.659
17	Minnesota Twins	7	★★★	2,857	4,317	.662
18	Detroit Tigers	11	★★★	2,847	4,296	.663
19	Baltimore Orioles	14	★★★	2,850	4,297	.663
20	Miami Marlins	81	★★	2,925	4,309	.679
21	Arizona Diamondbacks	119	★★	2,952	4,292	.688
22	Chicago Cubs	133	★★	3,008	4,355	.691
22	Texas Rangers	133	★★	2,983	4,317	.691
24	Oakland Athletics	217	★★	3,053	4,297	.710
25	Boston Red Sox	224	★	3,064	4,302	.712
26	Pittsburgh Pirates	240	★	3,088	4,314	.716
27	Kansas City Royals	330	★	3,139	4,256	.738
28	Cincinnati Reds	425	★	3,237	4,260	.760
29	Colorado Rockies	428	★	3,257	4,286	.760
30	Washington Nationals	486	★	3,292	4,251	.774

Run Prevention (2022): ERV [pitch]

Rank	Team	ERV [pitch]	Rating	IP	ER	ERA
1	Los Angeles Dodgers	-188	★★★★★	1,451.1	451	2.80
2	Houston Astros	-171	★★★★★	1,445.1	465	2.90
3	New York Yankees	-107	★★★★★	1,451.2	532	3.30
4	Tampa Bay Rays	-88	★★★★★	1,435.2	544	3.41
5	Atlanta Braves	-82	★★★★★	1,448.0	556	3.46
6	Cleveland Guardians	-81	★★★★★	1,456.0	560	3.46
7	New York Mets	-63	★★★★	1,438.2	570	3.57
8	Seattle Mariners	-60	★★★★	1,447.0	577	3.59
9	Los Angeles Angels	-31	★★★★	1,435.2	601	3.77
10	St. Louis Cardinals	-27	★★★★	1,435.2	605	3.79
11	San Diego Padres	-24	★★★★	1,443.1	611	3.81
12	Milwaukee Brewers	-22	★★★	1,446.0	615	3.83
13	San Francisco Giants	-18	★★★	1,433.0	613	3.85
14	Miami Marlins	-16	★★★	1,437.1	617	3.86
15	Toronto Blue Jays	-15	★★★	1,441.1	620	3.87
16	Chicago White Sox	-6	★★★	1,447.2	631	3.92
17	Baltimore Orioles	1	★★★	1,433.1	632	3.97
17	Philadelphia Phillies	1	★★★	1,428.1	630	3.97
19	Minnesota Twins	3	★★★	1,437.0	636	3.98
20	Chicago Cubs	6	★★★	1,443.2	642	4.00
21	Detroit Tigers	14	★★★	1,419.2	639	4.05
22	Texas Rangers	41	★★	1,435.0	673	4.22
23	Arizona Diamondbacks	46	★★	1,430.0	676	4.25
24	Oakland Athletics	89	★	1,426.1	717	4.52
25	Boston Red Sox	91	★	1,431.0	721	4.53
26	Pittsburgh Pirates	109	★	1,421.0	735	4.66
27	Kansas City Royals	117	★	1,416.0	740	4.70
28	Cincinnati Reds	141	★	1,423.1	768	4.86
29	Washington Nationals	163	★	1,411.2	785	5.00
30	Colorado Rockies	175	★	1,425.1	803	5.07

Power Prevention (2022): XV [pitch]

Rank	Team	XV [pitch]	Rating	AB	XB	ISO
1	Houston Astros	-168	★★★★★	5,295	638	.120
2	Atlanta Braves	-130	★★★★★	5,413	694	.128
3	St. Louis Cardinals	-94	★★★★★	5,409	729	.135
4	Los Angeles Dodgers	-89	★★★★★	5,336	723	.135
5	San Francisco Giants	-86	★★★★★	5,517	753	.136
6	New York Yankees	-85	★★★★★	5,380	734	.136
7	New York Mets	-60	★★★★	5,408	763	.141
8	Cleveland Guardians	-47	★★★★	5,447	782	.144
9	San Diego Padres	-40	★★★★	5,433	787	.145
10	Chicago White Sox	-38	★★★★	5,498	799	.145
11	Philadelphia Phillies	-34	★★★★	5,430	792	.146
12	Detroit Tigers	-32	★★★★	5,405	790	.146
13	Tampa Bay Rays	-28	★★★★	5,424	797	.147
14	Los Angeles Angels	-22	★★★★	5,386	798	.148
15	Texas Rangers	-8	★★★	5,452	822	.151
16	Baltimore Orioles	-5	★★★	5,490	830	.151
17	Pittsburgh Pirates	1	★★★	5,539	844	.152
18	Toronto Blue Jays	2	★★★	5,493	838	.153
19	Kansas City Royals	6	★★★	5,505	844	.153
20	Seattle Mariners	10	★★★	5,429	836	.154
21	Minnesota Twins	32	★★	5,458	862	.158
22	Milwaukee Brewers	39	★★	5,406	862	.159
23	Boston Red Sox	62	★★	5,517	901	.163
24	Miami Marlins	64	★★	5,423	889	.164
25	Arizona Diamondbacks	78	★	5,445	907	.167
26	Chicago Cubs	98	★	5,506	936	.170
27	Oakland Athletics	118	★	5,491	954	.174
28	Colorado Rockies	124	★	5,569	971	.174
29	Cincinnati Reds	141	★	5,439	969	.178
30	Washington Nationals	189	★	5,522	1,029	.186

Strikeout Pitching (2022): BPV [pitch]

Rank	Team	BPV [pitch]	Rating	AB	BP	CT
1	New York Mets	-215	★★★★★	5,408	3,843	.711
2	Atlanta Braves	-203	★★★★★	5,413	3,859	.713
3	Houston Astros	-202	★★★★★	5,295	3,771	.712
4	Milwaukee Brewers	-180	★★★★★	5,406	3,876	.717
5	Los Angeles Dodgers	-133	★★★★★	5,336	3,871	.725
6	New York Yankees	-116	★★★★★	5,380	3,921	.729
7	San Diego Padres	-95	★★★★	5,433	3,982	.733
8	Miami Marlins	-83	★★★★	5,423	3,986	.735
9	Chicago White Sox	-77	★★★★	5,498	4,048	.736
10	Philadelphia Phillies	-67	★★★★	5,430	4,007	.738
11	Cincinnati Reds	-56	★★★★	5,439	4,025	.740
12	Los Angeles Angels	-38	★★★★	5,386	4,003	.743
13	Seattle Mariners	-36	★★★★	5,429	4,038	.744
14	Cleveland Guardians	-30	★★★	5,447	4,057	.745
14	Tampa Bay Rays	-30	★★★	5,424	4,040	.745
16	Toronto Blue Jays	-19	★★★	5,493	4,103	.747
17	Chicago Cubs	-8	★★★	5,506	4,123	.749
18	San Francisco Giants	7	★★★	5,517	4,147	.752
19	Minnesota Twins	27	★★★	5,458	4,122	.755
20	Boston Red Sox	31	★★★	5,517	4,171	.756
21	Texas Rangers	47	★★	5,452	4,138	.759
22	Pittsburgh Pirates	133	★	5,539	4,289	.774
23	Arizona Diamondbacks	143	★	5,445	4,229	.777
24	Detroit Tigers	154	★	5,405	4,210	.779
25	Baltimore Orioles	157	★	5,490	4,276	.779
26	Washington Nationals	159	★	5,522	4,302	.779
27	Oakland Athletics	168	★	5,491	4,288	.781
28	St. Louis Cardinals	173	★	5,409	4,232	.782
29	Kansas City Royals	183	★	5,505	4,314	.784
30	Colorado Rockies	203	★	5,569	4,382	.787

Control Pitching (2022): BBV [pitch]

Rank	Team	BBV [pitch]	Rating	PA-IBB	UBB	EY
1	Tampa Bay Rays	-99	★★★★★	5,915	369	.062
2	Los Angeles Dodgers	-69	★★★★★	5,852	394	.067
2	Toronto Blue Jays	-69	★★★★★	6,038	409	.068
4	New York Mets	-55	★★★★★	5,937	415	.070
5	San Francisco Giants	-54	★★★★★	6,054	425	.070
6	Cleveland Guardians	-52	★★★★★	5,975	421	.070
7	Seattle Mariners	-49	★★★★★	5,962	423	.071
8	Baltimore Orioles	-44	★★★★	6,050	435	.072
9	New York Yankees	-35	★★★★	5,928	434	.073
10	Minnesota Twins	-28	★★★★	6,023	449	.075
11	Philadelphia Phillies	-27	★★★★	5,990	447	.075
12	Oakland Athletics	-16	★★★★	6,084	466	.077
12	San Diego Padres	-16	★★★★	6,041	462	.076
14	Houston Astros	-11	★★★	5,850	452	.077
15	Atlanta Braves	3	★★★	6,010	479	.080
15	St. Louis Cardinals	3	★★★	6,003	478	.080
17	Arizona Diamondbacks	7	★★★	6,047	486	.080
18	Miami Marlins	14	★★	6,037	492	.081
19	Boston Red Sox	22	★★	6,150	509	.083
20	Detroit Tigers	24	★★	6,038	502	.083
21	Milwaukee Brewers	30	★★	6,045	509	.084
22	Chicago White Sox	33	★★	6,130	518	.085
23	Colorado Rockies	34	★★	6,228	527	.085
24	Chicago Cubs	35	★★	6,143	521	.085
25	Los Angeles Angels	41	★★	6,015	517	.086
26	Washington Nationals	54	★	6,208	546	.088
27	Pittsburgh Pirates	69	★	6,240	563	.090
28	Texas Rangers	78	★	6,151	565	.092
29	Kansas City Royals	80	★	6,234	574	.092
30	Cincinnati Reds	100	★	6,199	591	.095

Fan Support Index (2022)

Rank	Team	Attendance (2022)	W	Att:W	FSI
1	Colorado Rockies	2,597,428	68	38,197	143.8
2	Washington Nationals	2,026,401	55	36,844	138.7
3	St. Louis Cardinals	3,320,551	93	35,705	134.4
4	Chicago Cubs	2,616,780	74	35,362	133.1
5	Los Angeles Dodgers	3,861,408	111	34,787	130.9
6	Boston Red Sox	2,625,089	78	33,655	126.7
6	Los Angeles Angels	2,457,461	73	33,664	126.7
8	San Diego Padres	2,987,470	89	33,567	126.3
9	New York Yankees	3,136,207	99	31,679	119.2
10	Atlanta Braves	3,129,931	101	30,989	116.6
11	San Francisco Giants	2,482,686	81	30,650	115.4
12	Texas Rangers	2,011,381	68	29,579	111.3
13	Toronto Blue Jays	2,653,830	92	28,846	108.6
14	Milwaukee Brewers	2,422,420	86	28,168	106.0
15	Philadelphia Phillies	2,276,736	87	26,169	98.5
16	Seattle Mariners	2,287,267	90	25,414	95.7
17	New York Mets	2,564,737	101	25,393	95.6
18	Houston Astros	2,688,998	106	25,368	95.5
19	Chicago White Sox	2,009,359	81	24,807	93.4
20	Detroit Tigers	1,575,544	66	23,872	89.9
21	Minnesota Twins	1,801,128	78	23,091	86.9
22	Cincinnati Reds	1,395,770	62	22,512	84.7
23	Arizona Diamondbacks	1,605,199	74	21,692	81.7
24	Pittsburgh Pirates	1,257,458	62	20,282	76.3
25	Kansas City Royals	1,277,686	65	19,657	74.0
26	Baltimore Orioles	1,368,367	83	16,486	62.1
27	Cleveland Guardians	1,295,870	92	14,086	53.0
28	Miami Marlins	907,487	69	13,152	49.5
29	Oakland Athletics	787,902	60	13,132	49.4
29	Tampa Bay Rays	1,128,127	86	13,118	49.4

2022: BEST PERFORMANCES

Aaron Judge and Paul Goldschmidt won the respective Most Valuable Player Awards for the American and National Leagues in 2022. Both deserved the honor.

Judge, an outfielder for the New York Yankees, led the AL in overall base value, the best statistical measure of a player's total performance. He posted an impressive OBV of 255. The league's runner-up was Shohei Ohtani, a pitcher and designated hitter for the Los Angeles Angels, who finished far behind with an overall value of 186.

Goldschmidt, who plays for the St. Louis Cardinals, topped the NL's rankings for OBV. His mark of 159 gave him a comfortable lead over the league's second-ranked player, fellow first baseman Freddie Freeman of the Los Angeles Dodgers, at 139.

Overall base value, as we've already discussed, is calculated by subtracting BV [pitch], the base value for pitchers, from BV [bat], the base value for batters. Optimal pitching performances are expressed in negative values, but subtraction flips them to positive signs. That means the higher a player's OBV goes, the more bases he reached and/or prevented above the big-league average of zero, and the more valuable he was to his club.

Subtraction is essential in determining the overall base value for a team, but it rarely comes into play for individuals in this era of the universal DH. A hitter's OBV is almost always the same as his BV [bat], while a pitcher's is the inverse of his BV [pitch]. Ohtani, the rare double threat who hits and pitches effectively, is an obvious exception. His 2022 mark was a combination of his values of plus-102 as a batter and minus-84 as a pitcher, equaling an OBV of plus-186.

The American League's leaders in overall base value were almost evenly balanced between the two sides. The top 10 players included five batters, four pitchers, and the multitalented Ohtani. But the scales tipped heavily toward batters in the National League. They occupied seven of the top 10 OBV slots, leaving only three for pitchers.

Separate rankings of the past season's 25 best players in each league, as determined by OBV, can be found toward the end of this chapter. You'll also see an array of other tables, enumerating the best performances in a wide range of categories.

The following summary touches briefly on the highlights. All of the concepts, formulas, and abbreviations used in this chapter were already explained on previous pages. If you're uncertain about any, flip back to find the answer.

American League

Scoring

Aaron Judge led the league in runs scored, runs batted in, and home runs. So, of course, he led the league in scoring with an SC of 202. Jose Ramirez, a third baseman for the Cleveland Guardians, came second at 187.

Season Values for Batters

Base production: We already know about Judge's BV [bat] of 255. He finished 103 ahead of runner-up Yordan Alvarez (152), a designated hitter for the Houston Astros.

Run production: Judge again. His SCV of 66 indicates that he directly generated 66 more runs than the average player would have produced under the same circumstances.

Power hitting: Any doubts about this one? Judge finished with an XV of 127, meaning that he exceeded the big-league norm by that amount for extra bases reached through doubles, triples, and homers.

Contact hitting: Luis Arraez, an infielder for the Minnesota Twins, struck out only 43 times in 603 plate appearances. His BPV shows that he put 94 more balls in play than would have been expected. Are you at all surprised that he also led the league in batting average?

Batting eye: The typical batter in Jesse Winker's shoes would have drawn 43 unintentional walks in 2022. But the left fielder for the Seattle Mariners coaxed 83, giving him an AL-leading BBV of 40.

Season Values for Pitchers

Base prevention: Justin Verlander won the American League's Cy Young Award in 2022, and deservedly so. The ace for the Houston Astros allowed 127 fewer bases than the average major-league pitcher would have surrendered under the same conditions. It was the only triple-digit negative BV [pitch] in the AL.

Run prevention: There's an obvious connection between preventing bases and preventing earned runs. That's why Verlander also finished as the leader in this category with an ERV of minus-43.

Power prevention: Another starter for the Astros, Framber Valdez, excelled at neutralizing the long ball. Valdez gave up only 61 extra bases in 2022, putting him 52 below average. The latter was the best XV in the league.

Strikeout pitching: Gerrit Cole of the New York Yankees topped the American League with 257 strikeouts, 30 more than runner-up Dylan Cease of the Chicago White Sox. Cole's resulting BPV, which also paced the league, was minus-73, which means he allowed 73 fewer balls in play than average.

Control pitching: Corey Kluber worked 164 innings for the Tampa Bay Rays and issued only 21 unintentional walks. That gave him an AL-leading walk value (BBV) of minus-34.

Extreme Games for Batters

Three or more hits in a game: This chapter also features tables of the most frequent occurrences of three positive events for individual batters and three more for pitchers. Amed Rosario, a shortstop for the Cleveland Guardians, and the aforementioned Luis Arraez tied for first place in this category. Each rapped at least three hits in 17 different games in 2022.

Two or more homers in a game: Yes, yes, yes, it's Aaron Judge. He homered at least twice on 11 separate occasions.

Five or more RBIs in a game: You might be expecting Judge once again, but you're wrong. Jose Ramirez of the Guardians was the AL leader here. He drove home five or more runs in three games.

Extreme Games for Pitchers

Two or fewer earned runs in seven or more innings: A pitcher is credited with a quality start when he works at least six innings and allows no more than three earned runs. But that can translate to an ERA as high as 4.50, considerably worse than the big-league average of 3.96. This category measures what could be called *true* quality starts, requiring at least seven innings with no more than two earned runs. Shane Bieber of the Guardians met that standard 12 times in 2022, leading the league.

Ten or more strikeouts in a game: Shohei Ohtani was the only American League pitcher to register double-digit strikeouts in double-digit games, 10 in all.

No baserunners in a save: This category might also be known as *clean* saves. It counts the number of times a reliever didn't allow a single baserunner while being credited with a save. Emmanuel Clase of the Guardians topped the AL with 22.

National League

Scoring

Freddie Freeman was the most effective National League player in terms of run generation, totaling an SC of 196 for the Dodgers. Second place was a tie between Paul Goldschmidt of the Cardinals and another first baseman, Pete Alonso of the New York Mets, at 186 apiece.

Season Values for Batters

Base production: Goldschmidt topped the league in OBV, so it stands to reason that his BV [bat] of 159 would be first in this category, too. Freeman was the runner-up at 139.

Run production: The same names keep popping up. This was an especially tight race between the three powerful first basemen mentioned above. Goldschmidt exceeded the big-league norm for scoring value (SCV) by 59, edging out Freeman at 58 and Alonso at 52.

Power hitting: Kyle Schwarber, a free-swinging left fielder for the Philadelphia Phillies, accumulated 165 extra bases through doubles, triples, and homers. The typical batter in the same circumstances would have reached 88. That gave Schwarber an XV of plus-77, the best in the National League.

Contact hitting: Jeff McNeil, a second baseman for the Mets, exceeded the norm for balls in play by 72, pacing the NL in BPV. He also posted the league's best batting average, duplicating the feat of Luis Arraez, the American League's BPV leader. Is there a message here?

Batting eye: No batter in either league knows the strike zone as well as Juan Soto, a right fielder who split his season between the Washington Nationals and San Diego Padres. Soto drew 129 unintentional walks in 2022, 77 more than the typical batter would have gotten. His BBV of 77 was easily the league's best.

Season Values for Pitchers

Base prevention: Sandy Alcantara of the Miami Marlins won the NL's Cy Young Award, but he was edged out by Max Fried of the Atlanta Braves in this key category. Fried allowed 105 fewer bases than average, the lowest (and best) BV [pitch] in the league. Zac Gallen of the Arizona Diamondbacks finished second at minus-93, followed by Alcantara at minus-92.

Run prevention: Alcantara surged to the forefront in earned run value (ERV) at minus-43. The runners-up were Julio Urias of the Dodgers at minus-35 and Fried at minus-31.

Power prevention: It's Fried again. No NL pitcher was better at keeping opposing batters from going long. Fried surrendered only 65 extra bases through doubles, triples, and homers, leaving him with an XV of minus-40.

Strikeout pitching: Spencer Strider of the Atlanta Braves burst onto the scene in 2022, finishing second in balloting for the National League Rookie of the Year Award. He went one better in this category, taking first place by allowing 83 fewer balls in play than average (as measured by BPV).

Control pitching: Aaron Nola was a master of control for the Philadelphia Phillies, working 205 innings and giving up just 28 unintentional walks. The latter total was 36 less than average, as reflected in Nola's walk value (BBV) of minus-36.

Extreme Games for Batters

Three or more hits in a game: Freddie Freeman rapped at least three hits in 20 different games, the highest total in the National League. Jeff McNeil, the batting-average champ, came in second with 16 games.

Two or more homers in a game: Kyle Schwarber topped the league with 46 home runs. He also led in multi-homer games with eight.

Five or more RBIs in a game: Pete Alonso set the pace by driving home at least five runs for the Mets in four games.

Extreme Games for Pitchers

Two or fewer earned runs in seven or more innings: Sandy Alcantara proved his Cy Young worthiness in this category. The ace for the Marlins accumulated 20 true quality starts, defined as two or fewer earned runs in at least seven innings. No other NL pitcher had more than 11.

Ten or more strikeouts in a game: Carlos Rodon of the San Francisco Giants piled up at least 10 strikeouts on 11 occasions last season. The two runners-up worked for the Milwaukee Brewers: Corbin Burnes (nine games of double-digit strikeouts) and Brandon Woodruff (seven).

No baserunners in a save: Kenley Jansen of the Braves earned 21 clean saves, allowing no runners while closing the door on the opposition. It was the NL's highest total in 2022.

American League Season Leaders

AL Overall Performance: OBV

Rank	Player	Team	BV [bat]	BV [pitch]	OBV
1	Aaron Judge	Yankees	255	0	255
2	Shohei Ohtani	Angels	102	-84	186
3	Yordan Alvarez	Astros	152	0	152
4	Justin Verlander	Astros	0	-127	127
5	Mike Trout	Angels	126	0	126
6	Jose Altuve	Astros	123	0	123
7	Jose Ramirez	Guardians	113	0	113
8	Shane McClanahan	Rays	0	-91	91
9	Nestor Cortes	Yankees	0	-89	89
10	Alek Manoah	Blue Jays	0	-87	87
11	Shane Bieber	Guardians	0	-85	85
11	Framber Valdez	Astros	0	-85	85
13	Julio Rodriguez	Mariners	83	0	83
14	Rafael Devers	Red Sox	81	0	81
15	Andres Gimenez	Guardians	75	0	75
16	Emmanuel Clase	Guardians	0	-74	74
17	Triston McKenzie	Guardians	0	-71	71
18	Alex Bregman	Astros	70	0	70
19	Kyle Tucker	Astros	69	0	69
20	Xander Bogaerts	Red Sox	66	0	66
20	Dylan Cease	White Sox	0	-66	66
22	Nathaniel Lowe	Rangers	65	0	65
22	George Springer	Blue Jays	65	0	65
24	Cristian Javier	Astros	0	-64	64
24	Taylor Ward	Angels	64	0	64

AL Scoring: SC

Rank	Player	Team	R	(+) RBI	(-) HR	(=) SC
1	Aaron Judge	Yankees	133	131	62	202
2	Jose Ramirez	Guardians	90	126	29	187
3	Alex Bregman	Astros	93	93	23	163
4	Adolis Garcia	Rangers	88	101	27	162
5	Bo Bichette	Blue Jays	91	93	24	160
6	Marcus Semien	Rangers	101	83	26	158
7	Yordan Alvarez	Astros	95	97	37	155
7	Vladimir Guerrero Jr.	Blue Jays	90	97	32	155
9	Shohei Ohtani	Angels	90	95	34	151
10	Kyle Tucker	Astros	71	107	30	148
11	Amed Rosario	Guardians	86	71	11	146
12	Jose Abreu	White Sox	85	75	15	145
12	Rafael Devers	Red Sox	84	88	27	145
14	Xander Bogaerts	Red Sox	84	73	15	142
14	Bobby Witt	Royals	82	80	20	142
16	Randy Arozarena	Rays	72	89	20	141
16	Corey Seager	Rangers	91	83	33	141
18	George Springer	Blue Jays	89	76	25	140
19	Alex Verdugo	Red Sox	75	74	11	138
20	Cedric Mullins	Orioles	89	64	16	137
21	Steven Kwan	Guardians	89	52	6	135
22	Anthony Santander	Orioles	78	89	33	134
23	Jose Altuve	Astros	103	57	28	132
23	Matt Chapman	Blue Jays	83	76	27	132
23	Eugenio Suarez	Mariners	76	87	31	132

AL Base Production: BV [bat]

Rank	Batter	Team	B	O	BPO	BV [bat]
1	Aaron Judge	Yankees	529	415	1.275	255
2	Yordan Alvarez	Astros	380	346	1.098	152
3	Mike Trout	Angels	338	321	1.053	126
4	Jose Altuve	Astros	376	384	.979	123
5	Jose Ramirez	Guardians	413	454	.910	113
6	Shohei Ohtani	Angels	395	444	.890	102
7	Julio Rodriguez	Mariners	334	381	.877	83

Rank	Batter	Team	B	O	BPO	BV [bat]
8	Rafael Devers	Red Sox	351	409	.858	81
9	Andres Gimenez	Guardians	315	364	.865	75
10	Alex Bregman	Astros	358	436	.821	70

AL Run Production: SCV [bat]

Rank	Batter	Team	PA	SC	SE	SCV [bat]
1	Aaron Judge	Yankees	696	202	.290	66
2	Jose Ramirez	Guardians	685	187	.273	53
3	Yordan Alvarez	Astros	561	155	.276	46
4	Alex Bregman	Astros	656	163	.248	35
5	Adolis Garcia	Rangers	657	162	.247	34
6	Kyle Tucker	Astros	609	148	.243	29
7	Mike Trout	Angels	499	125	.251	28
8	Trevor Story	Red Sox	396	103	.260	26
8	George Springer	Blue Jays	583	140	.240	26
10	Rafael Devers	Red Sox	614	145	.236	25

AL Power Hitting: XV [bat]

Rank	Batter	Team	AB	XB	ISO	XV [bat]
1	Aaron Judge	Yankees	570	214	.375	127
2	Mike Trout	Angels	438	152	.347	85
3	Yordan Alvarez	Astros	470	144	.306	72
4	Shohei Ohtani	Angels	586	144	.246	55
5	Byron Buxton	Twins	340	103	.303	51
6	Jose Ramirez	Guardians	601	141	.235	50
7	Anthony Rizzo	Yankees	465	119	.256	48
8	Cal Raleigh	Mariners	370	103	.278	47
9	Jose Altuve	Astros	527	123	.233	43
10	Rafael Devers	Red Sox	555	125	.225	41

AL Contact Hitting: BPV [bat]

Rank	Batter	Team	AB	BP	CT	BPV [bat]
1	Luis Arraez	Twins	547	504	.921	94
2	Steven Kwan	Guardians	563	503	.893	81
3	Jose Ramirez	Guardians	601	519	.864	68
4	Yuli Gurriel	Astros	545	472	.866	63
5	Adam Frazier	Mariners	541	468	.865	62
5	Alex Verdugo	Red Sox	593	507	.855	62
7	Alex Bregman	Astros	548	471	.859	60
8	Alejandro Kirk	Blue Jays	470	412	.877	59
9	Yandy Diaz	Rays	473	413	.873	58
10	Tony Kemp	Athletics	497	428	.861	55

AL Batting Eye: BBV [bat]

Rank	Batter	Team	PA-IBB	UBB	EY	BBV [bat]
1	Jesse Winker	Mariners	546	83	.152	40
2	Aaron Judge	Yankees	677	92	.136	38
3	Alex Bregman	Astros	655	86	.131	34
4	Yandy Diaz	Rays	556	76	.137	32
5	Carlos Santana	Royals-Mariners	504	69	.137	29
6	Jorge Polanco	Twins	444	63	.142	28
6	Adley Rutschman	Orioles	470	65	.138	28
8	Yordan Alvarez	Astros	552	69	.125	25
9	DJ LeMahieu	Yankees	541	67	.124	24
10	Aaron Hicks	Yankees	450	59	.131	23
10	MJ Melendez	Royals	533	65	.122	23
10	Eugenio Suarez	Mariners	629	73	.116	23

AL Base Prevention: BV [pitch]

Rank	Pitcher	Team	B	O	BPO	BV [pitch]
1	Justin Verlander	Astros	220	526	.418	-127
2	Shane McClanahan	Rays	238	499	.477	-91
3	Nestor Cortes	Yankees	225	475	.474	-89
4	Alek Manoah	Blue Jays	304	592	.514	-87
5	Shane Bieber	Guardians	312	602	.518	-85
5	Framber Valdez	Astros	316	608	.520	-85

Rank	Pitcher	Team	B	O	BPO	BV [pitch]
7	Shohei Ohtani	Angels	246	500	.492	-84
8	Emmanuel Clase	Guardians	75	226	.332	-74
9	Triston McKenzie	Guardians	305	569	.536	-71
10	Dylan Cease	White Sox	297	550	.540	-66

AL Run Prevention: ERV [pitch]

Rank	Pitcher	Team	IP	ER	ERA	ERV [pitch]
1	Justin Verlander	Astros	175.0	34	1.75	-43
2	Alek Manoah	Blue Jays	196.2	49	2.24	-38
3	Dylan Cease	White Sox	184.0	45	2.20	-36
4	Shohei Ohtani	Angels	166.0	43	2.33	-30
5	Nestor Cortes	Yankees	158.1	43	2.44	-27
6	Shane McClanahan	Rays	166.1	47	2.54	-26
6	Framber Valdez	Astros	201.1	63	2.82	-26
8	Shane Bieber	Guardians	200.0	64	2.88	-24
9	Cristian Javier	Astros	148.2	42	2.54	-23
9	Martin Perez	Rangers	196.1	63	2.89	-23
9	Jeffrey Springs	Rays	135.1	37	2.46	-23

AL Power Prevention: XV [pitch]

Rank	Pitcher	Team	AB	XB	ISO	XV [pitch]
1	Framber Valdez	Astros	745	61	.082	-52
2	Martin Perez	Rangers	738	70	.095	-42
2	Justin Verlander	Astros	625	53	.085	-42
4	Patrick Sandoval	Angels	565	49	.087	-37
5	Alek Manoah	Blue Jays	713	80	.112	-28
6	Shane Bieber	Guardians	747	87	.116	-27
7	Dylan Cease	White Sox	663	77	.116	-24
7	Emmanuel Clase	Guardians	258	15	.058	-24
7	Shohei Ohtani	Angels	610	69	.113	-24
10	Jason Foley	Tigers	242	16	.066	-21

AL Strikeout Pitching: BPV [pitch]

Rank	Pitcher	Team	AB	BP	CT	BPV [pitch]
1	Gerrit Cole	Yankees	738	481	.652	-73
2	Shohei Ohtani	Angels	610	391	.641	-67
3	Cristian Javier	Astros	524	330	.630	-63
4	Dylan Cease	White Sox	663	436	.658	-61
5	Shane McClanahan	Rays	597	403	.675	-45
6	Andres Munoz	Mariners	227	131	.577	-39
7	Robbie Ray	Mariners	705	493	.699	-36
8	Bryan Abreu	Astros	217	129	.594	-34
9	Kevin Gausman	Blue Jays	690	485	.703	-33
9	Liam Hendriks	White Sox	210	125	.595	-33

AL Control Pitching: BBV [pitch]

Rank	Pitcher	Team	PA-IBB	UBB	EY	BBV [pitch]
1	Corey Kluber	Rays	689	21	.030	-34
2	Kevin Gausman	Blue Jays	725	28	.039	-29
3	Shane Bieber	Guardians	791	36	.046	-27
4	Jameson Taillon	Yankees	728	32	.044	-26
5	Cole Irvin	Athletics	738	33	.045	-25
6	Justin Verlander	Astros	666	29	.044	-24
7	Lance Lynn	White Sox	512	19	.037	-22
7	Ross Stripling	Blue Jays	536	20	.037	-22
9	George Kirby	Mariners	542	22	.041	-21
10	Johnny Cueto	White Sox	649	31	.048	-20

National League Season Leaders

NL Overall Performance: OBV

Rank	Player	Team	BV [bat]	BV [pitch]	OBV
1	Paul Goldschmidt	Cardinals	159	0	159
2	Freddie Freeman	Dodgers	139	0	139
3	Juan Soto	Nationals-Padres	111	0	111
4	Max Fried	Braves	0	-105	105
5	Manny Machado	Padres	104	0	104
6	Mookie Betts	Dodgers	99	0	99
6	Austin Riley	Braves	99	0	99
8	Pete Alonso	Mets	97	0	97
9	Zac Gallen	Diamondbacks	0	-93	93
10	Sandy Alcantara	Marlins	0	-92	92
11	Nolan Arenado	Cardinals	90	0	90
11	Aaron Nola	Phillies	0	-90	90
13	Kyle Schwarber	Phillies	87	0	87
14	Spencer Strider	Braves	0	-83	83
15	Corbin Burnes	Brewers	0	-81	81
16	Yu Darvish	Padres	0	-80	80
17	Tony Gonsolin	Dodgers	0	-77	77
17	Clayton Kershaw	Dodgers	0	-77	77
19	Carlos Rodon	Giants	0	-75	75
19	Max Scherzer	Mets	0	-75	75
19	Julio Urias	Dodgers	0	-75	75
22	Trea Turner	Dodgers	71	0	71
23	J.T. Realmuto	Phillies	70	0	70
24	Tyler Anderson	Dodgers	-1	-70	69
25	Bryce Harper	Phillies	67	0	67

NL Scoring: SC

Rank	Player	Team	R	(+) RBI	(-) HR	(=) SC
1	Freddie Freeman	Dodgers	117	100	21	196
2	Pete Alonso	Mets	95	131	40	186
2	Paul Goldschmidt	Cardinals	106	115	35	186
4	Trea Turner	Dodgers	101	100	21	180
5	Francisco Lindor	Mets	98	107	26	179
6	Manny Machado	Padres	100	102	32	170
6	Dansby Swanson	Braves	99	96	25	170
8	Mookie Betts	Dodgers	117	82	35	164
9	Jake Cronenworth	Padres	88	88	17	159
10	Matt Olson	Braves	86	103	34	155
11	C.J. Cron	Rockies	79	102	29	152
12	Willy Adames	Brewers	83	98	31	150
12	Brandon Nimmo	Mets	102	64	16	150
14	Kyle Schwarber	Phillies	100	94	46	148
15	Nolan Arenado	Cardinals	73	103	30	146
15	Brandon Drury	Reds-Padres	87	87	28	146
17	Austin Riley	Braves	90	93	38	145
18	Christian Walker	Diamondbacks	84	94	36	142
18	Christian Yelich	Brewers	99	57	14	142
20	Tommy Edman	Cardinals	95	57	13	139
21	Alec Bohm	Phillies	79	72	13	138
22	J.T. Realmuto	Phillies	75	84	22	137
23	Josh Bell	Nationals-Padres	78	71	17	132
24	Will Smith	Dodgers	68	87	24	131
25	Rhys Hoskins	Phillies	81	79	30	130

NL Base Production: BV [bat]

Rank	Batter	Team	B	O	BPO	BV [bat]
1	Paul Goldschmidt	Cardinals	419	394	1.063	159
2	Freddie Freeman	Dodgers	422	429	.984	139
3	Juan Soto	Nationals-Padres	382	411	.929	111
4	Manny Machado	Padres	382	421	.907	104
5	Mookie Betts	Dodgers	384	432	.889	99
5	Austin Riley	Braves	405	464	.873	99
7	Pete Alonso	Mets	402	462	.870	97

Rank	Batter	Team	B	O	BPO	BV [bat]
8	Nolan Arenado	Cardinals	365	416	.877	90
9	Kyle Schwarber	Phillies	393	464	.847	87
10	Trea Turner	Dodgers	385	476	.809	71

NL Run Production: SCV [bat]

Rank	Batter	Team	PA	SC	SE	SCV [bat]
1	Paul Goldschmidt	Cardinals	651	186	.286	59
2	Freddie Freeman	Dodgers	708	196	.277	58
3	Pete Alonso	Mets	685	186	.272	52
4	Manny Machado	Padres	644	170	.264	44
5	Trea Turner	Dodgers	708	180	.254	42
6	Francisco Lindor	Mets	706	179	.254	41
7	Mookie Betts	Dodgers	639	164	.257	39
8	Brandon Drury	Reds-Padres	568	146	.257	35
9	Dansby Swanson	Braves	696	170	.244	34
9	Michael Harris	Braves	441	120	.272	34

NL Power Hitting: XV [bat]

Rank	Batter	Team	AB	XB	ISO	XV [bat]
1	Kyle Schwarber	Phillies	577	165	.286	77
2	Mookie Betts	Dodgers	572	151	.264	64
3	Austin Riley	Braves	615	157	.255	63
4	Paul Goldschmidt	Cardinals	561	146	.260	61
5	Pete Alonso	Mets	597	147	.246	56
6	Matt Olson	Braves	616	146	.237	52
7	Nolan Arenado	Cardinals	557	134	.241	49
8	Rowdy Tellez	Brewers	529	128	.242	48
8	Christian Walker	Diamondbacks	583	137	.235	48
10	Manny Machado	Padres	578	135	.234	47

NL Contact Hitting: BPV [bat]

Rank	Batter	Team	AB	BP	CT	BPV [bat]
1	Jeff McNeil	Mets	533	472	.886	72
2	Nolan Arenado	Cardinals	557	485	.871	67
3	Nico Hoerner	Cubs	481	424	.881	63
4	Miguel Rojas	Marlins	471	410	.870	57
5	Jose Iglesias	Rockies	439	383	.872	54
6	Freddie Freeman	Dodgers	612	510	.833	51
7	Keibert Ruiz	Nationals	394	344	.873	48
8	Jurickson Profar	Padres	575	472	.821	41
9	Mookie Betts	Dodgers	572	468	.818	39
10	Joey Wendle	Marlins	347	297	.856	37

NL Batting Eye: BBV [bat]

Rank	Batter	Team	PA-IBB	UBB	EY	BBV [bat]
1	Juan Soto	Nationals-Padres	658	129	.196	77
2	Max Muncy	Dodgers	564	89	.158	44
3	Daniel Vogelbach	Pirates-Mets	459	71	.155	35
4	Kyle Schwarber	Phillies	666	83	.125	30
4	Christian Yelich	Brewers	666	83	.125	30
6	Paul Goldschmidt	Cardinals	650	78	.120	27
7	Josh Bell	Nationals-Padres	643	77	.120	26
8	Lars Nootbaar	Cardinals	346	50	.145	23
9	Brendan Donovan	Cardinals	467	59	.126	22
10	Jurickson Profar	Padres	658	73	.111	21

NL Base Prevention: BV [pitch]

Rank	Pitcher	Team	B	O	BPO	BV [pitch]
1	Max Fried	Braves	265	560	.473	-105
2	Zac Gallen	Diamondbacks	269	549	.490	-93
3	Sandy Alcantara	Marlins	356	678	.525	-92
4	Aaron Nola	Phillies	318	618	.515	-90
5	Spencer Strider	Braves	180	398	.452	-83
6	Corbin Burnes	Brewers	320	608	.526	-81
7	Yu Darvish	Padres	307	586	.524	-80
8	Tony Gonsolin	Dodgers	182	393	.463	-77

Rank	Pitcher	Team	B	O	BPO	BV [pitch]
8	Clayton Kershaw	Dodgers	175	382	.458	-77
10	Carlos Rodon	Giants	278	535	.520	-75
10	Max Scherzer	Mets	213	436	.489	-75
10	Julio Urias	Dodgers	277	533	.520	-75

NL Run Prevention: ERV [pitch]

Rank	Pitcher	Team	IP	ER	ERA	ERV [pitch]
1	Sandy Alcantara	Marlins	228.2	58	2.28	-43
2	Julio Urias	Dodgers	175.0	42	2.16	-35
3	Max Fried	Braves	185.1	51	2.48	-31
4	Zac Gallen	Diamondbacks	184.0	52	2.54	-29
5	Tyler Anderson	Dodgers	178.2	51	2.57	-28
6	Max Scherzer	Mets	145.1	37	2.29	-27
7	Tony Gonsolin	Dodgers	130.1	31	2.14	-26
8	Clayton Kershaw	Dodgers	126.1	32	2.28	-24
9	Corbin Burnes	Brewers	202.0	66	2.94	-23
9	Logan Webb	Giants	192.1	62	2.90	-23

NL Power Prevention: XV [pitch]

Rank	Pitcher	Team	AB	XB	ISO	XV [pitch]
1	Max Fried	Braves	692	65	.094	-40
2	Alex Cobb	Giants	580	51	.088	-37
3	Jose Quintana	Pirates-Cardinals	626	61	.097	-34
4	Sandy Alcantara	Marlins	820	92	.112	-33
4	Spencer Strider	Braves	478	40	.084	-33
4	Logan Webb	Giants	726	77	.106	-33
7	Carlos Rodon	Giants	649	69	.106	-30
8	Dakota Hudson	Cardinals	517	53	.103	-26
8	Justin Steele	Cubs	454	43	.095	-26
10	Clayton Kershaw	Dodgers	465	48	.103	-23
10	Adam Wainwright	Cardinals	736	89	.121	-23

NL Strikeout Pitching: BPV [pitch]

Rank	Pitcher	Team	AB	BP	CT	BPV [pitch]
1	Spencer Strider	Braves	478	276	.577	-83
2	Carlos Rodon	Giants	649	412	.635	-75
3	Edwin Diaz	Mets	213	95	.446	-65
4	Corbin Burnes	Brewers	731	488	.668	-60
5	Blake Snell	Padres	476	305	.641	-52
6	Brandon Woodruff	Brewers	568	378	.665	-48
7	Hunter Greene	Reds	469	305	.650	-47
8	Jacob deGrom	Mets	229	127	.555	-45
8	Charlie Morton	Braves	640	435	.680	-45
8	Devin Williams	Brewers	205	109	.532	-45

NL Control Pitching: BBV [pitch]

Rank	Pitcher	Team	PA-IBB	UBB	EY	BBV [pitch]
1	Aaron Nola	Phillies	806	28	.035	-36
2	Max Fried	Braves	731	30	.041	-28
3	Miles Mikolas	Cardinals	805	39	.048	-25
4	Yu Darvish	Padres	771	37	.048	-24
5	Tyler Anderson	Dodgers	707	34	.048	-22
6	Sandy Alcantara	Marlins	885	49	.055	-21
6	Max Scherzer	Mets	565	24	.042	-21
8	Joe Musgrove	Padres	739	41	.055	-18
9	Clayton Kershaw	Dodgers	493	23	.047	-16
10	Paolo Espino	Nationals	487	24	.049	-15
10	Zack Wheeler	Phillies	606	33	.054	-15
10	Alex Wood	Giants	554	29	.052	-15

American League Extreme Games

AL Batters With 3+ Hits in Game

Rank	Batter	Team	G (3+ H)
1	Amed Rosario	Guardians	17
1	Luis Arraez	Twins	17
3	Steven Kwan	Guardians	16
3	Xander Bogaerts	Red Sox	16
5	Gio Urshela	Twins	15
5	Harold Castro	Tigers	15
5	Jose Altuve	Astros	15
8	Julio Rodriguez	Mariners	14
8	Randy Arozarena	Rays	14
10	Aaron Judge	Yankees	13
10	Marcus Semien	Rangers	13
10	Rafael Devers	Red Sox	13
10	Ty France	Mariners	13

AL Batters With 2+ Home Runs in Game

Rank	Batter	Team	G (2+ HR)
1	Aaron Judge	Yankees	11
2	Shohei Ohtani	Angels	6
3	Anthony Santander	Orioles	5
3	Yordan Alvarez	Astros	5
5	Byron Buxton	Twins	4
5	Carlos Santana	Royals-Mariners	4
5	Eugenio Suarez	Mariners	4
5	Mike Trout	Angels	4
9	Bo Bichette	Blue Jays	3
9	Gleyber Torres	Yankees	3
9	Isaac Paredes	Rays	3
9	Jose Ramirez	Guardians	3
9	Matt Carpenter	Yankees	3
9	Ryan Mountcastle	Orioles	3

AL Batters With 5+ RBIs in Game

Rank	Batter	Team	G (5+ RBI)
1	Jose Ramirez	Guardians	3
2	Adolis Garcia	Rangers	2
2	Carlos Santana	Royals-Mariners	2
2	Danny Jansen	Blue Jays	2
2	Gleyber Torres	Yankees	2
2	Lourdes Gurriel Jr.	Blue Jays	2
2	Matt Carpenter	Yankees	2
2	Rafael Devers	Red Sox	2
2	Shohei Ohtani	Angels	2
2	Yoan Moncada	White Sox	2

AL Pitchers With 0-2 Earned Runs in 7+ Innings

Rank	Pitcher	Team	G (0-2 ER in 7+ IP)
1	Shane Bieber	Guardians	12
2	Framber Valdez	Astros	10
2	Justin Verlander	Astros	10
4	Alek Manoah	Blue Jays	9
4	Gerrit Cole	Yankees	9
4	Martin Perez	Rangers	9
7	Shane McClanahan	Rays	8
7	Shohei Ohtani	Angels	8
7	Triston McKenzie	Guardians	8
10	Brady Singer	Royals	7
10	Nick Pivetta	Red Sox	7

AL Pitchers With 10+ Strikeouts in Game

Rank	Pitcher	Team	G (10+ SO)
1	Shohei Ohtani	Angels	10
2	Gerrit Cole	Yankees	9
3	Robbie Ray	Mariners	7
4	Dylan Cease	White Sox	4
4	Justin Verlander	Astros	4
4	Kevin Gausman	Blue Jays	4
4	Nestor Cortes	Yankees	4

Rank	Pitcher	Team	G (10+ SO)
4	Shane McClanahan	Rays	4
9	Cristian Javier	Astros	3
9	Framber Valdez	Astros	3
9	Shane Bieber	Guardians	3
9	Triston McKenzie	Guardians	3

AL Pitchers With No Baserunners in Save

Rank	Pitcher	Team	G (0 BR in SV)
1	Emmanuel Clase	Guardians	22
2	Liam Hendriks	White Sox	17
3	Jordan Romano	Blue Jays	15
4	Ryan Pressly	Astros	14
5	Scott Barlow	Royals	12
6	Gregory Soto	Tigers	11
6	Paul Sewald	Mariners	11
8	Clay Holmes	Yankees	10
9	Raisel Iglesias	Angels	9
10	Joe Barlow	Rangers	7

National League Extreme Games

NL Batters With 3+ Hits in Game

Rank	Batter	Team	G (3+ H)
1	Freddie Freeman	Dodgers	20
2	Jeff McNeil	Mets	16
3	Paul Goldschmidt	Cardinals	15
4	Austin Riley	Braves	14
4	Dansby Swanson	Braves	14
4	Manny Machado	Padres	14
4	Nico Hoerner	Cubs	14
8	Mookie Betts	Dodgers	13
8	Nolan Arenado	Cardinals	13
8	Pete Alonso	Mets	13

NL Batters With 2+ Home Runs in Game

Rank	Batter	Team	G (2+ HR)
1	Kyle Schwarber	Phillies	8
2	Rowdy Tellez	Brewers	5
3	Albert Pujols	Cardinals	4
3	Mookie Betts	Dodgers	4
5	C.J. Cron	Rockies	3
5	Christian Walker	Diamondbacks	3
5	Hunter Renfroe	Brewers	3
5	Manny Machado	Padres	3
5	Marcell Ozuna	Braves	3
5	Paul Goldschmidt	Cardinals	3
5	Pete Alonso	Mets	3
5	Rhys Hoskins	Phillies	3
5	William Contreras	Braves	3

NL Batters With 5+ RBIs in Game

Rank	Batter	Team	G (5+ RBI)
1	Pete Alonso	Mets	4
2	C.J. Cron	Rockies	3
2	Rowdy Tellez	Brewers	3
4	Albert Pujols	Cardinals	2
4	Alfonso Rivas	Cubs	2
4	Bryan Reynolds	Pirates	2
4	Eduardo Escobar	Mets	2
4	Freddie Freeman	Dodgers	2
4	Joc Pederson	Giants	2
4	Paul Goldschmidt	Cardinals	2
4	Rhys Hoskins	Phillies	2

NL Pitchers With 0-2 Earned Runs in 7+ Innings

Rank	Pitcher	Team	G (0-2 ER in 7+ IP)
1	Sandy Alcantara	Marlins	20
2	Aaron Nola	Phillies	11
2	Corbin Burnes	Brewers	11
2	Merrill Kelly	Diamondbacks	11
2	Miles Mikolas	Cardinals	11
6	Adam Wainwright	Cardinals	10
6	Yu Darvish	Padres	10
6	Zac Gallen	Diamondbacks	10
9	Max Fried	Braves	8
9	Max Scherzer	Mets	8
9	Tyler Anderson	Dodgers	8
9	Zack Wheeler	Phillies	8

NL Pitchers With 10+ Strikeouts in Game

Rank	Pitcher	Team	G (10+ SO)
1	Carlos Rodon	Giants	11
2	Corbin Burnes	Brewers	9
3	Brandon Woodruff	Brewers	7
4	Max Scherzer	Mets	6
4	Sandy Alcantara	Marlins	6
4	Spencer Strider	Braves	6
7	Aaron Nola	Phillies	5
7	Blake Snell	Padres	5
7	Charlie Morton	Braves	5
7	Jacob deGrom	Mets	5

NL Pitchers With No Baserunners in Save

Rank	Pitcher	Team	G (0 BR in SV)
1	Kenley Jansen	Braves	21
2	Daniel Bard	Rockies	17
3	Josh Hader	Brewers-Padres	14
4	Edwin Diaz	Mets	13
4	Taylor Rogers	Padres-Brewers	13
6	Devin Williams	Brewers	11
7	David Robertson	Cubs-Phillies	10
8	Camilo Doval	Giants	8
8	David Bednar	Pirates	8
8	Mark Melancon	Diamondbacks	8
8	Ryan Helsley	Cardinals	8

2022: WORST PERFORMANCES

THE PREVIOUS CHAPTER FOCUSED solely on the best performances of 2022. Most of the remaining sections of this publication have a similar bias toward the positive.

But not this chapter. It's time for us to consider the parenthetical portion of this book's title, the *"(and Worst)"* part. Hence the following compendium of 2022's most disappointing individual statistics.

If there were such a thing as a Least Valuable Player Award, last season's versions would have been presented to Jonathan Schoop in the American League and Patrick Corbin in the National League, the respective tailenders in overall base value.

Schoop, a second baseman for the Detroit Tigers, batted an anemic .202 in 131 games. The typical big leaguer would have attained 266 bases in Schoop's circumstances, but he reached only 189. His resulting BV [bat] of minus-77 was the worst in the AL. The same dismal rank was appended to his OBV, an identical minus-77.

Corbin pitched 152.2 innings in 31 starts for the Washington Nationals. He finished with an unfortunate record of 6-19 and a bloated earned run average of 6.31. His BV [pitch] of plus-100 translated to an OBV of minus-100, easily the NL's worst.

Batters (six) outnumbered pitchers (four) on the list of the American League's 10 lowest overall base values. But pitchers were dominant in the National League, filling eight of the 10 worst slots for OBV, including all six with the most heavily negative values.

Tables of the worst OBV performances are located toward the end of this chapter, along with a plethora of other tables that have the same negative bent.

The following summary looks at what can appropriately be called the lowlights of 2022.

American League

Season Values for Batters

Base production: Any element of surprise was removed in the introductory portion of this chapter, where it was revealed that Jonathan Schoop posted the AL's worst BV [bat] of minus-77. Next was Leury Garcia, a utility player for the Chicago White Sox, at minus-67.

Run production: Catcher Yasmani Grandal has enjoyed productive seasons in his career, notably in 2019, when he scored 79 runs and drove in 77 for the Milwaukee Brewers. But his 2022 performance for the White Sox came nowhere close to those standards. Grandal was directly responsible for only 37 runs, falling 36 short of expectations. The latter was the league's lowest scoring value (SCV).

Power hitting: A single stat encapsulates Myles Straw's lack of power. The center fielder for the Cleveland Guardians hit zero home runs in the entire 2022 season. Zero. He reached only 28 extra bases through doubles, triples, and homers in 152 games, saddling him with an XV of minus-53, the worst in the AL.

Contact hitting: A swing and a miss. That was a common phrase when Eugenio Suarez stood at the plate for the Seattle Mariners. The third baseman had the dubious distinction of being the American League's leader in strikeouts (196). He also posted the worst BPV, minus-60, indicating that he put 60 fewer balls into play than expected.

Batting eye: Amed Rosario knows how to hit. The Cleveland shortstop batted a solid .283 and led the AL with nine triples in 2022. He just doesn't like to walk. Rosario drew only 25 unintentional walks, falling 28 below average for a big-league batter with the same number of plate appearances (670). His minus-28 BBV made him the tailender in this category.

Season Values for Pitchers

Base prevention: The typical major-league pitcher allowed .660 bases per out in 2022. Kris Bubic's BPO for the Kansas City Royals was much higher, .839. His resulting BV [pitch] soared to plus-69, the highest (and consequently the worst) figure in the American League.

Run prevention: The Toronto Blue Jays had strong expectations for Jose Berrios, a starter who had whittled his ERA to 3.52 in 2021, the lowest figure in his six-year career. So they were sadly disappointed by his 2022 rise to an ERA of 5.23. Berrios yielded 24 earned runs more than average, tying him with Dallas Keuchel for the league's highest earned run value. Keuchel's ERV of plus-24 was notable because he compiled it in just 42 innings for the Chicago White Sox and Texas Rangers, compared to 172 innings for Berrios.

Power prevention: Bruce Zimmermann had trouble keeping the ball in the park last season. The starter for the Baltimore Orioles gave up 21 home runs in just 73.2 innings of work. He allowed 88 extra bases in all, counting one XB for each double, two for each triple, and three for each homer. His XV of plus-42 was the AL's worst.

Strikeout pitching: Marco Gonzales is no power pitcher. The Seattle starter notched only 103 strikeouts in 183 innings in 2022. Hitters put 614 balls in play against him, exceeding the big-league average by 76. The latter number, his BPV of plus-76, was the highest for any AL pitcher.

Control pitching: Yusei Kikuchi of the Blue Jays waged a season-long battle with the strike zone. Kikuchi issued 58 unintentional walks, translating to a walk value (BBV) of plus-22. No other AL pitcher did worse than plus-19.

Extreme Games for Batters

No hits in five or more at-bats: The back portion of this chapter also features tables of the most frequent occurrences of two negative events for individual batters and another two for pitchers. Marcus Semien, a second baseman for the Texas Rangers, went hitless in five or more at-bats on 10 occasions in 2022, an unhappy distinction unsurpassed by anyone else in the American League.

Four or more strikeouts in a game: Two free-swinging designated hitters tied for the lead in this category. Franmil Reyes of the Guardians and Giancarlo Stanton of the Yankees both struck out at least four times in five different games.

Extreme Games for Pitchers

Ten or more baserunners in a game: Marco Gonzales, Jose Berrios, and Kris Bubic were all mentioned earlier in this chapter. They make a return appearance in this category: Gonzales as the AL leader with 11 games in which he allowed at least 10 baserunners, Berrios and Bubic as runners-up with 10 such appearances apiece.

One or more earned runs in a save: This could be named the *messy* save, an instance in which a reliever is credited in the SV column despite giving up at least one earned run. Liam Hendriks of the Chicago White Sox and Ryan Pressly of the Houston Astros topped the American League with five messy saves each.

National League

Season Values for Batters

Base production: Maikel Franco, a third baseman for the Washington Nationals, batted just .229 and drew only 12 walks in 388 plate appearances last season. That's a recipe for a poor BV [bat], and his mark of minus-58 proved to be the very worst in the National League. Franco accumulated just 145 bases, falling 58 short of expectations.

Run production: Shortstop Miguel Rojas scored only 34 runs and drove home 36 in 140 games for the Miami Marlins. His scoring value of minus-35 was 12 below the corresponding SCV for any other NL batter.

Power hitting: Another member of the Nationals earns the dubious honor of recognition in this chapter. Second baseman Cesar Hernandez played 147 games for Washington in 2022, yet he hit just one home run. Hernandez reached only 39 extra bases through doubles, triples, and homers, leaving him with a league-worst XV of minus-46.

Contact hitting: Contact is not the first word that comes to mind in describing Chicago third baseman Patrick Wisdom. His contact rate for the Cubs last season was an abysmal .610, which means that 39 percent of his at-bats ended in strikeouts. Wisdom put 66 fewer balls into play than average, establishing him as the tailender in BPV.

Batting eye: There was a three-way tie on this list between Philadelphia third baseman Alec Bohm, Washington infielder Luis Garcia, and Colorado shortstop Jose Iglesias. Each finished 2022 with a walk value (BBV) of minus-20, indicating that he drew 20 fewer walks than expected.

Season Values for Pitchers

Base prevention: We already know that Washington's Patrick Corbin posted the worst BV [pitch] in the National League. He was, in fact, the only pitcher in either league to finish 2022 with a positive triple-digit mark, ending the year at precisely plus-100.

Run prevention: Corbin again. His earned run value (ERV) of plus-40 indicates that his total of 107 earned runs exceeded the big-league average by 40 last season. No other NL pitcher had an ERV worse than plus-27.

Power prevention: Another Washington pitcher takes the spotlight. Josiah Gray was shelled by opposing hitters in 2022; they blasted 38 home runs off of him in 148.2 innings. Gray yielded a grand total of 142 extra bases, giving him an NL-worst XV of plus-55.

Strikeout pitching: St. Louis starter Dakota Hudson often showed an inability to get a third strike when he needed it in 2022. He finished the season with only 78 strikeouts in 139.2 innings. Hudson's BPV of plus-51, the highest in the league, signified that batters put 51 more balls in play against him than the major-league average.

Control pitching: Tanner Scott issued 45 unintentional walks in only 62.2 innings of relief for the Miami Marlins. His resulting walk value (BBV) of plus-22 was the worst in the National League, outpacing even those starters who worked three times as many innings.

Extreme Games for Batters

No hits in five or more at-bats: The Milwaukee Brewers were a free-swinging team in 2022, as evidenced by their one-star rating for contact hitting. It was an approach that didn't always pay off. Milwaukee first baseman Rowdy Tellez topped this list by going hitless in five or more trips on 12 different occasions. Teammate Andrew McCutchen, a designated hitter, was the runner-up with nine such games.

Four or more strikeouts in a game: Five players had the misfortune of tying for first place on this list. Each of them suffered at least four strikeouts in four games: Austin Riley of the Braves, Kyle Schwarber of the Phillies, Lane Thomas of the Nationals, Oneil Cruz of the Pirates, and Luke Voit, who split his season between the Padres and Nationals.

Extreme Games for Pitchers

Ten or more baserunners in a game: It seemed that the basepaths were often congested in 2022 for German Marquez of the Colorado Rockies and Patrick Corbin of the Washington Nationals, each of whom allowed 10 or more baserunners in 12 separate starts.

One or more earned runs in a save: Kenley Jansen picked up seven messy saves for the Atlanta Braves, allowing an earned run on each occasion, yet still getting an SV credit. Craig Kimbrel of the Los Angeles Dodgers was right behind Jansen with six.

American League Season Tailenders

AL Overall Performance: OBV

Rank	Player	Team	BV [bat]	BV [pitch]	OBV
1	Jonathan Schoop	Tigers	-77	0	-77
2	Kris Bubic	Royals	0	69	-69
3	Nicky Lopez	Royals	-61	7	-68
4	Leury Garcia	White Sox	-67	0	-67
5	Austin Hedges	Guardians	-60	0	-60
5	Yusei Kikuchi	Blue Jays	0	60	-60
5	Cristian Pache	Athletics	-60	0	-60
8	Adam Oller	Athletics	0	59	-59
9	Bruce Zimmermann	Orioles	0	58	-58
10	Myles Straw	Guardians	-55	0	-55
11	Jackie Bradley Jr.	Red Sox-Blue Jays	-52	0	-52
11	Adam Frazier	Mariners	-52	0	-52
13	Tucker Barnhart	Tigers	-48	2	-50
13	Daniel Lynch	Royals	0	50	-50
15	Nick Allen	Athletics	-49	0	-49
15	Jose Berrios	Blue Jays	0	49	-49
17	Dane Dunning	Rangers	0	47	-47
17	Jonathan Heasley	Royals	0	47	-47
17	Zach Logue	Athletics	0	47	-47
17	Taylor Walls	Rays	-47	0	-47
21	Kole Calhoun	Rangers	-46	0	-46
21	Spencer Howard	Rangers	0	46	-46
21	Max Stassi	Angels	-46	0	-46
24	Lucas Giolito	White Sox	0	45	-45
24	Elvin Rodriguez	Tigers	0	45	-45
24	Abraham Toro	Mariners	-45	0	-45

AL Base Production: BV [bat]

Rank	Batter	Team	B	O	BPO	BV [bat]
1	Jonathan Schoop	Tigers	189	403	.469	-77
2	Leury Garcia	White Sox	97	248	.391	-67
3	Nicky Lopez	Royals	176	359	.490	-61
4	Austin Hedges	Guardians	119	271	.439	-60
4	Cristian Pache	Athletics	79	211	.374	-60
6	Myles Straw	Guardians	228	428	.533	-55
7	Jackie Bradley Jr.	Red Sox-Blue Jays	135	284	.475	-52
7	Adam Frazier	Mariners	240	443	.542	-52
9	Nick Allen	Athletics	117	251	.466	-49
10	Tucker Barnhart	Tigers	102	227	.449	-48

AL Run Production: SCV [bat]

Rank	Batter	Team	PA	SC	SE	SCV [bat]
1	Yasmani Grandal	White Sox	376	37	.098	-36
2	Tucker Barnhart	Tigers	308	31	.101	-29
3	J.P. Crawford	Mariners	603	93	.154	-25
4	Jonathan Schoop	Tigers	510	75	.147	-24
5	Nicky Lopez	Royals	480	71	.148	-23
6	Miguel Cabrera	Tigers	433	63	.145	-21
6	Spencer Torkelson	Tigers	404	58	.144	-21
8	Max Stassi	Angels	375	53	.141	-20
8	Matt Duffy	Angels	247	28	.113	-20
8	Luis Rengifo	Angels	511	80	.157	-20

AL Power Hitting: XV [bat]

Rank	Batter	Team	AB	XB	ISO	XV [bat]
1	Myles Straw	Guardians	535	28	.052	-53
2	Nicky Lopez	Royals	436	20	.046	-46
3	Adam Frazier	Mariners	541	39	.072	-43
4	Isiah Kiner-Falefa	Yankees	483	32	.066	-41
5	Miguel Cabrera	Tigers	397	25	.063	-35
6	J.P. Crawford	Mariners	518	48	.093	-31
7	Tucker Barnhart	Tigers	281	13	.046	-30

Rank	Batter	Team	AB	XB	ISO	XV [bat]
8	Leury Garcia	White Sox	300	17	.057	-29
8	Steven Kwan	Guardians	563	57	.101	-29
10	Yasmani Grandal	White Sox	327	22	.067	-28

AL Contact Hitting: BPV [bat]

Rank	Batter	Team	AB	BP	CT	BPV [bat]
1	Eugenio Suarez	Mariners	543	347	.639	-60
2	Joey Gallo	Yankees	233	127	.545	-48
3	Brandon Marsh	Angels	292	175	.599	-44
3	Brett Phillips	Rays-Orioles	201	107	.532	-44
5	Jo Adell	Angels	268	161	.601	-40
6	Kole Calhoun	Rangers	388	252	.649	-39
6	Bobby Dalbec	Red Sox	317	199	.628	-39
6	Andrew Velazquez	Angels	322	203	.630	-39
9	Franmil Reyes	Guardians	263	159	.605	-38
9	Giancarlo Stanton	Yankees	398	261	.656	-38

AL Batting Eye: BBV [bat]

Rank	Batter	Team	PA-IBB	UBB	EY	BBV [bat]
1	Amed Rosario	Guardians	670	25	.037	-28
2	Luis Rengifo	Angels	511	17	.033	-23
3	Javier Baez	Tigers	589	25	.042	-22
3	Jeremy Pena	Astros	558	22	.039	-22
3	Jonathan Schoop	Tigers	509	18	.035	-22
3	Bobby Witt	Royals	630	28	.044	-22
7	Salvador Perez	Royals	471	16	.034	-21
8	Harold Castro	Tigers	442	16	.036	-19
9	Leury Garcia	White Sox	315	7	.022	-18
9	Raimel Tapia	Blue Jays	433	16	.037	-18

AL Base Prevention: BV [pitch]

Rank	Pitcher	Team	B	O	BPO	BV [pitch]
1	Kris Bubic	Royals	323	385	.839	69
2	Yusei Kikuchi	Blue Jays	261	304	.859	60
3	Adam Oller	Athletics	206	222	.928	59
4	Bruce Zimmermann	Orioles	205	222	.923	58
5	Daniel Lynch	Royals	315	401	.786	50
6	Jose Berrios	Blue Jays	387	512	.756	49
7	Dane Dunning	Rangers	349	457	.764	47
7	Jonathan Heasley	Royals	255	315	.810	47
7	Zach Logue	Athletics	159	170	.935	47
10	Spencer Howard	Rangers	121	114	1.061	46

AL Run Prevention: ERV [pitch]

Rank	Pitcher	Team	IP	ER	ERA	ERV [pitch]
1	Jose Berrios	Blue Jays	172.0	100	5.23	24
1	Dallas Keuchel	White Sox-Rangers	42.0	42	9.00	24
3	Kris Bubic	Royals	129.0	80	5.58	23
4	Elvin Rodriguez	Tigers	29.2	35	10.62	22
5	Carlos Hernandez	Royals	56.0	46	7.39	21
6	Adam Oller	Athletics	74.1	52	6.30	19
7	Brad Keller	Royals	139.2	79	5.09	18
7	Zach Logue	Athletics	57.0	43	6.79	18
7	Mitch White	Blue Jays	43.0	37	7.74	18
10	Lucas Giolito	White Sox	161.2	88	4.90	17
10	Daniel Lynch	Royals	131.2	75	5.13	17
10	Bruce Zimmermann	Orioles	73.2	49	5.99	17

AL Power Prevention: XV [pitch]

Rank	Pitcher	Team	AB	XB	ISO	XV [pitch]
1	Bruce Zimmermann	Orioles	302	88	.291	42
2	Yusei Kikuchi	Blue Jays	383	96	.251	38
3	Adam Oller	Athletics	293	79	.270	34
4	Zach Logue	Athletics	232	63	.272	28
4	Robbie Ray	Mariners	705	135	.191	28
6	Elvin Rodriguez	Tigers	127	45	.354	26

Rank	Pitcher	Team	AB	XB	ISO	XV [pitch]
6	Jose Urquidy	Astros	630	122	.194	26
8	Marco Gonzales	Mariners	717	134	.187	25
8	Spencer Howard	Rangers	162	50	.309	25
10	Jonathan Heasley	Royals	404	85	.210	24

AL Strikeout Pitching: BPV [pitch]

Rank	Pitcher	Team	AB	BP	CT	BPV [pitch]
1	Marco Gonzales	Mariners	717	614	.856	76
2	Zack Greinke	Royals	549	476	.867	64
3	Johnny Cueto	White Sox	604	502	.831	49
4	Cal Quantrill	Guardians	702	574	.818	47
5	Dylan Bundy	Twins	558	464	.832	45
5	Cole Irvin	Athletics	693	565	.815	45
7	Spenser Watkins	Orioles	423	360	.851	43
8	Tyler Alexander	Tigers	393	332	.845	37
8	Chris Flexen	Mariners	529	434	.820	37
10	Drew Hutchison	Tigers	417	349	.837	36
10	Brad Keller	Royals	553	451	.816	36

AL Control Pitching: BBV [pitch]

Rank	Pitcher	Team	PA-IBB	UBB	EY	BBV [pitch]
1	Yusei Kikuchi	Blue Jays	454	58	.128	22
2	Jake Diekman	Red Sox-White Sox	267	40	.150	19
3	Michael Kopech	White Sox	494	57	.115	18
4	Kris Bubic	Royals	587	63	.107	17
4	Dylan Cease	White Sox	745	76	.102	17
6	Amir Garrett	Royals	196	32	.163	16
6	Glenn Otto	Rangers	587	62	.106	16
8	Matt Brash	Mariners	221	32	.145	15
8	Aroldis Chapman	Yankees	160	28	.175	15
8	Josh Staumont	Royals	176	29	.165	15

National League Season Tailenders

NL Overall Performance: OBV

Rank	Player	Team	BV [bat]	BV [pitch]	OBV
1	Patrick Corbin	Nationals	0	100	-100
2	Mike Minor	Reds	0	88	-88
3	Chad Kuhl	Rockies	0	78	-78
4	Josiah Gray	Nationals	0	72	-72
5	Erick Fedde	Nationals	0	70	-70
6	Madison Bumgarner	Diamondbacks	0	69	-69
7	Yadier Molina	Cardinals	-54	10	-64
8	Maikel Franco	Nationals	-58	0	-58
8	Kyle Freeland	Rockies	0	58	-58
10	Elieser Hernandez	Marlins	0	56	-56
11	Vladimir Gutierrez	Reds	0	54	-54
12	Miguel Rojas	Marlins	-53	0	-53
13	Avisail Garcia	Marlins	-52	0	-52
13	German Marquez	Rockies	0	52	-52
15	Geraldo Perdomo	Diamondbacks	-51	0	-51
15	Jacob Stallings	Marlins	-51	0	-51
17	Jose Barrero	Reds	-49	0	-49
18	Joan Adon	Nationals	0	48	-48
18	Trevor Rogers	Marlins	0	48	-48
20	Antonio Senzatela	Rockies	0	47	-47
20	Josh VanMeter	Pirates	-20	27	-47
22	Jason Alexander	Brewers	0	45	-45
22	Cesar Hernandez	Nationals	-45	0	-45
22	Bryse Wilson	Pirates	0	45	-45
25	Frank Schwindel	Cubs	-29	15	-44

NL Base Production: BV [bat]

Rank	Batter	Team	B	O	BPO	BV [bat]
1	Maikel Franco	Nationals	145	307	.472	-58
2	Yadier Molina	Cardinals	89	217	.410	-54
3	Miguel Rojas	Marlins	197	379	.520	-53
4	Avisail Garcia	Marlins	140	291	.481	-52
5	Geraldo Perdomo	Diamondbacks	191	366	.522	-51
5	Jacob Stallings	Marlins	139	288	.483	-51
7	Jose Barrero	Reds	47	145	.324	-49
8	Cesar Hernandez	Nationals	245	439	.558	-45
9	Tomas Nido	Mets	121	244	.496	-40
10	Nick Senzel	Reds	160	302	.530	-39

NL Run Production: SCV [bat]

Rank	Batter	Team	PA	SC	SE	SCV [bat]
1	Miguel Rojas	Marlins	507	64	.126	-35
2	Cesar Hernandez	Nationals	617	97	.157	-23
3	Keibert Ruiz	Nationals	433	62	.143	-22
4	Jacob Stallings	Marlins	384	55	.143	-20
4	Ke'Bryan Hayes	Pirates	560	89	.159	-20
6	Nick Madrigal	Cubs	228	26	.114	-18
6	Omar Narvaez	Brewers	296	40	.135	-18
6	Jesus Aguilar	Marlins	456	71	.156	-18
6	Brandon Belt	Giants	298	40	.134	-18
10	Nick Senzel	Reds	420	65	.155	-17
10	Luis Guillorme	Mets	335	48	.143	-17
10	Donovan Solano	Reds	304	42	.138	-17

NL Power Hitting: XV [bat]

Rank	Batter	Team	AB	XB	ISO	XV [bat]
1	Cesar Hernandez	Nationals	560	39	.070	-46
2	Geraldo Perdomo	Diamondbacks	431	29	.067	-37
3	Miguel Rojas	Marlins	471	41	.087	-31
4	Nick Senzel	Reds	373	28	.075	-29
4	Jacob Stallings	Marlins	346	24	.069	-29
6	Jose Iglesias	Rockies	439	39	.089	-28
7	Yonathan Daza	Rockies	372	31	.083	-26
7	Ke'Bryan Hayes	Pirates	505	51	.101	-26
7	Austin Nola	Padres	347	27	.078	-26
10	Luis Guillorme	Mets	297	20	.067	-25
10	Nick Madrigal	Cubs	209	7	.033	-25

NL Contact Hitting: BPV [bat]

Rank	Batter	Team	AB	BP	CT	BPV [bat]
1	Patrick Wisdom	Cubs	469	286	.610	-66
2	Chris Taylor	Dodgers	402	242	.602	-60
3	Kyle Schwarber	Phillies	577	377	.653	-56
4	Luke Voit	Padres-Nationals	500	321	.642	-54
5	Keston Hiura	Brewers	234	123	.526	-53
6	Joey Bart	Giants	261	149	.571	-47
7	Oneil Cruz	Pirates	331	205	.619	-43
7	J.D. Davis	Mets-Giants	318	196	.616	-43
9	Christopher Morel	Cubs	379	242	.639	-42
10	Trayce Thompson	Padres-Dodgers	219	126	.575	-38

NL Batting Eye: BBV [bat]

Rank	Batter	Team	PA-IBB	UBB	EY	BBV [bat]
1	Alec Bohm	Phillies	630	30	.048	-20
1	Luis Garcia	Nationals	376	10	.027	-20
1	Jose Iglesias	Rockies	467	17	.036	-20
4	CJ Abrams	Padres-Nationals	302	5	.017	-19
4	Maikel Franco	Nationals	388	12	.031	-19
4	Randal Grichuk	Rockies	538	24	.045	-19
7	Charlie Blackmon	Rockies	573	28	.049	-17

Rank	Batter	Team	PA-IBB	UBB	EY	BBV [bat]
7	Nico Hoerner	Cubs	513	24	.047	-17
9	Michael Chavis	Pirates	425	18	.042	-16
9	Yadier Molina	Cardinals	270	5	.019	-16

NL Base Prevention: BV [pitch]

Rank	Pitcher	Team	B	O	BPO	BV [pitch]
1	Patrick Corbin	Nationals	408	466	.876	100
2	Mike Minor	Reds	283	295	.959	88
3	Chad Kuhl	Rockies	350	412	.850	78
4	Josiah Gray	Nationals	368	448	.821	72
5	Erick Fedde	Nationals	321	381	.843	70
6	Madison Bumgarner	Diamondbacks	386	480	.804	69
7	Kyle Freeland	Rockies	407	529	.769	58
8	Elieser Hernandez	Marlins	180	188	.957	56
9	Vladimir Gutierrez	Reds	125	108	1.157	54
10	German Marquez	Rockies	415	550	.755	52

NL Run Prevention: ERV [pitch]

Rank	Pitcher	Team	IP	ER	ERA	ERV [pitch]
1	Patrick Corbin	Nationals	152.2	107	6.31	40
2	Chad Kuhl	Rockies	137.0	87	5.72	27
3	Erick Fedde	Nationals	127.0	82	5.81	26
4	Joan Adon	Nationals	64.2	51	7.10	23
4	Mike Minor	Reds	98.0	66	6.06	23
6	Austin Gomber	Rockies	124.2	77	5.56	22
7	German Marquez	Rockies	181.2	101	5.00	21
8	Ryan Feltner	Rockies	97.1	63	5.83	20
8	Kyle Gibson	Phillies	167.2	94	5.05	20
8	Bryse Wilson	Pirates	115.2	71	5.52	20

NL Power Prevention: XV [pitch]

Rank	Pitcher	Team	AB	XB	ISO	XV [pitch]
1	Josiah Gray	Nationals	569	142	.250	55
2	Elieser Hernandez	Marlins	249	79	.317	41
3	German Marquez	Rockies	704	145	.206	38
4	Chad Kuhl	Rockies	546	118	.216	35
4	Mike Minor	Reds	405	97	.240	35
6	Madison Bumgarner	Diamondbacks	637	131	.206	34
7	Sean Manaea	Padres	611	123	.201	30
8	Patrick Corbin	Nationals	655	126	.192	26
9	Paolo Espino	Nationals	456	94	.206	25
10	Matt Swarmer	Cubs	132	44	.333	24

NL Strikeout Pitching: BPV [pitch]

Rank	Pitcher	Team	AB	BP	CT	BPV [pitch]
1	Dakota Hudson	Cardinals	517	439	.849	51
2	Madison Bumgarner	Diamondbacks	637	525	.824	47
3	Kyle Freeland	Rockies	687	556	.809	41
3	Antonio Senzatela	Rockies	381	327	.858	41
3	Adam Wainwright	Cardinals	736	593	.806	41
6	Patrick Corbin	Nationals	655	527	.805	36
6	Bryse Wilson	Pirates	460	381	.828	36
8	Graham Ashcraft	Reds	423	352	.832	35
8	Miles Mikolas	Cardinals	751	598	.796	35
10	Erick Fedde	Nationals	508	414	.815	33
10	Zach Thompson	Pirates	493	403	.817	33

NL Control Pitching: BBV [pitch]

Rank	Pitcher	Team	PA-IBB	UBB	EY	BBV [pitch]
1	Tanner Scott	Marlins	288	45	.156	22
2	Ian Anderson	Braves	493	54	.110	15
3	Joan Adon	Nationals	309	38	.123	14
3	Josiah Gray	Nationals	648	65	.100	14
3	Jordan Hicks	Cardinals	263	35	.133	14
3	Dakota Hudson	Cardinals	596	61	.102	14
3	Ryan Pepiot	Dodgers	160	27	.169	14
3	Caleb Smith	Diamondbacks	301	38	.126	14
9	Erick Fedde	Nationals	573	58	.101	13
9	MacKenzie Gore	Padres	309	37	.120	13
9	Tyler Matzek	Braves	182	27	.148	13
9	David Robertson	Cubs-Phillies	263	34	.129	13

American League Extreme Games

AL Batters With 0 Hits in 5+ At-Bats

Rank	Batter	Team	G (0 H in 5+ AB)
1	Marcus Semien	Rangers	10
2	Yoan Moncada	White Sox	9
3	Bo Bichette	Blue Jays	8
4	Adam Frazier	Mariners	7
4	Adolis Garcia	Rangers	7
4	Anthony Santander	Orioles	7
4	DJ LeMahieu	Yankees	7
4	Luis Arraez	Twins	7
4	Salvador Perez	Royals	7
4	Vladimir Guerrero Jr.	Blue Jays	7

AL Batters With 4+ Strikeouts in Game

Rank	Batter	Team	G (4+ SO)
1	Franmil Reyes	Guardians	5
1	Giancarlo Stanton	Yankees	5
3	Eugenio Suarez	Mariners	3
3	Mike Trout	Angels	3
5	Brandon Marsh	Angels	2
5	Eli White	Rangers	2
5	Gunnar Henderson	Orioles	2
5	Jake Cave	Twins	2
5	Jarren Duran	Red Sox	2
5	Joey Gallo	Yankees	2
5	Josh Jung	Rangers	2
5	Kole Calhoun	Rangers	2
5	Matt Chapman	Blue Jays	2
5	Nathaniel Lowe	Rangers	2
5	Riley Greene	Tigers	2
5	Ryan McKenna	Orioles	2
5	Shohei Ohtani	Angels	2
5	Steven Duggar	Rangers-Angels	2
5	Trevor Story	Red Sox	2
5	Vladimir Guerrero Jr.	Blue Jays	2

AL Pitchers With 10+ Baserunners in Game

Rank	Pitcher	Team	G (10+ BR)
1	Marco Gonzales	Mariners	11
2	Jose Berrios	Blue Jays	10
2	Kris Bubic	Royals	10
4	Framber Valdez	Astros	9
5	Dane Dunning	Rangers	8
5	Jordan Lyles	Orioles	8
5	Nick Pivetta	Red Sox	8
8	Cal Quantrill	Guardians	7
8	Johnny Cueto	White Sox	7
8	Martin Perez	Rangers	7
8	Patrick Sandoval	Angels	7

AL Pitchers With 1+ Earned Runs in Save

Rank	Pitcher	Team	G (1+ ER in SV)
1	Liam Hendriks	White Sox	5
1	Ryan Pressly	Astros	5
3	Paul Sewald	Mariners	4
4	Felix Bautista	Orioles	3
4	Gregory Soto	Tigers	3
4	Rafael Montero	Astros	3
7	Andrew Kittredge	Rays	2
7	Aroldis Chapman	Yankees	2
7	Clay Holmes	Yankees	2
7	Garrett Whitlock	Red Sox	2
7	Jordan Romano	Blue Jays	2
7	Kendall Graveman	White Sox	2
7	Scott Barlow	Royals	2

National League Extreme Games

NL Batters With 0 Hits in 5+ At-Bats

Rank	Batter	Team	G (0 H in 5+ AB)
1	Rowdy Tellez	Brewers	12
2	Andrew McCutchen	Brewers	9
3	Dylan Carlson	Cardinals	8
3	Ronald Acuna Jr.	Braves	8
5	Cesar Hernandez	Nationals	7
5	Charlie Blackmon	Rockies	7
5	Ian Happ	Cubs	7
5	Mookie Betts	Dodgers	7
5	Willy Adames	Brewers	7
10	Dansby Swanson	Braves	6
10	J.T. Realmuto	Phillies	6
10	Jesus Aguilar	Marlins	6
10	Jonathan India	Reds	6
10	Josh Bell	Nationals-Padres	6
10	Kyle Schwarber	Phillies	6

NL Batters With 4+ Strikeouts in Game

Rank	Batter	Team	G (4+ SO)
1	Austin Riley	Braves	4
1	Kyle Schwarber	Phillies	4
1	Lane Thomas	Nationals	4
1	Luke Voit	Padres-Nationals	4
1	Oneil Cruz	Pirates	4
6	Aristides Aquino	Reds	3
6	Michael Chavis	Pirates	3
8	Charlie Blackmon	Rockies	2
8	Christian Yelich	Brewers	2
8	Christopher Morel	Cubs	2
8	Edmundo Sosa	Cardinals-Phillies	2
8	Ian Happ	Cubs	2
8	Jack Suwinski	Pirates	2
8	Jonathan India	Reds	2

Rank	Batter	Team	G (4+ SO)
8	Matt Olson	Braves	2
8	Nelson Velazquez	Cubs	2
8	Patrick Wisdom	Cubs	2
8	Tyler Naquin	Reds-Mets	2

NL Pitchers With 10+ Baserunners in Game

Rank	Pitcher	Team	G (10+ BR)
1	German Marquez	Rockies	12
1	Patrick Corbin	Nationals	12
3	Adam Wainwright	Cardinals	11
3	Kyle Freeland	Rockies	11
3	Madison Bumgarner	Diamondbacks	11
6	Graham Ashcraft	Reds	10
7	Chad Kuhl	Rockies	9
7	JT Brubaker	Pirates	9
7	Mike Minor	Reds	9
10	Dakota Hudson	Cardinals	8

NL Pitchers With 1+ Earned Runs in Save

Rank	Pitcher	Team	G (1+ ER in SV)
1	Kenley Jansen	Braves	7
2	Craig Kimbrel	Dodgers	6
3	Taylor Rogers	Padres-Brewers	5
4	Alexis Diaz	Reds	3
4	Josh Hader	Brewers-Padres	3
4	Nick Martinez	Padres	3
4	Ryan Helsley	Cardinals	3
8	Alex Colome	Rockies	2
8	Daniel Bard	Rockies	2
8	Edwin Diaz	Mets	2
8	Giovanny Gallegos	Cardinals	2
8	Hunter Strickland	Reds	2
8	Tanner Scott	Marlins	2

2023: PREDICTIONS

NOBODY KNOWS HOW THE 2023 baseball season will turn out. Nobody.

The rosters for all 30 clubs were in flux as the calendar flipped into the new year, and they're certain to remain unstable all spring. Free agents will keep hopping from team to team as January, February, and March drag on. Trading activity will continue unabated as the weather gets warmer. Phenoms will pop up in spring-training games in Florida and Arizona. Marginal players will be waived, and equally marginal replacements will be signed.

It's a fool's errand to predict 2023's standings in the midst of such uncertainty, yet a plethora of preseason magazines, sports websites, columnists, and beat writers will issue their fearless forecasts prior to opening day. This book is joining the parade.

A yearbook, by definition, looks back at the previous season, but it's also expected to gaze into its crystal ball. This chapter uses a unique mechanism to accomplish the latter task.

I developed a computer program to compare each team's record during the past three seasons (2020-2022) against the corresponding marks for 1,258 clubs that played during the era of free agency, which began in 1976. (A couple of notes: Expansion teams obviously couldn't be added to this mix until they played three seasons. And I cut off the comparisons after 2020, so that all of the clubs involved would have at least two years of future data.)

The aim was to find parallels from history that might offer hints about the future, to gain insights into each present-day team by studying what eventually happened to its close matches from the past.

The 2020-2022 team scores for a current club were compared to the corresponding scores for every team in the comparison pool. The absolute differences between each set of scores were added on a 3-2-1 basis, putting the strongest emphasis on the most recent pair.

Here's a closer look at the formula, accompanied by an example that pits the 2020-2022 Milwaukee Brewers against the 1987-1989 Boston Red Sox:

Diff (TS) = (3 • Diff (2022)) + (2 • Diff (2021)) + Diff (2020)

Diff (TS) = 3 • | (51.203 − 51.960) | + 2 • | (60.272 − 61.593) | + | (42.825 - 43.608) | = 5.696

You might remember the pipe symbol (|) from your school days. It's the sign for absolute value, indicating that the result of each subtraction above is to displayed as a positive number, no matter which side of the equation is larger.

The TS for the 2022 Brewers was 51.203, extremely close to the 1989 Red Sox at 51.960. The absolute difference between the two was 0.757. That was the most recent pair in this example, so it was tripled to 2.271. Then we stepped back a year to compare the 2021 Brewers and the 1988 Red Sox, just 1.321 points apart, doubled to 2.642. Then to the 2020 Brewers and the 1987 Red Sox, just 0.783 from each other. The sum of these absolute differences was 5.696, a very close match.

Here's another example, this time showing a wide gap between two clubs. The 2020-2022 Brewers are involved again, this time along with the 2003-2005 Kansas City Royals:

Diff (TS) = (3 • Diff (2022)) + (2 • Diff (2021)) + Diff (2020)

Diff (TS) = 3 • | (51.203 - 10.715) | + 2 • | (60.272 - 14.882) | + | (42.825 - 43.371) | = 212.790

The sum of 212.790 points was enormous, telling us that these versions of the Brewers and Royals had virtually nothing in common. It proved to be one of the eight worst matches for Milwaukee in the entire pool of 1,258 comparisons.

But our initial example, involving the Brewers and Red Sox, had a much different outcome. It emerged as Milwaukee's very best match of all. No other club from the period of free agency came closer to the 2020-2022 Brewers than the Red Sox from 1987 to 1989.

I compiled a list of the 50 closest matches (CMs) for each current club, culling the top 4 percent of all 1,258 candidates, the 4 percent with the smallest sums of absolute differences.

I then examined the subsequent performance of each of the 50 CMs. We've already evaluated the team scores for the 1987-1989 Red Sox, for example, but how did Boston perform in its next season, 1990? The same question was repeated for all 50 look-alikes.

And that's how the predictions for this chapter were generated. The next-year records for each current club's 50 closest matches were tabulated, generating separate breakdowns of playoff qualifiers, league champions, and World Series winners.

You'll find those numbers in the divisional tables at the end of this chapter, along with the 2022 record for each current team, and the name and three-year span for its very best match. (You'll also see a list of every club's 25 closest matches—all that space will allow—on the final page of its profile in the back of this book.)

The Red Sox, by the way, went 88-74 in 1990 and qualified for the playoffs, which is a positive sign for Milwaukee's 2023 prospects. But the second-best match for the 2020-2022 Brewers—the 1998-2000 Cincinnati Reds—stumbled to a 66-96 mark in 2001, giving cause for concern.

Thirty-three of Milwaukee's 50 closest matches played better than .500 ball the following season. Twenty-two made the playoffs, four won league championships (the Orioles in 1979, Red Sox in 1986, Giants in 1989, and Astros in 2017), and one (the Astros) won a World Series. Those are good omens for the Brewers, but their fans should keep in mind that the 2001 Reds, 2009 Diamondbacks (70-92), 2009 Indians (65-97), and 2017 Mets (70-92) also fit Milwaukee's template for 2023.

How accurate is my prediction system? The only honest answer is that I'm not sure. I suspect it's as reliable as the guesswork or direct extrapolations favored by many prognosticators. But we won't know for certain until October.

Divisional Forecasts

The final two pages of this chapter contain statistical summaries of the 50 closest matches for each of the 30 current teams. Clubs are listed in their predicted order of finish for 2023.

Divisional standings for the upcoming season were determined by a three-step process: (1) Teams were ranked by the number of their 50 closest matches who subsequently qualified for the playoffs. (2) Any ties were broken by the number of league championships. (3) If any ties persisted after the first two steps, they were broken by the number of World Series winners.

Below is a quick rundown of the predictions.

American League East

Most experts believe that the 2023 race in the AL East—whose members brag of being the toughest division in baseball—will be extremely tight. My system agrees. It gives a slight nod to the Toronto Blue Jays, with 23 of their 50 closest matches making it to the playoffs. Right on their heels are the Tampa Bay Rays and New York Yankees, who have 21 qualifying CMs apiece. The first tiebreaker favors Tampa Bay for second place, based on its 11 league championships to five for New York.

American League Central

The Cleveland Guardians shocked most experts by winning the AL Central in 2022, but history suggests that a 2023 repeat should come as no surprise. Fourteen of the 50 CMs for the 2020-2022 Indians/Guardians played into the postseason the following year. That's the best total in the division, followed by the Chicago White Sox with 11 and the Minnesota Twins with eight.

American League West

Who could disagree with this one? The Houston Astros have dominated the AL West since 2017—taking five of the past six divisional crowns—a period they bookended with World Series titles in 2017 and 2022. My computer anticipates more of the same. Thirty-one of Houston's 50 CMs went to the playoffs, dwarfing the 14 for the runner-up Seattle Mariners.

National League East

The battle for the NL East raged to the end of the season in 2022, as the Atlanta Braves and New York Mets finished with identical 101-61 marks. The title went to Atlanta, based on its head-to-head advantage in games against New York. What about 2023? The Braves again hold an edge, with 26 of their 50 CMs pushing into the postseason. The Mets are second with 21 qualifiers, and don't forget about the Philadelphia Phillies with 19.

National League Central

If you ignore 2020's truncated schedule, recent championships in the NL Central have been traded between the St. Louis Cardinals (2019 and 2022) and Milwaukee Brewers (2018 and 2021). The forecast for 2023 calls for a dead heat between the same two clubs. Milwaukee has 22 playoff qualifiers among its 50 closest matches, while St. Louis has 21. The division's other three clubs are all far behind.

National League West

The trend in the NL West is obvious to everyone. The Los Angeles Dodgers finished in first place nine times during the past 10 seasons. The sole exception was 2021, when L.A. notched 106 victories, only to fall one game short of the San Francisco Giants. Look for another divisional repeat in 2023. Thirty-four of the Dodgers' 50 CMs were playoff-bound. The runners-up are San Francisco (16 qualifiers) and the San Diego Padres (12).

American League Closest Matches (2023)

American League East

Rank	Team	CM	WS	LC	PQ	2022	Top Match
1	Toronto Blue Jays	50	3	7	23	92-70 (P)	Pirates (2012-2014)
2	Tampa Bay Rays	50	5	11	21	86-76 (P)	Orioles (1979-1981)
3	New York Yankees	50	2	5	21	99-63 (P)	Brewers (1980-1982)
4	Boston Red Sox	50	1	2	13	78-84	Cardinals (1995-1997)
5	Baltimore Orioles	50	0	2	7	83-79	Mariners (2007-2009)

American League Central

Rank	Team	CM	WS	LC	PQ	2022	Top Match
1	Cleveland Guardians	50	1	1	14	92-70 (P)	White Sox (2008-2010)
2	Chicago White Sox	50	1	1	11	81-81	Dodgers (1982-1984)
3	Minnesota Twins	50	1	2	8	78-84	Astros (1986-1988)
4	Kansas City Royals	50	1	1	5	65-97	Royals (2016-2018)
5	Detroit Tigers	50	1	1	3	66-96	White Sox (2015-2017)

American League West

Rank	Team	CM	WS	LC	PQ	2022	Top Match
1	Houston Astros	50	8	14	31	106-56 (WLP)	Indians (1993-1995)
2	Seattle Mariners	50	0	3	14	90-72 (P)	Rays (2016-2018)
3	Los Angeles Angels	50	1	2	8	73-89	Athletics (1983-1985)
4	Texas Rangers	50	0	0	7	68-94	Phillies (1988-1990)
5	Oakland Athletics	50	0	0	3	60-102	Rangers (2012-2014)

National League Closest Matches (2023)

National League East

Rank	Team	CM	WS	LC	PQ	2022	Top Match
1	Atlanta Braves	50	3	6	26	101-61 (P)	Astros (1997-1999)
2	New York Mets	50	3	6	21	101-61 (P)	Padres (1994-1996)
3	Philadelphia Phillies	50	3	6	19	87-75 (LP)	Astros (1984-1986)
4	Miami Marlins	50	0	1	4	69-93	Brewers (1997-1999)
5	Washington Nationals	50	0	0	2	55-107	Marlins (2011-2013)

National League Central

Rank	Team	CM	WS	LC	PQ	2022	Top Match
1	Milwaukee Brewers	50	1	4	22	86-76	Red Sox (1987-1989)
2	St. Louis Cardinals	50	1	6	21	93-69 (P)	Royals (1987-1989)
3	Cincinnati Reds	50	1	1	5	62-100	Angels (1990-1992)
4	Chicago Cubs	50	0	0	4	74-88	Mets (2016-2018)
5	Pittsburgh Pirates	50	0	2	3	62-100	Orioles (2009-2011)

National League West

Rank	Team	CM	WS	LC	PQ	2022	Top Match
1	Los Angeles Dodgers	50	8	15	34	111-51 (P)	Braves (1997-1999)
2	San Francisco Giants	50	4	5	16	81-81	Marlins (2002-2004)
3	San Diego Padres	50	0	4	12	89-73 (P)	Dodgers (2009-2011)
4	Arizona Diamondbacks	50	0	1	8	74-88	Expos (1975-1977)
5	Colorado Rockies	50	1	1	3	68-94	Rockies (2012-2014)

Part 2
TEAM PROFILES

KEY TO THE PROFILES

THE REMAINDER OF THIS book comprises 30 team profiles, which are identical in format and length. Each 10-page chapter focuses on the 2022 performances and 2023 prospects for a given big-league club. Every chapter is divided into the same 23 sections, encompassing 25 tables and four graphs. Teams are profiled in alphabetical order.

Individual statistics apply only to a player's tenure with a specific club. Juan Soto's stats for the Washington Nationals, for example, do not include the two months he spent with the San Diego Padres after being traded. A few transactions kept prominent players from being listed at all. Josh Hader made 37 appearances as the Milwaukee Brewers' closer before being traded. But the qualifying threshold for a reliever is 41 games with a single club, so Hader isn't included in the listing of Milwaukee's pitchers.

Profile Sections

MOST OF THE PROFILE material—I hope—is self-explanatory. But there's no point in leaving anything to chance. Hence this key, which offers details for all 23 sections.

Past 10 Seasons (2013-2022)

The franchise's records during the past decade are listed in chronological order, including wins, losses, winning percentages, postseason outcomes, and team scores. The final column (ME%) indicates the percentage of all 1,656 Modern Era (1961-2022) clubs that each year's team outperformed. The franchise's ME% readings between 2013 and

2022 are displayed in the accompanying graph. If the team qualified for the playoffs, the corresponding bar is black. All non-playoff bars are gray.

Best Seasons of Modern Era (1961-2022)

This table has the same format as its predecessor. It ranks the franchise's 10 best team scores during the Modern Era, shown in descending order. (If the franchise was created after 1961, the header begins with the appropriate year.)

Worst Seasons of Modern Era (1961-2022)

This table ranks the franchise's 10 worst team scores during the Modern Era, shown in ascending order.

Season Breakdown (2022)

Eight aspects of the club's 2022 season are highlighted, beginning with its overall record. Subsequent lines focus on home and away games; the first and second halves of the season (81 games apiece); and games against clubs that finished in first place in their divisions, teams that qualified for the postseason, and teams that missed the playoffs.

Season as Nine-Inning Game (2022)

The 162-game schedule can be neatly divided into nine segments of 18 games apiece, equating the year to a nine-inning game. This table enumerates each team's wins and losses in 2022's nine increments, from the first (games 1-18) to the last (games 145-162). The accompanying graph shows the number of wins in each 18-game inning, plotting the club's ebb and flow.

Scoring by Game (2022)

This table focuses on the number of runs scored by the team in each game in 2022. Games at each run level are totaled, with subsequent columns indicating the club's win-loss record, winning percentage, and the average number of runs it scored and allowed.

Scoring Allowed by Game (2022)

This table has the same format as its predecessor. It shows the number of runs allowed by the team in each game in 2022.

Margins (2022)

This table displays the club's 2022 records in games with margins of different sizes. Games are divided into three groups, based on the final scores. Close margins are defined as differentials of one or two runs, medium margins are three or four runs, and distant margins are five or more runs. The table shows the team's number of games at each level, win-loss record, winning percentage, game share, and win share. The last two columns are the percentages of the team's total games and wins within the corresponding margin.

Individual Scoring Leaders (2022)

This is a listing of the club's top 10 scorers in 2022, based on the SC formula, which adds runs and runs batted in, and subtracts home runs.

Team Ratings (2022)

The second chapter of this book revealed 11 sets of ratings for all 30 big-league franchises. The 2022 ratings for a specific club are collected in this table. Successive columns indicate the quality (overall performance, base production, etc.) and type of play (overall, batting, or pitching) being measured, the statistical indicator involved, its numerical value, and the resulting rating on a five-star scale. Star ratings are depicted in the accompanying graph.

Team Batting Stats (2022)

Seven team batting statistics for 2022 are included in this table: runs scored, hits, home runs, bases per out, batting average, on-base percentage, and slugging average. Each stat is followed by the club's category ranks within its division, its league, and the major leagues, as well as the best performance by any big-league team in 2022. (The best rank in each batting category goes to the club with the highest number.) Division and league names are listed at the bottom of the table.

Team Pitching Stats (2022)

Seven team pitching statistics for 2022 are included in this table: earned run average, strikeouts, walks, bases per out, batting average, on-base percentage, and slugging average. Ranks are presented in the same manner as in the previous table. (The best ranks in six pitching categories go to the clubs with the lowest numbers. The exception is strikeouts, where highest is best.)

Individual Batting Stats (2022)

Every batter who made at least 324 plate appearances for a given team in 2022 is represented in this table. Names are listed alphabetically. Subsequent columns show the batter's appearances and seven production rates: bases per out, batting average, on-base percentage, slugging average, isolated power average, contact rate, and batting eye rate.

Individual Pitching Stats for Starters (2022)

Every pitcher who worked at least 100 innings for a given team in 2022 is included in this table. Some started all of their games; others blended starts and relief appearances. The stats for each pitcher cover his full body of work. Names are listed alphabetically. Columns give the pitcher's innings and seven allowance rates: bases per out, earned run average, batting average, slugging average, isolated power average, contact rate, and batting eye rate.

Individual Pitching Stats for Relievers (2022)

Every pitcher who made at least 41 relief appearances for a given team in 2022 is included in this table. The stats for each pitcher cover his full body of work, even if he also started games. Names are listed alphabetically. Columns show the pitcher's number of games relieved and the same seven allowance rates previously displayed for starters.

Best Stats on Team (2022)

This header encompasses two tables of 2022's best individual statistics. Batters are shown on the left, with team leaders in 22 categories. Pitchers are on the right, with the club's top performances in 21 stats. A minimum of 324 plate appearances is required for eligibility in the eight rates for batters (abbreviated BA, BPO, CT, EY, ISO, OBP, SA, and SE). The other 14 batting categories are open to everyone. The highest numbers are the best for all batting stats. A minimum of 100 innings is required for eligibility in eight rates for pitchers (BA, BPO-S, CT,

ERA-S, EY, ISO, OBP, SA); at least 41 relief appearances are required for the other two rates (BPO-R and ERA-R). The remaining 11 pitching categories are open to everyone. The lowest numbers are the best for most pitching stats, with six exceptions where the highest are best: games relieved, games started, innings, strikeouts, saves, and wins.

Worst Stats on Team (2022)

These two tables are laid out similarly to the preceding pair, with batters on the left and pitchers on the right. Eligibility standards are also the same. The club's worst individual stats for 2022 are listed for 14 batting and 17 pitching categories. The lowest numbers are the worst for all batting stats, except for strikeouts, where the highest total is the least desirable. The highest numbers are the worst for all pitching stats.

Overall Base Value Leaders (2022)

This table ranks the 10 players who were most valuable to the team in 2022. Overall base value (OBV) is calculated by subtracting a player's pitching base value from his batting base value.

Fan Support in Past 10 Seasons (2013-2022)

Home attendance figures from eight of the past 10 years are included in this table. The 2020 and 2021 seasons are excluded because of Covid-related irregularities. The final three columns show the club's total wins (home and away) in a given season, its ratio of attendance per win, and its fan support index. The FSI is tied to a benchmark of 100 points; anything exceeding that level indicates support above the big-league norm. The accompanying graph displays the annual FSI readings, with black bars for years above 100 and gray bars for the rest.

Extreme Games for Batters (2022)

This table contains team totals and individual leaders for five extreme batting events during the 2022 season: a single game with three or more hits, two or more home runs, five or more runs batted in, no hits in five or more at-bats, or four or more strikeouts. The team total reflects the number of times that all individual players achieved the listed stat in any game. (The total for 3+ H, for example, is the number of times that separate batters made at least three hits in a game, not the number of games in which the team collectively got at least three hits.)

Extreme Games for Pitchers (2022)

This table contains team totals and individual leaders for five extreme pitching events during the 2022 season: a single game with two or fewer earned runs in seven or more innings pitched, 10 or more strikeouts, no baserunners allowed while picking up a save, 10 or more baserunners allowed, or one or more earned runs allowed while picking up a save. A team total reflects the number of times that all individual players achieved the listed stat in any game.

Predictions for Coming Season (2023)

The 2020-2022 team scores for each franchise were compared against three years of scores for 1,258 clubs between 1976-1978 and 2018-2020, generating a list of the 50 closest matches. The next-season record for each match was then tabulated, offering a clue to the current club's 2023 prospects. (The 1975-1977 Montreal Expos, for example, bore the closest resemblance to the 2020-2022 Arizona Diamondbacks. Montreal's 1978 record was used in Arizona's 2023 calculations.) This table offers separate breakdowns for the 10, 25, and 50 closest matches. Each line contains the next-season stats for a specified group: average wins, losses, and winning percentage, along with the number of teams that won the World Series, won a league championship, or qualified for the playoffs.

25 Closest Matches (2023)

This table ranks the current club's 25 closest matches (starting with the very best), as determined by the three-year analysis described above. Each match is listed with the record for its next season, the data that generated the previous table. Any World Series title, league championship, or playoff berth is denoted by an X.

Abbreviations

YOU'LL ENCOUNTER THE FOLLOWING abbreviations in the profiles. Most are familiar to any baseball fan. A few are unique to this book. If you're

KEY TO THE PROFILES • 115

looking for detailed explanations, your best move is to flip back to The Stats, the very first chapter.

2B: Doubles.
3B: Triples.
AB: At-bats.
Attendance: Home attendance for a season.
Att:W: Attendance-win ratio.
BA: Batting average.
BB: Walks.
BBV: Walk value.
BPO: Bases per out.
BPO-R: Bases per out allowed by a relief pitcher.
BPO-S: Bases per out allowed by a starting pitcher.
BPV: Ball in play value.
BR: Baserunners.
BV: Base value.
CT: Contact rate.
Div: Division.
ER: Earned runs.
ERA: Earned run average.
ERA-R: Earned run average for a relief pitcher.
ERA-S: Earned run average for a starting pitcher.
ERV: Earned run value.
EY: Batting eye rate.
FSI: Fan support index.
G: Games.
GR: Games relieved.
GS: Games started.
GShr: Game share.
H: Hits.
HR: Home runs.
IP: Innings pitched.
ISO: Isolated power average.
L: Losses.
LC: League championships.

Lg: League.

ME%: Percentage of Modern Era clubs outranked in team score by a given team.

MLB: Major League Baseball.

Next: The season immediately following a designated three-year period in a list of closest matches.

OBP: On-base percentage.

OBV: Overall base value.

PA: Plate appearances.

Pct.: Winning percentage.

Post: Postseason results.

PQ: Playoff qualifiers.

R: Runs scored.

R/G: Runs scored per game.

RA: Runs allowed.

RA/G: Runs allowed per game.

Rating: Five-star system that denotes performances as excellent (★★★★★), above average (★★★★), average (★★★), below average (★★), or poor (★).

RBI: Runs batted in.

SA: Slugging average.

SB: Stolen bases.

SC: Scoring.

SCV: Scoring value.

SE: Scoring efficiency rate.

SO: Strikeouts.

SV: Saves.

TS: Team score.

W: Wins.

WS: World Series championships.

WShr: Win share.

XV: Extra base value.

ARIZONA DIAMONDBACKS

Past 10 Seasons (2013-2022)

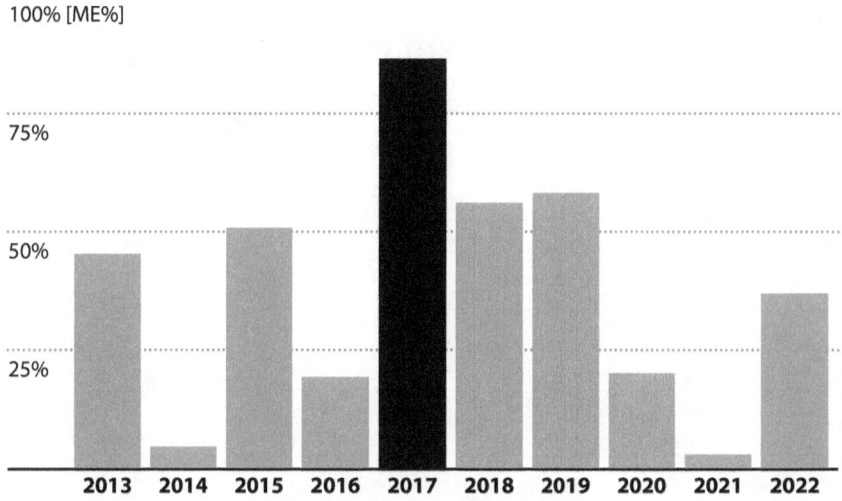

Year	Team	W	L	Pct.	Post	TS	ME%
2013	Arizona Diamondbacks	81	81	.500	—	43.601	45.3%
2014	Arizona Diamondbacks	64	98	.395	—	19.252	4.5%
2015	Arizona Diamondbacks	79	83	.488	—	46.387	50.8%
2016	Arizona Diamondbacks	69	93	.426	—	30.398	19.3%
2017	Arizona Diamondbacks	93	69	.574	P	64.767	86.5%
2018	Arizona Diamondbacks	82	80	.506	—	49.169	56.1%
2019	Arizona Diamondbacks	85	77	.525	—	50.350	58.2%
2020	Arizona Diamondbacks	25	35	.417	—	30.931	20.1%
2021	Arizona Diamondbacks	52	110	.321	—	16.829	2.9%
2022	Arizona Diamondbacks	74	88	.457	—	39.806	36.9%

Best Seasons of Modern Era (1998-2022)

Year	Team	W	L	Pct.	Post	TS	ME%
2001	Arizona Diamondbacks	92	70	.568	WLP	81.168	97.5%
1999	Arizona Diamondbacks	100	62	.617	P	71.067	91.7%
2002	Arizona Diamondbacks	98	64	.605	P	67.533	89.1%
2017	Arizona Diamondbacks	93	69	.574	P	64.767	86.5%
2011	Arizona Diamondbacks	94	68	.580	P	61.130	80.3%
2007	Arizona Diamondbacks	90	72	.556	P	52.105	62.8%
2000	Arizona Diamondbacks	85	77	.525	—	51.954	62.5%
2012	Arizona Diamondbacks	81	81	.500	—	51.535	61.5%
2008	Arizona Diamondbacks	82	80	.506	—	51.340	60.7%
2003	Arizona Diamondbacks	84	78	.519	—	50.915	59.2%

Worst Seasons of Modern Era (1998-2022)

Year	Team	W	L	Pct.	Post	TS	ME%
2004	Arizona Diamondbacks	51	111	.315	—	10.445	0.7%
2021	Arizona Diamondbacks	52	110	.321	—	16.829	2.9%
2014	Arizona Diamondbacks	64	98	.395	—	19.252	4.5%
2010	Arizona Diamondbacks	65	97	.401	—	26.584	12.8%
1998	Arizona Diamondbacks	65	97	.401	—	28.902	16.4%
2016	Arizona Diamondbacks	69	93	.426	—	30.398	19.3%
2020	Arizona Diamondbacks	25	35	.417	—	30.931	20.1%
2005	Arizona Diamondbacks	77	85	.475	—	31.820	21.3%
2009	Arizona Diamondbacks	70	92	.432	—	36.950	30.9%
2022	Arizona Diamondbacks	74	88	.457	—	39.806	36.9%

Season Breakdown (2022)

Category	W	L	Pct.	R	RA	R/G	RA/G
Overall record in 2022	74	88	.457	702	740	4.33	4.57
Home games	40	41	.494	353	360	4.36	4.44
Away games	34	47	.420	349	380	4.31	4.69
First half of 2022 season	37	44	.457	343	384	4.23	4.74
Second half of 2022 season	37	44	.457	359	356	4.43	4.40
Against first-place teams	12	27	.308	129	196	3.31	5.03
Against playoff teams	22	48	.314	247	356	3.53	5.09
Against non-playoff teams	52	40	.565	455	384	4.95	4.17

Season as Nine-Inning Game (2022)

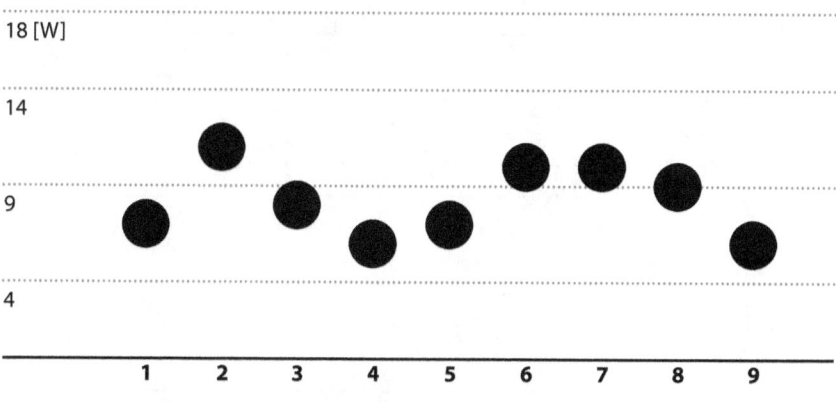

Result	1	2	3	4	5	6	7	8	9	Total
Wins	7	11	8	6	7	10	10	9	6	74
Losses	11	7	10	12	11	8	8	9	12	88

Scoring by Game (2022)

Runs Scored	G	W	L	Pct.	R/G	RA/G
Overall record	162	74	88	.457	4.33	4.57
0	15	0	15	.000	0.00	4.40
1	14	0	14	.000	1.00	5.29
2	17	2	15	.118	2.00	4.76
3	25	8	17	.320	3.00	4.84
4	18	9	9	.500	4.00	4.28
5	26	14	12	.538	5.00	4.19
6	11	9	2	.818	6.00	3.45
7	14	12	2	.857	7.00	4.29
8	7	6	1	.857	8.00	6.71
9	5	5	0	1.000	9.00	3.20
10 or more	10	9	1	.900	11.20	5.10

Scoring Allowed by Game (2022)

Runs Allowed	G	W	L	Pct.	R/G	RA/G
Overall record	162	74	88	.457	4.33	4.57
0	10	10	0	1.000	4.80	0.00
1	12	10	2	.833	4.67	1.00
2	22	18	4	.818	4.64	2.00
3	26	15	11	.577	4.35	3.00
4	21	8	13	.381	3.29	4.00
5	17	3	14	.176	3.53	5.00
6	26	6	20	.231	4.50	6.00
7	10	4	6	.400	6.50	7.00
8	2	0	2	.000	4.50	8.00
9	0	0	0	—	—	—
10 or more	16	0	16	.000	3.94	12.19

Margins (2022)

Category	Margin	G	W	L	Pct.	GShr	WShr
Overall record	—	162	74	88	.457	—	—
Close	1 or 2 runs	74	30	44	.405	45.7%	40.5%
Medium	3 or 4 runs	43	21	22	.488	26.5%	28.4%
Distant	5 or more runs	45	23	22	.511	27.8%	31.1%

Individual Scoring Leaders (2022)

Team Rank	Batter	R	(+) RBI	(-) HR	(=) SC
1	Christian Walker	84	94	36	142
2	Daulton Varsho	79	74	27	126
3	Josh Rojas	66	56	9	113
4	Ketel Marte	68	52	12	108
5	Geraldo Perdomo	58	40	5	93
6	Jake McCarthy	53	43	8	88
7	Alek Thomas	45	39	8	76
8	Carson Kelly	40	35	7	68
9	David Peralta	29	41	12	58
10	Pavin Smith	24	33	9	48

Team Ratings (2022)

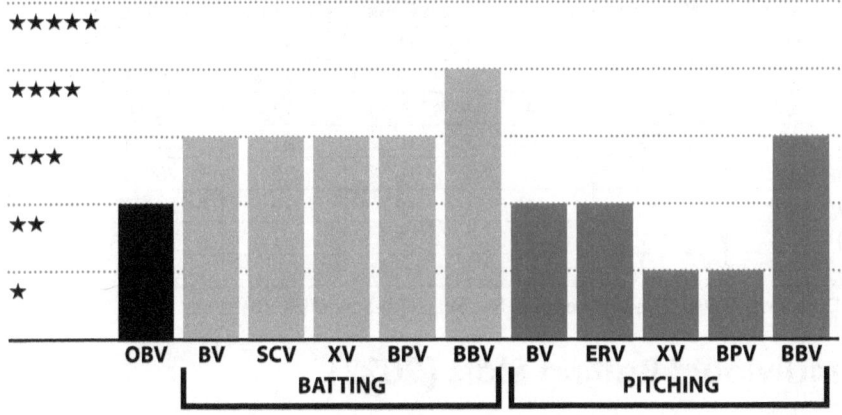

Quality	Type	Indicator	Value	Rating
Overall performance	Overall	OBV	-138	★★
Base production	Batting	BV	-19	★★★
Run production	Batting	SCV	12	★★★
Power hitting	Batting	XV	15	★★★
Contact hitting	Batting	BPV	-5	★★★
Batting eye	Batting	BBV	41	★★★★
Base prevention	Pitching	BV	119	★★
Run prevention	Pitching	ERV	46	★★
Power prevention	Pitching	XV	78	★
Strikeout pitching	Pitching	BPV	143	★
Control pitching	Pitching	BBV	7	★★★

Team Batting Stats (2022)

Stat	Number	Div Rank	Lg Rank	MLB Rank	MLB Best
R	702	4	9	14	847 (Dodgers)
H	1,232	5	14	28	1,464 (Blue Jays)
HR	173	3	7	14	254 (Yankees)
BPO	.656	4	9	15	.764 (Dodgers)
BA	.230	5	13	26	.264 (Blue Jays)
OBP	.304	5	12	23	.333 (Dodgers)
SA	.385	4	10	20	.443 (Braves)

Division: NL West, 5 teams. **League:** National, 15 teams. **MLB:** 30 teams.

Team Pitching Stats (2022)

Stat	Number	Div Rank	Lg Rank	MLB Rank	MLB Best
ERA	4.25	4	11	23	2.80 (Dodgers)
SO	1,216	4	13	24	1,565 (Mets)
BB	504	4	8	17	384 (Rays)
BPO	.688	4	10	21	.551 (Astros)
BA	.247	3	10	20	.209 (Dodgers)
OBP	.315	4	10	19	.273 (Dodgers)
SA	.414	4	11	23	.332 (Astros)

Division: NL West, 5 teams. **League:** National, 15 teams. **MLB:** 30 teams.

Individual Batting Stats (2022)

Batter	PA	BPO	BA	OBP	SA	ISO	CT	EY
Carson Kelly	354	.549	.211	.282	.334	.123	.776	.082
Ketel Marte	558	.691	.240	.321	.407	.167	.795	.094
Jake McCarthy	354	.804	.283	.342	.427	.143	.763	.065
Geraldo Perdomo	500	.522	.195	.285	.262	.067	.761	.100
Josh Rojas	510	.765	.269	.349	.391	.122	.779	.104
Alek Thomas	411	.537	.231	.275	.344	.113	.806	.054
Daulton Varsho	592	.728	.235	.302	.443	.207	.727	.078
Christian Walker	667	.781	.242	.327	.477	.235	.775	.101

Individual Pitching Stats for Starters (2022)

Pitcher	IP	BPO	ERA	BA	SA	ISO	CT	EY
Madison Bumgarner	158.2	.804	4.88	.281	.487	.206	.824	.070
Zach Davies	134.1	.682	4.09	.241	.412	.172	.799	.091
Zac Gallen	184.0	.490	2.54	.186	.307	.121	.705	.066
Merrill Kelly	200.1	.597	3.37	.226	.371	.145	.760	.074

Individual Pitching Stats for Relievers (2022)

Pitcher	GR	BPO	ERA	BA	SA	ISO	CT	EY
Ian Kennedy	57	.864	5.36	.278	.502	.224	.785	.083
Joe Mantiply	69	.539	2.85	.255	.359	.104	.736	.025
Mark Melancon	62	.679	4.66	.281	.393	.112	.844	.078
Kyle Nelson	42	.518	2.19	.194	.299	.104	.776	.093
Noe Ramirez	55	.800	5.22	.245	.451	.207	.723	.113
Caleb Smith	43	.730	4.11	.218	.429	.211	.751	.126

Best Stats on Team (2022)

Stat	Batter	Number
2B	Ketel Marte	42
3B	Daulton Varsho, Jake McCarthy, Cooper Hummel	3
BA	Jake McCarthy	.283
BB	Christian Walker	69
BBV	Christian Walker	14
BPO	Jake McCarthy	.804
BPV	Ketel Marte	22
BV	Christian Walker	56
CT	Alek Thomas	.806
EY	Josh Rojas	.104
H	Christian Walker	141
HR	Christian Walker	36
ISO	Christian Walker	.235
OBP	Josh Rojas	.349
R	Christian Walker	84
RBI	Christian Walker	94
SA	Christian Walker	.477
SB	Josh Rojas, Jake McCarthy	23
SC	Christian Walker	142
SCV	Jake McCarthy	19
SE	Jake McCarthy	.249
XV	Christian Walker	48

Stat	Pitcher	Number
BA	Zac Gallen	.186
BBV	Joe Mantiply	-13
BPO-R	Kyle Nelson	.518
BPO-S	Zac Gallen	.490
BPV	Zac Gallen	-29
BV	Zac Gallen	-93
CT	Zac Gallen	.705
ERA-R	Kyle Nelson	2.19
ERA-S	Zac Gallen	2.54
ERV	Zac Gallen	-29
EY	Zac Gallen	.066
GR	Joe Mantiply	69
GS	Merrill Kelly	33
IP	Merrill Kelly	200.1
ISO	Zac Gallen	.121
OBP	Zac Gallen	.252
SA	Zac Gallen	.307
SO	Zac Gallen	192
SV	Mark Melancon	18
W	Merrill Kelly	13
XV	Zac Gallen	-20

Worst Stats on Team (2022)

Stat	Batter	Number
BA	Geraldo Perdomo	.195
BBV	Alek Thomas	-11
BPO	Geraldo Perdomo	.522
BPV	Cooper Hummel	-20
BV	Geraldo Perdomo	-51
CT	Daulton Varsho	.727
EY	Alek Thomas	.054
ISO	Geraldo Perdomo	.067
OBP	Alek Thomas	.275
SA	Geraldo Perdomo	.262
SCV	Seth Beer	-13
SE	Alek Thomas	.185
SO	Daulton Varsho	145
XV	Geraldo Perdomo	-37

Stat	Pitcher	Number
BA	Madison Bumgarner	.281
BB	Merrill Kelly	61
BBV	Caleb Smith	14
BPO-R	Ian Kennedy	.864
BPO-S	Madison Bumgarner	.804
BPV	Madison Bumgarner	47
BV	Madison Bumgarner	69
CT	Madison Bumgarner	.824
ERA-R	Ian Kennedy	5.36
ERA-S	Madison Bumgarner	4.88
ERV	Madison Bumgarner	16
EY	Zach Davies	.091
ISO	Madison Bumgarner	.206
L	Madison Bumgarner	15
OBP	Madison Bumgarner	.340
SA	Madison Bumgarner	.487
XV	Madison Bumgarner	34

Overall Base Value Leaders (2022)

Team Rank	Player	BV [bat]	(-) BV [pitch]	(=) OBV
1	Zac Gallen	0	-93	93
2	Christian Walker	56	0	56
3	Merrill Kelly	0	-37	37
4	Josh Rojas	36	0	36
5	Jake McCarthy	35	0	35
6	Daulton Varsho	29	0	29
7	Joe Mantiply	0	-22	22
8	Kyle Nelson	0	-16	16
8	David Peralta	16	0	16
10	Corbin Carroll	13	0	13

Fan Support in Past 10 Seasons (2013-2022)

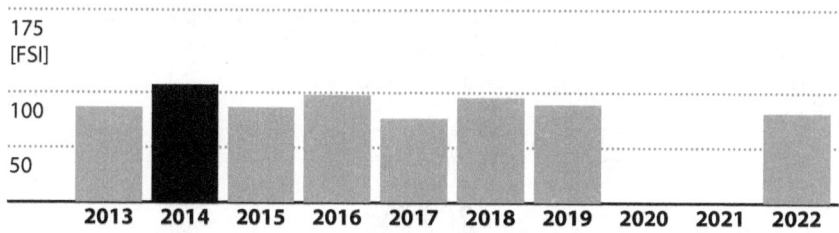

Year	Team	Attendance	W	Att:W	FSI
2013	Arizona Diamondbacks	2,134,895	81	26,357	86.6
2014	Arizona Diamondbacks	2,073,730	64	32,402	106.8
2015	Arizona Diamondbacks	2,080,145	79	26,331	86.7
2016	Arizona Diamondbacks	2,036,216	69	29,510	97.9
2017	Arizona Diamondbacks	2,134,375	93	22,950	76.7
2018	Arizona Diamondbacks	2,242,695	82	27,350	95.4
2019	Arizona Diamondbacks	2,135,510	85	25,124	89.1
2022	Arizona Diamondbacks	1,605,199	74	21,692	81.7

Extreme Games for Batters (2022)

Stat	Team Total	Individual Leader	G
3+ H	54	Christian Walker, Josh Rojas	8
2+ HR	10	Christian Walker	3
5+ RBI	2	Geraldo Perdomo, Jake McCarthy	1
0 H in 5+ AB	24	Christian Walker, Daulton Varsho	5
4+ SO	0	[none]	0

Extreme Games for Pitchers (2022)

Stat	Team Total	Individual Leader	G
0-2 ER in 7+ IP	28	Merrill Kelly	11
10+ SO	4	Zac Gallen	4
0 BR in SV	14	Mark Melancon	8
10+ BR	24	Madison Bumgarner	11
1+ ER in SV	2	Ian Kennedy, Mark Melancon	1

Predictions for Coming Season (2023)

Group	Next W	Next L	Next Pct.	WS	LC	PQ
10 closest matches (avg. W-L)	78.2	83.8	.483	0	1	1
25 closest matches (avg. W-L)	74.0	81.0	.477	0	1	4
50 closest matches (avg. W-L)	73.5	80.9	.476	0	1	8

25 Closest Matches (2023)

Rank	Team	Next	W	L	Pct.	WS	LC	PQ
1	Expos (1975-1977)	1978	76	86	.469	—	—	—
2	Marlins (2012-2014)	2015	71	91	.438	—	—	—
3	Twins (1994-1996)	1997	68	94	.420	—	—	—
4	Blue Jays (1980-1982)	1983	89	73	.549	—	—	—
5	Astros (1990-1992)	1993	85	77	.525	—	—	—
6	Mariners (1985-1987)	1988	68	93	.422	—	—	—
7	Athletics (1996-1998)	1999	87	75	.537	—	—	—
8	Indians (1986-1988)	1989	73	89	.451	—	—	—
9	Rockies (2004-2006)	2007	90	73	.552	—	X	X
10	Pirates (2000-2002)	2003	75	87	.463	—	—	—
11	Reds (2017-2019)	2020	31	29	.517	—	—	X
12	Mets (1992-1994)	1995	69	75	.479	—	—	—
13	Phillies (1996-1998)	1999	77	85	.475	—	—	—
14	Athletics (2015-2017)	2018	97	65	.599	—	—	X
15	Padres (1980-1982)	1983	81	81	.500	—	—	—
16	Mets (2002-2004)	2005	83	79	.512	—	—	—
17	Indians (2009-2011)	2012	68	94	.420	—	—	—
18	Rockies (2011-2013)	2014	66	96	.407	—	—	—
19	Blue Jays (1994-1996)	1997	76	86	.469	—	—	—
20	Braves (1978-1980)	1981	50	56	.472	—	—	—
21	Phillies (1988-1990)	1991	78	84	.481	—	—	—
22	White Sox (2014-2016)	2017	67	95	.414	—	—	—
23	Mariners (2007-2009)	2010	61	101	.377	—	—	—
24	Marlins (1998-2000)	2001	76	86	.469	—	—	—
25	Rockies (2014-2016)	2017	87	75	.537	—	—	X

ATLANTA BRAVES

Past 10 Seasons (2013-2022)

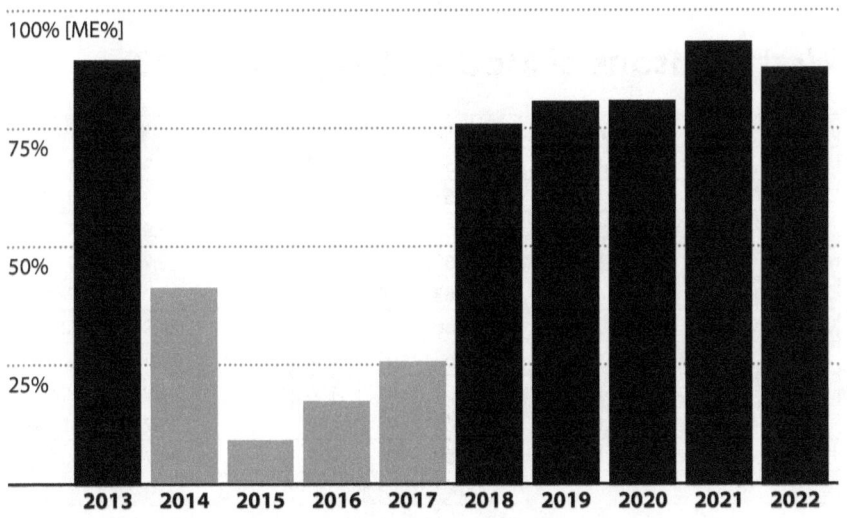

Year	Team	W	L	Pct.	Post	TS	ME%
2013	Atlanta Braves	96	66	.593	P	67.754	89.4%
2014	Atlanta Braves	79	83	.488	—	41.718	41.3%
2015	Atlanta Braves	67	95	.414	—	23.755	9.0%
2016	Atlanta Braves	68	93	.422	—	29.254	17.3%
2017	Atlanta Braves	72	90	.444	—	33.833	25.7%
2018	Atlanta Braves	90	72	.556	P	58.272	75.9%
2019	Atlanta Braves	97	65	.599	P	61.197	80.7%
2020	Atlanta Braves	35	25	.583	P	61.310	80.8%
2021	Atlanta Braves	88	73	.547	WLP	73.126	93.3%
2022	Atlanta Braves	101	61	.623	P	66.029	87.8%

Best Seasons of Modern Era (1961-2022)

Year	Team	W	L	Pct.	Post	TS	ME%
1995	Atlanta Braves	90	54	.625	WLP	84.662	98.7%
1996	Atlanta Braves	96	66	.593	LP	83.372	98.4%
1992	Atlanta Braves	98	64	.605	LP	80.453	97.2%
1999	Atlanta Braves	103	59	.636	LP	78.705	96.7%
1997	Atlanta Braves	101	61	.623	P	78.525	96.6%
1998	Atlanta Braves	106	56	.654	P	77.144	95.9%
1991	Atlanta Braves	94	68	.580	LP	76.629	95.7%
2021	Atlanta Braves	88	73	.547	WLP	73.126	93.3%
2003	Atlanta Braves	101	61	.623	P	72.536	92.9%
1993	Atlanta Braves	104	58	.642	P	72.282	92.4%

Worst Seasons of Modern Era (1961-2022)

Year	Team	W	L	Pct.	Post	TS	ME%
1988	Atlanta Braves	54	106	.338	—	12.913	1.3%
1977	Atlanta Braves	61	101	.377	—	16.259	2.5%
1990	Atlanta Braves	65	97	.401	—	20.029	5.0%
1978	Atlanta Braves	69	93	.426	—	22.794	7.7%
1989	Atlanta Braves	63	97	.394	—	23.101	8.0%
1985	Atlanta Braves	66	96	.407	—	23.327	8.5%
2015	Atlanta Braves	67	95	.414	—	23.755	9.0%
1975	Atlanta Braves	67	94	.416	—	24.915	9.7%
1979	Atlanta Braves	66	94	.413	—	25.711	11.4%
1987	Atlanta Braves	69	92	.429	—	28.705	16.0%

Season Breakdown (2022)

Category	W	L	Pct.	R	RA	R/G	RA/G
Overall record in 2022	101	61	.623	789	609	4.87	3.76
Home games	55	26	.679	395	282	4.88	3.48
Away games	46	35	.568	394	327	4.86	4.04
First half of 2022 season	47	34	.580	384	332	4.74	4.10
Second half of 2022 season	54	27	.667	405	277	5.00	3.42
Against first-place teams	8	8	.500	69	59	4.31	3.69
Against playoff teams	33	31	.516	288	274	4.50	4.28
Against non-playoff teams	68	30	.694	501	335	5.11	3.42

Season as Nine-Inning Game (2022)

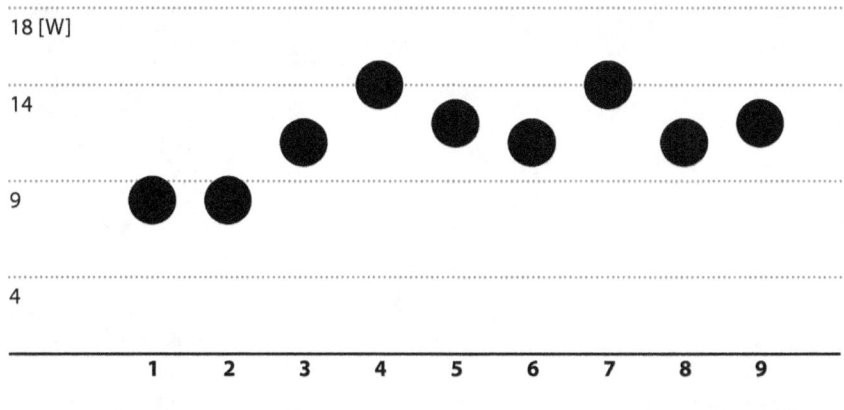

Result	1	2	3	4	5	6	7	8	9	Total
Wins	8	8	11	14	12	11	14	11	12	101
Losses	10	10	7	4	6	7	4	7	6	61

Scoring by Game (2022)

Runs Scored	G	W	L	Pct.	R/G	RA/G
Overall record	162	101	61	.623	4.87	3.76
0	5	0	5	.000	0.00	2.00
1	15	1	14	.067	1.00	4.60
2	15	5	10	.333	2.00	3.67
3	28	14	14	.500	3.00	3.54
4	19	11	8	.579	4.00	4.32
5	21	19	2	.905	5.00	2.76
6	19	17	2	.895	6.00	3.32
7	11	7	4	.636	7.00	5.00
8	10	10	0	1.000	8.00	3.20
9	7	6	1	.857	9.00	5.00
10 or more	12	11	1	.917	12.08	4.25

Scoring Allowed by Game (2022)

Runs Allowed	G	W	L	Pct.	R/G	RA/G
Overall record	162	101	61	.623	4.87	3.76
0	9	9	0	1.000	4.22	0.00
1	26	23	3	.885	4.54	1.00
2	29	28	1	.966	6.03	2.00
3	29	19	10	.655	3.83	3.00
4	19	11	8	.579	5.47	4.00
5	9	3	6	.333	4.33	5.00
6	15	4	11	.267	4.73	6.00
7	11	3	8	.273	4.73	7.00
8	3	0	3	.000	6.33	8.00
9	6	1	5	.167	5.00	9.00
10 or more	6	0	6	.000	5.33	12.00

Margins (2022)

Category	Margin	G	W	L	Pct.	GShr	WShr
Overall record	—	162	101	61	.623	—	—
Close	1 or 2 runs	70	42	28	.600	43.2%	41.6%
Medium	3 or 4 runs	58	33	25	.569	35.8%	32.7%
Distant	5 or more runs	34	26	8	.765	21.0%	25.7%

Individual Scoring Leaders (2022)

Team Rank	Batter	R	(+) RBI	(-) HR	(=) SC
1	Dansby Swanson	99	96	25	170
2	Matt Olson	86	103	34	155
3	Austin Riley	90	93	38	145
4	Michael Harris	75	64	19	120
5	Ronald Acuna Jr.	71	50	15	106
6	Travis d'Arnaud	61	60	18	103
7	Marcell Ozuna	56	56	23	89
8	William Contreras	51	45	20	76
9	Ozzie Albies	36	35	8	63
9	Adam Duvall	39	36	12	63

Team Ratings (2022)

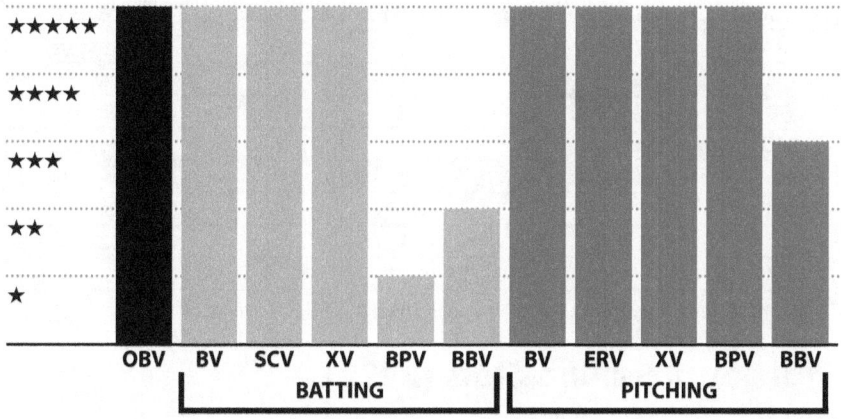

Quality	Type	Indicator	Value	Rating
Overall performance	Overall	OBV	538	★★★★★
Base production	Batting	BV	274	★★★★★
Run production	Batting	SCV	113	★★★★★
Power hitting	Batting	XV	211	★★★★★
Contact hitting	Batting	BPV	-123	★
Batting eye	Batting	BBV	-24	★★
Base prevention	Pitching	BV	-264	★★★★★
Run prevention	Pitching	ERV	-82	★★★★★
Power prevention	Pitching	XV	-130	★★★★★
Strikeout pitching	Pitching	BPV	-203	★★★★★
Control pitching	Pitching	BBV	3	★★★

Team Batting Stats (2022)

Stat	Number	Div Rank	Lg Rank	MLB Rank	MLB Best
R	789	1	2	3	847 (Dodgers)
H	1,394	2	4	8	1,464 (Blue Jays)
HR	243	1	1	2	254 (Yankees)
BPO	.724	1	2	3	.764 (Dodgers)
BA	.253	3	5	9	.264 (Blue Jays)
OBP	.317	2	5	9	.333 (Dodgers)
SA	.443	1	1	1	.443 (Braves)

Division: NL East, 5 teams. **League:** National, 15 teams. **MLB:** 30 teams.

Team Pitching Stats (2022)

Stat	Number	Div Rank	Lg Rank	MLB Rank	MLB Best
ERA	3.46	1	2	5	2.80 (Dodgers)
SO	1,554	2	2	2	1,565 (Mets)
BB	500	3	7	15	384 (Rays)
BPO	.600	1	2	4	.551 (Astros)
BA	.226	1	2	4	.209 (Dodgers)
OBP	.297	1	2	6	.273 (Dodgers)
SA	.354	1	2	3	.332 (Astros)

Division: NL East, 5 teams. **League:** National, 15 teams. **MLB:** 30 teams.

Individual Batting Stats (2022)

Batter	PA	BPO	BA	OBP	SA	ISO	CT	EY
Ronald Acuna Jr.	533	.789	.266	.351	.413	.148	.730	.093
William Contreras	376	.859	.278	.354	.506	.228	.689	.101
Travis d'Arnaud	426	.719	.268	.319	.472	.205	.773	.045
Michael Harris	441	.864	.297	.339	.514	.217	.742	.048
Matt Olson	699	.777	.240	.325	.477	.237	.724	.100
Marcell Ozuna	507	.612	.226	.274	.413	.187	.740	.061
Austin Riley	693	.873	.273	.349	.528	.255	.727	.081
Dansby Swanson	696	.741	.277	.329	.447	.170	.716	.070

Individual Pitching Stats for Starters (2022)

Pitcher	IP	BPO	ERA	BA	SA	ISO	CT	EY
Ian Anderson	111.2	.713	5.00	.264	.408	.144	.778	.110
Max Fried	185.1	.473	2.48	.225	.319	.094	.754	.041
Charlie Morton	172.0	.702	4.34	.233	.411	.178	.680	.087
Spencer Strider	131.2	.452	2.67	.180	.264	.084	.577	.083
Kyle Wright	180.1	.557	3.19	.232	.351	.119	.741	.072

Individual Pitching Stats for Relievers (2022)

Pitcher	GR	BPO	ERA	BA	SA	ISO	CT	EY
Jesse Chavez	45	.608	2.72	.244	.383	.139	.697	.064
Kenley Jansen	65	.606	3.38	.192	.346	.154	.637	.074
Dylan Lee	46	.487	2.13	.212	.323	.111	.688	.045
Tyler Matzek	42	.603	3.50	.173	.280	.107	.760	.148
Collin McHugh	58	.466	2.60	.203	.299	.096	.701	.048
A.J. Minter	75	.502	2.06	.198	.306	.109	.621	.055
Will Smith	41	.779	4.38	.240	.425	.185	.719	.107

Best Stats on Team (2022)

Stat	Batter	Number
2B	Matt Olson	44
3B	Michael Harris	3
BA	Michael Harris	.297
BB	Matt Olson	75
BBV	Matt Olson	14
BPO	Austin Riley	.873
BPV	Ozzie Albies	15
BV	Austin Riley	99
CT	Travis d'Arnaud	.773
EY	William Contreras	.101
H	Dansby Swanson	177
HR	Austin Riley	38
ISO	Austin Riley	.255
OBP	William Contreras	.354
R	Dansby Swanson	99
RBI	Matt Olson	103
SA	Austin Riley	.528
SB	Ronald Acuna Jr.	29
SC	Dansby Swanson	170
SCV	Dansby Swanson, Michael Harris	34
SE	Michael Harris	.272
XV	Austin Riley	63

Stat	Pitcher	Number
BA	Spencer Strider	.180
BBV	Max Fried	-28
BPO-R	Collin McHugh	.466
BPO-S	Spencer Strider	.452
BPV	Spencer Strider	-83
BV	Max Fried	-105
CT	Spencer Strider	.577
ERA-R	A.J. Minter	2.06
ERA-S	Max Fried	2.48
ERV	Max Fried	-31
EY	Max Fried	.041
GR	A.J. Minter	75
GS	Charlie Morton	31
IP	Max Fried	185.1
ISO	Spencer Strider	.084
OBP	Spencer Strider	.254
SA	Spencer Strider	.264
SO	Charlie Morton	205
SV	Kenley Jansen	41
W	Kyle Wright	21
XV	Max Fried	-40

Worst Stats on Team (2022)

Stat	Batter	Number
BA	Marcell Ozuna	.226
BBV	Travis d'Arnaud	-15
BPO	Marcell Ozuna	.612
BPV	Adam Duvall	-29
BV	Eddie Rosario	-29
CT	William Contreras	.689
EY	Travis d'Arnaud	.045
ISO	Ronald Acuna Jr.	.148
OBP	Marcell Ozuna	.274
SA	Marcell Ozuna	.413
SCV	Marcell Ozuna	-10
SE	Marcell Ozuna	.176
SO	Dansby Swanson	182
XV	Eddie Rosario	-9

Stat	Pitcher	Number
BA	Ian Anderson	.264
BB	Charlie Morton	63
BBV	Ian Anderson	15
BPO-R	Will Smith	.779
BPO-S	Ian Anderson	.713
BPV	Ian Anderson	12
BV	Charlie Morton, Jake Odorizzi	22
CT	Ian Anderson	.778
ERA-R	Will Smith	4.38
ERA-S	Ian Anderson	5.00
ERV	Ian Anderson	13
EY	Ian Anderson	.110
ISO	Charlie Morton	.178
L	Max Fried	7
OBP	Ian Anderson	.345
SA	Charlie Morton	.411
XV	Charlie Morton	17

Overall Base Value Leaders (2022)

Team Rank	Player	BV [bat]	(-) BV [pitch]	(=) OBV
1	Max Fried	0	-105	105
2	Austin Riley	99	0	99
3	Spencer Strider	0	-83	83
4	Michael Harris	61	0	61
5	Matt Olson	57	0	57
6	Kyle Wright	0	-56	56
7	William Contreras	49	0	49
8	Ronald Acuna Jr.	47	0	47
9	Collin McHugh	0	-40	40
10	Dansby Swanson	39	0	39

Fan Support in Past 10 Seasons (2013-2022)

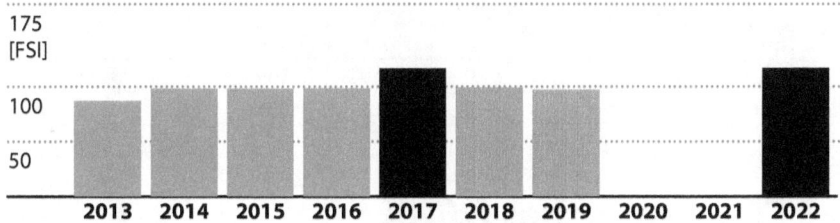

Year	Team	Attendance	W	Att:W	FSI
2013	Atlanta Braves	2,548,679	96	26,549	87.2
2014	Atlanta Braves	2,354,305	79	29,801	98.2
2015	Atlanta Braves	2,001,392	67	29,872	98.4
2016	Atlanta Braves	2,020,914	68	29,719	98.6
2017	Atlanta Braves	2,505,252	72	34,795	116.3
2018	Atlanta Braves	2,555,781	90	28,398	99.1
2019	Atlanta Braves	2,654,920	97	27,370	97.0
2022	Atlanta Braves	3,129,931	101	30,989	116.6

Extreme Games for Batters (2022)

Stat	Team Total	Individual Leader	G
3+ H	85	Austin Riley, Dansby Swanson	14
2+ HR	16	Marcell Ozuna, William Contreras	3
5+ RBI	4	Austin Riley, Eddie Rosario, Matt Olson, Travis d'Arnaud	1
0 H in 5+ AB	31	Ronald Acuna Jr.	8
4+ SO	7	Austin Riley	4

Extreme Games for Pitchers (2022)

Stat	Team Total	Individual Leader	G
0-2 ER in 7+ IP	21	Max Fried	8
10+ SO	13	Spencer Strider	6
0 BR in SV	25	Kenley Jansen	21
10+ BR	27	Charlie Morton, Ian Anderson, Kyle Wright	6
1+ ER in SV	9	Kenley Jansen	7

Predictions for Coming Season (2023)

Group	Next W	Next L	Next Pct.	WS	LC	PQ
10 closest matches (avg. W-L)	87.5	74.5	.540	0	0	5
25 closest matches (avg. W-L)	85.0	69.9	.549	1	3	13
50 closest matches (avg. W-L)	87.8	70.3	.555	3	6	26

25 Closest Matches (2023)

Rank	Team	Next	W	L	Pct.	WS	LC	PQ
1	Astros (1997-1999)	2000	72	90	.444	—	—	—
2	Athletics (2000-2002)	2003	96	66	.593	—	—	X
3	Giants (2001-2003)	2004	91	71	.562	—	—	—
4	Pirates (1990-1992)	1993	75	87	.463	—	—	—
5	Yankees (2005-2007)	2008	89	73	.549	—	—	—
6	Yankees (2010-2012)	2013	85	77	.525	—	—	—
7	Yankees (2002-2004)	2005	95	67	.586	—	—	X
8	Dodgers (2013-2015)	2016	91	71	.562	—	—	X
9	Dodgers (1980-1982)	1983	91	71	.562	—	—	X
10	Braves (2002-2004)	2005	90	72	.556	—	—	X
11	Phillies (2008-2010)	2011	102	60	.630	—	—	X
12	Orioles (1978-1980)	1981	59	46	.562	—	—	—
13	Yankees (1984-1986)	1987	89	73	.549	—	—	—
14	Nationals (2015-2017)	2018	82	80	.506	—	—	—
15	Braves (1992-1994)	1995	90	54	.625	X	X	X
16	Cardinals (2010-2012)	2013	97	65	.599	—	X	X
17	Athletics (2012-2014)	2015	68	94	.420	—	—	—
18	Mets (2005-2007)	2008	89	73	.549	—	—	—
19	Phillies (1975-1977)	1978	90	72	.556	—	—	X
20	Yankees (2017-2019)	2020	33	27	.550	—	—	X
21	Phillies (1976-1978)	1979	84	78	.519	—	—	—
22	Tigers (2011-2013)	2014	90	72	.556	—	—	X
23	Mets (1987-1989)	1990	91	71	.562	—	—	—
24	Indians (1998-2000)	2001	91	71	.562	—	—	X
25	Giants (1999-2001)	2002	95	66	.590	—	X	X

BALTIMORE ORIOLES

Past 10 Seasons (2013-2022)

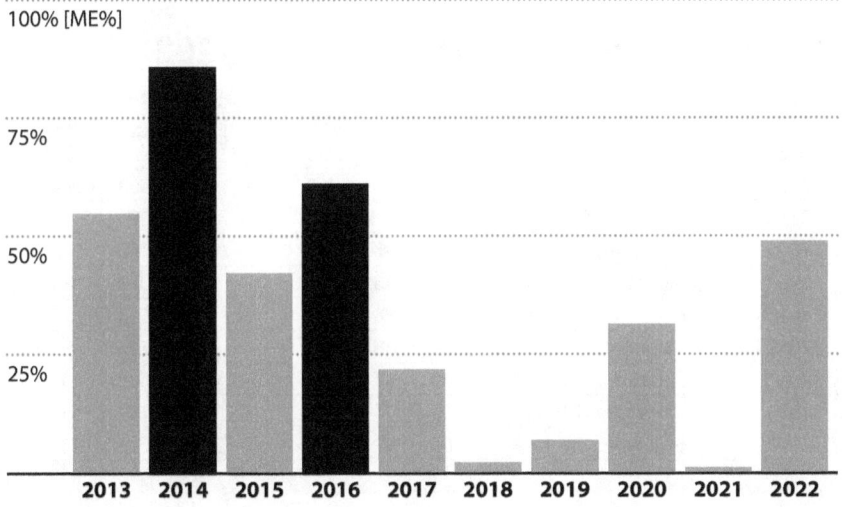

Year	Team	W	L	Pct.	Post	TS	ME%
2013	Baltimore Orioles	85	77	.525	—	48.453	54.7%
2014	Baltimore Orioles	96	66	.593	P	64.226	85.7%
2015	Baltimore Orioles	81	81	.500	—	42.089	42.2%
2016	Baltimore Orioles	89	73	.549	P	51.407	61.0%
2017	Baltimore Orioles	75	87	.463	—	32.320	21.8%
2018	Baltimore Orioles	47	115	.290	—	15.199	2.1%
2019	Baltimore Orioles	54	108	.333	—	21.747	6.8%
2020	Baltimore Orioles	25	35	.417	—	37.071	31.4%
2021	Baltimore Orioles	52	110	.321	—	11.059	1.0%
2022	Baltimore Orioles	83	79	.512	—	45.422	48.9%

Best Seasons of Modern Era (1961-2022)

Year	Team	W	L	Pct.	Post	TS	ME%
1966	Baltimore Orioles	97	63	.606	WLP	88.282	99.6%
1970	Baltimore Orioles	108	54	.667	WLP	87.901	99.5%
1969	Baltimore Orioles	109	53	.673	LP	86.161	99.0%
1971	Baltimore Orioles	101	57	.639	LP	83.333	98.3%
1983	Baltimore Orioles	98	64	.605	WLP	81.677	97.6%
1979	Baltimore Orioles	102	57	.642	LP	77.612	96.2%
1973	Baltimore Orioles	97	65	.599	P	71.917	92.3%
1997	Baltimore Orioles	98	64	.605	P	67.599	89.2%
1980	Baltimore Orioles	100	62	.617	—	66.988	88.6%
2014	Baltimore Orioles	96	66	.593	P	64.226	85.7%

Worst Seasons of Modern Era (1961-2022)

Year	Team	W	L	Pct.	Post	TS	ME%
1988	Baltimore Orioles	54	107	.335	—	9.850	0.4%
2021	Baltimore Orioles	52	110	.321	—	11.059	1.0%
2018	Baltimore Orioles	47	115	.290	—	15.199	2.1%
2009	Baltimore Orioles	64	98	.395	—	18.700	4.3%
1987	Baltimore Orioles	67	95	.414	—	21.072	6.2%
2010	Baltimore Orioles	66	96	.407	—	21.513	6.5%
2019	Baltimore Orioles	54	108	.333	—	21.747	6.8%
2011	Baltimore Orioles	69	93	.426	—	25.687	11.2%
1991	Baltimore Orioles	67	95	.414	—	25.757	11.4%
2008	Baltimore Orioles	68	93	.422	—	25.795	11.6%

Season Breakdown (2022)

Category	W	L	Pct.	R	RA	R/G	RA/G
Overall record in 2022	83	79	.512	674	688	4.16	4.25
Home games	45	36	.556	343	335	4.23	4.14
Away games	38	43	.469	331	353	4.09	4.36
First half of 2022 season	37	44	.457	329	354	4.06	4.37
Second half of 2022 season	46	35	.568	345	334	4.26	4.12
Against first-place teams	16	19	.457	124	146	3.54	4.17
Against playoff teams	36	43	.456	308	360	3.90	4.56
Against non-playoff teams	47	36	.566	366	328	4.41	3.95

Season as Nine-Inning Game (2022)

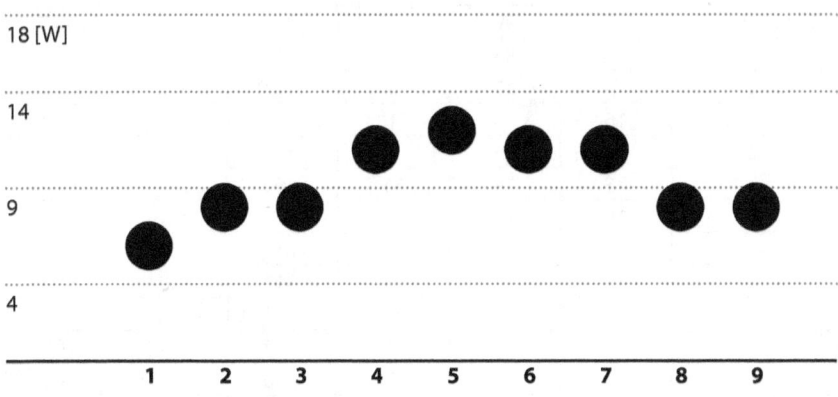

Result	1	2	3	4	5	6	7	8	9	Total
Wins	6	8	8	11	12	11	11	8	8	83
Losses	12	10	10	7	6	7	7	10	10	79

Scoring by Game (2022)

Runs Scored	G	W	L	Pct.	R/G	RA/G
Overall record	162	83	79	.512	4.16	4.25
0	11	0	11	.000	0.00	5.36
1	23	4	19	.174	1.00	4.22
2	23	8	15	.348	2.00	3.57
3	21	7	14	.333	3.00	3.95
4	18	10	8	.556	4.00	4.11
5	17	14	3	.824	5.00	3.82
6	19	13	6	.684	6.00	4.21
7	7	7	0	1.000	7.00	3.14
8	5	4	1	.800	8.00	4.40
9	9	8	1	.889	9.00	5.11
10 or more	9	8	1	.889	11.22	6.44

Scoring Allowed by Game (2022)

Runs Allowed	G	W	L	Pct.	R/G	RA/G
Overall record	162	83	79	.512	4.16	4.25
0	15	15	0	1.000	3.47	0.00
1	16	15	1	.938	3.81	1.00
2	20	15	5	.750	4.55	2.00
3	25	14	11	.560	3.88	3.00
4	18	10	8	.556	4.28	4.00
5	19	4	15	.211	3.32	5.00
6	16	5	11	.313	4.25	6.00
7	11	1	10	.091	5.55	7.00
8	9	2	7	.222	4.00	8.00
9	2	1	1	.500	6.50	9.00
10 or more	11	1	10	.091	5.00	11.55

Margins (2022)

Category	Margin	G	W	L	Pct.	GShr	WShr
Overall record	—	162	83	79	.512	—	—
Close	1 or 2 runs	83	43	40	.518	51.2%	51.8%
Medium	3 or 4 runs	42	22	20	.524	25.9%	26.5%
Distant	5 or more runs	37	18	19	.486	22.8%	21.7%

Individual Scoring Leaders (2022)

Team Rank	Batter	R	(+) RBI	(-) HR	(=) SC
1	Cedric Mullins	89	64	16	137
2	Anthony Santander	78	89	33	134
3	Ryan Mountcastle	62	85	22	125
4	Austin Hays	66	60	16	110
5	Jorge Mateo	63	50	13	100
6	Adley Rutschman	70	42	13	99
7	Rougned Odor	49	53	13	89
8	Ramon Urias	50	51	16	85
9	Trey Mancini	39	41	10	70
10	Ryan McKenna	23	11	2	32

Team Ratings (2022)

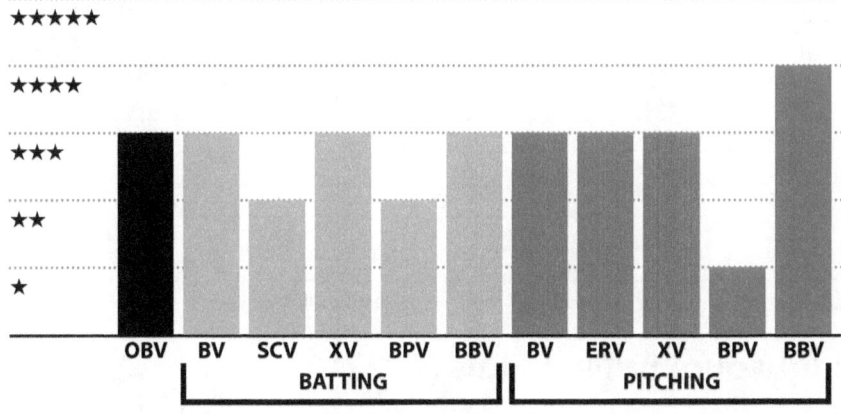

Quality	Type	Indicator	Value	Rating
Overall performance	Overall	OBV	-43	★★★
Base production	Batting	BV	-29	★★★
Run production	Batting	SCV	-37	★★
Power hitting	Batting	XV	12	★★★
Contact hitting	Batting	BPV	-35	★★
Batting eye	Batting	BBV	-12	★★★
Base prevention	Pitching	BV	14	★★★
Run prevention	Pitching	ERV	1	★★★
Power prevention	Pitching	XV	-5	★★★
Strikeout pitching	Pitching	BPV	157	★
Control pitching	Pitching	BBV	-44	★★★★

Team Batting Stats (2022)

Stat	Number	Div Rank	Lg Rank	MLB Rank	MLB Best
R	674	4	10	20	847 (Dodgers)
H	1,281	5	11	20	1,464 (Blue Jays)
HR	171	3	8	15	254 (Yankees)
BPO	.653	4	8	18	.764 (Dodgers)
BA	.236	5	11	20	.264 (Blue Jays)
OBP	.305	5	11	22	.333 (Dodgers)
SA	.390	4	7	14	.443 (Braves)

Division: AL East, 5 teams. **League:** American, 15 teams. **MLB:** 30 teams.

Team Pitching Stats (2022)

Stat	Number	Div Rank	Lg Rank	MLB Rank	MLB Best
ERA	3.97	4	9	17	2.80 (Dodgers)
SO	1,214	5	12	25	1,565 (Mets)
BB	443	3	4	7	384 (Rays)
BPO	.663	4	11	19	.551 (Astros)
BA	.256	5	14	26	.209 (Dodgers)
OBP	.317	4	11	21	.273 (Dodgers)
SA	.407	4	12	21	.332 (Astros)

Division: AL East, 5 teams. **League:** American, 15 teams. **MLB:** 30 teams.

Individual Batting Stats (2022)

Batter	PA	BPO	BA	OBP	SA	ISO	CT	EY
Austin Hays	582	.644	.250	.306	.413	.163	.787	.058
Trey Mancini	401	.714	.268	.347	.404	.136	.757	.083
Jorge Mateo	533	.636	.221	.267	.379	.158	.702	.051
Ryan Mountcastle	609	.672	.250	.305	.423	.173	.723	.069
Cedric Mullins	672	.724	.258	.318	.403	.145	.793	.067
Rougned Odor	472	.580	.207	.275	.357	.150	.744	.066
Adley Rutschman	470	.832	.254	.362	.445	.191	.784	.138
Anthony Santander	647	.731	.240	.318	.455	.214	.787	.084
Ramon Urias	445	.662	.248	.305	.414	.166	.757	.065

Individual Pitching Stats for Starters (2022)

Pitcher	IP	BPO	ERA	BA	SA	ISO	CT	EY
Kyle Bradish	117.2	.705	4.90	.265	.419	.154	.753	.090
Dean Kremer	125.1	.628	3.23	.262	.390	.128	.814	.066
Jordan Lyles	179.0	.732	4.42	.276	.454	.177	.797	.067
Spenser Watkins	105.1	.696	4.70	.281	.423	.142	.851	.065
Tyler Wells	103.2	.633	4.25	.231	.406	.175	.805	.066

Individual Pitching Stats for Relievers (2022)

Pitcher	GR	BPO	ERA	BA	SA	ISO	CT	EY
Keegan Akin	44	.556	3.20	.227	.375	.148	.747	.061
Bryan Baker	64	.543	3.49	.230	.310	.080	.709	.086
Felix Bautista	65	.495	2.19	.167	.291	.123	.612	.087
Joey Krehbiel	56	.697	3.90	.242	.434	.192	.795	.070
Jorge Lopez	44	.490	1.68	.174	.267	.093	.686	.082
Cionel Perez	66	.486	1.40	.220	.278	.057	.737	.086
Dillon Tate	67	.541	3.05	.213	.341	.127	.775	.048

Best Stats on Team (2022)

Stat	Batter	Number
2B	Austin Hays, Adley Rutschman	35
3B	Jorge Mateo	7
BA	Trey Mancini	.268
BB	Adley Rutschman	65
BBV	Adley Rutschman	28
BPO	Adley Rutschman	.832
BPV	Cedric Mullins	26
BV	Adley Rutschman	52
CT	Cedric Mullins	.793
EY	Adley Rutschman	.138
H	Cedric Mullins	157
HR	Anthony Santander	33
ISO	Anthony Santander	.214
OBP	Adley Rutschman	.362
R	Cedric Mullins	89
RBI	Anthony Santander	89
SA	Anthony Santander	.455
SB	Jorge Mateo	35
SC	Cedric Mullins	137
SCV	Anthony Santander	8
SE	Adley Rutschman	.211
XV	Anthony Santander	36

Stat	Pitcher	Number
BA	Tyler Wells	.231
BBV	Bruce Zimmermann	-13
BPO-R	Cionel Perez	.486
BPO-S	Dean Kremer	.628
BPV	Felix Bautista	-31
BV	Felix Bautista	-33
CT	Kyle Bradish	.753
ERA-R	Cionel Perez	1.40
ERA-S	Dean Kremer	3.23
ERV	Cionel Perez	-16
EY	Spenser Watkins	.065
GR	Dillon Tate	67
GS	Jordan Lyles	32
IP	Jordan Lyles	179.0
ISO	Dean Kremer	.128
OBP	Tyler Wells	.285
SA	Dean Kremer	.390
SO	Jordan Lyles	144
SV	Jorge Lopez	19
W	Jordan Lyles	12
XV	Cionel Perez	-20

Worst Stats on Team (2022)

Stat	Batter	Number
BA	Rougned Odor	.207
BBV	Jorge Mateo	-15
BPO	Rougned Odor	.580
BPV	Jorge Mateo	-24
BV	Robinson Chirinos, Rougned Odor	-28
CT	Jorge Mateo	.702
EY	Jorge Mateo	.051
ISO	Trey Mancini	.136
OBP	Jorge Mateo	.267
SA	Rougned Odor	.357
SCV	Robinson Chirinos	-15
SE	Trey Mancini	.175
SO	Ryan Mountcastle	154
XV	Tyler Nevin	-14

Stat	Pitcher	Number
BA	Spenser Watkins	.281
BB	Jordan Lyles	52
BBV	Kyle Bradish	6
BPO-R	Joey Krehbiel	.697
BPO-S	Jordan Lyles	.732
BPV	Spenser Watkins	43
BV	Bruce Zimmermann	58
CT	Spenser Watkins	.851
ERA-R	Joey Krehbiel	3.90
ERA-S	Kyle Bradish	4.90
ERV	Bruce Zimmermann	17
EY	Kyle Bradish	.090
ISO	Jordan Lyles	.177
L	Jordan Lyles	11
OBP	Kyle Bradish	.340
SA	Jordan Lyles	.454
XV	Bruce Zimmermann	42

Overall Base Value Leaders (2022)

Team Rank	Player	BV [bat]	(-) BV [pitch]	(=) OBV
1	Adley Rutschman	52	0	52
2	Felix Bautista	0	-33	33
3	Anthony Santander	32	0	32
4	Cionel Perez	0	-31	31
5	Cedric Mullins	30	0	30
6	Dillon Tate	0	-27	27
7	Keegan Akin	0	-26	26
8	Jorge Lopez	0	-25	25
9	Bryan Baker	0	-24	24
10	Trey Mancini	14	0	14

Fan Support in Past 10 Seasons (2013-2022)

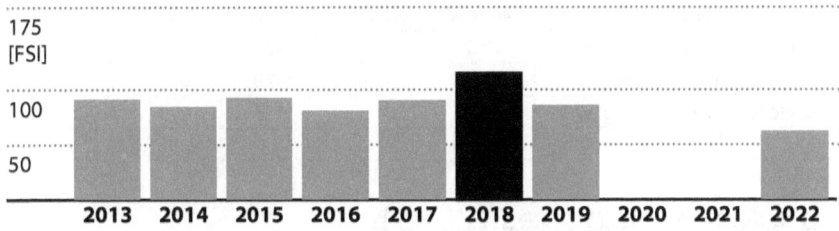

Year	Team	Attendance	W	Att:W	FSI
2013	Baltimore Orioles	2,357,561	85	27,736	91.1
2014	Baltimore Orioles	2,464,473	96	25,672	84.6
2015	Baltimore Orioles	2,281,202	81	28,163	92.7
2016	Baltimore Orioles	2,172,344	89	24,408	81.0
2017	Baltimore Orioles	2,028,424	75	27,046	90.4
2018	Baltimore Orioles	1,564,192	47	33,281	116.1
2019	Baltimore Orioles	1,307,807	54	24,219	85.9
2022	Baltimore Orioles	1,368,367	83	16,486	62.1

Extreme Games for Batters (2022)

Stat	Team Total	Individual Leader	G
3+ H	56	Anthony Santander	9
2+ HR	10	Anthony Santander	5
5+ RBI	1	Jorge Mateo	1
0 H in 5+ AB	28	Anthony Santander	7
4+ SO	9	Gunnar Henderson, Ryan McKenna	2

Extreme Games for Pitchers (2022)

Stat	Team Total	Individual Leader	G
0-2 ER in 7+ IP	15	Jordan Lyles	6
10+ SO	2	Kyle Bradish	2
0 BR in SV	11	Jorge Lopez	4
10+ BR	28	Jordan Lyles	8
1+ ER in SV	4	Felix Bautista	3

Predictions for Coming Season (2023)

Group	Next W	Next L	Next Pct.	WS	LC	PQ
10 closest matches (avg. W-L)	74.2	82.6	.473	0	1	2
25 closest matches (avg. W-L)	74.1	83.6	.470	0	1	2
50 closest matches (avg. W-L)	76.5	81.3	.485	0	2	7

25 Closest Matches (2023)

Rank	Team	Next	W	L	Pct.	WS	LC	PQ
1	Mariners (2007-2009)	2010	61	101	.377	—	—	—
2	Indians (1984-1986)	1987	61	101	.377	—	—	—
3	Twins (2015-2017)	2018	78	84	.481	—	—	—
4	Diamondbacks (2013-2015)	2016	69	93	.426	—	—	—
5	Athletics (1978-1980)	1981	64	45	.587	—	—	X
6	Padres (1980-1982)	1983	81	81	.500	—	—	—
7	Tigers (1988-1990)	1991	84	78	.519	—	—	—
8	Tigers (1995-1997)	1998	65	97	.401	—	—	—
9	Rockies (2004-2006)	2007	90	73	.552	—	X	X
10	Blue Jays (1980-1982)	1983	89	73	.549	—	—	—
11	Orioles (1987-1989)	1990	76	85	.472	—	—	—
12	Mariners (1985-1987)	1988	68	93	.422	—	—	—
13	Expos (1975-1977)	1978	76	86	.469	—	—	—
14	Indians (1986-1988)	1989	73	89	.451	—	—	—
15	Indians (1990-1992)	1993	76	86	.469	—	—	—
16	Athletics (1996-1998)	1999	87	75	.537	—	—	—
17	Mariners (1991-1993)	1994	49	63	.438	—	—	—
18	Marlins (2012-2014)	2015	71	91	.438	—	—	—
19	Rangers (1981-1983)	1984	69	92	.429	—	—	—
20	Twins (1994-1996)	1997	68	94	.420	—	—	—
21	Padres (1986-1988)	1989	89	73	.549	—	—	—
22	Tigers (2002-2004)	2005	71	91	.438	—	—	—
23	Mets (1982-1984)	1985	98	64	.605	—	—	—
24	Padres (1976-1978)	1979	68	93	.422	—	—	—
25	White Sox (1975-1977)	1978	71	90	.441	—	—	—

BOSTON RED SOX

Past 10 Seasons (2013-2022)

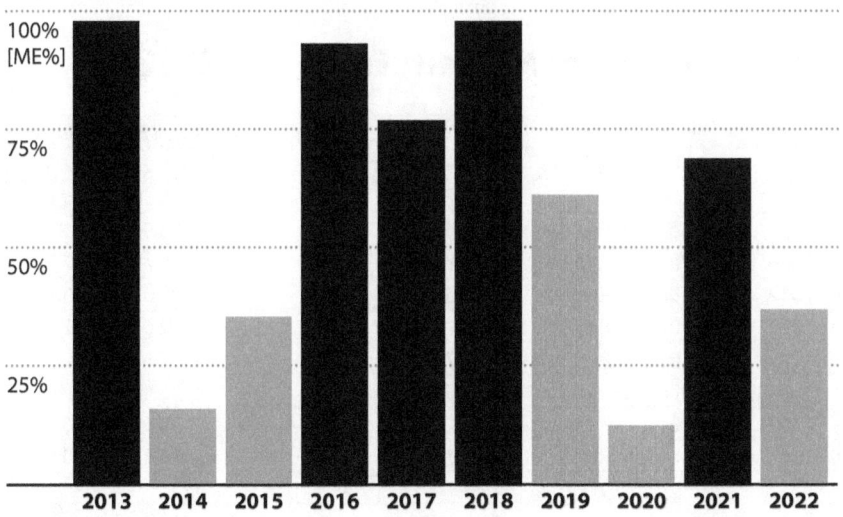

Year	Team	W	L	Pct.	Post	TS	ME%
2013	Boston Red Sox	97	65	.599	WLP	81.732	97.8%
2014	Boston Red Sox	71	91	.438	—	28.587	15.8%
2015	Boston Red Sox	78	84	.481	—	39.135	35.3%
2016	Boston Red Sox	93	69	.574	P	72.624	93.0%
2017	Boston Red Sox	93	69	.574	P	58.930	76.8%
2018	Boston Red Sox	108	54	.667	WLP	81.765	97.8%
2019	Boston Red Sox	84	78	.519	—	51.375	61.0%
2020	Boston Red Sox	24	36	.400	—	26.276	12.3%
2021	Boston Red Sox	92	70	.568	P	54.899	68.8%
2022	Boston Red Sox	78	84	.481	—	39.805	36.8%

Best Seasons of Modern Era (1961-2022)

Year	Team	W	L	Pct.	Post	TS	ME%
2007	Boston Red Sox	96	66	.593	WLP	85.711	99.0%
2004	Boston Red Sox	98	64	.605	WLP	84.936	98.7%
2018	Boston Red Sox	108	54	.667	WLP	81.765	97.8%
2013	Boston Red Sox	97	65	.599	WLP	81.732	97.8%
1986	Boston Red Sox	95	66	.590	LP	74.764	94.6%
1967	Boston Red Sox	92	70	.568	LP	73.514	93.6%
2016	Boston Red Sox	93	69	.574	P	72.624	93.0%
1975	Boston Red Sox	95	65	.594	LP	70.338	91.2%
2008	Boston Red Sox	95	67	.586	P	68.829	90.4%
2003	Boston Red Sox	95	67	.586	P	64.926	86.8%

Worst Seasons of Modern Era (1961-2022)

Year	Team	W	L	Pct.	Post	TS	ME%
2020	Boston Red Sox	24	36	.400	—	26.276	12.3%
2014	Boston Red Sox	71	91	.438	—	28.587	15.8%
1965	Boston Red Sox	62	100	.383	—	28.843	16.2%
1966	Boston Red Sox	72	90	.444	—	29.204	17.1%
2012	Boston Red Sox	69	93	.426	—	29.636	18.0%
1964	Boston Red Sox	72	90	.444	—	32.571	22.5%
1992	Boston Red Sox	73	89	.451	—	32.636	22.7%
1994	Boston Red Sox	54	61	.470	—	36.460	29.8%
1962	Boston Red Sox	76	84	.475	—	36.633	30.2%
1961	Boston Red Sox	76	86	.469	—	36.826	30.6%

Season Breakdown (2022)

Category	W	L	Pct.	R	RA	R/G	RA/G
Overall record in 2022	78	84	.481	735	787	4.54	4.86
Home games	43	38	.531	392	411	4.84	5.07
Away games	35	46	.432	343	376	4.23	4.64
First half of 2022 season	45	36	.556	382	323	4.72	3.99
Second half of 2022 season	33	48	.407	353	464	4.36	5.73
Against first-place teams	18	21	.462	168	207	4.31	5.31
Against playoff teams	34	50	.405	338	448	4.02	5.33
Against non-playoff teams	44	34	.564	397	339	5.09	4.35

Season as Nine-Inning Game (2022)

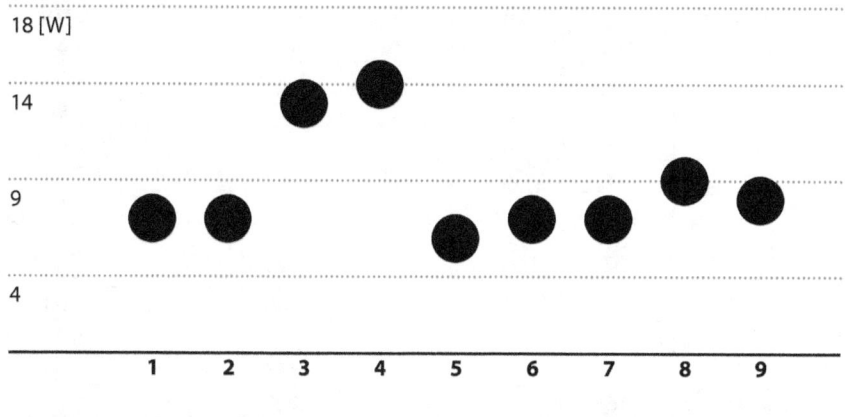

Result	1	2	3	4	5	6	7	8	9	Total
Wins	7	7	13	14	6	7	7	9	8	78
Losses	11	11	5	4	12	11	11	9	10	84

Scoring by Game (2022)

Runs Scored	G	W	L	Pct.	R/G	RA/G
Overall record	162	78	84	.481	4.54	4.86
0	8	0	8	.000	0.00	6.25
1	18	3	15	.167	1.00	4.06
2	22	4	18	.182	2.00	4.32
3	16	6	10	.375	3.00	4.25
4	24	12	12	.500	4.00	4.92
5	27	13	14	.481	5.00	6.26
6	16	13	3	.813	6.00	4.19
7	8	7	1	.875	7.00	2.88
8	7	5	2	.714	8.00	5.29
9	5	5	0	1.000	9.00	5.60
10 or more	11	10	1	.909	12.82	5.36

Scoring Allowed by Game (2022)

Runs Allowed	G	W	L	Pct.	R/G	RA/G
Overall record	162	78	84	.481	4.54	4.86
0	10	10	0	1.000	3.40	0.00
1	17	15	2	.882	4.65	1.00
2	15	12	3	.800	4.47	2.00
3	32	21	11	.656	4.78	3.00
4	16	7	9	.438	4.63	4.00
5	16	6	10	.375	4.13	5.00
6	12	2	10	.167	5.00	6.00
7	10	2	8	.200	5.50	7.00
8	11	2	9	.182	4.18	8.00
9	7	1	6	.143	4.57	9.00
10 or more	16	0	16	.000	4.31	12.94

Margins (2022)

Category	Margin	G	W	L	Pct.	GShr	WShr
Overall record	—	162	78	84	.481	—	—
Close	1 or 2 runs	79	39	40	.494	48.8%	50.0%
Medium	3 or 4 runs	33	17	16	.515	20.4%	21.8%
Distant	5 or more runs	50	22	28	.440	30.9%	28.2%

Individual Scoring Leaders (2022)

Team Rank	Batter	R	(+) RBI	(-) HR	(=) SC
1	Rafael Devers	84	88	27	145
2	Xander Bogaerts	84	73	15	142
3	Alex Verdugo	75	74	11	138
4	J.D. Martinez	76	62	16	122
5	Trevor Story	53	66	16	103
6	Enrique Hernandez	48	45	6	87
7	Bobby Dalbec	40	39	12	67
7	Christian Vazquez	33	42	8	67
9	Christian Arroyo	32	36	6	62
10	Franchy Cordero	36	29	8	57

Team Ratings (2022)

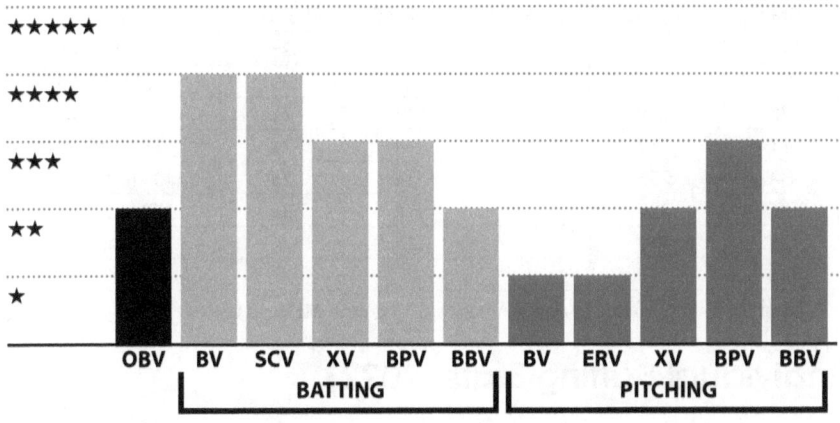

Quality	Type	Indicator	Value	Rating
Overall performance	Overall	OBV	-156	★★
Base production	Batting	BV	68	★★★★
Run production	Batting	SCV	86	★★★★
Power hitting	Batting	XV	-2	★★★
Contact hitting	Batting	BPV	10	★★★
Batting eye	Batting	BBV	-30	★★
Base prevention	Pitching	BV	224	★
Run prevention	Pitching	ERV	91	★
Power prevention	Pitching	XV	62	★★
Strikeout pitching	Pitching	BPV	31	★★★
Control pitching	Pitching	BBV	22	★★

Team Batting Stats (2022)

Stat	Number	Div Rank	Lg Rank	MLB Rank	MLB Best
R	735	3	4	9	847 (Dodgers)
H	1,427	2	3	3	1,464 (Blue Jays)
HR	155	4	9	20	254 (Yankees)
BPO	.676	3	4	10	.764 (Dodgers)
BA	.258	2	2	3	.264 (Blue Jays)
OBP	.321	3	3	6	.333 (Dodgers)
SA	.409	3	4	9	.443 (Braves)

Division: AL East, 5 teams. **League:** American, 15 teams. **MLB:** 30 teams.

Team Pitching Stats (2022)

Stat	Number	Div Rank	Lg Rank	MLB Rank	MLB Best
ERA	4.53	5	14	25	2.80 (Dodgers)
SO	1,346	4	9	19	1,565 (Mets)
BB	526	5	11	21	384 (Rays)
BPO	.712	5	14	25	.551 (Astros)
BA	.256	4	13	25	.209 (Dodgers)
OBP	.326	5	14	25	.273 (Dodgers)
SA	.419	5	13	25	.332 (Astros)

Division: AL East, 5 teams. **League:** American, 15 teams. **MLB:** 30 teams.

Individual Batting Stats (2022)

Batter	PA	BPO	BA	OBP	SA	ISO	CT	EY
Xander Bogaerts	631	.822	.307	.377	.456	.149	.788	.087
Bobby Dalbec	353	.605	.215	.283	.369	.155	.628	.082
Rafael Devers	614	.858	.295	.358	.521	.225	.795	.065
Enrique Hernandez	402	.547	.222	.291	.338	.116	.803	.085
J.D. Martinez	596	.731	.274	.341	.448	.174	.728	.086
Trevor Story	396	.726	.238	.303	.434	.196	.658	.071
Alex Verdugo	644	.649	.280	.328	.405	.125	.855	.062

Individual Pitching Stats for Starters (2022)

Pitcher	IP	BPO	ERA	BA	SA	ISO	CT	EY
Nathan Eovaldi	109.1	.684	3.87	.264	.457	.193	.763	.043
Rich Hill	124.1	.695	4.27	.258	.432	.174	.775	.070
Nick Pivetta	179.2	.742	4.56	.253	.425	.172	.747	.094
Michael Wacha	127.1	.625	3.32	.233	.410	.176	.782	.060

Individual Pitching Stats for Relievers (2022)

Pitcher	GR	BPO	ERA	BA	SA	ISO	CT	EY
Matt Barnes	44	.675	4.31	.240	.333	.093	.773	.114
Ryan Brasier	68	.770	5.78	.280	.481	.202	.737	.046
Austin Davis	47	.759	5.47	.260	.386	.126	.716	.111
Jake Diekman	44	.781	4.23	.203	.376	.173	.617	.171
Hirokazu Sawamura	49	.618	3.73	.238	.339	.101	.788	.114
John Schreiber	64	.503	2.22	.195	.312	.117	.680	.074
Matt Strahm	50	.642	3.83	.224	.353	.129	.694	.083

Best Stats on Team (2022)

Stat	Batter	Number
2B	J.D. Martinez	43
3B	Jarren Duran	3
BA	Xander Bogaerts	.307
BB	Xander Bogaerts	57
BBV	Triston Casas	11
BPO	Rafael Devers	.858
BPV	Alex Verdugo	62
BV	Rafael Devers	81
CT	Alex Verdugo	.855
EY	Xander Bogaerts	.087
H	Xander Bogaerts	171
HR	Rafael Devers	27
ISO	Rafael Devers	.225
OBP	Xander Bogaerts	.377
R	Rafael Devers, Xander Bogaerts	84
RBI	Rafael Devers	88
SA	Rafael Devers	.521
SB	Trevor Story	13
SC	Rafael Devers	145
SCV	Trevor Story	26
SE	Trevor Story	.260
XV	Rafael Devers	41

Stat	Pitcher	Number
BA	Michael Wacha	.233
BBV	Nathan Eovaldi	-16
BPO-R	John Schreiber	.503
BPO-S	Michael Wacha	.625
BPV	Jake Diekman	-18
BV	John Schreiber	-31
CT	Nick Pivetta	.747
ERA-R	John Schreiber	2.22
ERA-S	Michael Wacha	3.32
ERV	John Schreiber	-13
EY	Nathan Eovaldi	.043
GR	Ryan Brasier	68
GS	Nick Pivetta	33
IP	Nick Pivetta	179.2
ISO	Nick Pivetta	.172
OBP	Michael Wacha	.283
SA	Michael Wacha	.410
SO	Nick Pivetta	175
SV	John Schreiber, Tanner Houck, Matt Barnes	8
W	Michael Wacha	11
XV	Tanner Houck	-18

Worst Stats on Team (2022)

Stat	Batter	Number
BA	Bobby Dalbec	.215
BBV	Christian Arroyo	-13
BPO	Enrique Hernandez	.547
BPV	Bobby Dalbec	-39
BV	Jackie Bradley Jr.	-39
CT	Bobby Dalbec	.628
EY	Alex Verdugo	.062
ISO	Enrique Hernandez	.116
OBP	Bobby Dalbec	.283
SA	Enrique Hernandez	.338
SCV	Jackie Bradley Jr.	-10
SE	Bobby Dalbec	.190
SO	J.D. Martinez	145
XV	Alex Verdugo	-16

Stat	Pitcher	Number
BA	Nathan Eovaldi	.264
BB	Nick Pivetta	73
BBV	Jake Diekman	16
BPO-R	Jake Diekman	.781
BPO-S	Nick Pivetta	.742
BPV	Josh Winckowski	27
BV	Nick Pivetta	44
CT	Michael Wacha	.782
ERA-R	Ryan Brasier	5.78
ERA-S	Nick Pivetta	4.56
ERV	Josh Winckowski, Connor Seabold	15
EY	Nick Pivetta	.094
ISO	Nathan Eovaldi	.193
L	Nick Pivetta	12
OBP	Nick Pivetta	.327
SA	Nathan Eovaldi	.457
XV	Nathan Eovaldi	18

Overall Base Value Leaders (2022)

Team Rank	Player	BV [bat]	(-) BV [pitch]	(=) OBV
1	Rafael Devers	81	0	81
2	Xander Bogaerts	66	0	66
3	John Schreiber	0	-31	31
4	J.D. Martinez	29	0	29
5	Rob Refsnyder	28	0	28
6	Garrett Whitlock	0	-21	21
7	Tanner Houck	0	-20	20
8	Trevor Story	19	0	19
9	Reese McGuire	12	-2	14
10	Michael Wacha	0	-13	13

Fan Support in Past 10 Seasons (2013-2022)

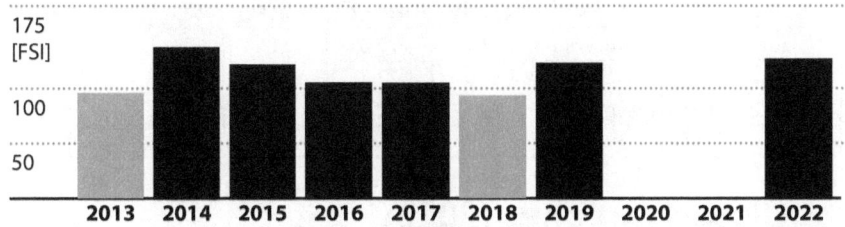

Year	Team	Attendance	W	Att:W	FSI
2013	Boston Red Sox	2,833,333	97	29,210	95.9
2014	Boston Red Sox	2,956,089	71	41,635	137.2
2015	Boston Red Sox	2,880,694	78	36,932	121.6
2016	Boston Red Sox	2,955,434	93	31,779	105.4
2017	Boston Red Sox	2,917,678	93	31,373	104.9
2018	Boston Red Sox	2,895,575	108	26,811	93.5
2019	Boston Red Sox	2,915,502	84	34,708	123.1
2022	Boston Red Sox	2,625,089	78	33,655	126.7

Extreme Games for Batters (2022)

Stat	Team Total	Individual Leader	G
3+ H	81	Xander Bogaerts	16
2+ HR	6	Rafael Devers	2
5+ RBI	5	Rafael Devers	2
0 H in 5+ AB	24	Kike Hernandez, Rafael Devers	5
4+ SO	8	Jarren Duran, Trevor Story	2

Extreme Games for Pitchers (2022)

Stat	Team Total	Individual Leader	G
0-2 ER in 7+ IP	14	Nick Pivetta	7
10+ SO	4	Nick Pivetta	2
0 BR in SV	19	Garrett Whitlock, Matt Barnes, Tanner Houck	4
10+ BR	27	Nick Pivetta	8
1+ ER in SV	3	Garrett Whitlock	2

Predictions for Coming Season (2023)

Group	Next W	Next L	Next Pct.	WS	LC	PQ
10 closest matches (avg. W-L)	77.1	77.0	.500	1	1	1
25 closest matches (avg. W-L)	81.0	77.7	.510	1	2	7
50 closest matches (avg. W-L)	79.4	78.2	.504	1	2	13

25 Closest Matches (2023)

Rank	Team	Next	W	L	Pct.	WS	LC	PQ
1	Cardinals (1995-1997)	1998	83	79	.512	—	—	—
2	White Sox (2007-2009)	2010	88	74	.543	—	—	—
3	Mariners (2015-2017)	2018	89	73	.549	—	—	—
4	Tigers (1992-1994)	1995	60	84	.417	—	—	—
5	Cardinals (1978-1980)	1981	59	43	.578	—	—	—
6	Expos (1995-1997)	1998	65	97	.401	—	—	—
7	Rangers (1985-1987)	1988	70	91	.435	—	—	—
8	Rockies (1999-2001)	2002	73	89	.451	—	—	—
9	White Sox (2009-2011)	2012	85	77	.525	—	—	—
10	Angels (1999-2001)	2002	99	63	.611	X	X	X
11	Cardinals (1997-1999)	2000	95	67	.586	—	—	X
12	White Sox (1995-1997)	1998	80	82	.494	—	—	—
13	Padres (2009-2011)	2012	76	86	.469	—	—	—
14	Royals (1981-1983)	1984	84	78	.519	—	—	X
15	Cubs (2000-2002)	2003	88	74	.543	—	—	X
16	Padres (1988-1990)	1991	84	78	.519	—	—	—
17	Royals (1993-1995)	1996	75	86	.466	—	—	—
18	Mariners (2013-2015)	2016	86	76	.531	—	—	—
19	Padres (1981-1983)	1984	92	70	.568	—	X	X
20	Rangers (2003-2005)	2006	80	82	.494	—	—	—
21	Phillies (1985-1987)	1988	65	96	.404	—	—	—
22	Padres (2003-2005)	2006	88	74	.543	—	—	X
23	Twins (2016-2018)	2019	101	61	.623	—	—	X
24	Braves (2006-2008)	2009	86	76	.531	—	—	—
25	White Sox (1976-1978)	1979	73	87	.456	—	—	—

CHICAGO CUBS

Past 10 Seasons (2013-2022)

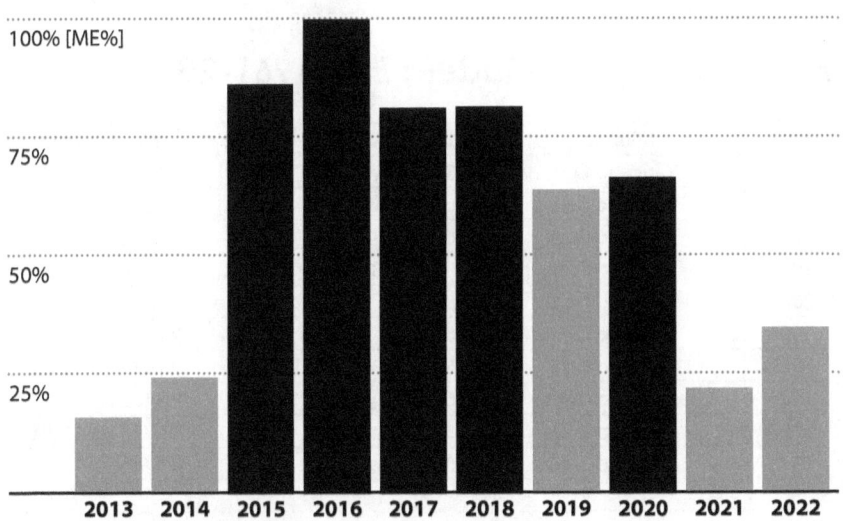

Year	Team	W	L	Pct.	Post	TS	ME%
2013	Chicago Cubs	66	96	.407	—	28.566	15.7%
2014	Chicago Cubs	73	89	.451	—	33.106	24.1%
2015	Chicago Cubs	97	65	.599	P	64.366	86.0%
2016	Chicago Cubs	103	58	.640	WLP	92.166	99.8%
2017	Chicago Cubs	92	70	.568	P	61.476	81.0%
2018	Chicago Cubs	95	68	.583	P	61.549	81.3%
2019	Chicago Cubs	84	78	.519	—	52.490	63.7%
2020	Chicago Cubs	34	26	.567	P	53.847	66.2%
2021	Chicago Cubs	71	91	.438	—	32.261	21.7%
2022	Chicago Cubs	74	88	.457	—	38.643	34.5%

Best Seasons of Modern Era (1961-2022)

Year	Team	W	L	Pct.	Post	TS	ME%
2016	Chicago Cubs	103	58	.640	WLP	92.166	99.8%
2008	Chicago Cubs	97	64	.602	P	72.913	93.2%
1984	Chicago Cubs	96	65	.596	P	69.775	90.8%
2015	Chicago Cubs	97	65	.599	P	64.366	86.0%
1989	Chicago Cubs	93	69	.574	P	63.654	84.7%
2018	Chicago Cubs	95	68	.583	P	61.549	81.3%
2017	Chicago Cubs	92	70	.568	P	61.476	81.0%
1970	Chicago Cubs	84	78	.519	—	58.954	76.9%
2004	Chicago Cubs	89	73	.549	—	58.802	76.6%
1972	Chicago Cubs	85	70	.548	—	58.763	76.6%

Worst Seasons of Modern Era (1961-2022)

Year	Team	W	L	Pct.	Post	TS	ME%
1981	Chicago Cubs	38	65	.369	—	17.954	3.8%
1980	Chicago Cubs	64	98	.395	—	18.364	4.0%
2012	Chicago Cubs	61	101	.377	—	19.962	4.8%
1966	Chicago Cubs	59	103	.364	—	20.238	5.3%
2006	Chicago Cubs	66	96	.407	—	20.558	5.6%
2000	Chicago Cubs	65	97	.401	—	24.576	9.5%
1962	Chicago Cubs	59	103	.364	—	25.070	10.0%
1999	Chicago Cubs	67	95	.414	—	25.702	11.3%
1997	Chicago Cubs	68	94	.420	—	25.827	11.7%
1974	Chicago Cubs	66	96	.407	—	27.781	14.7%

Season Breakdown (2022)

Category	W	L	Pct.	R	RA	R/G	RA/G
Overall record in 2022	74	88	.457	657	731	4.06	4.51
Home games	37	44	.457	324	343	4.00	4.23
Away games	37	44	.457	333	388	4.11	4.79
First half of 2022 season	33	48	.407	357	420	4.41	5.19
Second half of 2022 season	41	40	.506	300	311	3.70	3.84
Against first-place teams	9	26	.257	101	192	2.89	5.49
Against playoff teams	23	38	.377	213	306	3.49	5.02
Against non-playoff teams	51	50	.505	444	425	4.40	4.21

Season as Nine-Inning Game (2022)

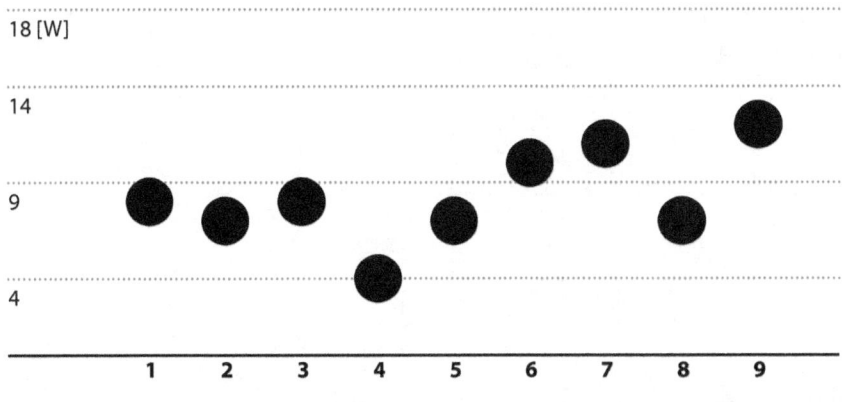

Result	1	2	3	4	5	6	7	8	9	Total
Wins	8	7	8	4	7	10	11	7	12	74
Losses	10	11	10	14	11	8	7	11	6	88

Scoring by Game (2022)

Runs Scored	G	W	L	Pct.	R/G	RA/G
Overall record	162	74	88	.457	4.06	4.51
0	12	0	12	.000	0.00	5.50
1	18	1	17	.056	1.00	5.06
2	25	10	15	.400	2.00	3.16
3	27	8	19	.296	3.00	4.37
4	24	14	10	.583	4.00	4.08
5	13	5	8	.385	5.00	8.00
6	17	13	4	.765	6.00	4.29
7	10	8	2	.800	7.00	4.40
8	6	6	0	1.000	8.00	4.00
9	4	3	1	.750	9.00	3.50
10 or more	6	6	0	1.000	15.17	3.33

Scoring Allowed by Game (2022)

Runs Allowed	G	W	L	Pct.	R/G	RA/G
Overall record	162	74	88	.457	4.06	4.51
0	11	11	0	1.000	6.00	0.00
1	15	14	1	.933	3.53	1.00
2	23	20	3	.870	4.57	2.00
3	21	12	9	.571	3.95	3.00
4	23	5	18	.217	3.35	4.00
5	24	9	15	.375	4.67	5.00
6	9	0	9	.000	2.56	6.00
7	13	3	10	.231	4.08	7.00
8	8	0	8	.000	2.63	8.00
9	4	0	4	.000	4.25	9.00
10 or more	11	0	11	.000	4.27	13.64

Margins (2022)

Category	Margin	G	W	L	Pct.	GShr	WShr
Overall record	—	162	74	88	.457	—	—
Close	1 or 2 runs	91	43	48	.473	56.2%	58.1%
Medium	3 or 4 runs	26	12	14	.462	16.0%	16.2%
Distant	5 or more runs	45	19	26	.422	27.8%	25.7%

Individual Scoring Leaders (2022)

Team Rank	Batter	R	(+) RBI	(-) HR	(=) SC
1	Ian Happ	72	72	17	127
2	Patrick Wisdom	67	66	25	108
3	Nico Hoerner	60	55	10	105
4	Willson Contreras	65	55	22	98
5	Christopher Morel	55	47	16	86
5	Seiya Suzuki	54	46	14	86
7	Rafael Ortega	35	35	7	63
8	Frank Schwindel	23	36	8	51
9	Alfonso Rivas	27	25	3	49
10	P.J. Higgins	23	30	6	47

Team Ratings (2022)

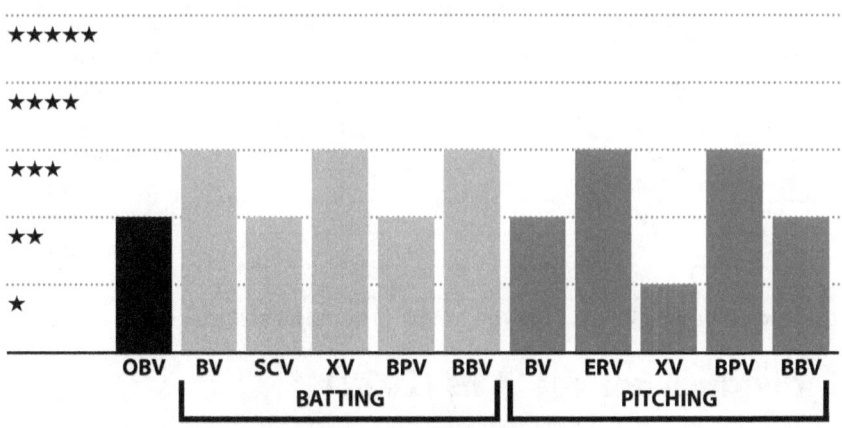

Quality	Type	Indicator	Value	Rating
Overall performance	Overall	OBV	-153	★★
Base production	Batting	BV	-20	★★★
Run production	Batting	SCV	-66	★★
Power hitting	Batting	XV	-21	★★★
Contact hitting	Batting	BPV	-94	★★
Batting eye	Batting	BBV	11	★★★
Base prevention	Pitching	BV	133	★★
Run prevention	Pitching	ERV	6	★★★
Power prevention	Pitching	XV	98	★
Strikeout pitching	Pitching	BPV	-8	★★★
Control pitching	Pitching	BBV	35	★★

Team Batting Stats (2022)

Stat	Number	Div Rank	Lg Rank	MLB Rank	MLB Best
R	657	3	11	22	847 (Dodgers)
H	1,293	2	9	19	1,464 (Blue Jays)
HR	159	3	9	17	254 (Yankees)
BPO	.655	3	10	16	.764 (Dodgers)
BA	.238	2	9	19	.264 (Blue Jays)
OBP	.311	3	10	17	.333 (Dodgers)
SA	.387	3	9	19	.443 (Braves)

Division: NL Central, 5 teams. **League:** National, 15 teams. **MLB:** 30 teams.

Team Pitching Stats (2022)

Stat	Number	Div Rank	Lg Rank	MLB Rank	MLB Best
ERA	4.00	3	10	20	2.80 (Dodgers)
SO	1,383	3	9	16	1,565 (Mets)
BB	540	3	12	24	384 (Rays)
BPO	.691	3	11	22	.551 (Astros)
BA	.244	2	7	15	.209 (Dodgers)
OBP	.318	3	11	22	.273 (Dodgers)
SA	.414	4	12	24	.332 (Astros)

Division: NL Central, 5 teams. **League:** National, 15 teams. **MLB:** 30 teams.

Individual Batting Stats (2022)

Batter	PA	BPO	BA	OBP	SA	ISO	CT	EY
Willson Contreras	487	.808	.243	.349	.466	.224	.752	.092
Ian Happ	641	.753	.271	.342	.440	.169	.740	.085
Nico Hoerner	517	.701	.281	.327	.410	.129	.881	.047
Christopher Morel	425	.714	.235	.308	.433	.198	.639	.089
Rafael Ortega	371	.675	.241	.331	.358	.117	.766	.114
Seiya Suzuki	446	.744	.262	.336	.433	.171	.723	.088
Patrick Wisdom	534	.705	.207	.298	.426	.220	.610	.098

Individual Pitching Stats for Starters (2022)

Pitcher	IP	BPO	ERA	BA	SA	ISO	CT	EY
Adrian Sampson	104.1	.589	3.11	.253	.383	.130	.817	.063
Drew Smyly	106.1	.671	3.47	.243	.422	.178	.781	.058
Justin Steele	119.0	.604	3.18	.244	.339	.095	.722	.098
Marcus Stroman	138.2	.597	3.50	.234	.377	.143	.773	.063
Keegan Thompson	115.0	.669	3.76	.239	.411	.172	.749	.089

Individual Pitching Stats for Relievers (2022)

Pitcher	GR	BPO	ERA	BA	SA	ISO	CT	EY
Scott Effross	46	.478	2.66	.220	.299	.079	.695	.046
Brandon Hughes	57	.640	3.12	.200	.395	.195	.676	.076
Michael Rucker	41	.636	3.95	.242	.396	.155	.758	.087
Rowan Wick	64	.845	4.22	.305	.475	.170	.734	.092

Best Stats on Team (2022)

Stat	Batter	Number
2B	Ian Happ	42
3B	Nico Hoerner	5
BA	Nico Hoerner	.281
BB	Ian Happ	58
BBV	Rafael Ortega	13
BPO	Willson Contreras	.808
BPV	Nico Hoerner	63
BV	Willson Contreras	49
CT	Nico Hoerner	.881
EY	Rafael Ortega	.114
H	Ian Happ	155
HR	Patrick Wisdom	25
ISO	Willson Contreras	.224
OBP	Willson Contreras	.349
R	Ian Happ	72
RBI	Ian Happ	72
SA	Willson Contreras	.466
SB	Nico Hoerner	20
SC	Ian Happ	127
SCV	Patrick Wisdom, Nico Hoerner	4
SE	Nico Hoerner	.203
XV	Patrick Wisdom	32

Stat	Pitcher	Number
BA	Marcus Stroman	.234
BBV	Drew Smyly, Marcus Stroman	-9
BPO-R	Scott Effross	.478
BPO-S	Adrian Sampson	.589
BPV	Brandon Hughes, David Robertson	-16
BV	Marcus Stroman	-26
CT	Justin Steele	.722
ERA-R	Scott Effross	2.66
ERA-S	Adrian Sampson	3.11
ERV	Justin Steele, Adrian Sampson	-10
EY	Drew Smyly	.058
GR	Rowan Wick	64
GS	Marcus Stroman	25
IP	Marcus Stroman	138.2
ISO	Justin Steele	.095
OBP	Marcus Stroman	.287
SA	Justin Steele	.339
SO	Justin Steele	126
SV	David Robertson	14
W	Keegan Thompson	10
XV	Justin Steele	-26

Worst Stats on Team (2022)

Stat	Batter	Number
BA	Patrick Wisdom	.207
BBV	Nico Hoerner	-17
BPO	Rafael Ortega	.675
BPV	Patrick Wisdom	-66
BV	Yan Gomes	-34
CT	Patrick Wisdom	.610
EY	Nico Hoerner	.047
ISO	Rafael Ortega	.117
OBP	Patrick Wisdom	.298
SA	Rafael Ortega	.358
SCV	Nick Madrigal	-18
SE	Rafael Ortega	.170
SO	Patrick Wisdom	183
XV	Nick Madrigal	-25

Stat	Pitcher	Number
BA	Adrian Sampson	.253
BB	Justin Steele	50
BBV	Daniel Norris	10
BPO-R	Rowan Wick	.845
BPO-S	Drew Smyly	.671
BPV	Adrian Sampson	27
BV	Rowan Wick	36
CT	Adrian Sampson	.817
ERA-R	Rowan Wick	4.22
ERA-S	Keegan Thompson	3.76
ERV	Sean Newcomb	13
EY	Justin Steele	.098
ISO	Drew Smyly	.178
L	Drew Smyly	8
OBP	Justin Steele	.321
SA	Drew Smyly	.422
XV	Matt Swarmer	24

Overall Base Value Leaders (2022)

Team Rank	Player	BV [bat]	(-) BV [pitch]	(=) OBV
1	Willson Contreras	49	0	49
2	Ian Happ	41	0	41
3	Marcus Stroman	0	-26	26
3	Seiya Suzuki	26	0	26
5	Scott Effross	0	-24	24
6	Adrian Sampson	0	-22	22
7	Justin Steele	0	-20	20
8	Patrick Wisdom	18	0	18
9	Christopher Morel	17	0	17
10	Nico Hoerner	15	0	15
10	David Robertson	-1	-16	15

Fan Support in Past 10 Seasons (2013-2022)

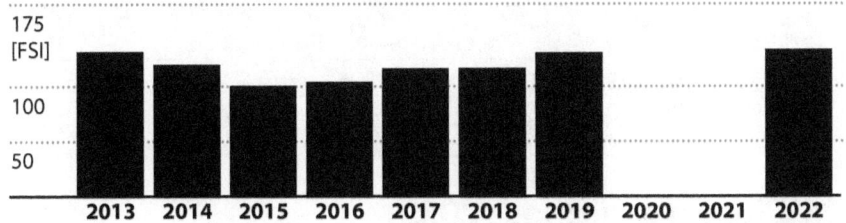

Year	Team	Attendance	W	Att:W	FSI
2013	Chicago Cubs	2,642,682	66	40,041	131.5
2014	Chicago Cubs	2,652,113	73	36,330	119.7
2015	Chicago Cubs	2,959,812	97	30,514	100.5
2016	Chicago Cubs	3,232,420	103	31,383	104.1
2017	Chicago Cubs	3,199,562	92	34,778	116.3
2018	Chicago Cubs	3,181,089	95	33,485	116.8
2019	Chicago Cubs	3,094,865	84	36,844	130.6
2022	Chicago Cubs	2,616,780	74	35,362	133.1

Extreme Games for Batters (2022)

Stat	Team Total	Individual Leader	G
3+ H	63	Nico Hoerner	14
2+ HR	9	Ian Happ, Willson Contreras	2
5+ RBI	5	Alfonso Rivas	2
0 H in 5+ AB	25	Ian Happ	7
4+ SO	10	Christopher Morel, Ian Happ, Nelson Velazquez, Patrick Wisdom	2

Extreme Games for Pitchers (2022)

Stat	Team Total	Individual Leader	G
0-2 ER in 7+ IP	18	Marcus Stroman	6
10+ SO	2	Justin Steele	2
0 BR in SV	14	David Robertson	6
10+ BR	15	Keegan Thompson, Kyle Hendricks, Marcus Stroman	3
1+ ER in SV	3	Brandon Hughes, Robert Gsellman, Rowan Wick	1

Predictions for Coming Season (2023)

Group	Next W	Next L	Next Pct.	WS	LC	PQ
10 closest matches (avg. W-L)	77.4	84.4	.478	0	0	0
25 closest matches (avg. W-L)	73.3	80.6	.476	0	0	0
50 closest matches (avg. W-L)	75.7	80.8	.484	0	0	4

25 Closest Matches (2023)

Rank	Team	Next	W	L	Pct.	WS	LC	PQ
1	Mets (2016-2018)	2019	86	76	.531	—	—	—
2	Giants (2004-2006)	2007	71	91	.438	—	—	—
3	Brewers (2014-2016)	2017	86	76	.531	—	—	—
4	White Sox (1977-1979)	1980	70	90	.438	—	—	—
5	Blue Jays (2011-2013)	2014	83	79	.512	—	—	—
6	Padres (2010-2012)	2013	76	86	.469	—	—	—
7	Cubs (1989-1991)	1992	78	84	.481	—	—	—
8	Rangers (2006-2008)	2009	87	75	.537	—	—	—
9	Indians (1982-1984)	1985	60	102	.370	—	—	—
10	Mariners (1987-1989)	1990	77	85	.475	—	—	—
11	Giants (1975-1977)	1978	89	73	.549	—	—	—
12	Rangers (2017-2019)	2020	22	38	.367	—	—	—
13	Reds (1996-1998)	1999	96	67	.589	—	—	—
14	Reds (2000-2002)	2003	69	93	.426	—	—	—
15	Athletics (2007-2009)	2010	81	81	.500	—	—	—
16	Rockies (2001-2003)	2004	68	94	.420	—	—	—
17	Astros (1974-1976)	1977	81	81	.500	—	—	—
18	Blue Jays (2016-2018)	2019	67	95	.414	—	—	—
19	Royals (1994-1996)	1997	67	94	.416	—	—	—
20	Indians (2001-2003)	2004	80	82	.494	—	—	—
21	Athletics (1981-1983)	1984	77	85	.475	—	—	—
22	Red Sox (1991-1993)	1994	54	61	.470	—	—	—
23	Giants (1978-1980)	1981	56	55	.505	—	—	—
24	Mets (2008-2010)	2011	77	85	.475	—	—	—
25	Padres (2012-2014)	2015	74	88	.457	—	—	—

CHICAGO WHITE SOX

Past 10 Seasons (2013-2022)

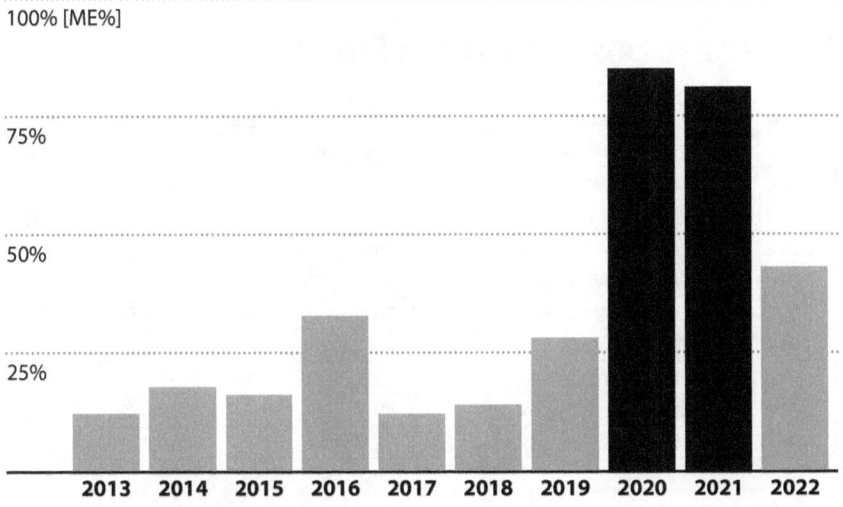

Year	Team	W	L	Pct.	Post	TS	ME%
2013	Chicago White Sox	63	99	.389	—	26.209	12.2%
2014	Chicago White Sox	73	89	.451	—	29.452	17.8%
2015	Chicago White Sox	76	86	.469	—	28.839	16.1%
2016	Chicago White Sox	78	84	.481	—	37.921	32.8%
2017	Chicago White Sox	67	95	.414	—	26.072	12.1%
2018	Chicago White Sox	62	100	.383	—	27.388	14.0%
2019	Chicago White Sox	72	89	.447	—	35.518	28.1%
2020	Chicago White Sox	35	25	.583	P	63.906	84.9%
2021	Chicago White Sox	93	69	.574	P	61.531	81.1%
2022	Chicago White Sox	81	81	.500	—	42.539	43.1%

Best Seasons of Modern Era (1961-2022)

Year	Team	W	L	Pct.	Post	TS	ME%
2005	Chicago White Sox	99	63	.611	WLP	75.291	94.8%
1994	Chicago White Sox	67	46	.593	—	70.266	91.1%
1983	Chicago White Sox	99	63	.611	P	69.732	90.8%
1993	Chicago White Sox	94	68	.580	P	68.047	89.6%
2000	Chicago White Sox	95	67	.586	P	66.438	88.0%
1964	Chicago White Sox	98	64	.605	—	65.632	87.3%
2020	Chicago White Sox	35	25	.583	P	63.906	84.9%
1963	Chicago White Sox	94	68	.580	—	63.155	84.0%
2021	Chicago White Sox	93	69	.574	P	61.531	81.1%
1990	Chicago White Sox	94	68	.580	—	61.168	80.5%

Worst Seasons of Modern Era (1961-2022)

Year	Team	W	L	Pct.	Post	TS	ME%
1970	Chicago White Sox	56	106	.346	—	17.195	3.3%
1976	Chicago White Sox	64	97	.398	—	20.772	5.8%
2017	Chicago White Sox	67	95	.414	—	26.072	12.1%
2013	Chicago White Sox	63	99	.389	—	26.209	12.2%
2018	Chicago White Sox	62	100	.383	—	27.388	14.0%
2007	Chicago White Sox	72	90	.444	—	28.389	15.3%
2015	Chicago White Sox	76	86	.469	—	28.839	16.1%
1988	Chicago White Sox	71	90	.441	—	28.884	16.3%
2014	Chicago White Sox	73	89	.451	—	29.452	17.8%
1968	Chicago White Sox	67	95	.414	—	29.822	18.3%

Season Breakdown (2022)

Category	W	L	Pct.	R	RA	R/G	RA/G
Overall record in 2022	81	81	.500	686	717	4.23	4.43
Home games	37	44	.457	331	416	4.09	5.14
Away games	44	37	.543	355	301	4.38	3.72
First half of 2022 season	39	42	.481	343	388	4.23	4.79
Second half of 2022 season	42	39	.519	343	329	4.23	4.06
Against first-place teams	14	22	.389	142	197	3.94	5.47
Against playoff teams	26	31	.456	223	295	3.91	5.18
Against non-playoff teams	55	50	.524	463	422	4.41	4.02

Season as Nine-Inning Game (2022)

Result	1	2	3	4	5	6	7	8	9	Total
Wins	7	11	8	8	11	10	8	11	7	81
Losses	11	7	10	10	7	8	10	7	11	81

Scoring by Game (2022)

Runs Scored	G	W	L	Pct.	R/G	RA/G
Overall record	162	81	81	.500	4.23	4.43
0	6	0	6	.000	0.00	4.67
1	18	1	17	.056	1.00	4.22
2	23	6	17	.261	2.00	4.26
3	35	17	18	.486	3.00	4.40
4	23	16	7	.696	4.00	3.52
5	18	10	8	.556	5.00	5.44
6	6	5	1	.833	6.00	4.33
7	10	6	4	.600	7.00	6.40
8	6	6	0	1.000	8.00	2.83
9	7	4	3	.571	9.00	7.86
10 or more	10	10	0	1.000	11.80	2.00

Scoring Allowed by Game (2022)

Runs Allowed	G	W	L	Pct.	R/G	RA/G
Overall record	162	81	81	.500	4.23	4.43
0	14	14	0	1.000	5.93	0.00
1	15	15	0	1.000	3.80	1.00
2	28	23	5	.821	4.54	2.00
3	21	15	6	.714	4.10	3.00
4	19	7	12	.368	3.74	4.00
5	15	3	12	.200	3.33	5.00
6	14	2	12	.143	3.93	6.00
7	8	1	7	.125	4.00	7.00
8	10	1	9	.100	3.50	8.00
9	4	0	4	.000	4.25	9.00
10 or more	14	0	14	.000	5.21	12.57

Margins (2022)

Category	Margin	G	W	L	Pct.	GShr	WShr
Overall record	—	162	81	81	.500	—	—
Close	1 or 2 runs	75	46	29	.613	46.3%	56.8%
Medium	3 or 4 runs	46	15	31	.326	28.4%	18.5%
Distant	5 or more runs	41	20	21	.488	25.3%	24.7%

Individual Scoring Leaders (2022)

Team Rank	Batter	R	(+) RBI	(-) HR	(=) SC
1	Jose Abreu	85	75	15	145
2	Andrew Vaughn	60	76	17	119
3	AJ Pollock	61	56	14	103
4	Luis Robert	54	56	12	98
5	Yoan Moncada	41	51	12	80
6	Eloy Jimenez	40	54	16	78
7	Gavin Sheets	34	53	15	72
8	Josh Harrison	50	27	7	70
9	Tim Anderson	50	25	6	69
10	Leury Garcia	38	20	3	55

Team Ratings (2022)

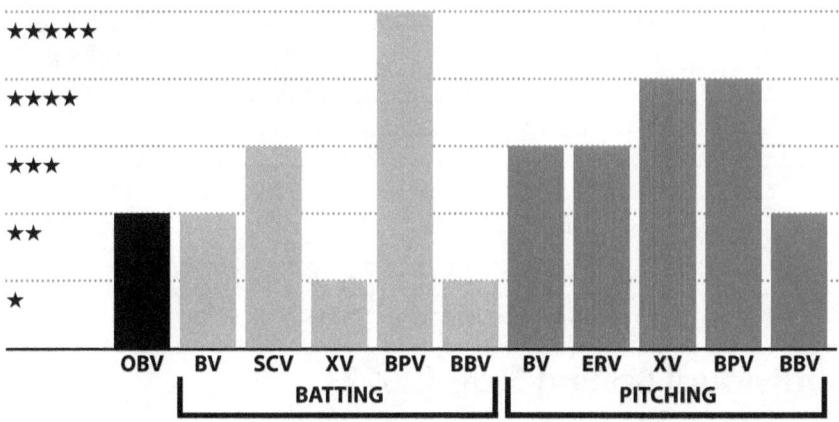

Quality	Type	Indicator	Value	Rating
Overall performance	Overall	OBV	-135	★★
Base production	Batting	BV	-139	★★
Run production	Batting	SCV	-3	★★★
Power hitting	Batting	XV	-117	★
Contact hitting	Batting	BPV	132	★★★★★
Batting eye	Batting	BBV	-105	★
Base prevention	Pitching	BV	-4	★★★
Run prevention	Pitching	ERV	-6	★★★
Power prevention	Pitching	XV	-38	★★★★
Strikeout pitching	Pitching	BPV	-77	★★★★
Control pitching	Pitching	BBV	33	★★

Team Batting Stats (2022)

Stat	Number	Div Rank	Lg Rank	MLB Rank	MLB Best
R	686	3	9	19	847 (Dodgers)
H	1,435	1	2	2	1,464 (Blue Jays)
HR	149	2	10	22	254 (Yankees)
BPO	.628	4	13	24	.764 (Dodgers)
BA	.256	1	3	5	.264 (Blue Jays)
OBP	.310	3	8	18	.333 (Dodgers)
SA	.387	2	10	18	.443 (Braves)

Division: AL Central, 5 teams. **League:** American, 15 teams. **MLB:** 30 teams.

Team Pitching Stats (2022)

Stat	Number	Div Rank	Lg Rank	MLB Rank	MLB Best
ERA	3.92	2	8	16	2.80 (Dodgers)
SO	1,450	1	3	8	1,565 (Mets)
BB	533	4	12	22	384 (Rays)
BPO	.659	2	8	16	.551 (Astros)
BA	.242	3	8	14	.209 (Dodgers)
OBP	.312	3	9	15	.273 (Dodgers)
SA	.387	2	6	11	.332 (Astros)

Division: AL Central, 5 teams. **League:** American, 15 teams. **MLB:** 30 teams.

Individual Batting Stats (2022)

Batter	PA	BPO	BA	OBP	SA	ISO	CT	EY
Jose Abreu	679	.785	.304	.378	.446	.141	.817	.089
Tim Anderson	351	.674	.301	.339	.395	.093	.834	.037
Yasmani Grandal	376	.509	.202	.301	.269	.067	.758	.117
Josh Harrison	425	.611	.256	.317	.370	.114	.816	.049
Eloy Jimenez	327	.830	.295	.358	.500	.205	.753	.086
Yoan Moncada	433	.556	.212	.273	.353	.141	.713	.070
AJ Pollock	527	.597	.245	.292	.389	.143	.800	.061
Luis Robert	401	.688	.284	.319	.426	.142	.797	.040
Gavin Sheets	410	.631	.241	.295	.411	.170	.772	.066
Andrew Vaughn	555	.677	.271	.321	.429	.159	.812	.056

Individual Pitching Stats for Starters (2022)

Pitcher	IP	BPO	ERA	BA	SA	ISO	CT	EY
Dylan Cease	184.0	.540	2.20	.190	.306	.116	.658	.102
Johnny Cueto	158.1	.630	3.35	.267	.409	.142	.831	.048
Lucas Giolito	161.2	.753	4.90	.272	.455	.183	.718	.086
Michael Kopech	119.1	.634	3.54	.198	.347	.149	.755	.115
Lance Lynn	121.2	.620	3.99	.249	.412	.162	.742	.037

Individual Pitching Stats for Relievers (2022)

Pitcher	GR	BPO	ERA	BA	SA	ISO	CT	EY
Matt Foster	48	.657	4.40	.247	.391	.144	.759	.083
Kendall Graveman	65	.655	3.18	.257	.364	.107	.739	.085
Liam Hendriks	58	.609	2.81	.210	.352	.143	.595	.064
Joe Kelly	42	.745	6.08	.252	.357	.105	.629	.135
Reynaldo Lopez	60	.508	2.76	.218	.312	.094	.731	.040
Jose Ruiz	63	.760	4.60	.231	.410	.179	.703	.125

Best Stats on Team (2022)

Stat	Batter	Number
2B	Jose Abreu	40
3B	Josh Harrison	2
BA	Jose Abreu	.304
BB	Jose Abreu	62
BBV	Yasmani Grandal	14
BPO	Eloy Jimenez	.830
BPV	Jose Abreu	40
BV	Jose Abreu	55
CT	Tim Anderson	.834
EY	Yasmani Grandal	.117
H	Jose Abreu	183
HR	Andrew Vaughn	17
ISO	Eloy Jimenez	.205
OBP	Jose Abreu	.378
R	Jose Abreu	85
RBI	Andrew Vaughn	76
SA	Eloy Jimenez	.500
SB	Tim Anderson	13
SC	Jose Abreu	145
SCV	Luis Robert	20
SE	Luis Robert	.244
XV	Eloy Jimenez	16

Stat	Pitcher	Number
BA	Dylan Cease	.190
BBV	Lance Lynn	-22
BPO-R	Reynaldo Lopez	.508
BPO-S	Dylan Cease	.540
BPV	Dylan Cease	-61
BV	Dylan Cease	-66
CT	Dylan Cease	.658
ERA-R	Reynaldo Lopez	2.76
ERA-S	Dylan Cease	2.20
ERV	Dylan Cease	-36
EY	Lance Lynn	.037
GR	Kendall Graveman	65
GS	Dylan Cease	32
IP	Dylan Cease	184.0
ISO	Dylan Cease	.116
OBP	Dylan Cease	.278
SA	Dylan Cease	.306
SO	Dylan Cease	227
SV	Liam Hendriks	37
W	Dylan Cease	14
XV	Dylan Cease	-24

Worst Stats on Team (2022)

Stat	Batter	Number
BA	Yasmani Grandal	.202
BBV	Leury Garcia	-18
BPO	Yasmani Grandal	.509
BPV	Seby Zavala	-20
BV	Leury Garcia	-67
CT	Yoan Moncada	.713
EY	Tim Anderson	.037
ISO	Yasmani Grandal	.067
OBP	Yoan Moncada	.273
SA	Yasmani Grandal	.269
SCV	Yasmani Grandal	-36
SE	Yasmani Grandal	.098
SO	Yoan Moncada	114
XV	Leury Garcia	-29

Stat	Pitcher	Number
BA	Lucas Giolito	.272
BB	Dylan Cease	78
BBV	Michael Kopech	18
BPO-R	Jose Ruiz	.760
BPO-S	Lucas Giolito	.753
BPV	Johnny Cueto	49
BV	Lucas Giolito	45
CT	Johnny Cueto	.831
ERA-R	Joe Kelly	6.08
ERA-S	Lucas Giolito	4.90
ERV	Lucas Giolito	17
EY	Michael Kopech	.115
ISO	Lucas Giolito	.183
L	Johnny Cueto	10
OBP	Lucas Giolito	.338
SA	Lucas Giolito	.455
XV	Lucas Giolito	19

Overall Base Value Leaders (2022)

Team Rank	Player	BV [bat]	(-) BV [pitch]	(=) OBV
1	Dylan Cease	0	-66	66
2	Jose Abreu	55	0	55
3	Eloy Jimenez	37	0	37
4	Reynaldo Lopez	0	-30	30
5	Tanner Banks	0	-25	25
6	Elvis Andrus	17	0	17
7	Lance Lynn	0	-15	15
8	Johnny Cueto	0	-14	14
9	Liam Hendriks	0	-9	9
9	Michael Kopech	0	-9	9

Fan Support in Past 10 Seasons (2013-2022)

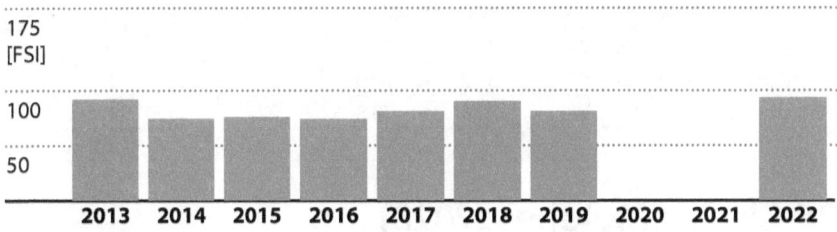

Year	Team	Attendance	W	Att:W	FSI
2013	Chicago White Sox	1,768,413	63	28,070	92.2
2014	Chicago White Sox	1,650,821	73	22,614	74.5
2015	Chicago White Sox	1,755,810	76	23,103	76.1
2016	Chicago White Sox	1,746,293	78	22,388	74.3
2017	Chicago White Sox	1,629,470	67	24,320	81.3
2018	Chicago White Sox	1,608,817	62	25,949	90.5
2019	Chicago White Sox	1,649,775	72	22,914	81.2
2022	Chicago White Sox	2,009,359	81	24,807	93.4

Extreme Games for Batters (2022)

Stat	Team Total	Individual Leader	G
3+ H	79	Andrew Vaughn	12
2+ HR	3	Gavin Sheets, Jose Abreu, Yoan Moncada	1
5+ RBI	5	Yoan Moncada	2
0 H in 5+ AB	39	Yoan Moncada	9
4+ SO	2	Seby Zavala, Yasmani Grandal	1

Extreme Games for Pitchers (2022)

Stat	Team Total	Individual Leader	G
0-2 ER in 7+ IP	19	Dylan Cease, Johnny Cueto	6
10+ SO	7	Dylan Cease	4
0 BR in SV	19	Liam Hendriks	17
10+ BR	25	Johnny Cueto	7
1+ ER in SV	8	Liam Hendriks	5

Predictions for Coming Season (2023)

Group	Next W	Next L	Next Pct.	WS	LC	PQ
10 closest matches (avg. W-L)	78.7	83.3	.486	0	0	2
25 closest matches (avg. W-L)	81.2	78.6	.508	1	1	7
50 closest matches (avg. W-L)	78.8	78.8	.500	1	1	11

25 Closest Matches (2023)

Rank	Team	Next	W	L	Pct.	WS	LC	PQ
1	Dodgers (1982-1984)	1985	95	67	.586	—	—	X
2	Astros (1994-1996)	1997	84	78	.519	—	—	X
3	Reds (2012-2014)	2015	64	98	.395	—	—	—
4	Rays (2012-2014)	2015	80	82	.494	—	—	—
5	Angels (2008-2010)	2011	86	76	.531	—	—	—
6	Astros (1980-1982)	1983	85	77	.525	—	—	—
7	Pirates (2014-2016)	2017	75	87	.463	—	—	—
8	Twins (1987-1989)	1990	74	88	.457	—	—	—
9	Brewers (2007-2009)	2010	77	85	.475	—	—	—
10	Braves (2012-2014)	2015	67	95	.414	—	—	—
11	Yankees (2011-2013)	2014	84	78	.519	—	—	—
12	Mariners (1996-1998)	1999	79	83	.488	—	—	—
13	Royals (1988-1990)	1991	82	80	.506	—	—	—
14	Mets (1989-1991)	1992	72	90	.444	—	—	—
15	Braves (1982-1984)	1985	66	96	.407	—	—	—
16	Astros (1998-2000)	2001	93	69	.574	—	—	X
17	Twins (2005-2007)	2008	88	75	.540	—	—	—
18	Phillies (1977-1979)	1980	91	71	.562	X	X	X
19	White Sox (1993-1995)	1996	85	77	.525	—	—	—
20	Orioles (2013-2015)	2016	89	73	.549	—	—	X
21	Braves (2004-2006)	2007	84	78	.519	—	—	—
22	Red Sox (1978-1980)	1981	59	49	.546	—	—	—
23	Rangers (1995-1997)	1998	88	74	.543	—	—	X
24	Angels (2011-2013)	2014	98	64	.605	—	—	X
25	Phillies (1983-1985)	1986	86	75	.534	—	—	—

CINCINNATI REDS

Past 10 Seasons (2013-2022)

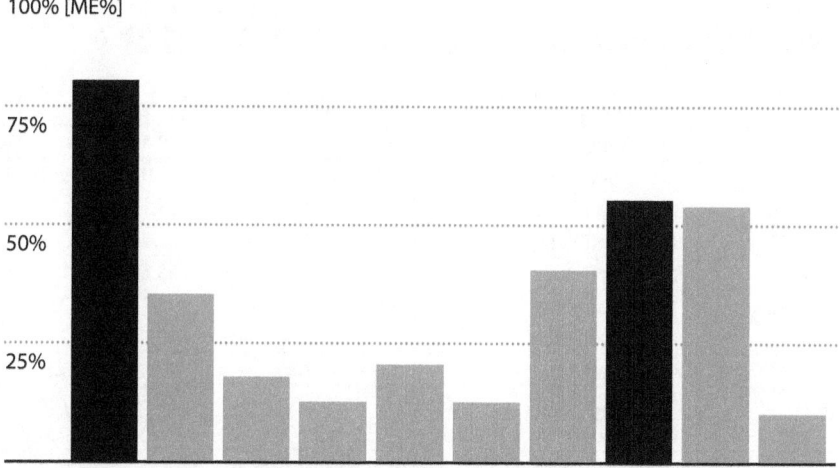

Year	Team	W	L	Pct.	Post	TS	ME%
2013	Cincinnati Reds	90	72	.556	P	61.161	80.4%
2014	Cincinnati Reds	76	86	.469	—	39.091	35.3%
2015	Cincinnati Reds	64	98	.395	—	29.609	17.9%
2016	Cincinnati Reds	68	94	.420	—	26.548	12.7%
2017	Cincinnati Reds	68	94	.420	—	31.000	20.5%
2018	Cincinnati Reds	67	95	.414	—	26.389	12.6%
2019	Cincinnati Reds	75	87	.463	—	41.347	40.5%
2020	Cincinnati Reds	31	29	.517	P	48.632	55.3%
2021	Cincinnati Reds	83	79	.512	—	48.109	54.0%
2022	Cincinnati Reds	62	100	.383	—	25.242	10.2%

Best Seasons of Modern Era (1961-2022)

Year	Team	W	L	Pct.	Post	TS	ME%
1975	Cincinnati Reds	108	54	.667	WLP	90.713	99.7%
1976	Cincinnati Reds	102	60	.630	WLP	87.331	99.3%
1970	Cincinnati Reds	102	60	.630	LP	80.511	97.2%
1990	Cincinnati Reds	91	71	.562	WLP	76.558	95.5%
1972	Cincinnati Reds	95	59	.617	LP	76.006	95.4%
1995	Cincinnati Reds	85	59	.590	P	72.385	92.5%
1961	Cincinnati Reds	93	61	.604	LP	68.297	89.9%
1973	Cincinnati Reds	99	63	.611	P	67.755	89.4%
1994	Cincinnati Reds	66	48	.579	—	65.978	87.7%
1974	Cincinnati Reds	98	64	.605	—	65.940	87.6%

Worst Seasons of Modern Era (1961-2022)

Year	Team	W	L	Pct.	Post	TS	ME%
1982	Cincinnati Reds	61	101	.377	—	18.446	4.1%
2003	Cincinnati Reds	69	93	.426	—	21.928	7.1%
1984	Cincinnati Reds	70	92	.432	—	23.138	8.2%
2022	Cincinnati Reds	62	100	.383	—	25.242	10.2%
2001	Cincinnati Reds	66	96	.407	—	25.653	11.2%
2018	Cincinnati Reds	67	95	.414	—	26.389	12.6%
2016	Cincinnati Reds	68	94	.420	—	26.548	12.7%
1983	Cincinnati Reds	74	88	.457	—	27.325	13.8%
2015	Cincinnati Reds	64	98	.395	—	29.609	17.9%
2017	Cincinnati Reds	68	94	.420	—	31.000	20.5%

Season Breakdown (2022)

Category	W	L	Pct.	R	RA	R/G	RA/G
Overall record in 2022	62	100	.383	648	815	4.00	5.03
Home games	33	48	.407	367	420	4.53	5.19
Away games	29	52	.358	281	395	3.47	4.88
First half of 2022 season	28	53	.346	343	448	4.23	5.53
Second half of 2022 season	34	47	.420	305	367	3.77	4.53
Against first-place teams	14	26	.350	142	210	3.55	5.25
Against playoff teams	20	45	.308	216	340	3.32	5.23
Against non-playoff teams	42	55	.433	432	475	4.45	4.90

Season as Nine-Inning Game (2022)

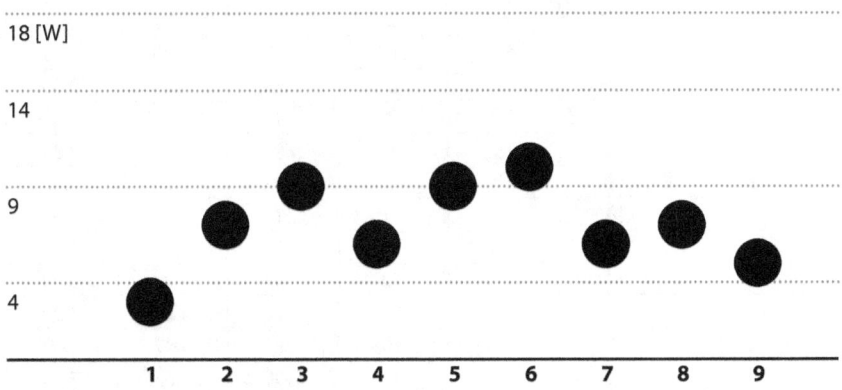

Result	1	2	3	4	5	6	7	8	9	Total
Wins	3	7	9	6	9	10	6	7	5	62
Losses	15	11	9	12	9	8	12	11	13	100

Scoring by Game (2022)

Runs Scored	G	W	L	Pct.	R/G	RA/G
Overall record	162	62	100	.383	4.00	5.03
0	9	0	9	.000	0.00	3.33
1	25	2	23	.080	1.00	4.52
2	18	4	14	.222	2.00	5.61
3	28	9	19	.321	3.00	4.96
4	27	9	18	.333	4.00	6.11
5	19	10	9	.526	5.00	5.21
6	10	4	6	.400	6.00	5.50
7	8	7	1	.875	7.00	4.88
8	6	5	1	.833	8.00	3.67
9	3	3	0	1.000	9.00	4.00
10 or more	9	9	0	1.000	12.11	4.44

Scoring Allowed by Game (2022)

Runs Allowed	G	W	L	Pct.	R/G	RA/G
Overall record	162	62	100	.383	4.00	5.03
0	6	6	0	1.000	4.33	0.00
1	17	14	3	.824	3.71	1.00
2	20	15	5	.750	4.20	2.00
3	18	13	5	.722	4.33	3.00
4	14	3	11	.214	2.43	4.00
5	23	7	16	.304	4.91	5.00
6	14	2	12	.143	3.07	6.00
7	16	0	16	.000	4.00	7.00
8	11	1	10	.091	4.45	8.00
9	6	0	6	.000	2.67	9.00
10 or more	17	1	16	.059	4.59	11.47

Margins (2022)

Category	Margin	G	W	L	Pct.	GShr	WShr
Overall record	—	162	62	100	.383	—	—
Close	1 or 2 runs	67	30	37	.448	41.4%	48.4%
Medium	3 or 4 runs	48	17	31	.354	29.6%	27.4%
Distant	5 or more runs	47	15	32	.319	29.0%	24.2%

Individual Scoring Leaders (2022)

Team Rank	Batter	R	(+) RBI	(-) HR	(=) SC
1	Kyle Farmer	58	78	14	122
2	Brandon Drury	62	59	20	101
3	Tommy Pham	57	39	11	85
4	Jonathan India	48	41	10	79
5	Nick Senzel	45	25	5	65
6	Joey Votto	31	41	11	61
7	Tyler Naquin	29	33	7	55
8	Tyler Stephenson	24	35	6	53
9	Matt Reynolds	31	23	3	51
10	Albert Almora	26	29	5	50
10	TJ Friedl	33	25	8	50

Team Ratings (2022)

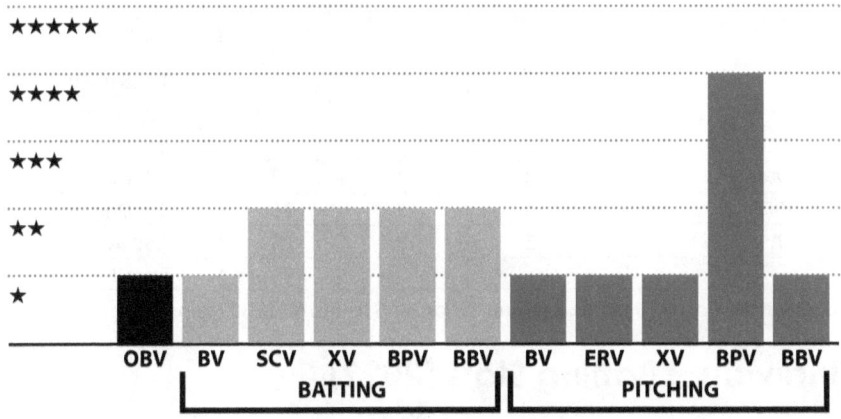

Quality	Type	Indicator	Value	Rating
Overall performance	Overall	OBV	-627	★
Base production	Batting	BV	-202	★
Run production	Batting	SCV	-55	★★
Power hitting	Batting	XV	-80	★★
Contact hitting	Batting	BPV	-87	★★
Batting eye	Batting	BBV	-27	★★
Base prevention	Pitching	BV	425	★
Run prevention	Pitching	ERV	141	★
Power prevention	Pitching	XV	141	★
Strikeout pitching	Pitching	BPV	-56	★★★★
Control pitching	Pitching	BBV	100	★

Team Batting Stats (2022)

Stat	Number	Div Rank	Lg Rank	MLB Rank	MLB Best
R	648	4	12	23	847 (Dodgers)
H	1,264	4	11	23	1,464 (Blue Jays)
HR	156	5	11	19	254 (Yankees)
BPO	.613	4	13	26	.764 (Dodgers)
BA	.235	3	10	21	.264 (Blue Jays)
OBP	.304	4	13	24	.333 (Dodgers)
SA	.372	4	13	26	.443 (Braves)

Division: NL Central, 5 teams. **League:** National, 15 teams. **MLB:** 30 teams.

Team Pitching Stats (2022)

Stat	Number	Div Rank	Lg Rank	MLB Rank	MLB Best
ERA	4.86	5	13	28	2.80 (Dodgers)
SO	1,414	2	8	11	1,565 (Mets)
BB	612	5	15	30	384 (Rays)
BPO	.760	5	13	28	.551 (Astros)
BA	.251	4	11	22	.209 (Dodgers)
OBP	.336	4	12	26	.273 (Dodgers)
SA	.429	5	13	28	.332 (Astros)

Division: NL Central, 5 teams. **League:** National, 15 teams. **MLB:** 30 teams.

Individual Batting Stats (2022)

Batter	PA	BPO	BA	OBP	SA	ISO	CT	EY
Brandon Drury	385	.830	.274	.335	.520	.246	.760	.075
Kyle Farmer	583	.624	.255	.315	.386	.131	.812	.057
Jonathan India	431	.649	.249	.327	.378	.130	.756	.070
Tommy Pham	387	.651	.238	.320	.374	.135	.706	.109
Nick Senzel	420	.530	.231	.296	.306	.075	.796	.071
Joey Votto	376	.655	.205	.319	.370	.165	.699	.117

Individual Pitching Stats for Starters (2022)

Pitcher	IP	BPO	ERA	BA	SA	ISO	CT	EY
Graham Ashcraft	105.0	.690	4.89	.281	.404	.123	.832	.063
Hunter Greene	125.2	.715	4.44	.222	.420	.198	.650	.090
Nick Lodolo	103.1	.704	3.66	.235	.392	.157	.658	.088
Tyler Mahle	104.1	.654	4.40	.232	.389	.158	.710	.089

Individual Pitching Stats for Relievers (2022)

Pitcher	GR	BPO	ERA	BA	SA	ISO	CT	EY
Alexis Diaz	59	.497	1.84	.131	.216	.085	.610	.119
Buck Farmer	44	.582	3.83	.211	.298	.088	.684	.126
Joel Kuhnel	53	.770	6.36	.291	.465	.174	.757	.051
Reiver Sanmartin	41	.822	6.32	.293	.476	.182	.791	.106
Hunter Strickland	66	.862	4.91	.253	.436	.183	.751	.113

Best Stats on Team (2022)

Stat	Batter	Number
2B	Kyle Farmer	25
3B	TJ Friedl	5
BA	Brandon Drury	.274
BB	Joey Votto	44
BBV	Joey Votto	14
BPO	Brandon Drury	.830
BPV	Kyle Farmer	32
BV	Brandon Drury	45
CT	Kyle Farmer	.812
EY	Joey Votto	.117
H	Kyle Farmer	134
HR	Brandon Drury	20
ISO	Brandon Drury	.246
OBP	Brandon Drury	.335
R	Brandon Drury	62
RBI	Kyle Farmer	78
SA	Brandon Drury	.520
SB	Nick Senzel	8
SC	Kyle Farmer	122
SCV	Brandon Drury	26
SE	Brandon Drury	.262
XV	Brandon Drury	33

Stat	Pitcher	Number
BA	Hunter Greene	.222
BBV	Graham Ashcraft	-8
BPO-R	Alexis Diaz	.497
BPO-S	Tyler Mahle	.654
BPV	Hunter Greene	-47
BV	Alexis Diaz	-31
CT	Hunter Greene	.650
ERA-R	Alexis Diaz	1.84
ERA-S	Nick Lodolo	3.66
ERV	Alexis Diaz	-15
EY	Graham Ashcraft	.063
GR	Hunter Strickland	66
GS	Hunter Greene	24
IP	Hunter Greene	125.2
ISO	Graham Ashcraft	.123
OBP	Tyler Mahle	.301
SA	Tyler Mahle	.389
SO	Hunter Greene	164
SV	Alexis Diaz	10
W	Alexis Diaz	7
XV	Alexis Diaz	-14

Worst Stats on Team (2022)

Stat	Batter	Number
BA	Joey Votto	.205
BBV	Kyle Farmer	-13
BPO	Nick Senzel	.530
BPV	Aristides Aquino	-36
BV	Jose Barrero	-49
CT	Joey Votto	.699
EY	Kyle Farmer	.057
ISO	Nick Senzel	.075
OBP	Nick Senzel	.296
SA	Nick Senzel	.306
SCV	Donovan Solano, Nick Senzel	-17
SE	Nick Senzel	.155
SO	Aristides Aquino	101
XV	Nick Senzel	-29

Stat	Pitcher	Number
BA	Graham Ashcraft	.281
BB	Hunter Greene	48
BBV	Hunter Strickland, Alexis Diaz	10
BPO-R	Hunter Strickland	.862
BPO-S	Hunter Greene	.715
BPV	Graham Ashcraft	35
BV	Mike Minor	88
CT	Graham Ashcraft	.832
ERA-R	Joel Kuhnel	6.36
ERA-S	Graham Ashcraft	4.89
ERV	Mike Minor	23
EY	Hunter Greene	.090
ISO	Hunter Greene	.198
L	Hunter Greene	13
OBP	Graham Ashcraft	.338
SA	Hunter Greene	.420
XV	Mike Minor	35

Overall Base Value Leaders (2022)

Team Rank	Player	BV [bat]	(-) BV [pitch]	(=) OBV
1	Brandon Drury	45	0	45
2	Alexis Diaz	0	-31	31
3	Luis Castillo	0	-28	28
3	Jake Fraley	28	0	28
5	Connor Overton	0	-24	24
6	Tyler Stephenson	19	0	19
7	TJ Friedl	18	0	18
8	Stuart Fairchild	15	0	15
9	Buck Farmer	0	-11	11
10	Tyler Naquin	7	0	7

Fan Support in Past 10 Seasons (2013-2022)

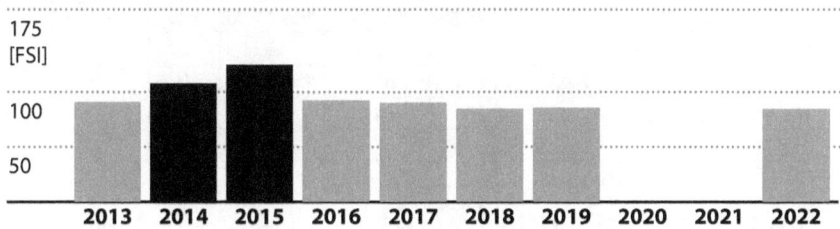

Year	Team	Attendance	W	Att:W	FSI
2013	Cincinnati Reds	2,492,101	90	27,690	90.9
2014	Cincinnati Reds	2,476,664	76	32,588	107.4
2015	Cincinnati Reds	2,419,506	64	37,805	124.5
2016	Cincinnati Reds	1,894,085	68	27,854	92.4
2017	Cincinnati Reds	1,836,917	68	27,013	90.3
2018	Cincinnati Reds	1,629,356	67	24,319	84.9
2019	Cincinnati Reds	1,809,075	75	24,121	85.5
2022	Cincinnati Reds	1,395,770	62	22,512	84.7

Extreme Games for Batters (2022)

Stat	Team Total	Individual Leader	G
3+ H	62	Donovan Solano	9
2+ HR	7	Aristides Aquino	2
5+ RBI	2	Colin Moran, Kyle Farmer	1
0 H in 5+ AB	27	Jonathan India	6
4+ SO	11	Aristides Aquino	3

Extreme Games for Pitchers (2022)

Stat	Team Total	Individual Leader	G
0-2 ER in 7+ IP	13	Graham Ashcraft, Luis Castillo	3
10+ SO	8	Hunter Greene, Luis Castillo, Nick Lodolo, Tyler Mahle	2
0 BR in SV	10	Hunter Strickland, Tony Santillan	2
10+ BR	42	Graham Ashcraft	10
1+ ER in SV	6	Alexis Diaz	3

Predictions for Coming Season (2023)

Group	Next W	Next L	Next Pct.	WS	LC	PQ
10 closest matches (avg. W-L)	66.8	80.5	.453	0	0	0
25 closest matches (avg. W-L)	72.4	81.6	.470	0	0	2
50 closest matches (avg. W-L)	70.9	84.6	.456	1	1	5

25 Closest Matches (2023)

Rank	Team	Next	W	L	Pct.	WS	LC	PQ
1	Angels (1990-1992)	1993	71	91	.438	—	—	—
2	Expos (2002-2004)	2005	81	81	.500	—	—	—
3	Padres (1991-1993)	1994	47	70	.402	—	—	—
4	Mariners (1990-1992)	1993	82	80	.506	—	—	—
5	White Sox (2011-2013)	2014	73	89	.451	—	—	—
6	Pirates (1983-1985)	1986	64	98	.395	—	—	—
7	Indians (2007-2009)	2010	69	93	.426	—	—	—
8	Pirates (2017-2019)	2020	19	41	.317	—	—	—
9	Blue Jays (2002-2004)	2005	80	82	.494	—	—	—
10	Angels (1997-1999)	2000	82	80	.506	—	—	—
11	Marlins (2005-2007)	2008	84	77	.522	—	—	—
12	Orioles (1998-2000)	2001	63	98	.391	—	—	—
13	Reds (1999-2001)	2002	78	84	.481	—	—	—
14	Rockies (1997-1999)	2000	82	80	.506	—	—	—
15	Angels (1978-1980)	1981	51	59	.464	—	—	—
16	Giants (2015-2017)	2018	73	89	.451	—	—	—
17	Cubs (1995-1997)	1998	90	73	.552	—	—	X
18	Cardinals (1976-1978)	1979	86	76	.531	—	—	—
19	Orioles (1989-1991)	1992	89	73	.549	—	—	—
20	Phillies (1998-2000)	2001	86	76	.531	—	—	—
21	Yankees (1987-1989)	1990	67	95	.414	—	—	—
22	Mets (1975-1977)	1978	66	96	.407	—	—	—
23	Cubs (2004-2006)	2007	85	77	.525	—	—	X
24	Rockies (2010-2012)	2013	74	88	.457	—	—	—
25	Orioles (1984-1986)	1987	67	95	.414	—	—	—

CLEVELAND GUARDIANS

Past 10 Seasons (2013-2022)

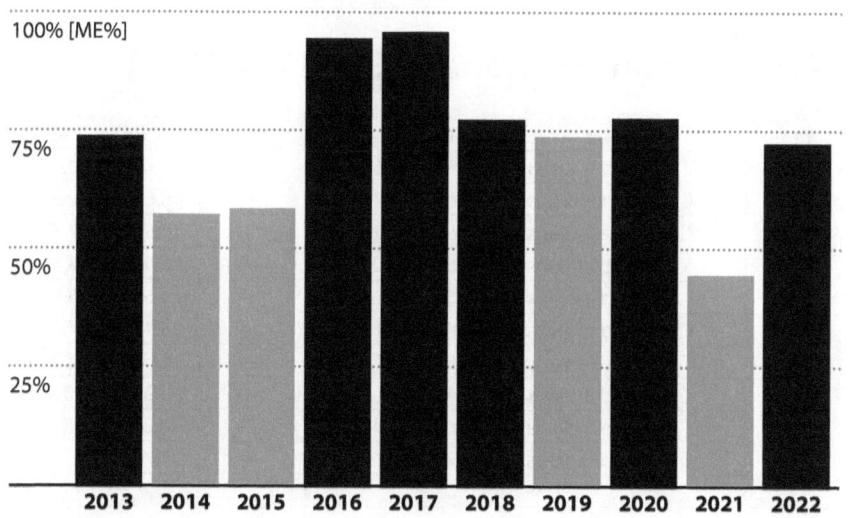

Year	Team	W	L	Pct.	Post	TS	ME%
2013	Cleveland Indians	92	70	.568	P	57.046	73.8%
2014	Cleveland Indians	85	77	.525	—	49.812	57.2%
2015	Cleveland Indians	81	80	.503	—	50.485	58.4%
2016	Cleveland Indians	94	67	.584	LP	74.722	94.4%
2017	Cleveland Indians	102	60	.630	P	76.821	95.8%
2018	Cleveland Indians	91	71	.562	P	59.447	77.3%
2019	Cleveland Indians	93	69	.574	—	56.940	73.7%
2020	Cleveland Indians	35	25	.583	P	59.522	77.6%
2021	Cleveland Indians	80	82	.494	—	43.352	44.5%
2022	Cleveland Guardians	92	70	.568	P	56.219	72.3%

Best Seasons of Modern Era (1961-2022)

Year	Team	W	L	Pct.	Post	TS	ME%
1995	Cleveland Indians	100	44	.694	LP	87.220	99.3%
2017	Cleveland Indians	102	60	.630	P	76.821	95.8%
2016	Cleveland Indians	94	67	.584	LP	74.722	94.4%
1996	Cleveland Indians	99	62	.615	P	71.320	92.0%
1999	Cleveland Indians	97	65	.599	P	67.480	89.1%
1997	Cleveland Indians	86	75	.534	LP	67.467	89.0%
1994	Cleveland Indians	66	47	.584	—	67.331	88.9%
2005	Cleveland Indians	93	69	.574	—	65.096	86.9%
2000	Cleveland Indians	90	72	.556	—	63.454	84.5%
2007	Cleveland Indians	96	66	.593	P	63.348	84.3%

Worst Seasons of Modern Era (1961-2022)

Year	Team	W	L	Pct.	Post	TS	ME%
1991	Cleveland Indians	57	105	.352	—	9.976	0.5%
1987	Cleveland Indians	61	101	.377	—	15.631	2.3%
1971	Cleveland Indians	60	102	.370	—	16.585	2.7%
1985	Cleveland Indians	60	102	.370	—	19.418	4.6%
2012	Cleveland Indians	68	94	.420	—	21.658	6.6%
1969	Cleveland Indians	62	99	.385	—	25.468	10.7%
2009	Cleveland Indians	65	97	.401	—	26.682	12.9%
1973	Cleveland Indians	71	91	.438	—	26.967	13.4%
2010	Cleveland Indians	69	93	.426	—	28.261	15.2%
1983	Cleveland Indians	70	92	.432	—	32.742	23.0%

Season Breakdown (2022)

Category	W	L	Pct.	R	RA	R/G	RA/G
Overall record in 2022	92	70	.568	698	634	4.31	3.91
Home games	46	35	.568	325	322	4.01	3.98
Away games	46	35	.568	373	312	4.60	3.85
First half of 2022 season	40	41	.494	344	361	4.25	4.46
Second half of 2022 season	52	29	.642	354	273	4.37	3.37
Against first-place teams	6	10	.375	40	75	2.50	4.69
Against playoff teams	19	21	.475	130	155	3.25	3.88
Against non-playoff teams	73	49	.598	568	479	4.66	3.93

Season as Nine-Inning Game (2022)

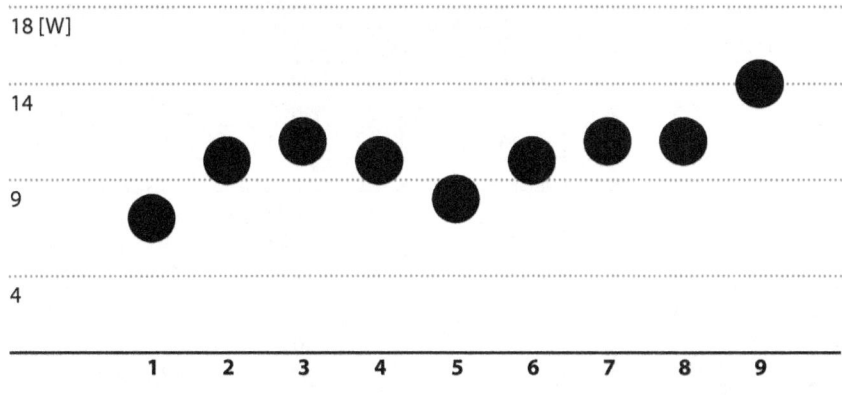

Result	1	2	3	4	5	6	7	8	9	Total
Wins	7	10	11	10	8	10	11	11	14	92
Losses	11	8	7	8	10	8	7	7	4	70

Scoring by Game (2022)

Runs Scored	G	W	L	Pct.	R/G	RA/G
Overall record	162	92	70	.568	4.31	3.91
0	12	0	12	.000	0.00	3.67
1	23	1	22	.043	1.00	4.17
2	15	5	10	.333	2.00	3.87
3	21	8	13	.381	3.00	4.38
4	25	17	8	.680	4.00	3.28
5	14	10	4	.714	5.00	4.07
6	15	15	0	1.000	6.00	3.60
7	13	13	0	1.000	7.00	4.08
8	11	10	1	.909	8.00	3.36
9	2	2	0	1.000	9.00	5.00
10 or more	11	11	0	1.000	11.36	4.64

Scoring Allowed by Game (2022)

Runs Allowed	G	W	L	Pct.	R/G	RA/G
Overall record	162	92	70	.568	4.31	3.91
0	8	8	0	1.000	5.00	0.00
1	22	20	2	.909	4.32	1.00
2	21	15	6	.714	3.90	2.00
3	30	22	8	.733	4.70	3.00
4	26	9	17	.346	3.65	4.00
5	17	9	8	.529	5.06	5.00
6	15	4	11	.267	3.60	6.00
7	7	2	5	.286	4.29	7.00
8	6	1	5	.167	3.33	8.00
9	3	1	2	.333	6.67	9.00
10 or more	7	1	6	.143	5.00	11.00

Margins (2022)

Category	Margin	G	W	L	Pct.	GShr	WShr
Overall record	—	162	92	70	.568	—	—
Close	1 or 2 runs	73	43	30	.589	45.1%	46.7%
Medium	3 or 4 runs	52	30	22	.577	32.1%	32.6%
Distant	5 or more runs	37	19	18	.514	22.8%	20.7%

Individual Scoring Leaders (2022)

Team Rank	Batter	R	(+) RBI	(-) HR	(=) SC
1	Jose Ramirez	90	126	29	187
2	Amed Rosario	86	71	11	146
3	Steven Kwan	89	52	6	135
4	Andres Gimenez	66	69	17	118
5	Josh Naylor	47	79	20	106
6	Myles Straw	72	32	0	104
7	Owen Miller	53	51	6	98
8	Oscar Gonzalez	39	43	11	71
9	Austin Hedges	26	30	7	49
10	Franmil Reyes	24	28	9	43

Team Ratings (2022)

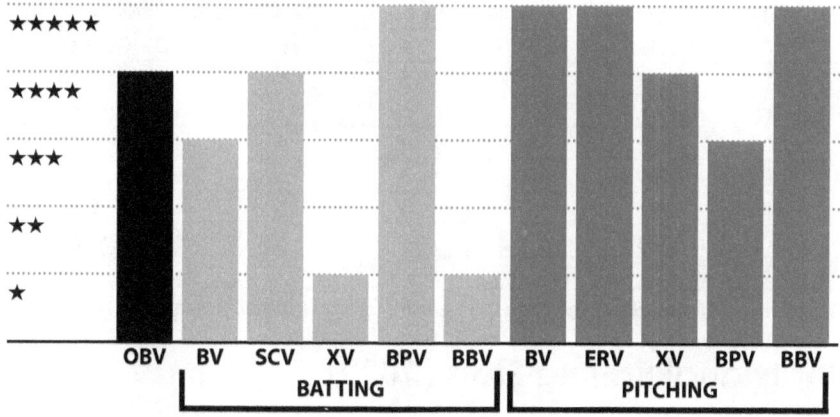

Quality	Type	Indicator	Value	Rating
Overall performance	Overall	OBV	191	★★★★
Base production	Batting	BV	-31	★★★
Run production	Batting	SCV	32	★★★★
Power hitting	Batting	XV	-130	★
Contact hitting	Batting	BPV	266	★★★★★
Batting eye	Batting	BBV	-71	★
Base prevention	Pitching	BV	-222	★★★★★
Run prevention	Pitching	ERV	-81	★★★★★
Power prevention	Pitching	XV	-47	★★★★
Strikeout pitching	Pitching	BPV	-30	★★★
Control pitching	Pitching	BBV	-52	★★★★★

Team Batting Stats (2022)

Stat	Number	Div Rank	Lg Rank	MLB Rank	MLB Best
R	698	1	6	15	847 (Dodgers)
H	1,410	2	4	6	1,464 (Blue Jays)
HR	127	4	14	29	254 (Yankees)
BPO	.653	2	9	19	.764 (Dodgers)
BA	.254	2	4	7	.264 (Blue Jays)
OBP	.316	2	6	12	.333 (Dodgers)
SA	.383	3	11	21	.443 (Braves)

Division: AL Central, 5 teams. **League:** American, 15 teams. **MLB:** 30 teams.

Team Pitching Stats (2022)

Stat	Number	Div Rank	Lg Rank	MLB Rank	MLB Best
ERA	3.46	1	4	6	2.80 (Dodgers)
SO	1,390	2	5	13	1,565 (Mets)
BB	435	1	3	5	384 (Rays)
BPO	.609	1	4	6	.551 (Astros)
BA	.230	1	3	6	.209 (Dodgers)
OBP	.292	1	4	5	.273 (Dodgers)
SA	.373	1	3	5	.332 (Astros)

Division: AL Central, 5 teams. **League:** American, 15 teams. **MLB:** 30 teams.

Individual Batting Stats (2022)

Batter	PA	BPO	BA	OBP	SA	ISO	CT	EY
Andres Gimenez	557	.865	.297	.371	.466	.169	.772	.054
Oscar Gonzalez	382	.709	.296	.327	.461	.166	.793	.034
Austin Hedges	338	.439	.163	.241	.248	.085	.735	.074
Steven Kwan	638	.769	.298	.373	.400	.101	.893	.094
Owen Miller	472	.589	.243	.301	.351	.108	.781	.066
Josh Naylor	498	.731	.256	.319	.452	.196	.822	.069
Jose Ramirez	685	.910	.280	.355	.514	.235	.864	.074
Amed Rosario	670	.636	.283	.312	.403	.121	.826	.037
Myles Straw	596	.533	.221	.291	.273	.052	.837	.091

Individual Pitching Stats for Starters (2022)

Pitcher	IP	BPO	ERA	BA	SA	ISO	CT	EY
Shane Bieber	200.0	.518	2.88	.230	.347	.116	.735	.046
Triston McKenzie	191.1	.536	2.96	.201	.358	.157	.724	.059
Zach Plesac	131.2	.672	4.31	.260	.426	.166	.809	.067
Cal Quantrill	186.1	.643	3.38	.254	.389	.135	.818	.061

Individual Pitching Stats for Relievers (2022)

Pitcher	GR	BPO	ERA	BA	SA	ISO	CT	EY
Emmanuel Clase	77	.332	1.36	.167	.225	.058	.702	.030
Enyel De Los Santos	50	.570	3.04	.208	.328	.120	.682	.075
Sam Hentges	57	.463	2.32	.186	.258	.072	.674	.074
Eli Morgan	49	.567	3.38	.192	.381	.188	.699	.051
Nick Sandlin	46	.534	2.25	.176	.248	.072	.732	.119
Bryan Shaw	58	.725	5.40	.252	.417	.165	.774	.096
Trevor Stephan	66	.613	2.69	.238	.329	.092	.658	.060

Best Stats on Team (2022)

Stat	Batter	Number	Stat	Pitcher	Number
2B	Jose Ramirez	44	BA	Triston McKenzie	.201
3B	Amed Rosario	9	BBV	Shane Bieber	-27
BA	Steven Kwan	.298	BPO-R	Emmanuel Clase	.332
BB	Jose Ramirez	69	BPO-S	Shane Bieber	.518
BBV	Steven Kwan	10	BPV	James Karinchak	-28
BPO	Jose Ramirez	.910	BV	Shane Bieber	-85
BPV	Steven Kwan	81	CT	Triston McKenzie	.724
BV	Jose Ramirez	113	ERA-R	Emmanuel Clase	1.36
CT	Steven Kwan	.893	ERA-S	Shane Bieber	2.88
EY	Steven Kwan	.094	ERV	Shane Bieber	-24
H	Amed Rosario	180	EY	Shane Bieber	.046
HR	Jose Ramirez	29	GR	Emmanuel Clase	77
ISO	Jose Ramirez	.235	GS	Cal Quantrill	32
OBP	Steven Kwan	.373	IP	Shane Bieber	200.0
R	Jose Ramirez	90	ISO	Shane Bieber	.116
RBI	Jose Ramirez	126	OBP	Triston McKenzie	.253
SA	Jose Ramirez	.514	SA	Shane Bieber	.347
SB	Myles Straw	21	SO	Shane Bieber	198
SC	Jose Ramirez	187	SV	Emmanuel Clase	42
SCV	Jose Ramirez	53	W	Cal Quantrill	15
SE	Jose Ramirez	.273	XV	Shane Bieber	-27
XV	Jose Ramirez	50			

Worst Stats on Team (2022)

Stat	Batter	Number
BA	Austin Hedges	.163
BBV	Amed Rosario	-28
BPO	Austin Hedges	.439
BPV	Franmil Reyes	-38
BV	Austin Hedges	-60
CT	Austin Hedges	.735
EY	Oscar Gonzalez	.034
ISO	Myles Straw	.052
OBP	Austin Hedges	.241
SA	Austin Hedges	.248
SCV	Austin Hedges	-17
SE	Austin Hedges	.145
SO	Andres Gimenez	112
XV	Myles Straw	-53

Stat	Pitcher	Number
BA	Zach Plesac	.260
BB	Cal Quantrill	47
BBV	Konnor Pilkington	12
BPO-R	Bryan Shaw	.725
BPO-S	Zach Plesac	.672
BPV	Cal Quantrill	47
BV	Hunter Gaddis	27
CT	Cal Quantrill	.818
ERA-R	Bryan Shaw	5.40
ERA-S	Zach Plesac	4.31
ERV	Hunter Gaddis	12
EY	Zach Plesac	.067
ISO	Zach Plesac	.166
L	Zach Plesac	12
OBP	Zach Plesac	.315
SA	Zach Plesac	.426
XV	Hunter Gaddis	18

Overall Base Value Leaders (2022)

Team Rank	Player	BV [bat]	(-) BV [pitch]	(=) OBV
1	Jose Ramirez	113	0	113
2	Shane Bieber	0	-85	85
3	Andres Gimenez	75	0	75
4	Emmanuel Clase	0	-74	74
5	Triston McKenzie	0	-71	71
6	Steven Kwan	45	0	45
7	Sam Hentges	0	-37	37
8	Josh Naylor	25	0	25
9	Eli Morgan	0	-19	19
10	Nick Sandlin	0	-16	16

Fan Support in Past 10 Seasons (2013-2022)

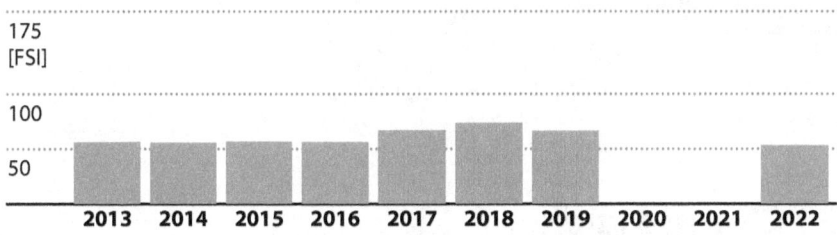

Year	Team	Attendance	W	Att:W	FSI
2013	Cleveland Indians	1,572,926	92	17,097	56.1
2014	Cleveland Indians	1,437,393	85	16,911	55.7
2015	Cleveland Indians	1,388,905	81	17,147	56.5
2016	Cleveland Indians	1,591,667	94	16,933	56.2
2017	Cleveland Indians	2,048,138	102	20,080	67.1
2018	Cleveland Indians	1,926,701	91	21,173	73.9
2019	Cleveland Indians	1,738,642	93	18,695	66.3
2022	Cleveland Guardians	1,295,870	92	14,086	53.0

Extreme Games for Batters (2022)

Stat	Team Total	Individual Leader	G
3+ H	77	Amed Rosario	17
2+ HR	7	Jose Ramirez	3
5+ RBI	7	Jose Ramirez	3
0 H in 5+ AB	24	Myles Straw	6
4+ SO	7	Franmil Reyes	5

Extreme Games for Pitchers (2022)

Stat	Team Total	Individual Leader	G
0-2 ER in 7+ IP	24	Shane Bieber	12
10+ SO	7	Shane Bieber, Triston McKenzie	3
0 BR in SV	27	Emmanuel Clase	22
10+ BR	23	Cal Quantrill	7
1+ ER in SV	1	Emmanuel Clase	1

Predictions for Coming Season (2023)

Group	Next W	Next L	Next Pct.	WS	LC	PQ
10 closest matches (avg. W-L)	83.7	78.3	.517	0	0	4
25 closest matches (avg. W-L)	81.2	77.0	.513	1	1	7
50 closest matches (avg. W-L)	82.9	77.1	.518	1	1	14

25 Closest Matches (2023)

Rank	Team	Next	W	L	Pct.	WS	LC	PQ
1	White Sox (2008-2010)	2011	79	83	.488	—	—	X
2	Rangers (1996-1998)	1999	95	67	.586	—	—	X
3	Rangers (1979-1981)	1982	64	98	.395	—	—	—
4	Astros (1995-1997)	1998	102	60	.630	—	—	X
5	Braves (2007-2009)	2010	91	71	.562	—	—	X
6	Dodgers (1998-2000)	2001	86	76	.531	—	—	—
7	Braves (2005-2007)	2008	72	90	.444	—	—	—
8	White Sox (1994-1996)	1997	80	81	.497	—	—	—
9	Twins (2006-2008)	2009	87	76	.534	—	—	X
10	Expos (1985-1987)	1988	81	81	.500	—	—	—
11	Dodgers (2002-2004)	2005	71	91	.438	—	—	—
12	Tigers (1991-1993)	1994	53	62	.461	—	—	—
13	Royals (1980-1982)	1983	79	83	.488	—	—	—
14	Cardinals (1979-1981)	1982	92	70	.568	X	X	X
15	Rangers (1991-1993)	1994	52	62	.456	—	—	—
16	Astros (2001-2003)	2004	92	70	.568	—	—	X
17	Red Sox (1988-1990)	1991	84	78	.519	—	—	—
18	Phillies (2001-2003)	2004	86	76	.531	—	—	—
19	Blue Jays (2008-2010)	2011	81	81	.500	—	—	—
20	Yankees (2013-2015)	2016	84	78	.519	—	—	—
21	Astros (1981-1983)	1984	80	82	.494	—	—	—
22	Dodgers (2000-2002)	2003	85	77	.525	—	—	—
23	Orioles (2014-2016)	2017	75	87	.463	—	—	—
24	Red Sox (1979-1981)	1982	89	73	.549	—	—	—
25	Dodgers (1993-1995)	1996	90	72	.556	—	—	X

COLORADO ROCKIES

Past 10 Seasons (2013-2022)

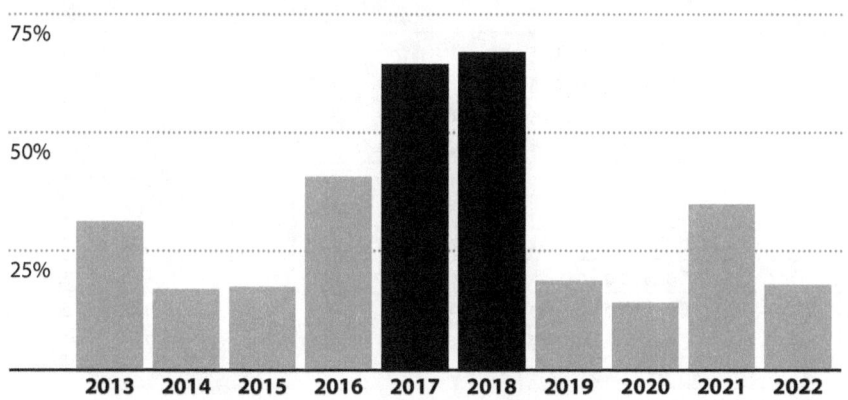

Year	Team	W	L	Pct.	Post	TS	ME%
2013	Colorado Rockies	74	88	.457	—	36.994	31.2%
2014	Colorado Rockies	66	96	.407	—	29.100	16.9%
2015	Colorado Rockies	68	94	.420	—	29.328	17.4%
2016	Colorado Rockies	75	87	.463	—	41.488	40.7%
2017	Colorado Rockies	87	75	.537	P	52.736	64.4%
2018	Colorado Rockies	91	72	.558	P	54.142	66.9%
2019	Colorado Rockies	71	91	.438	—	29.972	18.7%
2020	Colorado Rockies	26	34	.433	—	27.417	14.1%
2021	Colorado Rockies	74	87	.460	—	38.902	34.8%
2022	Colorado Rockies	68	94	.420	—	29.455	17.9%

Best Seasons of Modern Era (1993-2022)

Year	Team	W	L	Pct.	Post	TS	ME%
2007	Colorado Rockies	90	73	.552	LP	75.518	95.0%
2009	Colorado Rockies	92	70	.568	P	63.287	84.2%
2010	Colorado Rockies	83	79	.512	—	54.176	67.0%
2018	Colorado Rockies	91	72	.558	P	54.142	66.9%
2017	Colorado Rockies	87	75	.537	P	52.736	64.4%
1995	Colorado Rockies	77	67	.535	P	51.516	61.5%
2000	Colorado Rockies	82	80	.506	—	49.338	56.4%
1996	Colorado Rockies	83	79	.512	—	48.383	54.6%
1997	Colorado Rockies	83	79	.512	—	46.499	51.1%
2006	Colorado Rockies	76	86	.469	—	44.149	46.3%

Worst Seasons of Modern Era (1993-2022)

Year	Team	W	L	Pct.	Post	TS	ME%
2005	Colorado Rockies	67	95	.414	—	21.032	6.0%
1993	Colorado Rockies	67	95	.414	—	23.078	8.0%
2012	Colorado Rockies	64	98	.395	—	24.098	9.4%
2020	Colorado Rockies	26	34	.433	—	27.417	14.1%
1999	Colorado Rockies	72	90	.444	—	28.026	14.9%
2014	Colorado Rockies	66	96	.407	—	29.100	16.9%
2015	Colorado Rockies	68	94	.420	—	29.328	17.4%
2022	Colorado Rockies	68	94	.420	—	29.455	17.9%
2019	Colorado Rockies	71	91	.438	—	29.972	18.7%
2004	Colorado Rockies	68	94	.420	—	30.259	19.1%

Season Breakdown (2022)

Category	W	L	Pct.	R	RA	R/G	RA/G
Overall record in 2022	68	94	.420	698	873	4.31	5.39
Home games	41	40	.506	456	476	5.63	5.88
Away games	27	54	.333	242	397	2.99	4.90
First half of 2022 season	35	46	.432	365	438	4.51	5.41
Second half of 2022 season	33	48	.407	333	435	4.11	5.37
Against first-place teams	11	24	.314	130	185	3.71	5.29
Against playoff teams	25	43	.368	266	358	3.91	5.26
Against non-playoff teams	43	51	.457	432	515	4.60	5.48

Season as Nine-Inning Game (2022)

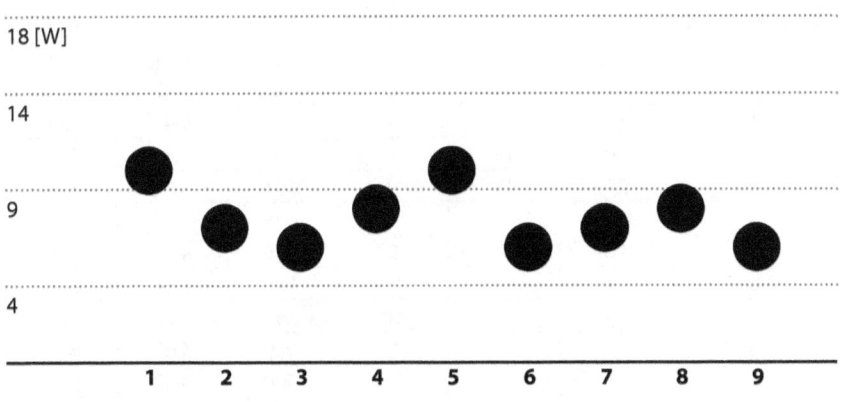

Result	1	2	3	4	5	6	7	8	9	Total
Wins	10	7	6	8	10	6	7	8	6	68
Losses	8	11	12	10	8	12	11	10	12	94

Scoring by Game (2022)

Runs Scored	G	W	L	Pct.	R/G	RA/G
Overall record	162	68	94	.420	4.31	5.39
0	12	0	12	.000	0.00	7.08
1	21	2	19	.095	1.00	4.52
2	18	4	14	.222	2.00	4.39
3	21	8	13	.381	3.00	4.86
4	25	13	12	.520	4.00	4.44
5	17	8	9	.471	5.00	5.53
6	14	8	6	.571	6.00	6.71
7	10	5	5	.500	7.00	6.70
8	7	5	2	.714	8.00	5.71
9	4	3	1	.750	9.00	6.75
10 or more	13	12	1	.923	11.31	6.08

Scoring Allowed by Game (2022)

Runs Allowed	G	W	L	Pct.	R/G	RA/G
Overall record	162	68	94	.420	4.31	5.39
0	6	6	0	1.000	2.17	0.00
1	10	10	0	1.000	4.40	1.00
2	20	13	7	.650	3.35	2.00
3	22	13	9	.591	3.68	3.00
4	16	10	6	.625	5.56	4.00
5	16	7	9	.438	4.75	5.00
6	21	4	17	.190	4.14	6.00
7	13	3	10	.231	5.08	7.00
8	6	0	6	.000	4.67	8.00
9	11	0	11	.000	3.82	9.00
10 or more	21	2	19	.095	5.00	11.86

Margins (2022)

Category	Margin	G	W	L	Pct.	GShr	WShr
Overall record	—	162	68	94	.420	—	—
Close	1 or 2 runs	73	36	37	.493	45.1%	52.9%
Medium	3 or 4 runs	49	22	27	.449	30.2%	32.4%
Distant	5 or more runs	40	10	30	.250	24.7%	14.7%

Individual Scoring Leaders (2022)

Team Rank	Batter	R	(+) RBI	(-) HR	(=) SC
1	C.J. Cron	79	102	29	152
2	Charlie Blackmon	60	78	16	122
2	Brendan Rodgers	72	63	13	122
4	Randal Grichuk	60	73	19	114
4	Ryan McMahon	67	67	20	114
6	Jose Iglesias	48	47	3	92
7	Yonathan Daza	56	34	2	88
8	Connor Joe	56	28	7	77
9	Elias Diaz	29	51	9	71
10	Garrett Hampson	29	15	2	42

Team Ratings (2022)

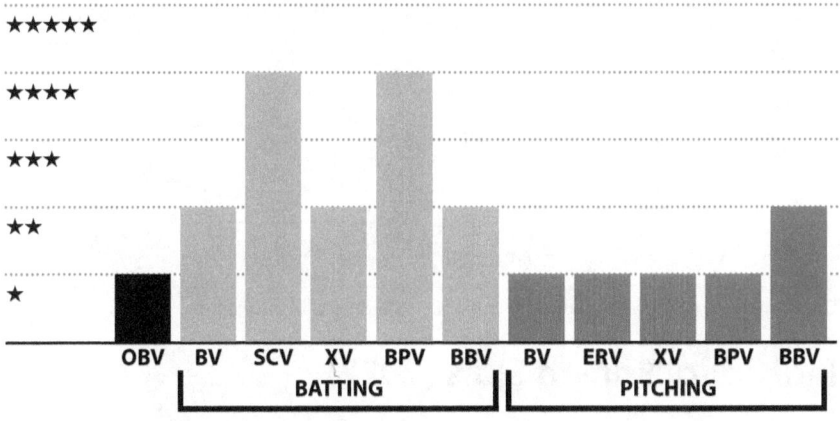

Quality	Type	Indicator	Value	Rating
Overall performance	Overall	OBV	-481	★
Base production	Batting	BV	-53	★★
Run production	Batting	SCV	28	★★★★
Power hitting	Batting	XV	-48	★★
Contact hitting	Batting	BPV	53	★★★★
Batting eye	Batting	BBV	-40	★★
Base prevention	Pitching	BV	428	★
Run prevention	Pitching	ERV	175	★
Power prevention	Pitching	XV	124	★
Strikeout pitching	Pitching	BPV	203	★
Control pitching	Pitching	BBV	34	★★

Team Batting Stats (2022)

Stat	Number	Div Rank	Lg Rank	MLB Rank	MLB Best
R	698	5	10	15	847 (Dodgers)
H	1,408	2	3	7	1,464 (Blue Jays)
HR	149	5	13	22	254 (Yankees)
BPO	.648	5	11	20	.764 (Dodgers)
BA	.254	2	3	6	.264 (Blue Jays)
OBP	.315	3	8	14	.333 (Dodgers)
SA	.398	2	7	12	.443 (Braves)

Division: NL West, 5 teams. **League:** National, 15 teams. **MLB:** 30 teams.

Team Pitching Stats (2022)

Stat	Number	Div Rank	Lg Rank	MLB Rank	MLB Best
ERA	5.07	5	15	30	2.80 (Dodgers)
SO	1,187	5	14	29	1,565 (Mets)
BB	539	5	11	23	384 (Rays)
BPO	.760	5	14	29	.551 (Astros)
BA	.272	5	15	30	.209 (Dodgers)
OBP	.340	5	15	29	.273 (Dodgers)
SA	.447	5	14	29	.332 (Astros)

Division: NL West, 5 teams. **League:** National, 15 teams. **MLB:** 30 teams.

Individual Batting Stats (2022)

Batter	PA	BPO	BA	OBP	SA	ISO	CT	EY
Charlie Blackmon	577	.669	.264	.314	.419	.155	.794	.049
C.J. Cron	632	.725	.257	.315	.468	.210	.715	.059
Yonathan Daza	408	.637	.301	.349	.384	.083	.844	.064
Elias Diaz	381	.562	.228	.281	.368	.140	.766	.066
Randal Grichuk	538	.645	.259	.299	.425	.166	.749	.045
Jose Iglesias	467	.601	.292	.328	.380	.089	.872	.036
Connor Joe	467	.671	.238	.338	.359	.121	.760	.118
Ryan McMahon	597	.714	.246	.327	.414	.168	.701	.101
Brendan Rodgers	581	.645	.266	.325	.408	.142	.808	.079

Individual Pitching Stats for Starters (2022)

Pitcher	IP	BPO	ERA	BA	SA	ISO	CT	EY
Kyle Freeland	174.2	.769	4.53	.281	.456	.175	.809	.069
Austin Gomber	124.2	.759	5.56	.281	.480	.199	.805	.063
Chad Kuhl	137.0	.850	5.72	.284	.500	.216	.799	.093
German Marquez	181.2	.755	5.00	.263	.469	.206	.787	.081

Individual Pitching Stats for Relievers (2022)

Pitcher	GR	BPO	ERA	BA	SA	ISO	CT	EY
Daniel Bard	57	.475	1.79	.162	.245	.083	.681	.098
Alex Colome	53	.872	5.74	.300	.484	.184	.832	.094
Carlos Estevez	62	.615	3.47	.211	.373	.163	.742	.094
Lucas Gilbreath	47	.680	4.19	.242	.320	.078	.680	.139
Robert Stephenson	45	.852	6.04	.291	.527	.236	.797	.061

Best Stats on Team (2022)

Stat	Batter	Number
2B	Brendan Rodgers, Jose Iglesias	30
3B	Charlie Blackmon	6
BA	Yonathan Daza	.301
BB	Ryan McMahon	60
BBV	Connor Joe	18
BPO	C.J. Cron	.725
BPV	Jose Iglesias	54
BV	C.J. Cron	29
CT	Jose Iglesias	.872
EY	Connor Joe	.118
H	C.J. Cron	148
HR	C.J. Cron	29
ISO	C.J. Cron	.210
OBP	Yonathan Daza	.349
R	C.J. Cron	79
RBI	C.J. Cron	102
SA	C.J. Cron	.468
SB	Garrett Hampson	12
SC	C.J. Cron	152
SCV	C.J. Cron	29
SE	C.J. Cron	.241
XV	C.J. Cron	34

Stat	Pitcher	Number
BA	German Marquez	.263
BBV	Antonio Senzatela	-10
BPO-R	Daniel Bard	.475
BPO-S	German Marquez	.755
BPV	Daniel Bard	-15
BV	Daniel Bard	-34
CT	German Marquez	.787
ERA-R	Daniel Bard	1.79
ERA-S	Kyle Freeland	4.53
ERV	Daniel Bard	-15
EY	Austin Gomber	.063
GR	Carlos Estevez	62
GS	German Marquez, Kyle Freeland	31
IP	German Marquez	181.2
ISO	Kyle Freeland	.175
OBP	German Marquez	.324
SA	Kyle Freeland	.456
SO	German Marquez	150
SV	Daniel Bard	34
W	German Marquez, Kyle Freeland	9
XV	Daniel Bard	-15

Worst Stats on Team (2022)

Stat	Batter	Number
BA	Elias Diaz	.228
BBV	Jose Iglesias	-20
BPO	Elias Diaz	.562
BPV	Ryan McMahon	-26
BV	Elias Diaz	-28
CT	Ryan McMahon	.701
EY	Jose Iglesias	.036
ISO	Yonathan Daza	.083
OBP	Elias Diaz	.281
SA	Connor Joe	.359
SCV	Connor Joe	-14
SE	Connor Joe	.165
SO	C.J. Cron	164
XV	Jose Iglesias	-28

Stat	Pitcher	Number
BA	Chad Kuhl	.284
BB	German Marquez	63
BBV	Lucas Gilbreath	11
BPO-R	Alex Colome	.872
BPO-S	Chad Kuhl	.850
BPV	Kyle Freeland, Antonio Senzatela	41
BV	Chad Kuhl	78
CT	Kyle Freeland	.809
ERA-R	Robert Stephenson	6.04
ERA-S	Chad Kuhl	5.72
ERV	Chad Kuhl	27
EY	Chad Kuhl	.093
ISO	Chad Kuhl	.216
L	German Marquez	13
OBP	Chad Kuhl	.355
SA	Chad Kuhl	.500
XV	German Marquez	38

Overall Base Value Leaders (2022)

Team Rank	Player	BV [bat]	(-) BV [pitch]	(=) OBV
1	Daniel Bard	0	-34	34
2	C.J. Cron	29	0	29
3	Sean Bouchard	24	0	24
4	Ryan McMahon	22	0	22
5	Kris Bryant	18	0	18
6	Tyler Kinley	0	-10	10
7	Carlos Estevez	0	-8	8
8	Charlie Blackmon	4	0	4
9	Connor Joe	3	0	3
10	Jordan Sheffield	0	0	0

Fan Support in Past 10 Seasons (2013-2022)

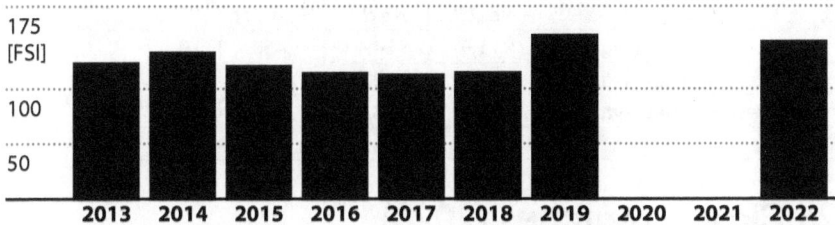

Year	Team	Attendance	W	Att:W	FSI
2013	Colorado Rockies	2,793,828	74	37,754	124.0
2014	Colorado Rockies	2,680,329	66	40,611	133.8
2015	Colorado Rockies	2,506,789	68	36,865	121.4
2016	Colorado Rockies	2,602,524	75	34,700	115.1
2017	Colorado Rockies	2,953,650	87	33,950	113.5
2018	Colorado Rockies	3,015,880	91	33,142	115.6
2019	Colorado Rockies	2,993,244	71	42,158	149.5
2022	Colorado Rockies	2,597,428	68	38,197	143.8

Extreme Games for Batters (2022)

Stat	Team Total	Individual Leader	G
3+ H	67	Brendan Rodgers	11
2+ HR	11	C.J. Cron	3
5+ RBI	7	C.J. Cron	3
0 H in 5+ AB	26	Charlie Blackmon	7
4+ SO	5	Charlie Blackmon	2

Extreme Games for Pitchers (2022)

Stat	Team Total	Individual Leader	G
0-2 ER in 7+ IP	15	German Marquez	7
10+ SO	0	[none]	0
0 BR in SV	19	Daniel Bard	17
10+ BR	48	German Marquez	12
1+ ER in SV	4	Alex Colome, Daniel Bard	2

Predictions for Coming Season (2023)

Group	Next W	Next L	Next Pct.	WS	LC	PQ
10 closest matches (avg. W-L)	71.9	84.4	.460	0	0	0
25 closest matches (avg. W-L)	70.7	88.8	.443	0	0	0
50 closest matches (avg. W-L)	73.9	86.9	.460	1	1	3

25 Closest Matches (2023)

Rank	Team	Next	W	L	Pct.	WS	LC	PQ
1	Rockies (2012-2014)	2015	68	94	.420	—	—	—
2	Twins (1995-1997)	1998	70	92	.432	—	—	—
3	White Sox (1978-1980)	1981	54	52	.509	—	—	—
4	Rockies (2002-2004)	2005	67	95	.414	—	—	—
5	White Sox (1986-1988)	1989	69	92	.429	—	—	—
6	Royals (2010-2012)	2013	86	76	.531	—	—	—
7	Padres (1975-1977)	1978	84	78	.519	—	—	—
8	White Sox (2015-2017)	2018	62	100	.383	—	—	—
9	Mariners (2011-2013)	2014	87	75	.537	—	—	—
10	Giants (2005-2007)	2008	72	90	.444	—	—	—
11	Nationals (2004-2006)	2007	73	89	.451	—	—	—
12	Pirates (1998-2000)	2001	62	100	.383	—	—	—
13	Rangers (2001-2003)	2004	89	73	.549	—	—	—
14	Royals (1999-2001)	2002	62	100	.383	—	—	—
15	Tigers (1999-2001)	2002	55	106	.342	—	—	—
16	Padres (1977-1979)	1980	73	89	.451	—	—	—
17	Cubs (1974-1976)	1977	81	81	.500	—	—	—
18	Astros (2007-2009)	2010	76	86	.469	—	—	—
19	Padres (2014-2016)	2017	71	91	.438	—	—	—
20	Royals (1995-1997)	1998	72	89	.447	—	—	—
21	Rangers (1982-1984)	1985	62	99	.385	—	—	—
22	White Sox (2013-2015)	2016	78	84	.481	—	—	—
23	Brewers (1998-2000)	2001	68	94	.420	—	—	—
24	Braves (1985-1987)	1988	54	106	.338	—	—	—
25	Mariners (1986-1988)	1989	73	89	.451	—	—	—

DETROIT TIGERS

Past 10 Seasons (2013-2022)

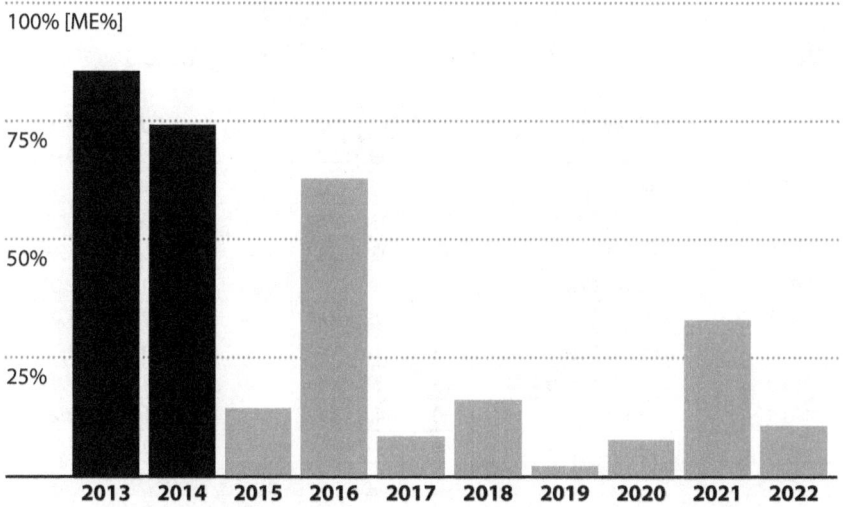

Year	Team	W	L	Pct.	Post	TS	ME%
2013	Detroit Tigers	93	69	.574	P	64.153	85.5%
2014	Detroit Tigers	90	72	.556	P	57.212	74.1%
2015	Detroit Tigers	74	87	.460	—	27.487	14.3%
2016	Detroit Tigers	86	75	.534	—	52.170	62.8%
2017	Detroit Tigers	64	98	.395	—	23.273	8.3%
2018	Detroit Tigers	64	98	.395	—	28.679	16.0%
2019	Detroit Tigers	47	114	.292	—	14.908	2.0%
2020	Detroit Tigers	23	35	.397	—	22.457	7.6%
2021	Detroit Tigers	77	85	.475	—	37.951	32.9%
2022	Detroit Tigers	66	96	.407	—	25.392	10.6%

Best Seasons of Modern Era (1961-2022)

Year	Team	W	L	Pct.	Post	TS	ME%
1984	Detroit Tigers	104	58	.642	WLP	97.109	100.0%
1968	Detroit Tigers	103	59	.636	WLP	87.102	99.2%
1987	Detroit Tigers	98	64	.605	P	71.911	92.2%
2006	Detroit Tigers	95	67	.586	LP	70.822	91.5%
1961	Detroit Tigers	101	61	.623	—	68.177	89.8%
2012	Detroit Tigers	88	74	.543	LP	64.777	86.6%
2013	Detroit Tigers	93	69	.574	P	64.153	85.5%
1967	Detroit Tigers	91	71	.562	—	63.023	83.9%
1983	Detroit Tigers	92	70	.568	—	62.554	83.4%
1986	Detroit Tigers	87	75	.537	—	60.274	78.9%

Worst Seasons of Modern Era (1961-2022)

Year	Team	W	L	Pct.	Post	TS	ME%
1996	Detroit Tigers	53	109	.327	—	5.197	0.0%
2003	Detroit Tigers	43	119	.265	—	7.040	0.1%
1989	Detroit Tigers	59	103	.364	—	8.859	0.2%
1975	Detroit Tigers	57	102	.358	—	13.022	1.4%
2019	Detroit Tigers	47	114	.292	—	14.908	2.0%
1974	Detroit Tigers	72	90	.444	—	16.924	3.0%
2002	Detroit Tigers	55	106	.342	—	17.911	3.7%
2020	Detroit Tigers	23	35	.397	—	22.457	7.6%
1995	Detroit Tigers	60	84	.417	—	23.133	8.2%
2017	Detroit Tigers	64	98	.395	—	23.273	8.3%

Season Breakdown (2022)

Category	W	L	Pct.	R	RA	R/G	RA/G
Overall record in 2022	66	96	.407	557	713	3.44	4.40
Home games	36	46	.439	285	357	3.48	4.35
Away games	30	50	.375	272	356	3.40	4.45
First half of 2022 season	34	47	.420	259	342	3.20	4.22
Second half of 2022 season	32	49	.395	298	371	3.68	4.58
Against first-place teams	11	24	.314	99	153	2.83	4.37
Against playoff teams	18	41	.305	179	279	3.03	4.73
Against non-playoff teams	48	55	.466	378	434	3.67	4.21

Season as Nine-Inning Game (2022)

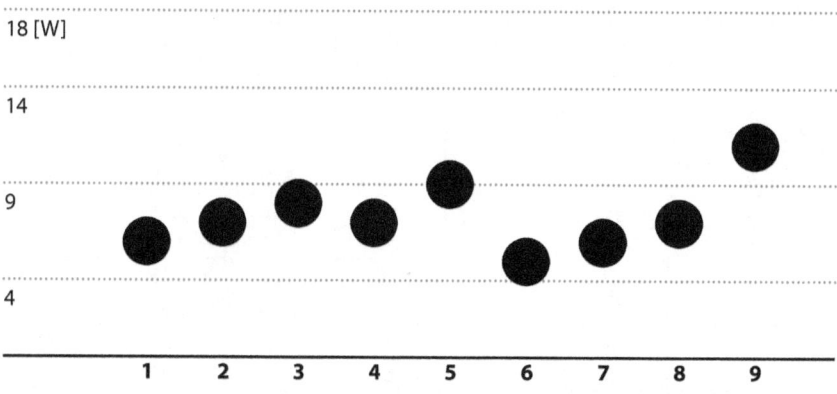

Result	1	2	3	4	5	6	7	8	9	Total
Wins	6	7	8	7	9	5	6	7	11	66
Losses	12	11	10	11	9	13	12	11	7	96

Scoring by Game (2022)

Runs Scored	G	W	L	Pct.	R/G	RA/G
Overall record	162	66	96	.407	3.44	4.40
0	22	0	22	.000	0.00	6.23
1	21	0	21	.000	1.00	5.48
2	22	4	18	.182	2.00	4.32
3	28	12	16	.429	3.00	3.64
4	27	16	11	.593	4.00	3.63
5	15	12	3	.800	5.00	3.67
6	6	3	3	.500	6.00	4.50
7	9	7	2	.778	7.00	5.22
8	2	2	0	1.000	8.00	3.00
9	2	2	0	1.000	9.00	4.50
10 or more	8	8	0	1.000	11.50	2.75

Scoring Allowed by Game (2022)

Runs Allowed	G	W	L	Pct.	R/G	RA/G
Overall record	162	66	96	.407	3.44	4.40
0	8	8	0	1.000	6.13	0.00
1	15	14	1	.933	3.67	1.00
2	22	18	4	.818	4.09	2.00
3	26	14	12	.538	3.38	3.00
4	17	6	11	.353	3.71	4.00
5	28	4	24	.143	3.18	5.00
6	11	0	11	.000	2.45	6.00
7	12	1	11	.083	3.00	7.00
8	8	1	7	.125	2.75	8.00
9	6	0	6	.000	3.67	9.00
10 or more	9	0	9	.000	1.78	11.11

Margins (2022)

Category	Margin	G	W	L	Pct.	GShr	WShr
Overall record	—	162	66	96	.407	—	—
Close	1 or 2 runs	80	38	42	.475	49.4%	57.6%
Medium	3 or 4 runs	38	13	25	.342	23.5%	19.7%
Distant	5 or more runs	44	15	29	.341	27.2%	22.7%

Individual Scoring Leaders (2022)

Team Rank	Batter	R	(+) RBI	(-) HR	(=) SC
1	Javier Baez	64	67	17	114
2	Jeimer Candelario	49	50	13	86
3	Riley Greene	46	42	5	83
4	Harold Castro	37	47	7	77
5	Jonathan Schoop	48	38	11	75
6	Eric Haase	41	44	14	71
7	Willi Castro	47	31	8	70
8	Miguel Cabrera	25	43	5	63
9	Victor Reyes	27	34	3	58
9	Spencer Torkelson	38	28	8	58

Team Ratings (2022)

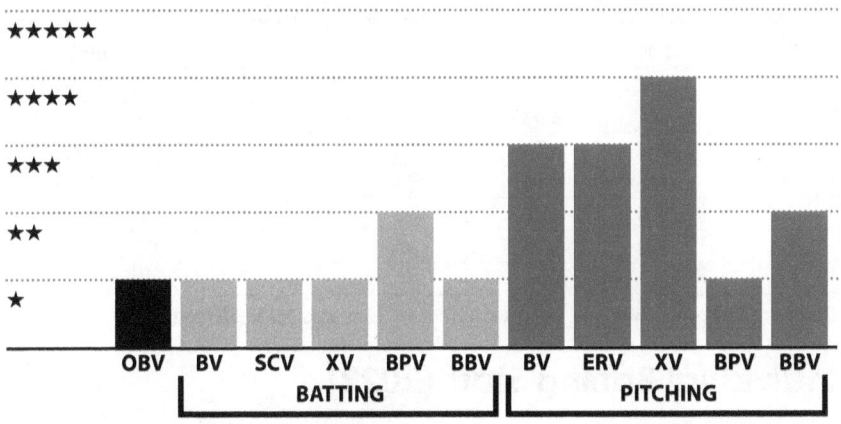

Quality	Type	Indicator	Value	Rating
Overall performance	Overall	OBV	-467	★
Base production	Batting	BV	-456	★
Run production	Batting	SCV	-167	★
Power hitting	Batting	XV	-199	★
Contact hitting	Batting	BPV	-70	★★
Batting eye	Batting	BBV	-92	★
Base prevention	Pitching	BV	11	★★★
Run prevention	Pitching	ERV	14	★★★
Power prevention	Pitching	XV	-32	★★★★
Strikeout pitching	Pitching	BPV	154	★
Control pitching	Pitching	BBV	24	★★

Team Batting Stats (2022)

Stat	Number	Div Rank	Lg Rank	MLB Rank	MLB Best
R	557	5	15	30	847 (Dodgers)
H	1,240	5	13	26	1,464 (Blue Jays)
HR	110	5	15	30	254 (Yankees)
BPO	.555	5	15	30	.764 (Dodgers)
BA	.231	5	13	25	.264 (Blue Jays)
OBP	.286	5	14	29	.333 (Dodgers)
SA	.346	5	15	30	.443 (Braves)

Division: AL Central, 5 teams. **League:** American, 15 teams. **MLB:** 30 teams.

Team Pitching Stats (2022)

Stat	Number	Div Rank	Lg Rank	MLB Rank	MLB Best
ERA	4.05	4	11	21	2.80 (Dodgers)
SO	1,195	4	14	27	1,565 (Mets)
BB	511	3	10	18	384 (Rays)
BPO	.663	4	10	18	.551 (Astros)
BA	.247	4	11	21	.209 (Dodgers)
OBP	.316	4	10	20	.273 (Dodgers)
SA	.394	3	8	16	.332 (Astros)

Division: AL Central, 5 teams. **League:** American, 15 teams. **MLB:** 30 teams.

Individual Batting Stats (2022)

Batter	PA	BPO	BA	OBP	SA	ISO	CT	EY
Javier Baez	590	.594	.238	.278	.393	.155	.735	.042
Miguel Cabrera	433	.522	.254	.305	.317	.063	.746	.058
Jeimer Candelario	467	.551	.217	.272	.361	.145	.746	.058
Harold Castro	443	.577	.271	.300	.381	.110	.812	.036
Willi Castro	392	.588	.241	.284	.367	.126	.775	.038
Riley Greene	418	.605	.253	.321	.362	.109	.681	.086
Eric Haase	351	.676	.254	.305	.443	.189	.700	.066
Victor Reyes	336	.552	.254	.289	.362	.108	.756	.039
Jonathan Schoop	510	.469	.202	.239	.322	.121	.778	.035
Spencer Torkelson	404	.526	.203	.285	.319	.117	.725	.092

Individual Pitching Stats for Starters (2022)

Pitcher	IP	BPO	ERA	BA	SA	ISO	CT	EY
Tyler Alexander	101.0	.744	4.81	.275	.473	.198	.845	.056
Drew Hutchison	105.1	.737	4.53	.273	.432	.158	.837	.089
Tarik Skubal	117.2	.576	3.52	.237	.372	.135	.733	.067

Individual Pitching Stats for Relievers (2022)

Pitcher	GR	BPO	ERA	BA	SA	ISO	CT	EY
Andrew Chafin	64	.549	2.83	.222	.329	.106	.690	.078
Jason Foley	60	.591	3.88	.298	.364	.066	.822	.043
Michael Fulmer	41	.580	3.20	.203	.273	.070	.727	.097
Joe Jimenez	62	.547	3.49	.226	.341	.115	.645	.056
Alex Lange	71	.620	3.69	.208	.316	.108	.645	.111
Gregory Soto	64	.643	3.28	.225	.317	.092	.725	.126
Will Vest	57	.635	4.00	.262	.367	.105	.734	.081

Best Stats on Team (2022)

Stat	Batter	Number
2B	Javier Baez	27
3B	Javier Baez, Riley Greene	4
BA	Harold Castro	.271
BB	Robbie Grossman	38
BBV	Robbie Grossman	13
BPO	Eric Haase	.676
BPV	Harold Castro	26
BV	Kerry Carpenter	9
CT	Harold Castro	.812
EY	Spencer Torkelson	.092
H	Javier Baez	132
HR	Javier Baez	17
ISO	Eric Haase	.189
OBP	Riley Greene	.321
R	Javier Baez	64
RBI	Javier Baez	67
SA	Eric Haase	.443
SB	Javier Baez, Willi Castro, Akil Baddoo	9
SC	Javier Baez	114
SCV	Eric Haase	3
SE	Eric Haase	.202
XV	Eric Haase	12

Stat	Pitcher	Number
BA	Tarik Skubal	.237
BBV	Tyler Alexander	-10
BPO-R	Joe Jimenez	.547
BPO-S	Tarik Skubal	.576
BPV	Alex Lange	-24
BV	Tarik Skubal	-30
CT	Tarik Skubal	.733
ERA-R	Andrew Chafin	2.83
ERA-S	Tarik Skubal	3.52
ERV	Jose Cisnero	-8
EY	Tyler Alexander	.056
GR	Alex Lange	71
GS	Tarik Skubal	21
IP	Tarik Skubal	117.2
ISO	Tarik Skubal	.135
OBP	Tarik Skubal	.288
SA	Tarik Skubal	.372
SO	Tarik Skubal	117
SV	Gregory Soto	30
W	Tarik Skubal, Alex Lange	7
XV	Jason Foley	-21

Worst Stats on Team (2022)

Stat	Batter	Number
BA	Jonathan Schoop	.202
BBV	Javier Baez, Jonathan Schoop	-22
BPO	Jonathan Schoop	.469
BPV	Riley Greene	-26
BV	Jonathan Schoop	-77
CT	Riley Greene	.681
EY	Jonathan Schoop	.035
ISO	Miguel Cabrera	.063
OBP	Jonathan Schoop	.239
SA	Miguel Cabrera	.317
SCV	Tucker Barnhart	-29
SE	Spencer Torkelson	.144
SO	Javier Baez	147
XV	Miguel Cabrera	-35

Stat	Pitcher	Number
BA	Tyler Alexander	.275
BB	Drew Hutchison	42
BBV	Gregory Soto	12
BPO-R	Gregory Soto	.643
BPO-S	Tyler Alexander	.744
BPV	Tyler Alexander	37
BV	Elvin Rodriguez	45
CT	Tyler Alexander	.845
ERA-R	Will Vest	4.00
ERA-S	Tyler Alexander	4.81
ERV	Elvin Rodriguez	22
EY	Drew Hutchison	.089
ISO	Tyler Alexander	.198
L	Tyler Alexander, Gregory Soto	11
OBP	Drew Hutchison	.341
SA	Tyler Alexander	.473
XV	Elvin Rodriguez	26

Overall Base Value Leaders (2022)

Team Rank	Player	BV [bat]	(-) BV [pitch]	(=) OBV
1	Tarik Skubal	0	-30	30
2	Andrew Chafin	0	-20	20
2	Joe Jimenez	0	-20	20
4	Matt Manning	0	-19	19
5	Jason Foley	0	-12	12
6	Jose Cisnero	0	-11	11
7	Drew Carlton	0	-10	10
7	Michael Fulmer	0	-10	10
9	Kerry Carpenter	9	0	9
10	Alex Lange	0	-8	8
10	Joey Wentz	0	-8	8

Fan Support in Past 10 Seasons (2013-2022)

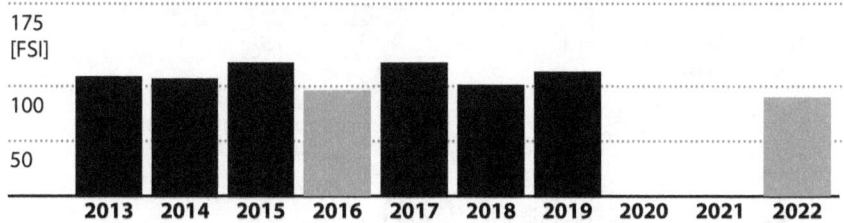

Year	Team	Attendance	W	Att:W	FSI
2013	Detroit Tigers	3,083,397	93	33,155	108.9
2014	Detroit Tigers	2,917,209	90	32,413	106.8
2015	Detroit Tigers	2,726,048	74	36,838	121.3
2016	Detroit Tigers	2,493,859	86	28,998	96.2
2017	Detroit Tigers	2,321,599	64	36,275	121.3
2018	Detroit Tigers	1,856,970	64	29,015	101.2
2019	Detroit Tigers	1,501,430	47	31,945	113.3
2022	Detroit Tigers	1,575,544	66	23,872	89.9

Extreme Games for Batters (2022)

Stat	Team Total	Individual Leader	G
3+ H	67	Harold Castro	15
2+ HR	3	Eric Haase, Harold Castro, Jeimer Candelario	1
5+ RBI	1	Harold Castro	1
0 H in 5+ AB	24	Riley Greene	5
4+ SO	6	Riley Greene	2

Extreme Games for Pitchers (2022)

Stat	Team Total	Individual Leader	G
0-2 ER in 7+ IP	8	Matt Manning	3
10+ SO	1	Tarik Skubal	1
0 BR in SV	13	Gregory Soto	11
10+ BR	18	Eduardo Rodriguez	4
1+ ER in SV	3	Gregory Soto	3

Predictions for Coming Season (2023)

Group	Next W	Next L	Next Pct.	WS	LC	PQ
10 closest matches (avg. W-L)	74.5	87.5	.460	0	0	1
25 closest matches (avg. W-L)	71.7	89.5	.445	1	1	3
50 closest matches (avg. W-L)	70.6	87.8	.446	1	1	3

25 Closest Matches (2023)

Rank	Team	Next	W	L	Pct.	WS	LC	PQ
1	White Sox (2015-2017)	2018	62	100	.383	—	—	—
2	Rockies (2012-2014)	2015	68	94	.420	—	—	—
3	Royals (2016-2018)	2019	59	103	.364	—	—	—
4	Twins (1995-1997)	1998	70	92	.432	—	—	—
5	Nationals (2004-2006)	2007	73	89	.451	—	—	—
6	Reds (2001-2003)	2004	76	86	.469	—	—	—
7	Padres (1975-1977)	1978	84	78	.519	—	—	—
8	Reds (2016-2018)	2019	75	87	.463	—	—	—
9	Royals (2010-2012)	2013	86	76	.531	—	—	—
10	Indians (2010-2012)	2013	92	70	.568	—	—	X
11	Phillies (1998-2000)	2001	86	76	.531	—	—	—
12	Orioles (2006-2008)	2009	64	98	.395	—	—	—
13	Twins (1984-1986)	1987	85	77	.525	X	X	X
14	Rangers (1982-1984)	1985	62	99	.385	—	—	—
15	Devil Rays (1998-2000)	2001	62	100	.383	—	—	—
16	Braves (1985-1987)	1988	54	106	.338	—	—	—
17	Pirates (2003-2005)	2006	67	95	.414	—	—	—
18	Mets (2001-2003)	2004	71	91	.438	—	—	—
19	Rockies (2002-2004)	2005	67	95	.414	—	—	—
20	Padres (1979-1981)	1982	81	81	.500	—	—	—
21	Royals (1999-2001)	2002	62	100	.383	—	—	—
22	Padres (2000-2002)	2003	64	98	.395	—	—	—
23	Angels (1992-1994)	1995	78	67	.538	—	—	—
24	Cubs (1995-1997)	1998	90	73	.552	—	—	X
25	Tigers (1999-2001)	2002	55	106	.342	—	—	—

HOUSTON ASTROS

Past 10 Seasons (2013-2022)

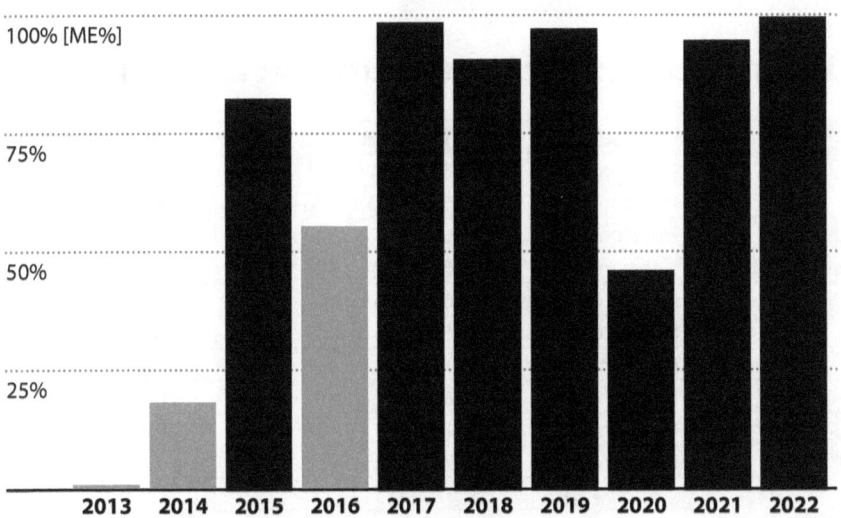

Year	Team	W	L	Pct.	Post	TS	ME%
2013	Houston Astros	51	111	.315	—	10.531	0.8%
2014	Houston Astros	70	92	.432	—	29.708	18.2%
2015	Houston Astros	86	76	.531	P	62.133	82.4%
2016	Houston Astros	84	78	.519	—	48.724	55.4%
2017	Houston Astros	101	61	.623	WLP	84.140	98.5%
2018	Houston Astros	103	59	.636	P	69.512	90.6%
2019	Houston Astros	107	55	.660	LP	80.425	97.1%
2020	Houston Astros	29	31	.483	P	43.887	46.0%
2021	Houston Astros	95	67	.586	LP	74.809	94.6%
2022	Houston Astros	106	56	.654	WLP	87.893	99.5%

Best Seasons of Modern Era (1962-2022)

Year	Team	W	L	Pct.	Post	TS	ME%
2022	Houston Astros	106	56	.654	WLP	87.893	99.5%
2017	Houston Astros	101	61	.623	WLP	84.140	98.5%
2019	Houston Astros	107	55	.660	LP	80.425	97.1%
2021	Houston Astros	95	67	.586	LP	74.809	94.6%
2005	Houston Astros	89	73	.549	LP	72.466	92.7%
1998	Houston Astros	102	60	.630	P	72.465	92.7%
2018	Houston Astros	103	59	.636	P	69.512	90.6%
1999	Houston Astros	97	65	.599	P	65.886	87.5%
1986	Houston Astros	96	66	.593	P	64.111	85.4%
1994	Houston Astros	66	49	.574	—	64.003	85.2%

Worst Seasons of Modern Era (1962-2022)

Year	Team	W	L	Pct.	Post	TS	ME%
2013	Houston Astros	51	111	.315	—	10.531	0.8%
2011	Houston Astros	56	106	.346	—	11.311	1.0%
2012	Houston Astros	55	107	.340	—	13.628	1.6%
1991	Houston Astros	65	97	.401	—	21.015	6.0%
1964	Houston Colt .45s	66	96	.407	—	23.309	8.4%
1963	Houston Colt .45s	66	96	.407	—	25.536	10.9%
1968	Houston Astros	72	90	.444	—	25.570	11.0%
1965	Houston Astros	65	97	.401	—	28.149	15.0%
2007	Houston Astros	73	89	.451	—	28.976	16.7%
2014	Houston Astros	70	92	.432	—	29.708	18.2%

Season Breakdown (2022)

Category	W	L	Pct.	R	RA	R/G	RA/G
Overall record in 2022	106	56	.654	737	518	4.55	3.20
Home games	55	26	.679	368	253	4.54	3.12
Away games	51	30	.630	369	265	4.56	3.27
First half of 2022 season	53	28	.654	363	273	4.48	3.37
Second half of 2022 season	53	28	.654	374	245	4.62	3.02
Against first-place teams	10	7	.588	64	55	3.76	3.24
Against playoff teams	35	20	.636	223	168	4.05	3.05
Against non-playoff teams	71	36	.664	514	350	4.80	3.27

Season as Nine-Inning Game (2022)

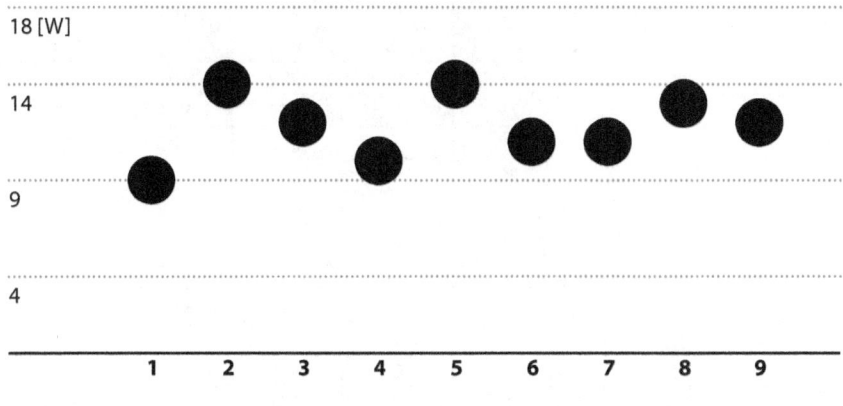

Result	1	2	3	4	5	6	7	8	9	Total
Wins	9	14	12	10	14	11	11	13	12	106
Losses	9	4	6	8	4	7	7	5	6	56

Scoring by Game (2022)

Runs Scored	G	W	L	Pct.	R/G	RA/G
Overall record	162	106	56	.654	4.55	3.20
0	11	0	11	.000	0.00	4.00
1	14	1	13	.071	1.00	4.57
2	20	8	12	.400	2.00	3.05
3	27	17	10	.630	3.00	2.78
4	21	15	6	.714	4.00	3.14
5	21	19	2	.905	5.00	2.14
6	11	9	2	.818	6.00	3.64
7	9	9	0	1.000	7.00	3.67
8	8	8	0	1.000	8.00	2.63
9	7	7	0	1.000	9.00	2.71
10 or more	13	13	0	1.000	12.08	3.85

Scoring Allowed by Game (2022)

Runs Allowed	G	W	L	Pct.	R/G	RA/G
Overall record	162	106	56	.654	4.55	3.20
0	18	18	0	1.000	5.00	0.00
1	27	26	1	.963	4.41	1.00
2	30	24	6	.800	4.00	2.00
3	28	20	8	.714	5.11	3.00
4	13	6	7	.462	5.23	4.00
5	14	6	8	.429	5.36	5.00
6	14	2	12	.143	2.57	6.00
7	13	3	10	.231	4.54	7.00
8	2	0	2	.000	4.50	8.00
9	0	0	0	—	—	—
10 or more	3	1	2	.333	6.00	11.33

Margins (2022)

Category	Margin	G	W	L	Pct.	GShr	WShr
Overall record	—	162	106	56	.654	—	—
Close	1 or 2 runs	72	47	25	.653	44.4%	44.3%
Medium	3 or 4 runs	42	24	18	.571	25.9%	22.6%
Distant	5 or more runs	48	35	13	.729	29.6%	33.0%

Individual Scoring Leaders (2022)

Team Rank	Batter	R	(+) RBI	(-) HR	(=) SC
1	Alex Bregman	93	93	23	163
2	Yordan Alvarez	95	97	37	155
3	Kyle Tucker	71	107	30	148
4	Jose Altuve	103	57	28	132
5	Jeremy Pena	72	63	22	113
6	Yuli Gurriel	53	53	8	98
7	Chas McCormick	47	44	14	77
8	Martin Maldonado	40	45	15	70
9	Aledmys Diaz	35	38	12	61
10	Michael Brantley	28	26	5	49

Team Ratings (2022)

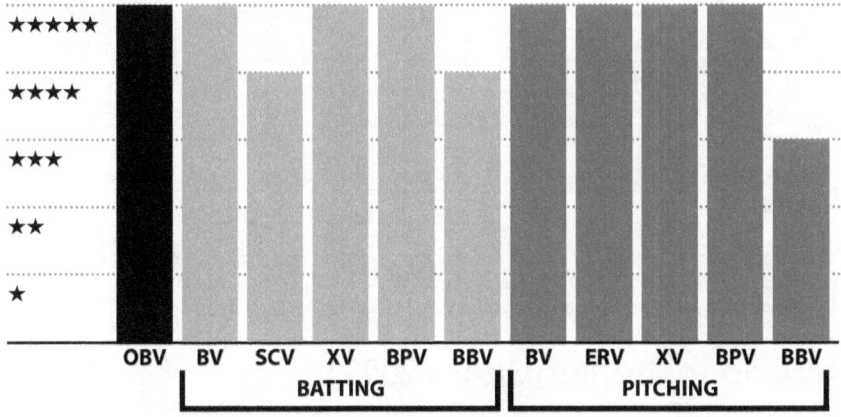

Quality	Type	Indicator	Value	Rating
Overall performance	Overall	OBV	679	★★★★★
Base production	Batting	BV	204	★★★★★
Run production	Batting	SCV	58	★★★★
Power hitting	Batting	XV	129	★★★★★
Contact hitting	Batting	BPV	171	★★★★★
Batting eye	Batting	BBV	32	★★★★
Base prevention	Pitching	BV	-475	★★★★★
Run prevention	Pitching	ERV	-171	★★★★★
Power prevention	Pitching	XV	-168	★★★★★
Strikeout pitching	Pitching	BPV	-202	★★★★★
Control pitching	Pitching	BBV	-11	★★★

Team Batting Stats (2022)

Stat	Number	Div Rank	Lg Rank	MLB Rank	MLB Best
R	737	1	3	8	847 (Dodgers)
H	1,341	1	6	13	1,464 (Blue Jays)
HR	214	1	2	4	254 (Yankees)
BPO	.708	1	3	6	.764 (Dodgers)
BA	.248	1	5	12	.264 (Blue Jays)
OBP	.319	1	4	7	.333 (Dodgers)
SA	.424	1	3	5	.443 (Braves)

Division: AL West, 5 teams. **League:** American, 15 teams. **MLB:** 30 teams.

Team Pitching Stats (2022)

Stat	Number	Div Rank	Lg Rank	MLB Rank	MLB Best
ERA	2.90	1	1	2	2.80 (Dodgers)
SO	1,524	1	1	4	1,565 (Mets)
BB	458	2	7	10	384 (Rays)
BPO	.551	1	1	1	.551 (Astros)
BA	.212	1	1	2	.209 (Dodgers)
OBP	.281	1	1	2	.273 (Dodgers)
SA	.332	1	1	1	.332 (Astros)

Division: AL West, 5 teams. **League:** American, 15 teams. **MLB:** 30 teams.

Individual Batting Stats (2022)

Batter	PA	BPO	BA	OBP	SA	ISO	CT	EY
Jose Altuve	604	.979	.300	.387	.533	.233	.835	.106
Yordan Alvarez	561	1.098	.306	.406	.613	.306	.774	.125
Alex Bregman	656	.821	.259	.366	.454	.195	.859	.131
Aledmys Diaz	327	.606	.243	.287	.403	.161	.826	.055
Yuli Gurriel	584	.566	.242	.288	.360	.117	.866	.051
Martin Maldonado	379	.534	.186	.248	.352	.166	.663	.058
Chas McCormick	407	.707	.245	.332	.407	.162	.705	.113
Jeremy Pena	558	.664	.253	.289	.426	.173	.741	.039
Kyle Tucker	609	.824	.257	.330	.478	.221	.825	.091

Individual Pitching Stats for Starters (2022)

Pitcher	IP	BPO	ERA	BA	SA	ISO	CT	EY
Luis Garcia	157.1	.619	3.72	.222	.399	.177	.733	.073
Cristian Javier	148.2	.517	2.54	.170	.305	.135	.630	.089
Jose Urquidy	164.1	.686	3.94	.244	.438	.194	.787	.056
Framber Valdez	201.1	.520	2.82	.223	.305	.082	.740	.081
Justin Verlander	175.0	.418	1.75	.186	.270	.085	.704	.044

Individual Pitching Stats for Relievers (2022)

Pitcher	GR	BPO	ERA	BA	SA	ISO	CT	EY
Bryan Abreu	55	.533	1.94	.207	.267	.060	.594	.105
Phil Maton	67	.693	3.84	.237	.408	.171	.702	.079
Rafael Montero	71	.483	2.37	.193	.267	.074	.700	.078
Hector Neris	70	.510	3.72	.205	.305	.100	.669	.065
Ryan Pressly	50	.425	2.98	.181	.277	.096	.608	.071
Ryne Stanek	59	.524	1.15	.188	.257	.068	.675	.135

Best Stats on Team (2022)

Stat	Batter	Number
2B	Yuli Gurriel	40
3B	Yordan Alvarez, Jeremy Pena, Chas McCormick, Jake Meyers, Jose Siri	2
BA	Yordan Alvarez	.306
BB	Alex Bregman	87
BBV	Alex Bregman	34
BPO	Yordan Alvarez	1.098
BPV	Yuli Gurriel	63
BV	Yordan Alvarez	152
CT	Yuli Gurriel	.866
EY	Alex Bregman	.131
H	Jose Altuve	158
HR	Yordan Alvarez	37
ISO	Yordan Alvarez	.306
OBP	Yordan Alvarez	.406
R	Jose Altuve	103
RBI	Kyle Tucker	107
SA	Yordan Alvarez	.613
SB	Kyle Tucker	25
SC	Alex Bregman	163
SCV	Yordan Alvarez	46
SE	Yordan Alvarez	.276
XV	Yordan Alvarez	72

Stat	Pitcher	Number
BA	Cristian Javier	.170
BBV	Justin Verlander	-24
BPO-R	Ryan Pressly	.425
BPO-S	Justin Verlander	.418
BPV	Cristian Javier	-63
BV	Justin Verlander	-127
CT	Cristian Javier	.630
ERA-R	Ryne Stanek	1.15
ERA-S	Justin Verlander	1.75
ERV	Justin Verlander	-43
EY	Justin Verlander	.044
GR	Rafael Montero	71
GS	Framber Valdez	31
IP	Framber Valdez	201.1
ISO	Framber Valdez	.082
OBP	Justin Verlander	.227
SA	Justin Verlander	.270
SO	Framber Valdez, Cristian Javier	194
SV	Ryan Pressly	33
W	Justin Verlander	18
XV	Framber Valdez	-52

Worst Stats on Team (2022)

Stat	Batter	Number
BA	Martin Maldonado	.186
BBV	Jeremy Pena	-22
BPO	Martin Maldonado	.534
BPV	Martin Maldonado	-30
BV	Yuli Gurriel	-40
CT	Martin Maldonado	.663
EY	Jeremy Pena	.039
ISO	Yuli Gurriel	.117
OBP	Martin Maldonado	.248
SA	Martin Maldonado	.352
SCV	Yuli Gurriel	-16
SE	Yuli Gurriel	.168
SO	Jeremy Pena	135
XV	Yuli Gurriel	-19

Stat	Pitcher	Number
BA	Jose Urquidy	.244
BB	Framber Valdez	67
BBV	Ryne Stanek	12
BPO-R	Phil Maton	.693
BPO-S	Jose Urquidy	.686
BPV	Jose Urquidy	23
BV	Jose Urquidy	13
CT	Jose Urquidy	.787
ERA-R	Phil Maton	3.84
ERA-S	Jose Urquidy	3.94
ERV	Pedro Baez, Ronel Blanco	2
EY	Cristian Javier	.089
ISO	Jose Urquidy	.194
L	Cristian Javier	9
OBP	Framber Valdez	.296
SA	Jose Urquidy	.438
XV	Jose Urquidy	26

Overall Base Value Leaders (2022)

Team Rank	Player	BV [bat]	(-) BV [pitch]	(=) OBV
1	Yordan Alvarez	152	0	152
2	Justin Verlander	0	-127	127
3	Jose Altuve	123	0	123
4	Framber Valdez	0	-85	85
5	Alex Bregman	70	0	70
6	Kyle Tucker	69	0	69
7	Cristian Javier	0	-64	64
8	Rafael Montero	0	-37	37
9	Ryan Pressly	0	-34	34
10	Hector Neris	0	-29	29

Fan Support in Past 10 Seasons (2013-2022)

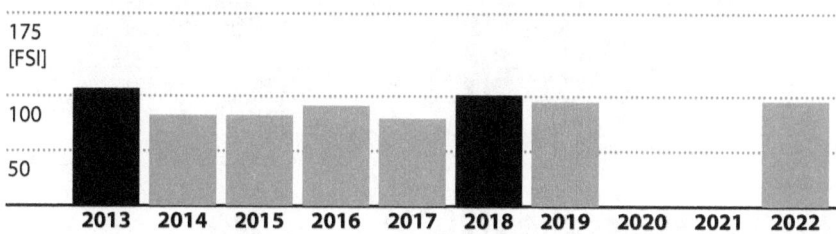

Year	Team	Attendance	W	Att:W	FSI
2013	Houston Astros	1,651,883	51	32,390	106.4
2014	Houston Astros	1,751,829	70	25,026	82.5
2015	Houston Astros	2,153,585	86	25,042	82.5
2016	Houston Astros	2,306,623	84	27,460	91.1
2017	Houston Astros	2,403,671	101	23,799	79.6
2018	Houston Astros	2,980,549	103	28,937	101.0
2019	Houston Astros	2,857,367	107	26,704	94.7
2022	Houston Astros	2,688,998	106	25,368	95.5

Extreme Games for Batters (2022)

Stat	Team Total	Individual Leader	G
3+ H	80	Jose Altuve	15
2+ HR	13	Yordan Alvarez	5
5+ RBI	4	Alex Bregman, Chas McCormick, Kyle Tucker, Trey Mancini	1
0 H in 5+ AB	31	Jeremy Pena	5
4+ SO	2	Chas McCormick, Jeremy Pena	1

Extreme Games for Pitchers (2022)

Stat	Team Total	Individual Leader	G
0-2 ER in 7+ IP	34	Framber Valdez, Justin Verlander	10
10+ SO	13	Justin Verlander	4
0 BR in SV	22	Ryan Pressly	14
10+ BR	24	Framber Valdez	9
1+ ER in SV	9	Ryan Pressly	5

Predictions for Coming Season (2023)

Group	Next W	Next L	Next Pct.	WS	LC	PQ
10 closest matches (avg. W-L)	89.9	67.4	.572	1	2	6
25 closest matches (avg. W-L)	91.9	68.2	.574	5	7	15
50 closest matches (avg. W-L)	88.7	66.7	.571	8	14	31

25 Closest Matches (2023)

Rank	Team	Next	W	L	Pct.	WS	LC	PQ
1	Indians (1993-1995)	1996	99	62	.615	—	—	X
2	Athletics (1987-1989)	1990	103	59	.636	—	X	X
3	Dodgers (1976-1978)	1979	79	83	.488	—	—	—
4	Indians (2015-2017)	2018	91	71	.562	—	—	X
5	Mariners (1999-2001)	2002	93	69	.574	—	—	—
6	Cubs (2014-2016)	2017	92	70	.568	—	—	X
7	Mets (1984-1986)	1987	92	70	.568	—	—	—
8	Red Sox (2002-2004)	2005	95	67	.586	—	—	X
9	Yankees (1975-1977)	1978	100	63	.613	X	X	X
10	Blue Jays (1991-1993)	1994	55	60	.478	—	—	—
11	Braves (1990-1992)	1993	104	58	.642	—	—	X
12	Orioles (1981-1983)	1984	85	77	.525	—	—	—
13	Rangers (2009-2011)	2012	93	69	.574	—	—	X
14	Yankees (1995-1997)	1998	114	48	.704	X	X	X
15	Yankees (1996-1998)	1999	98	64	.605	X	X	X
16	Braves (1994-1996)	1997	101	61	.623	—	—	X
17	Braves (1993-1995)	1996	96	66	.593	—	X	X
18	Reds (1974-1976)	1977	88	74	.543	—	—	—
19	Cardinals (2003-2005)	2006	83	78	.516	X	X	X
20	Dodgers (2016-2018)	2019	106	56	.654	—	—	X
21	Blue Jays (1990-1992)	1993	95	67	.586	X	X	X
22	Tigers (1982-1984)	1985	84	77	.522	—	—	—
23	Yankees (1979-1981)	1982	79	83	.488	—	—	—
24	Dodgers (1979-1981)	1982	88	74	.543	—	—	—
25	Athletics (1988-1990)	1991	84	78	.519	—	—	—

KANSAS CITY ROYALS

Past 10 Seasons (2013-2022)

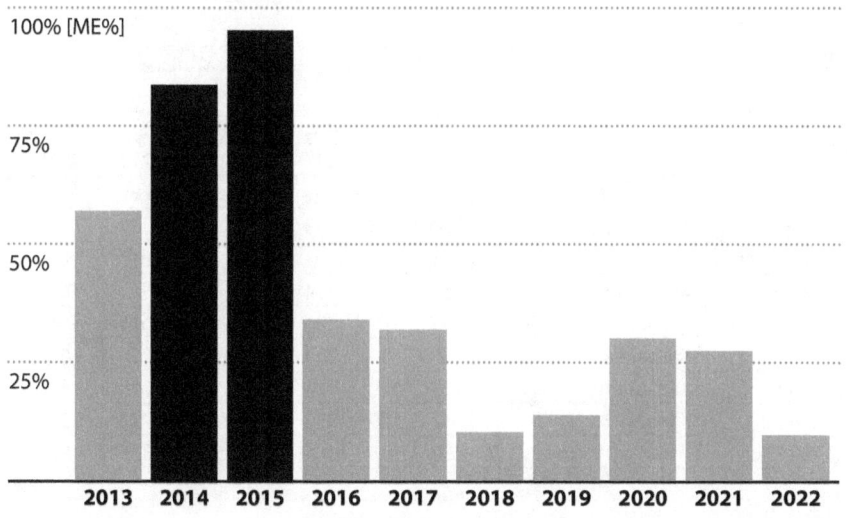

Year	Team	W	L	Pct.	Post	TS	ME%
2013	Kansas City Royals	86	76	.531	—	49.705	57.0%
2014	Kansas City Royals	89	73	.549	LP	62.588	83.6%
2015	Kansas City Royals	95	67	.586	WLP	75.761	95.2%
2016	Kansas City Royals	81	81	.500	—	38.442	34.0%
2017	Kansas City Royals	80	82	.494	—	37.495	31.9%
2018	Kansas City Royals	58	104	.358	—	25.256	10.3%
2019	Kansas City Royals	59	103	.364	—	27.329	13.9%
2020	Kansas City Royals	26	34	.433	—	36.579	30.1%
2021	Kansas City Royals	74	88	.457	—	35.262	27.4%
2022	Kansas City Royals	65	97	.401	—	24.678	9.6%

Best Seasons of Modern Era (1969-2022)

Year	Team	W	L	Pct.	Post	TS	ME%
2015	Kansas City Royals	95	67	.586	WLP	75.761	95.2%
1980	Kansas City Royals	97	65	.599	LP	72.071	92.4%
1985	Kansas City Royals	91	71	.562	WLP	71.710	92.1%
1977	Kansas City Royals	102	60	.630	P	68.760	90.3%
2014	Kansas City Royals	89	73	.549	LP	62.588	83.6%
1976	Kansas City Royals	90	72	.556	P	61.588	81.5%
1989	Kansas City Royals	92	70	.568	—	60.948	79.9%
1978	Kansas City Royals	92	70	.568	P	59.697	77.9%
1975	Kansas City Royals	91	71	.562	—	58.692	76.4%
1982	Kansas City Royals	90	72	.556	—	57.023	73.7%

Worst Seasons of Modern Era (1969-2022)

Year	Team	W	L	Pct.	Post	TS	ME%
2005	Kansas City Royals	56	106	.346	—	10.715	0.9%
2006	Kansas City Royals	62	100	.383	—	14.785	1.8%
2004	Kansas City Royals	58	104	.358	—	14.882	1.9%
2009	Kansas City Royals	65	97	.401	—	21.817	6.9%
2010	Kansas City Royals	67	95	.414	—	23.943	9.2%
2022	Kansas City Royals	65	97	.401	—	24.678	9.6%
2018	Kansas City Royals	58	104	.358	—	25.256	10.3%
2007	Kansas City Royals	69	93	.426	—	27.078	13.5%
2002	Kansas City Royals	62	100	.383	—	27.221	13.7%
2019	Kansas City Royals	59	103	.364	—	27.329	13.9%

Season Breakdown (2022)

Category	W	L	Pct.	R	RA	R/G	RA/G
Overall record in 2022	65	97	.401	640	810	3.95	5.00
Home games	39	42	.481	335	399	4.14	4.93
Away games	26	55	.321	305	411	3.77	5.07
First half of 2022 season	30	51	.370	318	420	3.93	5.19
Second half of 2022 season	35	46	.432	322	390	3.98	4.81
Against first-place teams	12	28	.300	141	233	3.53	5.83
Against playoff teams	20	43	.317	239	365	3.79	5.79
Against non-playoff teams	45	54	.455	401	445	4.05	4.49

Season as Nine-Inning Game (2022)

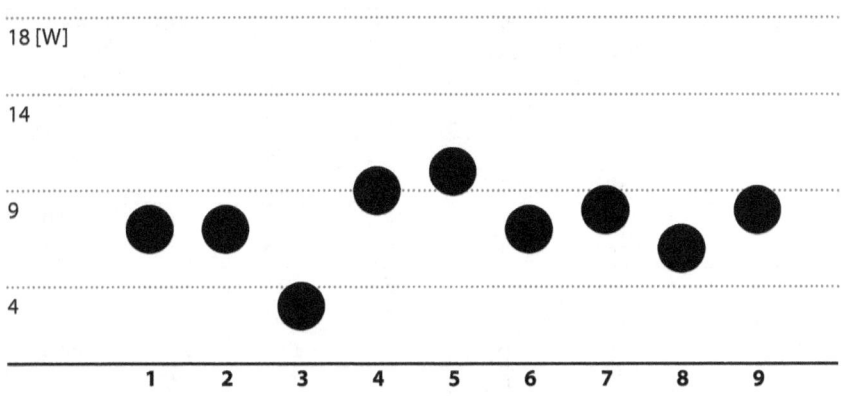

Result	1	2	3	4	5	6	7	8	9	Total
Wins	7	7	3	9	10	7	8	6	8	65
Losses	11	11	15	9	8	11	10	12	10	97

Scoring by Game (2022)

Runs Scored	G	W	L	Pct.	R/G	RA/G
Overall record	162	65	97	.401	3.95	5.00
0	16	0	16	.000	0.00	4.63
1	13	1	12	.077	1.00	4.77
2	24	6	18	.250	2.00	4.58
3	31	10	21	.323	3.00	5.65
4	19	7	12	.368	4.00	4.95
5	20	11	9	.550	5.00	4.80
6	10	7	3	.700	6.00	3.70
7	15	9	6	.600	7.00	5.67
8	6	6	0	1.000	8.00	3.83
9	2	2	0	1.000	9.00	3.50
10 or more	6	6	0	1.000	13.17	7.83

Scoring Allowed by Game (2022)

Runs Allowed	G	W	L	Pct.	R/G	RA/G
Overall record	162	65	97	.401	3.95	5.00
0	9	9	0	1.000	4.56	0.00
1	20	17	3	.850	3.35	1.00
2	17	14	3	.824	4.41	2.00
3	15	9	6	.600	4.00	3.00
4	24	7	17	.292	2.83	4.00
5	10	2	8	.200	4.10	5.00
6	14	1	13	.071	3.79	6.00
7	18	3	15	.167	4.61	7.00
8	8	0	8	.000	2.75	8.00
9	7	0	7	.000	3.57	9.00
10 or more	20	3	17	.150	5.25	11.40

Margins (2022)

Category	Margin	G	W	L	Pct.	GShr	WShr
Overall record	—	162	65	97	.401	—	—
Close	1 or 2 runs	72	33	39	.458	44.4%	50.8%
Medium	3 or 4 runs	48	20	28	.417	29.6%	30.8%
Distant	5 or more runs	42	12	30	.286	25.9%	18.5%

Individual Scoring Leaders (2022)

Team Rank	Batter	R	(+) RBI	(-) HR	(=) SC
1	Bobby Witt	82	80	20	142
2	MJ Melendez	57	62	18	101
2	Salvador Perez	48	76	23	101
4	Whit Merrifield	51	42	6	87
5	Michael A. Taylor	49	43	9	83
6	Hunter Dozier	51	41	12	80
7	Andrew Benintendi	40	39	3	76
8	Nicky Lopez	51	20	0	71
9	Kyle Isbel	32	28	5	55
10	Vinnie Pasquantino	25	26	10	41

Team Ratings (2022)

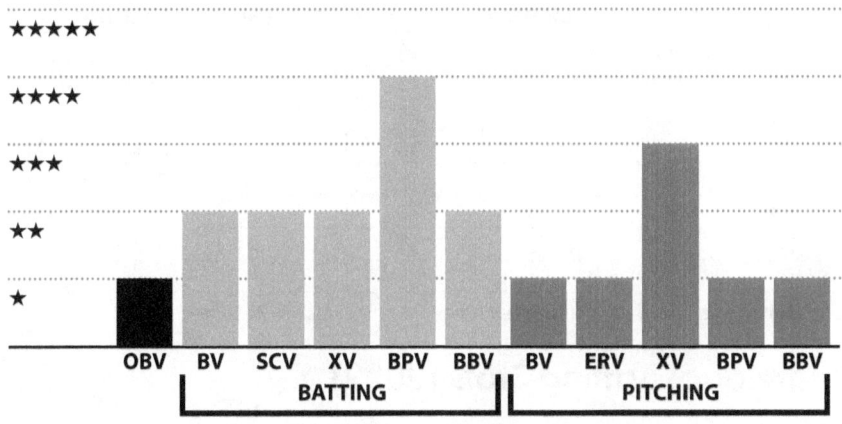

Quality	Type	Indicator	Value	Rating
Overall performance	Overall	OBV	-434	★
Base production	Batting	BV	-104	★★
Run production	Batting	SCV	-57	★★
Power hitting	Batting	XV	-90	★★
Contact hitting	Batting	BPV	70	★★★★
Batting eye	Batting	BBV	-22	★★
Base prevention	Pitching	BV	330	★
Run prevention	Pitching	ERV	117	★
Power prevention	Pitching	XV	6	★★★
Strikeout pitching	Pitching	BPV	183	★
Control pitching	Pitching	BBV	80	★

Team Batting Stats (2022)

Stat	Number	Div Rank	Lg Rank	MLB Rank	MLB Best
R	640	4	12	24	847 (Dodgers)
H	1,327	4	7	14	1,464 (Blue Jays)
HR	138	3	12	26	254 (Yankees)
BPO	.636	3	11	22	.764 (Dodgers)
BA	.244	4	7	14	.264 (Blue Jays)
OBP	.306	4	10	21	.333 (Dodgers)
SA	.380	4	12	23	.443 (Braves)

Division: AL Central, 5 teams. **League:** American, 15 teams. **MLB:** 30 teams.

Team Pitching Stats (2022)

Stat	Number	Div Rank	Lg Rank	MLB Rank	MLB Best
ERA	4.70	5	15	27	2.80 (Dodgers)
SO	1,191	5	15	28	1,565 (Mets)
BB	589	5	15	29	384 (Rays)
BPO	.738	5	15	27	.551 (Astros)
BA	.271	5	15	29	.209 (Dodgers)
OBP	.346	5	15	30	.273 (Dodgers)
SA	.425	5	14	26	.332 (Astros)

Division: AL Central, 5 teams. **League:** American, 15 teams. **MLB:** 30 teams.

Individual Batting Stats (2022)

Batter	PA	BPO	BA	OBP	SA	ISO	CT	EY
Andrew Benintendi	390	.749	.320	.387	.398	.078	.850	.100
Hunter Dozier	500	.596	.236	.292	.387	.152	.729	.068
Nicky Lopez	480	.490	.227	.281	.273	.046	.856	.060
MJ Melendez	534	.691	.217	.313	.393	.176	.715	.122
Whit Merrifield	420	.605	.240	.290	.352	.112	.841	.071
Salvador Perez	473	.683	.254	.292	.465	.211	.755	.034
Michael A. Taylor	456	.602	.254	.313	.357	.104	.737	.077
Bobby Witt	632	.697	.254	.294	.428	.174	.772	.044

Individual Pitching Stats for Starters (2022)

Pitcher	IP	BPO	ERA	BA	SA	ISO	CT	EY
Kris Bubic	129.0	.839	5.58	.306	.475	.169	.784	.107
Zack Greinke	137.0	.659	3.68	.286	.417	.131	.867	.046
Jonathan Heasley	104.0	.810	5.28	.267	.478	.210	.827	.101
Brad Keller	139.2	.726	5.09	.277	.427	.150	.816	.091
Daniel Lynch	131.2	.786	5.13	.290	.456	.166	.772	.084
Brady Singer	153.1	.589	3.23	.246	.378	.132	.736	.056

Individual Pitching Stats for Relievers (2022)

Pitcher	GR	BPO	ERA	BA	SA	ISO	CT	EY
Scott Barlow	69	.522	2.18	.198	.324	.126	.706	.073
Taylor Clarke	47	.644	4.04	.260	.427	.167	.750	.039
Dylan Coleman	68	.597	2.78	.194	.306	.112	.707	.125
Jose Cuas	47	.796	3.58	.264	.372	.108	.770	.124
Amir Garrett	60	.603	4.96	.177	.241	.063	.690	.163
Collin Snider	42	.770	6.55	.301	.444	.143	.835	.099
Josh Staumont	42	.866	6.45	.261	.423	.162	.697	.165

Best Stats on Team (2022)

Stat	Batter	Number
2B	Bobby Witt	31
3B	Bobby Witt	6
BA	Andrew Benintendi	.320
BB	MJ Melendez	66
BBV	MJ Melendez	23
BPO	Andrew Benintendi	.749
BPV	Nicky Lopez	46
BV	Vinnie Pasquantino	32
CT	Nicky Lopez	.856
EY	MJ Melendez	.122
H	Bobby Witt	150
HR	Salvador Perez	23
ISO	Salvador Perez	.211
OBP	Andrew Benintendi	.387
R	Bobby Witt	82
RBI	Bobby Witt	80
SA	Salvador Perez	.465
SB	Bobby Witt	30
SC	Bobby Witt	142
SCV	Bobby Witt	19
SE	Bobby Witt	.225
XV	Salvador Perez	26

Stat	Pitcher	Number
BA	Brady Singer	.246
BBV	Zack Greinke	-19
BPO-R	Scott Barlow	.522
BPO-S	Brady Singer	.589
BPV	Scott Barlow	-12
BV	Brady Singer	-33
CT	Brady Singer	.736
ERA-R	Scott Barlow	2.18
ERA-S	Brady Singer	3.23
ERV	Scott Barlow	-15
EY	Zack Greinke	.046
GR	Scott Barlow	69
GS	Kris Bubic, Daniel Lynch	27
IP	Brady Singer	153.1
ISO	Zack Greinke	.131
OBP	Brady Singer	.301
SA	Brady Singer	.378
SO	Brady Singer	150
SV	Scott Barlow	24
W	Brady Singer	10
XV	Amir Garrett	-14

Worst Stats on Team (2022)

Stat	Batter	Number
BA	MJ Melendez	.217
BBV	Bobby Witt	-22
BPO	Nicky Lopez	.490
BPV	Nick Pratto	-27
BV	Nicky Lopez	-61
CT	MJ Melendez	.715
EY	Salvador Perez	.034
ISO	Nicky Lopez	.046
OBP	Nicky Lopez	.281
SA	Nicky Lopez	.273
SCV	Nicky Lopez	-23
SE	Nicky Lopez	.148
SO	Bobby Witt	135
XV	Nicky Lopez	-46

Stat	Pitcher	Number
BA	Kris Bubic	.306
BB	Kris Bubic	63
BBV	Kris Bubic	17
BPO-R	Josh Staumont	.866
BPO-S	Kris Bubic	.839
BPV	Zack Greinke	64
BV	Kris Bubic	69
CT	Zack Greinke	.867
ERA-R	Collin Snider	6.55
ERA-S	Kris Bubic	5.58
ERV	Kris Bubic	23
EY	Kris Bubic	.107
ISO	Jonathan Heasley	.210
L	Brad Keller	14
OBP	Kris Bubic	.381
SA	Jonathan Heasley	.478
XV	Jonathan Heasley	24

Overall Base Value Leaders (2022)

Team Rank	Player	BV [bat]	(-) BV [pitch]	(=) OBV
1	Brady Singer	0	-33	33
2	Vinnie Pasquantino	32	0	32
3	Scott Barlow	0	-31	31
4	Andrew Benintendi	22	0	22
5	Bobby Witt	17	0	17
6	Dylan Coleman	0	-13	13
7	Nate Eaton	12	0	12
8	MJ Melendez	11	0	11
9	Drew Waters	9	0	9
10	Amir Garrett	0	-8	8
10	Salvador Perez	8	0	8

Fan Support in Past 10 Seasons (2013-2022)

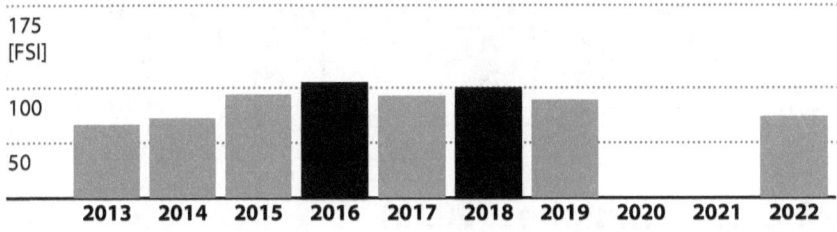

Year	Team	Attendance	W	Att:W	FSI
2013	Kansas City Royals	1,750,754	86	20,358	66.9
2014	Kansas City Royals	1,956,482	89	21,983	72.4
2015	Kansas City Royals	2,708,549	95	28,511	93.9
2016	Kansas City Royals	2,557,712	81	31,577	104.8
2017	Kansas City Royals	2,220,370	80	27,755	92.8
2018	Kansas City Royals	1,665,107	58	28,709	100.2
2019	Kansas City Royals	1,479,659	59	25,079	88.9
2022	Kansas City Royals	1,277,686	65	19,657	74.0

Extreme Games for Batters (2022)

Stat	Team Total	Individual Leader	G
3+ H	60	Andrew Benintendi	9
2+ HR	6	Salvador Perez	2
5+ RBI	2	Carlos Santana, MJ Melendez	1
0 H in 5+ AB	29	Salvador Perez	7
4+ SO	7	Adalberto Mondesi, Bobby Witt, Drew Waters, Edward Olivares, Nick Pratto, Salvador Perez, Whit Merrifield	1

Extreme Games for Pitchers (2022)

Stat	Team Total	Individual Leader	G
0-2 ER in 7+ IP	16	Brady Singer	7
10+ SO	3	Brady Singer	2
0 BR in SV	18	Scott Barlow	12
10+ BR	40	Kris Bubic	10
1+ ER in SV	2	Scott Barlow	2

Predictions for Coming Season (2023)

Group	Next W	Next L	Next Pct.	WS	LC	PQ
10 closest matches (avg. W-L)	71.1	90.9	.439	1	1	1
25 closest matches (avg. W-L)	74.3	87.7	.459	1	1	3
50 closest matches (avg. W-L)	73.3	86.3	.459	1	1	5

25 Closest Matches (2023)

Rank	Team	Next	W	L	Pct.	WS	LC	PQ
1	Royals (2016-2018)	2019	59	103	.364	—	—	—
2	Pirates (2003-2005)	2006	67	95	.414	—	—	—
3	Phillies (1998-2000)	2001	86	76	.531	—	—	—
4	Mets (2001-2003)	2004	71	91	.438	—	—	—
5	Brewers (1974-1976)	1977	67	95	.414	—	—	—
6	Padres (2000-2002)	2003	64	98	.395	—	—	—
7	Twins (1984-1986)	1987	85	77	.525	X	X	X
8	White Sox (2015-2017)	2018	62	100	.383	—	—	—
9	Padres (1975-1977)	1978	84	78	.519	—	—	—
10	Padres (2015-2017)	2018	66	96	.407	—	—	—
11	Padres (1985-1987)	1988	83	78	.516	—	—	—
12	Orioles (2004-2006)	2007	69	93	.426	—	—	—
13	Brewers (1999-2001)	2002	56	106	.346	—	—	—
14	Phillies (1994-1996)	1997	68	94	.420	—	—	—
15	Mariners (1984-1986)	1987	78	84	.481	—	—	—
16	Cardinals (1993-1995)	1996	88	74	.543	—	—	X
17	Reds (2014-2016)	2017	68	94	.420	—	—	—
18	Padres (1979-1981)	1982	81	81	.500	—	—	—
19	Cubs (1995-1997)	1998	90	73	.552	—	—	X
20	Padres (2014-2016)	2017	71	91	.438	—	—	—
21	Marlins (2011-2013)	2014	77	85	.475	—	—	—
22	Orioles (1989-1991)	1992	89	73	.549	—	—	—
23	Rockies (2003-2005)	2006	76	86	.469	—	—	—
24	Royals (1999-2001)	2002	62	100	.383	—	—	—
25	White Sox (1974-1976)	1977	90	72	.556	—	—	—

LOS ANGELES ANGELS

Past 10 Seasons (2013-2022)

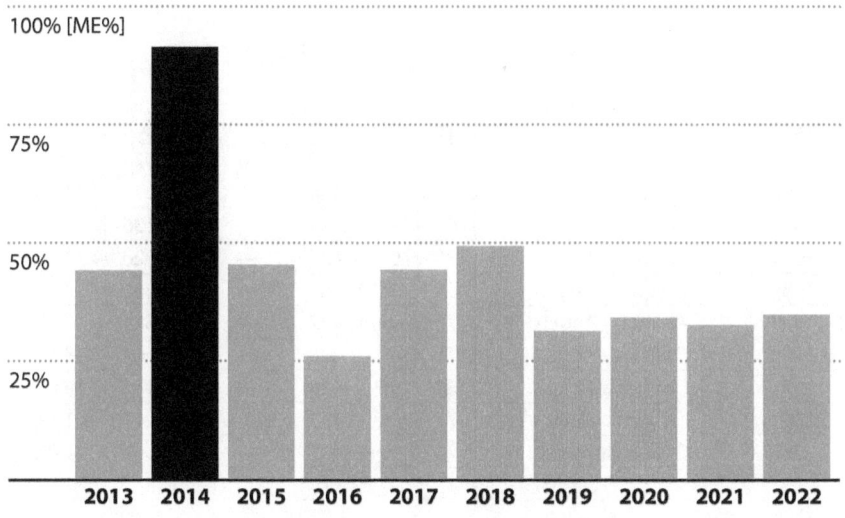

Year	Team	W	L	Pct.	Post	TS	ME%
2013	Los Angeles Angels	78	84	.481	—	43.138	44.2%
2014	Los Angeles Angels	98	64	.605	P	70.719	91.3%
2015	Los Angeles Angels	85	77	.525	—	43.677	45.4%
2016	Los Angeles Angels	74	88	.457	—	34.030	26.0%
2017	Los Angeles Angels	80	82	.494	—	43.175	44.3%
2018	Los Angeles Angels	80	82	.494	—	45.652	49.3%
2019	Los Angeles Angels	72	90	.444	—	37.054	31.3%
2020	Los Angeles Angels	26	34	.433	—	38.483	34.1%
2021	Los Angeles Angels	77	85	.475	—	37.806	32.6%
2022	Los Angeles Angels	73	89	.451	—	38.838	34.7%

Best Seasons of Modern Era (1961-2022)

Year	Team	W	L	Pct.	Post	TS	ME%
2002	Anaheim Angels	99	63	.611	WLP	77.467	96.1%
2014	Los Angeles Angels	98	64	.605	P	70.719	91.3%
1986	California Angels	92	70	.568	P	68.502	90.1%
1982	California Angels	93	69	.574	P	66.608	88.1%
2009	Los Angeles Angels	97	65	.599	P	61.875	81.9%
2008	Los Angeles Angels	100	62	.617	P	60.149	78.7%
2005	Los Angeles Angels	95	67	.586	P	59.484	77.3%
1989	California Angels	91	71	.562	—	59.259	77.2%
2007	Los Angeles Angels	94	68	.580	P	58.489	76.1%
2004	Anaheim Angels	92	70	.568	P	58.403	76.0%

Worst Seasons of Modern Era (1961-2022)

Year	Team	W	L	Pct.	Post	TS	ME%
1994	California Angels	47	68	.409	—	22.973	7.9%
1992	California Angels	72	90	.444	—	26.026	11.9%
1968	California Angels	67	95	.414	—	26.136	12.1%
1996	California Angels	70	91	.435	—	27.320	13.8%
1980	California Angels	65	95	.406	—	27.662	14.5%
1999	Anaheim Angels	70	92	.432	—	29.688	18.1%
1993	California Angels	71	91	.438	—	29.864	18.4%
1974	California Angels	68	94	.420	—	30.136	19.0%
1969	California Angels	71	91	.438	—	32.247	21.6%
1983	California Angels	70	92	.432	—	33.060	24.0%

Season Breakdown (2022)

Category	W	L	Pct.	R	RA	R/G	RA/G
Overall record in 2022	73	89	.451	623	668	3.85	4.12
Home games	40	41	.494	330	339	4.07	4.19
Away games	33	48	.407	293	329	3.62	4.06
First half of 2022 season	37	44	.457	331	344	4.09	4.25
Second half of 2022 season	36	45	.444	292	324	3.60	4.00
Against first-place teams	13	26	.333	119	179	3.05	4.59
Against playoff teams	29	49	.372	285	360	3.65	4.62
Against non-playoff teams	44	40	.524	338	308	4.02	3.67

Season as Nine-Inning Game (2022)

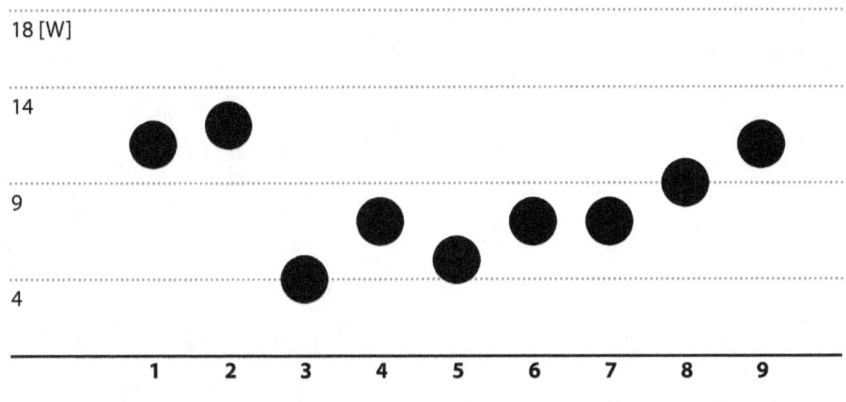

Result	1	2	3	4	5	6	7	8	9	Total
Wins	11	12	4	7	5	7	7	9	11	73
Losses	7	6	14	11	13	11	11	9	7	89

Scoring by Game (2022)

Runs Scored	G	W	L	Pct.	R/G	RA/G
Overall record	162	73	89	.451	3.85	4.12
0	12	0	12	.000	0.00	3.58
1	25	2	23	.080	1.00	5.12
2	21	6	15	.286	2.00	4.05
3	22	6	16	.273	3.00	4.14
4	29	19	10	.655	4.00	3.48
5	20	13	7	.650	5.00	4.15
6	6	5	1	.833	6.00	3.50
7	8	5	3	.625	7.00	5.00
8	5	5	0	1.000	8.00	3.20
9	5	5	0	1.000	9.00	4.00
10 or more	9	7	2	.778	10.78	4.44

Scoring Allowed by Game (2022)

Runs Allowed	G	W	L	Pct.	R/G	RA/G
Overall record	162	73	89	.451	3.85	4.12
0	17	17	0	1.000	4.94	0.00
1	23	20	3	.870	4.09	1.00
2	19	12	7	.632	3.26	2.00
3	19	13	6	.684	4.58	3.00
4	21	3	18	.143	2.14	4.00
5	13	3	10	.231	4.54	5.00
6	12	3	9	.250	4.83	6.00
7	13	2	11	.154	3.23	7.00
8	8	0	8	.000	2.75	8.00
9	7	0	7	.000	2.43	9.00
10 or more	10	0	10	.000	5.30	11.10

Margins (2022)

Category	Margin	G	W	L	Pct.	GShr	WShr
Overall record	—	162	73	89	.451	—	—
Close	1 or 2 runs	72	30	42	.417	44.4%	41.1%
Medium	3 or 4 runs	43	22	21	.512	26.5%	30.1%
Distant	5 or more runs	47	21	26	.447	29.0%	28.8%

Individual Scoring Leaders (2022)

Team Rank	Batter	R	(+) RBI	(-) HR	(=) SC
1	Shohei Ohtani	90	95	34	151
2	Mike Trout	85	80	40	125
3	Taylor Ward	73	65	23	115
4	Luis Rengifo	45	52	17	80
5	Jared Walsh	41	44	15	70
6	Brandon Marsh	34	37	8	63
7	Andrew Velazquez	37	28	9	56
8	Max Stassi	32	30	9	53
9	Jo Adell	22	27	8	41
10	David Fletcher	20	17	2	35

Team Ratings (2022)

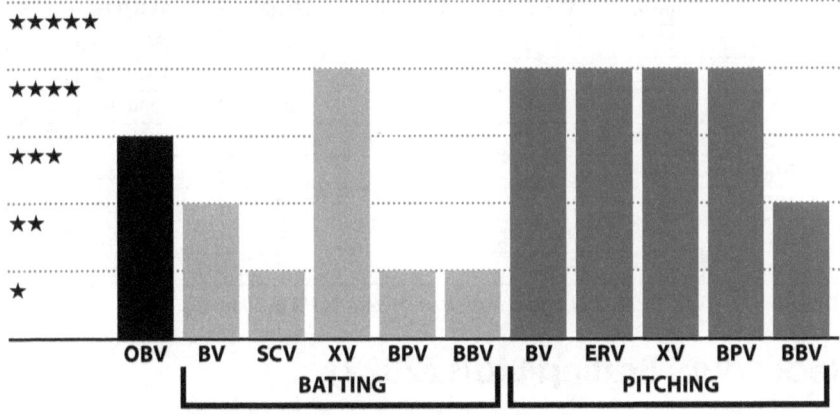

Quality	Type	Indicator	Value	Rating
Overall performance	Overall	OBV	-36	★★★
Base production	Batting	BV	-112	★★
Run production	Batting	SCV	-132	★
Power hitting	Batting	XV	26	★★★★
Contact hitting	Batting	BPV	-185	★
Batting eye	Batting	BBV	-50	★
Base prevention	Pitching	BV	-76	★★★★
Run prevention	Pitching	ERV	-31	★★★★
Power prevention	Pitching	XV	-22	★★★★
Strikeout pitching	Pitching	BPV	-38	★★★★
Control pitching	Pitching	BBV	41	★★

Team Batting Stats (2022)

Stat	Number	Div Rank	Lg Rank	MLB Rank	MLB Best
R	623	4	13	25	847 (Dodgers)
H	1,265	3	12	22	1,464 (Blue Jays)
HR	190	4	6	11	254 (Yankees)
BPO	.634	4	12	23	.764 (Dodgers)
BA	.233	3	12	24	.264 (Blue Jays)
OBP	.297	4	13	26	.333 (Dodgers)
SA	.390	3	8	15	.443 (Braves)

Division: AL West, 5 teams. **League:** American, 15 teams. **MLB:** 30 teams.

Team Pitching Stats (2022)

Stat	Number	Div Rank	Lg Rank	MLB Rank	MLB Best
ERA	3.77	3	6	9	2.80 (Dodgers)
SO	1,383	3	8	16	1,565 (Mets)
BB	540	4	13	24	384 (Rays)
BPO	.643	3	6	12	.551 (Astros)
BA	.230	2	4	7	.209 (Dodgers)
OBP	.306	3	6	11	.273 (Dodgers)
SA	.379	2	4	8	.332 (Astros)

Division: AL West, 5 teams. **League:** American, 15 teams. **MLB:** 30 teams.

Individual Batting Stats (2022)

Batter	PA	BPO	BA	OBP	SA	ISO	CT	EY
Shohei Ohtani	666	.890	.273	.356	.519	.246	.725	.089
Luis Rengifo	511	.636	.264	.294	.429	.166	.838	.033
Max Stassi	375	.498	.180	.267	.303	.123	.664	.101
Mike Trout	499	1.053	.283	.369	.630	.347	.683	.094
Andrew Velazquez	349	.522	.196	.236	.304	.109	.630	.043
Jared Walsh	454	.563	.215	.269	.374	.158	.674	.051
Taylor Ward	564	.835	.281	.360	.473	.192	.758	.106

Individual Pitching Stats for Starters (2022)

Pitcher	IP	BPO	ERA	BA	SA	ISO	CT	EY
Reid Detmers	129.0	.657	3.77	.231	.377	.147	.744	.084
Shohei Ohtani	166.0	.492	2.33	.203	.316	.113	.641	.067
Patrick Sandoval	148.2	.586	2.91	.246	.333	.087	.733	.094
Jose Suarez	109.0	.645	3.96	.243	.404	.161	.757	.067

Individual Pitching Stats for Relievers (2022)

Pitcher	GR	BPO	ERA	BA	SA	ISO	CT	EY
Jimmy Herget	48	.507	2.48	.196	.314	.118	.743	.046
Aaron Loup	65	.632	3.84	.235	.348	.113	.774	.074
Jose Quijada	42	.618	3.98	.172	.352	.179	.641	.103
Ryan Tepera	59	.577	3.61	.202	.341	.139	.774	.074
Andrew Wantz	41	.609	3.22	.206	.367	.161	.711	.103

Best Stats on Team (2022)

Stat	Batter	Number
2B	Shohei Ohtani	30
3B	Shohei Ohtani	6
BA	Mike Trout	.283
BB	Shohei Ohtani	72
BBV	Taylor Ward	15
BPO	Mike Trout	1.053
BPV	Luis Rengifo	43
BV	Mike Trout	126
CT	Luis Rengifo	.838
EY	Taylor Ward	.106
H	Shohei Ohtani	160
HR	Mike Trout	40
ISO	Mike Trout	.347
OBP	Mike Trout	.369
R	Shohei Ohtani	90
RBI	Shohei Ohtani	95
SA	Mike Trout	.630
SB	Andrew Velazquez	17
SC	Shohei Ohtani	151
SCV	Mike Trout	28
SE	Mike Trout	.251
XV	Mike Trout	85

Stat	Pitcher	Number
BA	Shohei Ohtani	.203
BBV	Jimmy Herget	-9
BPO-R	Jimmy Herget	.507
BPO-S	Shohei Ohtani	.492
BPV	Shohei Ohtani	-67
BV	Shohei Ohtani	-84
CT	Shohei Ohtani	.641
ERA-R	Jimmy Herget	2.48
ERA-S	Shohei Ohtani	2.33
ERV	Shohei Ohtani	-30
EY	Shohei Ohtani	.067
GR	Aaron Loup	65
GS	Shohei Ohtani	28
IP	Shohei Ohtani	166.0
ISO	Patrick Sandoval	.087
OBP	Shohei Ohtani	.258
SA	Shohei Ohtani	.316
SO	Shohei Ohtani	219
SV	Raisel Iglesias	16
W	Shohei Ohtani	15
XV	Patrick Sandoval	-37

Worst Stats on Team (2022)

Stat	Batter	Number
BA	Max Stassi	.180
BBV	Luis Rengifo	-23
BPO	Max Stassi	.498
BPV	Brandon Marsh	-44
BV	Max Stassi	-46
CT	Andrew Velazquez	.630
EY	Luis Rengifo	.033
ISO	Andrew Velazquez	.109
OBP	Andrew Velazquez	.236
SA	Max Stassi	.303
SCV	Luis Rengifo, Matt Duffy, Max Stassi	-20
SE	Max Stassi	.141
SO	Shohei Ohtani	161
XV	Matt Duffy	-21

Stat	Pitcher	Number
BA	Patrick Sandoval	.246
BB	Patrick Sandoval	60
BBV	Jose Marte	13
BPO-R	Aaron Loup	.632
BPO-S	Reid Detmers	.657
BPV	Jaime Barria	18
BV	Mike Mayers	26
CT	Jose Suarez	.757
ERA-R	Jose Quijada	3.98
ERA-S	Jose Suarez	3.96
ERV	Tucker Davidson	12
EY	Patrick Sandoval	.094
ISO	Jose Suarez	.161
L	Shohei Ohtani, Patrick Sandoval	9
OBP	Patrick Sandoval	.322
SA	Jose Suarez	.404
XV	Mike Mayers	21

Overall Base Value Leaders (2022)

Team Rank	Player	BV [bat]	(-) BV [pitch]	(=) OBV
1	Shohei Ohtani	102	-84	186
2	Mike Trout	126	0	126
3	Taylor Ward	64	0	64
4	Patrick Sandoval	0	-33	33
5	Jimmy Herget	0	-31	31
6	Jaime Barria	0	-17	17
7	Ryan Tepera	0	-15	15
8	Livan Soto	13	0	13
9	Michael Lorenzen	0	-10	10
10	Andrew Wantz	0	-8	8

Fan Support in Past 10 Seasons (2013-2022)

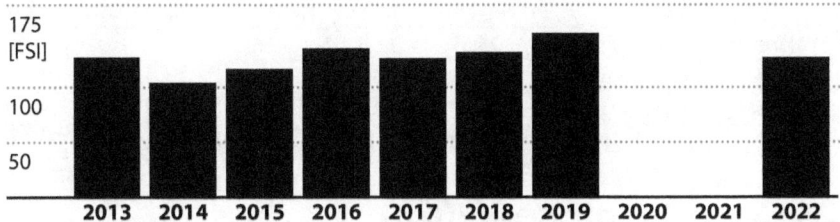

Year	Team	Attendance	W	Att:W	FSI
2013	Los Angeles Angels	3,019,505	78	38,712	127.1
2014	Los Angeles Angels	3,095,935	98	31,591	104.1
2015	Los Angeles Angels	3,012,765	85	35,444	116.7
2016	Los Angeles Angels	3,016,142	74	40,759	135.2
2017	Los Angeles Angels	3,019,585	80	37,745	126.2
2018	Los Angeles Angels	3,020,216	80	37,753	131.7
2019	Los Angeles Angels	3,023,012	72	41,986	148.9
2022	Los Angeles Angels	2,457,461	73	33,664	126.7

Extreme Games for Batters (2022)

Stat	Team Total	Individual Leader	G
3+ H	61	Shohei Ohtani	12
2+ HR	17	Shohei Ohtani	6
5+ RBI	3	Shohei Ohtani	2
0 H in 5+ AB	21	Luis Rengifo	5
4+ SO	10	Mike Trout	3

Extreme Games for Pitchers (2022)

Stat	Team Total	Individual Leader	G
0-2 ER in 7+ IP	20	Shohei Ohtani	8
10+ SO	12	Shohei Ohtani	10
0 BR in SV	22	Raisel Iglesias	9
10+ BR	18	Patrick Sandoval	7
1+ ER in SV	1	Ryan Tepera	1

Predictions for Coming Season (2023)

Group	Next W	Next L	Next Pct.	WS	LC	PQ
10 closest matches (avg. W-L)	75.5	86.5	.466	0	0	0
25 closest matches (avg. W-L)	75.9	86.0	.469	1	1	2
50 closest matches (avg. W-L)	75.8	80.8	.484	1	2	8

25 Closest Matches (2023)

Rank	Team	Next	W	L	Pct.	WS	LC	PQ
1	Athletics (1983-1985)	1986	76	86	.469	—	—	—
2	Indians (1988-1990)	1991	57	105	.352	—	—	—
3	Padres (1999-2001)	2002	66	96	.407	—	—	—
4	Giants (1975-1977)	1978	89	73	.549	—	—	—
5	Athletics (1984-1986)	1987	81	81	.500	—	—	—
6	Padres (2012-2014)	2015	74	88	.457	—	—	—
7	Athletics (2007-2009)	2010	81	81	.500	—	—	—
8	Rangers (2006-2008)	2009	87	75	.537	—	—	—
9	Mets (2011-2013)	2014	79	83	.488	—	—	—
10	Athletics (1994-1996)	1997	65	97	.401	—	—	—
11	Brewers (1995-1997)	1998	74	88	.457	—	—	—
12	Padres (2013-2015)	2016	68	94	.420	—	—	—
13	Mets (2010-2012)	2013	74	88	.457	—	—	—
14	Rangers (2000-2002)	2003	71	91	.438	—	—	—
15	Marlins (2014-2016)	2017	77	85	.475	—	—	—
16	Cubs (1990-1992)	1993	84	78	.519	—	—	—
17	Padres (2011-2013)	2014	77	85	.475	—	—	—
18	Blue Jays (1995-1997)	1998	88	74	.543	—	—	—
19	Indians (1976-1978)	1979	81	80	.503	—	—	—
20	Reds (2007-2009)	2010	91	71	.562	—	—	X
21	Marlins (2000-2002)	2003	91	71	.562	X	X	X
22	Indians (1977-1979)	1980	79	81	.494	—	—	—
23	Indians (1982-1984)	1985	60	102	.370	—	—	—
24	Marlins (2015-2017)	2018	63	98	.391	—	—	—
25	Cubs (1977-1979)	1980	64	98	.395	—	—	—

LOS ANGELES DODGERS

Past 10 Seasons (2013-2022)

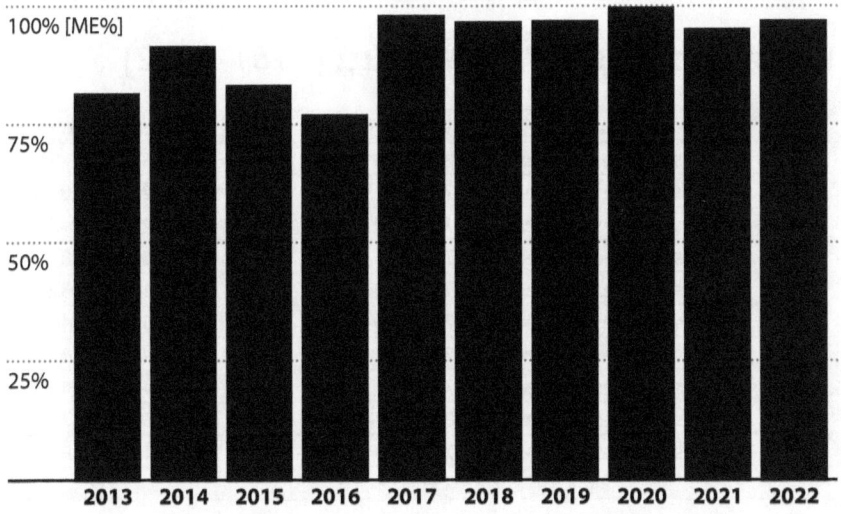

Year	Team	W	L	Pct.	Post	TS	ME%
2013	Los Angeles Dodgers	92	70	.568	P	61.642	81.6%
2014	Los Angeles Dodgers	94	68	.580	P	70.842	91.5%
2015	Los Angeles Dodgers	92	70	.568	P	62.476	83.3%
2016	Los Angeles Dodgers	91	71	.562	P	59.232	77.1%
2017	Los Angeles Dodgers	104	58	.642	LP	82.495	98.1%
2018	Los Angeles Dodgers	92	71	.564	LP	78.932	96.7%
2019	Los Angeles Dodgers	106	56	.654	P	79.532	96.9%
2020	Los Angeles Dodgers	43	17	.717	WLP	94.085	99.8%
2021	Los Angeles Dodgers	106	56	.654	P	75.648	95.2%
2022	Los Angeles Dodgers	111	51	.685	P	78.998	96.9%

Best Seasons of Modern Era (1961-2022)

Year	Team	W	L	Pct.	Post	TS	ME%
2020	Los Angeles Dodgers	43	17	.717	WLP	94.085	99.8%
2017	Los Angeles Dodgers	104	58	.642	LP	82.495	98.1%
1978	Los Angeles Dodgers	95	67	.586	LP	82.060	97.9%
1974	Los Angeles Dodgers	102	60	.630	LP	81.722	97.7%
2019	Los Angeles Dodgers	106	56	.654	P	79.532	96.9%
2022	Los Angeles Dodgers	111	51	.685	P	78.998	96.9%
2018	Los Angeles Dodgers	92	71	.564	LP	78.932	96.7%
1981	Los Angeles Dodgers	63	47	.573	WLP	78.333	96.5%
1977	Los Angeles Dodgers	98	64	.605	LP	77.512	96.1%
2021	Los Angeles Dodgers	106	56	.654	P	75.648	95.2%

Worst Seasons of Modern Era (1961-2022)

Year	Team	W	L	Pct.	Post	TS	ME%
1992	Los Angeles Dodgers	63	99	.389	—	23.311	8.5%
2005	Los Angeles Dodgers	71	91	.438	—	31.267	20.7%
1987	Los Angeles Dodgers	73	89	.451	—	33.288	24.5%
1967	Los Angeles Dodgers	73	89	.451	—	35.606	28.3%
1986	Los Angeles Dodgers	73	89	.451	—	38.124	33.3%
1968	Los Angeles Dodgers	76	86	.469	—	38.588	34.3%
1984	Los Angeles Dodgers	79	83	.488	—	43.410	44.7%
1999	Los Angeles Dodgers	77	85	.475	—	43.448	44.8%
2010	Los Angeles Dodgers	80	82	.494	—	44.504	47.1%
1989	Los Angeles Dodgers	77	83	.481	—	45.195	48.6%

Season Breakdown (2022)

Category	W	L	Pct.	R	RA	R/G	RA/G
Overall record in 2022	111	51	.685	847	513	5.23	3.17
Home games	57	24	.704	422	278	5.21	3.43
Away games	54	27	.667	425	235	5.25	2.90
First half of 2022 season	52	29	.642	405	261	5.00	3.22
Second half of 2022 season	59	22	.728	442	252	5.46	3.11
Against first-place teams	9	6	.600	63	52	4.20	3.47
Against playoff teams	29	19	.604	235	166	4.90	3.46
Against non-playoff teams	82	32	.719	612	347	5.37	3.04

Season as Nine-Inning Game (2022)

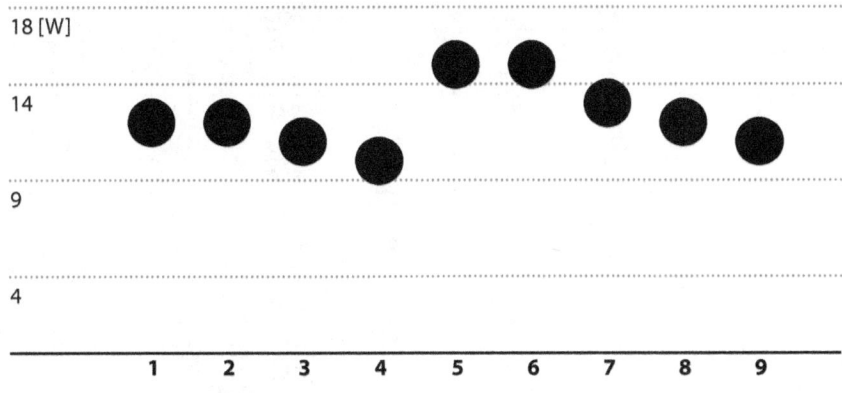

Result	1	2	3	4	5	6	7	8	9	Total
Wins	12	12	11	10	15	15	13	12	11	111
Losses	6	6	7	8	3	3	5	6	7	51

Scoring by Game (2022)

Runs Scored	G	W	L	Pct.	R/G	RA/G
Overall record	162	111	51	.685	5.23	3.17
0	7	0	7	.000	0.00	4.29
1	13	1	12	.077	1.00	3.46
2	12	5	7	.417	2.00	2.75
3	21	8	13	.381	3.00	3.76
4	23	15	8	.652	4.00	3.17
5	19	18	1	.947	5.00	2.53
6	12	11	1	.917	6.00	2.75
7	18	17	1	.944	7.00	2.72
8	10	10	0	1.000	8.00	2.90
9	8	8	0	1.000	9.00	3.13
10 or more	19	18	1	.947	11.05	3.63

Scoring Allowed by Game (2022)

Runs Allowed	G	W	L	Pct.	R/G	RA/G
Overall record	162	111	51	.685	5.23	3.17
0	15	15	0	1.000	4.87	0.00
1	35	34	1	.971	6.11	1.00
2	23	18	5	.783	4.83	2.00
3	25	20	5	.800	5.84	3.00
4	22	13	9	.591	4.55	4.00
5	20	4	16	.200	3.90	5.00
6	7	5	2	.714	7.29	6.00
7	5	0	5	.000	3.40	7.00
8	3	0	3	.000	3.33	8.00
9	5	2	3	.400	7.40	9.00
10 or more	2	0	2	.000	5.00	11.50

Margins (2022)

Category	Margin	G	W	L	Pct.	GShr	WShr
Overall record	—	162	111	51	.685	—	—
Close	1 or 2 runs	64	34	30	.531	39.5%	30.6%
Medium	3 or 4 runs	48	35	13	.729	29.6%	31.5%
Distant	5 or more runs	50	42	8	.840	30.9%	37.8%

Individual Scoring Leaders (2022)

Team Rank	Batter	R	(+) RBI	(-) HR	(=) SC
1	Freddie Freeman	117	100	21	196
2	Trea Turner	101	100	21	180
3	Mookie Betts	117	82	35	164
4	Will Smith	68	87	24	131
5	Justin Turner	61	81	13	129
6	Cody Bellinger	70	68	19	119
7	Max Muncy	69	69	21	117
8	Gavin Lux	66	42	6	102
9	Chris Taylor	45	43	10	78
10	Trayce Thompson	35	39	13	61

Team Ratings (2022)

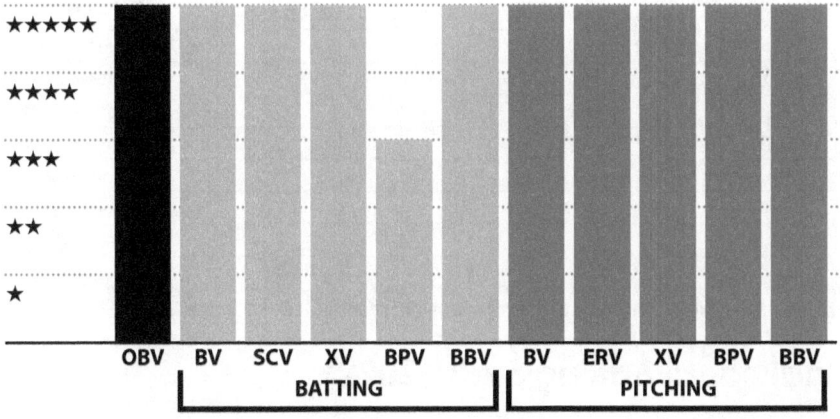

Quality	Type	Indicator	Value	Rating
Overall performance	Overall	OBV	904	★★★★★
Base production	Batting	BV	441	★★★★★
Run production	Batting	SCV	229	★★★★★
Power hitting	Batting	XV	182	★★★★★
Contact hitting	Batting	BPV	6	★★★
Batting eye	Batting	BBV	92	★★★★★
Base prevention	Pitching	BV	-463	★★★★★
Run prevention	Pitching	ERV	-188	★★★★★
Power prevention	Pitching	XV	-89	★★★★★
Strikeout pitching	Pitching	BPV	-133	★★★★★
Control pitching	Pitching	BBV	-69	★★★★★

Team Batting Stats (2022)

Stat	Number	Div Rank	Lg Rank	MLB Rank	MLB Best
R	847	1	1	1	847 (Dodgers)
H	1,418	1	2	5	1,464 (Blue Jays)
HR	212	1	3	5	254 (Yankees)
BPO	.764	1	1	1	.764 (Dodgers)
BA	.257	1	2	4	.264 (Blue Jays)
OBP	.333	1	1	1	.333 (Dodgers)
SA	.442	1	2	2	.443 (Braves)

Division: NL West, 5 teams. **League:** National, 15 teams. **MLB:** 30 teams.

Team Pitching Stats (2022)

Stat	Number	Div Rank	Lg Rank	MLB Rank	MLB Best
ERA	2.80	1	1	1	2.80 (Dodgers)
SO	1,465	1	4	5	1,565 (Mets)
BB	407	1	1	2	384 (Rays)
BPO	.555	1	1	2	.551 (Astros)
BA	.209	1	1	1	.209 (Dodgers)
OBP	.273	1	1	1	.273 (Dodgers)
SA	.344	1	1	2	.332 (Astros)

Division: NL West, 5 teams. **League:** National, 15 teams. **MLB:** 30 teams.

Individual Batting Stats (2022)

Batter	PA	BPO	BA	OBP	SA	ISO	CT	EY
Cody Bellinger	550	.618	.210	.265	.389	.179	.702	.069
Mookie Betts	639	.889	.269	.340	.533	.264	.818	.086
Freddie Freeman	708	.984	.325	.407	.511	.186	.833	.103
Gavin Lux	471	.719	.276	.346	.399	.124	.774	.100
Max Muncy	565	.738	.196	.329	.384	.188	.696	.158
Will Smith	578	.785	.260	.343	.465	.205	.811	.091
Chris Taylor	454	.660	.221	.304	.373	.152	.602	.093
Justin Turner	532	.758	.278	.350	.438	.160	.810	.092
Trea Turner	708	.809	.298	.343	.466	.169	.799	.062

Individual Pitching Stats for Starters (2022)

Pitcher	IP	BPO	ERA	BA	SA	ISO	CT	EY
Tyler Anderson	178.2	.529	2.57	.221	.350	.129	.790	.048
Tony Gonsolin	130.1	.463	2.14	.172	.299	.127	.740	.068
Clayton Kershaw	126.1	.458	2.28	.206	.310	.103	.705	.047
Julio Urias	175.0	.520	2.16	.199	.347	.149	.740	.060

Individual Pitching Stats for Relievers (2022)

Pitcher	GR	BPO	ERA	BA	SA	ISO	CT	EY
Phil Bickford	60	.701	4.72	.233	.449	.216	.705	.057
Brusdar Graterol	45	.500	3.26	.215	.320	.105	.762	.046
Craig Kimbrel	63	.646	3.75	.227	.351	.124	.680	.101
Evan Phillips	64	.364	1.14	.155	.211	.056	.638	.060
Alex Vesia	63	.488	2.15	.187	.247	.061	.601	.102

Best Stats on Team (2022)

Stat	Batter	Number
2B	Freddie Freeman	47
3B	Gavin Lux	7
BA	Freddie Freeman	.325
BB	Max Muncy	90
BBV	Max Muncy	44
BPO	Freddie Freeman	.984
BPV	Freddie Freeman	51
BV	Freddie Freeman	139
CT	Freddie Freeman	.833
EY	Max Muncy	.158
H	Freddie Freeman	199
HR	Mookie Betts	35
ISO	Mookie Betts	.264
OBP	Freddie Freeman	.407
R	Freddie Freeman, Mookie Betts	117
RBI	Trea Turner, Freddie Freeman	100
SA	Mookie Betts	.533
SB	Trea Turner	27
SC	Freddie Freeman	196
SCV	Freddie Freeman	58
SE	Freddie Freeman	.277
XV	Mookie Betts	64

Stat	Pitcher	Number
BA	Tony Gonsolin	.172
BBV	Tyler Anderson	-22
BPO-R	Evan Phillips	.364
BPO-S	Clayton Kershaw	.458
BPV	Andrew Heaney	-40
BV	Tony Gonsolin, Clayton Kershaw	-77
CT	Clayton Kershaw	.705
ERA-R	Evan Phillips	1.14
ERA-S	Tony Gonsolin	2.14
ERV	Julio Urias	-35
EY	Clayton Kershaw	.047
GR	Evan Phillips	64
GS	Julio Urias	31
IP	Tyler Anderson	178.2
ISO	Clayton Kershaw	.103
OBP	Tony Gonsolin	.237
SA	Tony Gonsolin	.299
SO	Julio Urias	166
SV	Craig Kimbrel	22
W	Julio Urias	17
XV	Clayton Kershaw	-23

Worst Stats on Team (2022)

Stat	Batter	Number
BA	Max Muncy	.196
BBV	Trea Turner	-12
BPO	Cody Bellinger	.618
BPV	Chris Taylor	-60
BV	Hanser Alberto	-23
CT	Chris Taylor	.602
EY	Trea Turner	.062
ISO	Gavin Lux	.124
OBP	Cody Bellinger	.265
SA	Chris Taylor	.373
SCV	Chris Taylor	-11
SE	Chris Taylor	.172
SO	Chris Taylor	160
XV	Gavin Lux	-12

Stat	Pitcher	Number
BA	Tyler Anderson	.221
BB	Julio Urias	41
BBV	Ryan Pepiot	14
BPO-R	Phil Bickford	.701
BPO-S	Tyler Anderson	.529
BPV	Tyler Anderson	26
BV	Michael Grove	12
CT	Tyler Anderson	.790
ERA-R	Phil Bickford	4.72
ERA-S	Tyler Anderson	2.57
ERV	Phil Bickford	5
EY	Tony Gonsolin	.068
ISO	Julio Urias	.149
L	Julio Urias, Craig Kimbrel	7
OBP	Tyler Anderson	.267
SA	Tyler Anderson	.350
XV	Andrew Heaney	17

Overall Base Value Leaders (2022)

Team Rank	Player	BV [bat]	(-) BV [pitch]	(=) OBV
1	Freddie Freeman	139	0	139
2	Mookie Betts	99	0	99
3	Tony Gonsolin	0	-77	77
3	Clayton Kershaw	0	-77	77
5	Julio Urias	0	-75	75
6	Trea Turner	71	0	71
7	Tyler Anderson	-1	-70	69
8	Evan Phillips	0	-55	55
9	Will Smith	49	0	49
10	Trayce Thompson	46	0	46

Fan Support in Past 10 Seasons (2013-2022)

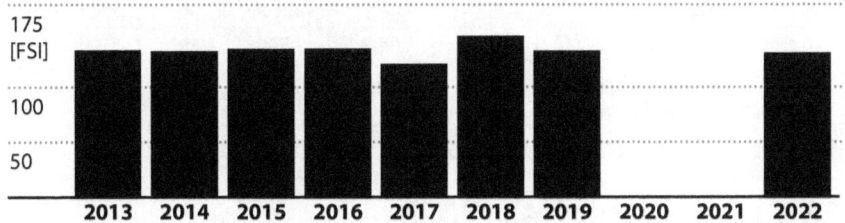

Year	Team	Attendance	W	Att:W	FSI
2013	Los Angeles Dodgers	3,743,527	92	40,691	133.6
2014	Los Angeles Dodgers	3,782,337	94	40,238	132.6
2015	Los Angeles Dodgers	3,764,815	92	40,922	134.8
2016	Los Angeles Dodgers	3,703,312	91	40,696	135.0
2017	Los Angeles Dodgers	3,765,856	104	36,210	121.1
2018	Los Angeles Dodgers	3,857,500	92	41,929	146.3
2019	Los Angeles Dodgers	3,974,309	106	37,493	132.9
2022	Los Angeles Dodgers	3,861,408	111	34,787	130.9

Extreme Games for Batters (2022)

Stat	Team Total	Individual Leader	G
3+ H	87	Freddie Freeman	20
2+ HR	10	Mookie Betts	4
5+ RBI	5	Freddie Freeman	2
0 H in 5+ AB	33	Mookie Betts	7
4+ SO	6	Cody Bellinger, Gavin Lux, Joey Gallo, Max Muncy, Mookie Betts, Trayce Thompson	1

Extreme Games for Pitchers (2022)

Stat	Team Total	Individual Leader	G
0-2 ER in 7+ IP	23	Tyler Anderson	8
10+ SO	9	Andrew Heaney, Clayton Kershaw	3
0 BR in SV	14	Craig Kimbrel	6
10+ BR	13	Dustin May, Tyler Anderson	3
1+ ER in SV	6	Craig Kimbrel	6

Predictions for Coming Season (2023)

Group	Next W	Next L	Next Pct.	WS	LC	PQ
10 closest matches (avg. W-L)	80.5	55.9	.590	1	3	7
25 closest matches (avg. W-L)	86.6	62.5	.581	3	6	18
50 closest matches (avg. W-L)	88.8	66.7	.571	8	15	34

25 Closest Matches (2023)

Rank	Team	Next	W	L	Pct.	WS	LC	PQ
1	Braves (1997-1999)	2000	95	67	.586	—	—	X
2	Dodgers (2017-2019)	2020	43	17	.717	X	X	X
3	Braves (1996-1998)	1999	103	59	.636	—	X	X
4	Mets (1986-1988)	1989	87	75	.537	—	—	—
5	Braves (1995-1997)	1998	106	56	.654	—	—	X
6	Yankees (1976-1978)	1979	89	71	.556	—	—	—
7	Astros (2017-2019)	2020	29	31	.483	—	—	X
8	Yankees (1998-2000)	2001	95	65	.594	—	X	X
9	Cardinals (2011-2013)	2014	90	72	.556	—	—	X
10	Braves (1991-1993)	1994	68	46	.596	—	—	—
11	Yankees (2001-2003)	2004	101	61	.623	—	—	X
12	Dodgers (2016-2018)	2019	106	56	.654	—	—	X
13	Yankees (1999-2001)	2002	103	58	.640	—	—	X
14	Indians (1995-1997)	1998	89	73	.549	—	—	X
15	Cardinals (2004-2006)	2007	78	84	.481	—	—	—
16	Phillies (2009-2011)	2012	81	81	.500	—	—	—
17	Blue Jays (1991-1993)	1994	55	60	.478	—	—	—
18	Indians (2015-2017)	2018	91	71	.562	—	—	X
19	Dodgers (1976-1978)	1979	79	83	.488	—	—	—
20	Giants (2000-2002)	2003	100	61	.621	—	—	X
21	Yankees (1975-1977)	1978	100	63	.613	X	X	X
22	Phillies (2007-2009)	2010	97	65	.599	—	—	X
23	Yankees (2009-2011)	2012	95	67	.586	—	—	X
24	Braves (1993-1995)	1996	96	66	.593	—	X	X
25	Braves (1992-1994)	1995	90	54	.625	X	X	X

MIAMI MARLINS

Past 10 Seasons (2013-2022)

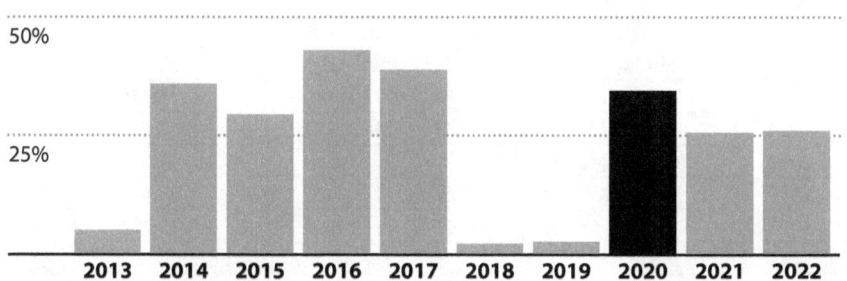

Year	Team	W	L	Pct.	Post	TS	ME%
2013	Miami Marlins	62	100	.383	—	20.020	4.9%
2014	Miami Marlins	77	85	.475	—	39.415	35.8%
2015	Miami Marlins	71	91	.438	—	36.367	29.4%
2016	Miami Marlins	79	82	.491	—	42.501	43.0%
2017	Miami Marlins	77	85	.475	—	40.779	38.9%
2018	Miami Marlins	63	98	.391	—	15.434	2.1%
2019	Miami Marlins	57	105	.352	—	16.109	2.5%
2020	Miami Marlins	31	29	.517	P	38.599	34.4%
2021	Miami Marlins	67	95	.414	—	33.754	25.6%
2022	Miami Marlins	69	93	.426	—	34.066	26.0%

Best Seasons of Modern Era (1993-2022)

Year	Team	W	L	Pct.	Post	TS	ME%
1997	Florida Marlins	92	70	.568	WLP	73.229	93.4%
2003	Florida Marlins	91	71	.562	WLP	72.426	92.6%
2009	Florida Marlins	87	75	.537	—	51.016	59.6%
2008	Florida Marlins	84	77	.522	—	50.568	58.5%
2005	Florida Marlins	83	79	.512	—	47.749	52.9%
2004	Florida Marlins	83	79	.512	—	47.024	51.8%
1996	Florida Marlins	80	82	.494	—	45.484	49.0%
2006	Florida Marlins	78	84	.481	—	44.906	47.9%
2010	Florida Marlins	80	82	.494	—	44.862	47.7%
2016	Miami Marlins	79	82	.491	—	42.501	43.0%

Worst Seasons of Modern Era (1993-2022)

Year	Team	W	L	Pct.	Post	TS	ME%
1998	Florida Marlins	54	108	.333	—	12.978	1.3%
2018	Miami Marlins	63	98	.391	—	15.434	2.1%
2019	Miami Marlins	57	105	.352	—	16.109	2.5%
2013	Miami Marlins	62	100	.383	—	20.020	4.9%
1999	Florida Marlins	64	98	.395	—	22.531	7.6%
1993	Florida Marlins	64	98	.395	—	25.416	10.6%
1994	Florida Marlins	51	64	.443	—	29.271	17.3%
2007	Florida Marlins	71	91	.438	—	29.805	18.2%
2012	Miami Marlins	69	93	.426	—	32.424	22.2%
2021	Miami Marlins	67	95	.414	—	33.754	25.6%

Season Breakdown (2022)

Category	W	L	Pct.	R	RA	R/G	RA/G
Overall record in 2022	69	93	.426	586	676	3.62	4.17
Home games	34	47	.420	296	347	3.65	4.28
Away games	35	46	.432	290	329	3.58	4.06
First half of 2022 season	39	42	.481	348	346	4.30	4.27
Second half of 2022 season	30	51	.370	238	330	2.94	4.07
Against first-place teams	11	24	.314	107	164	3.06	4.69
Against playoff teams	29	58	.333	277	397	3.18	4.56
Against non-playoff teams	40	35	.533	309	279	4.12	3.72

Season as Nine-Inning Game (2022)

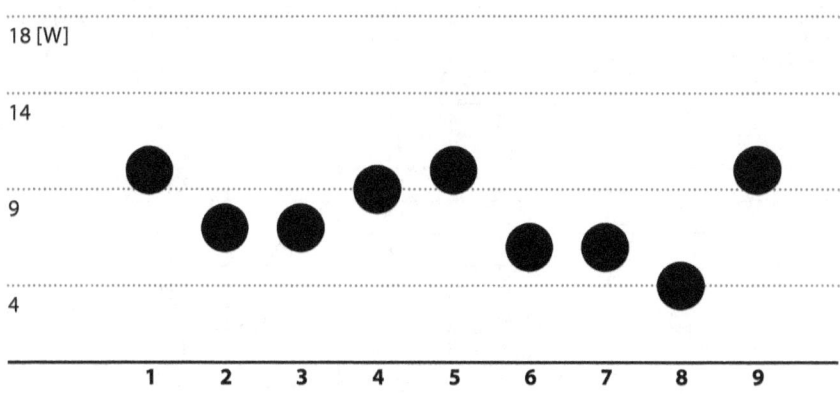

Result	1	2	3	4	5	6	7	8	9	Total
Wins	10	7	7	9	10	6	6	4	10	69
Losses	8	11	11	9	8	12	12	14	8	93

Scoring by Game (2022)

Runs Scored	G	W	L	Pct.	R/G	RA/G
Overall record	162	69	93	.426	3.62	4.17
0	14	0	14	.000	0.00	5.21
1	24	0	24	.000	1.00	3.83
2	23	7	16	.304	2.00	3.30
3	36	13	23	.361	3.00	4.39
4	21	10	11	.476	4.00	4.19
5	13	12	1	.923	5.00	2.69
6	8	6	2	.750	6.00	5.88
7	7	6	1	.857	7.00	4.43
8	4	4	0	1.000	8.00	2.25
9	3	3	0	1.000	9.00	6.00
10 or more	9	8	1	.889	11.44	5.44

Scoring Allowed by Game (2022)

Runs Allowed	G	W	L	Pct.	R/G	RA/G
Overall record	162	69	93	.426	3.62	4.17
0	10	10	0	1.000	3.70	0.00
1	17	15	2	.882	3.82	1.00
2	24	12	12	.500	2.96	2.00
3	29	15	14	.517	3.97	3.00
4	20	8	12	.400	3.55	4.00
5	20	2	18	.100	3.25	5.00
6	12	3	9	.250	3.92	6.00
7	7	1	6	.143	2.71	7.00
8	5	1	4	.200	3.60	8.00
9	7	2	5	.286	5.14	9.00
10 or more	11	0	11	.000	3.82	10.91

Margins (2022)

Category	Margin	G	W	L	Pct.	GShr	WShr
Overall record	—	162	69	93	.426	—	—
Close	1 or 2 runs	87	35	52	.402	53.7%	50.7%
Medium	3 or 4 runs	40	23	17	.575	24.7%	33.3%
Distant	5 or more runs	35	11	24	.314	21.6%	15.9%

Individual Scoring Leaders (2022)

Team Rank	Batter	R	(+) RBI	(-) HR	(=) SC
1	Garrett Cooper	37	50	9	78
2	Jesus Aguilar	37	49	15	71
2	Jon Berti	47	28	4	71
4	Jazz Chisholm Jr.	39	45	14	70
5	Bryan De La Cruz	38	43	13	68
6	Miguel Rojas	34	36	6	64
7	Brian Anderson	43	28	8	63
8	Jesus Sanchez	38	36	13	61
9	Avisail Garcia	31	35	8	58
10	Nick Fortes	41	24	9	56
10	Joey Wendle	27	32	3	56

Team Ratings (2022)

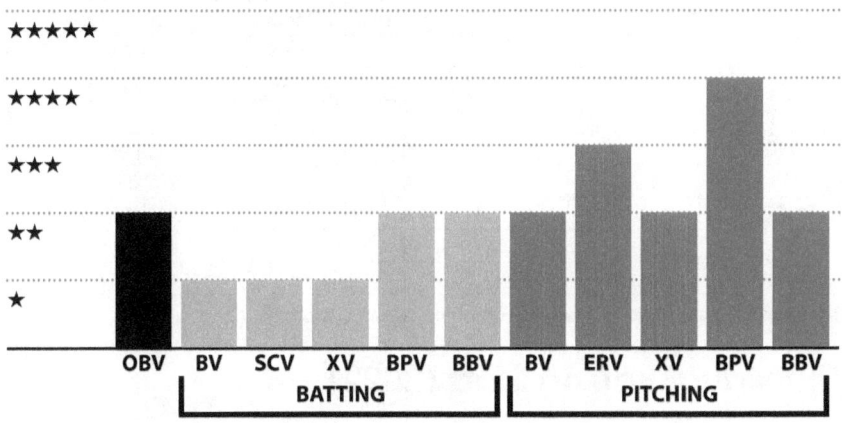

Quality	Type	Indicator	Value	Rating
Overall performance	Overall	OBV	-319	★★
Base production	Batting	BV	-238	★
Run production	Batting	SCV	-164	★
Power hitting	Batting	XV	-101	★
Contact hitting	Batting	BPV	-82	★★
Batting eye	Batting	BBV	-41	★★
Base prevention	Pitching	BV	81	★★
Run prevention	Pitching	ERV	-16	★★★
Power prevention	Pitching	XV	64	★★
Strikeout pitching	Pitching	BPV	-83	★★★★
Control pitching	Pitching	BBV	14	★★

Team Batting Stats (2022)

Stat	Number	Div Rank	Lg Rank	MLB Rank	MLB Best
R	586	5	15	28	847 (Dodgers)
H	1,241	5	13	25	1,464 (Blue Jays)
HR	144	4	14	24	254 (Yankees)
BPO	.605	5	14	27	.764 (Dodgers)
BA	.230	5	14	28	.264 (Blue Jays)
OBP	.294	5	14	27	.333 (Dodgers)
SA	.363	5	15	28	.443 (Braves)

Division: NL East, 5 teams. **League:** National, 15 teams. **MLB:** 30 teams.

Team Pitching Stats (2022)

Stat	Number	Div Rank	Lg Rank	MLB Rank	MLB Best
ERA	3.86	3	8	14	2.80 (Dodgers)
SO	1,437	3	6	9	1,565 (Mets)
BB	511	4	9	18	384 (Rays)
BPO	.679	4	9	20	.551 (Astros)
BA	.242	3	6	12	.209 (Dodgers)
OBP	.314	4	8	17	.273 (Dodgers)
SA	.406	4	9	20	.332 (Astros)

Division: NL East, 5 teams. **League:** National, 15 teams. **MLB:** 30 teams.

Individual Batting Stats (2022)

Batter	PA	BPO	BA	OBP	SA	ISO	CT	EY
Jesus Aguilar	456	.600	.236	.286	.388	.152	.745	.057
Brian Anderson	383	.601	.222	.311	.346	.124	.701	.092
Jon Berti	404	.732	.240	.324	.338	.098	.751	.104
Garrett Cooper	469	.716	.261	.337	.415	.155	.713	.085
Bryan De La Cruz	355	.663	.252	.294	.432	.179	.726	.054
Avisail Garcia	380	.481	.224	.266	.317	.092	.695	.045
Miguel Rojas	507	.520	.236	.283	.323	.087	.870	.049
Jesus Sanchez	343	.618	.214	.280	.403	.188	.706	.076
Jacob Stallings	384	.483	.223	.292	.292	.069	.760	.076
Joey Wendle	371	.594	.259	.297	.360	.101	.856	.040

Individual Pitching Stats for Starters (2022)

Pitcher	IP	BPO	ERA	BA	SA	ISO	CT	EY
Sandy Alcantara	228.2	.525	2.28	.212	.324	.112	.748	.055
Pablo Lopez	180.0	.636	3.75	.234	.404	.170	.741	.071
Jesus Luzardo	100.1	.536	3.32	.191	.335	.144	.668	.088
Trevor Rogers	107.0	.810	5.47	.274	.468	.194	.749	.094

Individual Pitching Stats for Relievers (2022)

Pitcher	GR	BPO	ERA	BA	SA	ISO	CT	EY
Anthony Bass	45	.422	1.41	.198	.272	.074	.722	.058
Richard Bleier	54	.742	3.55	.301	.459	.158	.847	.032
Dylan Floro	56	.524	3.02	.235	.338	.103	.765	.055
Steven Okert	60	.650	2.98	.186	.339	.153	.656	.110
Tanner Scott	67	.730	4.31	.236	.348	.112	.614	.156

Best Stats on Team (2022)

Stat	Batter	Number
2B	Garrett Cooper	33
3B	Jazz Chisholm Jr.	4
BA	Garrett Cooper	.261
BB	Jon Berti	42
BBV	JJ Bleday	11
BPO	Jon Berti	.732
BPV	Miguel Rojas	57
BV	Jazz Chisholm Jr.	43
CT	Miguel Rojas	.870
EY	Jon Berti	.104
H	Miguel Rojas	111
HR	Jesus Aguilar	15
ISO	Jesus Sanchez	.188
OBP	Garrett Cooper	.337
R	Jon Berti	47
RBI	Garrett Cooper	50
SA	Bryan De La Cruz	.432
SB	Jon Berti	41
SC	Garrett Cooper	78
SCV	Jazz Chisholm Jr.	23
SE	Bryan De La Cruz	.192
XV	Jazz Chisholm Jr.	28

Stat	Pitcher	Number
BA	Jesus Luzardo	.191
BBV	Sandy Alcantara	-21
BPO-R	Anthony Bass	.422
BPO-S	Sandy Alcantara	.525
BPV	Tanner Scott	-32
BV	Sandy Alcantara	-92
CT	Jesus Luzardo	.668
ERA-R	Anthony Bass	1.41
ERA-S	Sandy Alcantara	2.28
ERV	Sandy Alcantara	-43
EY	Sandy Alcantara	.055
GR	Tanner Scott	67
GS	Pablo Lopez, Sandy Alcantara	32
IP	Sandy Alcantara	228.2
ISO	Sandy Alcantara	.112
OBP	Sandy Alcantara	.263
SA	Sandy Alcantara	.324
SO	Sandy Alcantara	207
SV	Tanner Scott	20
W	Sandy Alcantara	14
XV	Sandy Alcantara	-33

Worst Stats on Team (2022)

Stat	Batter	Number
BA	Jesus Sanchez	.214
BBV	Miguel Rojas	-15
BPO	Avisail Garcia	.481
BPV	Jorge Soler	-23
BV	Miguel Rojas	-53
CT	Avisail Garcia	.695
EY	Joey Wendle	.040
ISO	Jacob Stallings	.069
OBP	Avisail Garcia	.266
SA	Jacob Stallings	.292
SCV	Miguel Rojas	-35
SE	Miguel Rojas	.126
SO	Garrett Cooper	119
XV	Miguel Rojas	-31

Stat	Pitcher	Number
BA	Trevor Rogers	.274
BB	Pablo Lopez	53
BBV	Tanner Scott	22
BPO-R	Richard Bleier	.742
BPO-S	Trevor Rogers	.810
BPV	Richard Bleier	20
BV	Elieser Hernandez	56
CT	Trevor Rogers	.749
ERA-R	Tanner Scott	4.31
ERA-S	Trevor Rogers	5.47
ERV	Trevor Rogers	18
EY	Trevor Rogers	.094
ISO	Trevor Rogers	.194
L	Trevor Rogers	11
OBP	Trevor Rogers	.348
SA	Trevor Rogers	.468
XV	Elieser Hernandez	41

Overall Base Value Leaders (2022)

Team Rank	Player	BV [bat]	(-) BV [pitch]	(=) OBV
1	Sandy Alcantara	0	-92	92
2	Jazz Chisholm Jr.	43	0	43
3	Jesus Luzardo	0	-37	37
4	Anthony Bass	0	-32	32
5	Dylan Floro	0	-22	22
6	Jon Berti	21	0	21
7	Garrett Cooper	18	0	18
8	Edward Cabrera	0	-13	13
8	Pablo Lopez	0	-13	13
10	Zach Pop	0	-5	5

Fan Support in Past 10 Seasons (2013-2022)

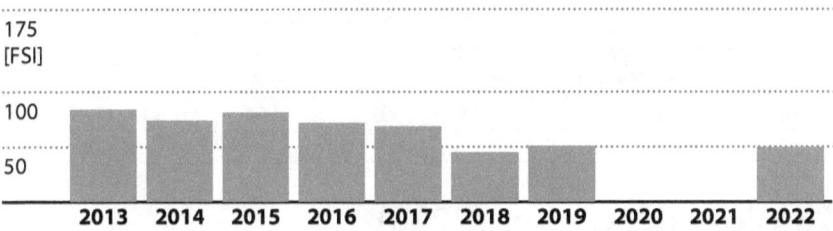

Year	Team	Attendance	W	Att:W	FSI
2013	Miami Marlins	1,586,322	62	25,586	84.0
2014	Miami Marlins	1,732,283	77	22,497	74.1
2015	Miami Marlins	1,752,235	71	24,679	81.3
2016	Miami Marlins	1,712,417	79	21,676	71.9
2017	Miami Marlins	1,583,014	77	20,559	68.7
2018	Miami Marlins	811,104	63	12,875	44.9
2019	Miami Marlins	811,302	57	14,233	50.5
2022	Miami Marlins	907,487	69	13,152	49.5

Extreme Games for Batters (2022)

Stat	Team Total	Individual Leader	G
3+ H	49	Garrett Cooper	8
2+ HR	8	Jazz Chisholm Jr.	2
5+ RBI	1	Jazz Chisholm Jr.	1
0 H in 5+ AB	27	Jesus Aguilar	6
4+ SO	6	Avisail Garcia, Billy Hamilton, Jesus Aguilar, Jesus Sanchez, JJ Bleday, Jon Berti	1

Extreme Games for Pitchers (2022)

Stat	Team Total	Individual Leader	G
0-2 ER in 7+ IP	32	Sandy Alcantara	20
10+ SO	13	Sandy Alcantara	6
0 BR in SV	12	Tanner Scott	6
10+ BR	18	Pablo Lopez, Sandy Alcantara, Trevor Rogers	4
1+ ER in SV	3	Tanner Scott	2

Predictions for Coming Season (2023)

Group	Next W	Next L	Next Pct.	WS	LC	PQ
10 closest matches (avg. W-L)	73.2	78.6	.482	0	1	2
25 closest matches (avg. W-L)	71.6	82.2	.466	0	1	2
50 closest matches (avg. W-L)	73.5	82.9	.470	0	1	4

25 Closest Matches (2023)

Rank	Team	Next	W	L	Pct.	WS	LC	PQ
1	Brewers (1997-1999)	2000	73	89	.451	—	—	—
2	Phillies (1990-1992)	1993	97	65	.599	—	X	X
3	Blue Jays (2017-2019)	2020	32	28	.533	—	—	X
4	Reds (2006-2008)	2009	78	84	.481	—	—	—
5	Angels (1974-1976)	1977	74	88	.457	—	—	—
6	Giants (2006-2008)	2009	88	74	.543	—	—	—
7	Mariners (1987-1989)	1990	77	85	.475	—	—	—
8	Brewers (1998-2000)	2001	68	94	.420	—	—	—
9	Padres (2014-2016)	2017	71	91	.438	—	—	—
10	Padres (2012-2014)	2015	74	88	.457	—	—	—
11	Cubs (1974-1976)	1977	81	81	.500	—	—	—
12	Cubs (1985-1987)	1988	77	85	.475	—	—	—
13	Padres (2013-2015)	2016	68	94	.420	—	—	—
14	Marlins (2010-2012)	2013	62	100	.383	—	—	—
15	Orioles (2001-2003)	2004	78	84	.481	—	—	—
16	Rockies (2001-2003)	2004	68	94	.420	—	—	—
17	Brewers (1996-1998)	1999	74	87	.460	—	—	—
18	Padres (2011-2013)	2014	77	85	.475	—	—	—
19	Indians (1988-1990)	1991	57	105	.352	—	—	—
20	Rangers (2001-2003)	2004	89	73	.549	—	—	—
21	Mets (2011-2013)	2014	79	83	.488	—	—	—
22	Indians (1976-1978)	1979	81	80	.503	—	—	—
23	Giants (2005-2007)	2008	72	90	.444	—	—	—
24	Royals (1998-2000)	2001	65	97	.401	—	—	—
25	Giants (2017-2019)	2020	29	31	.483	—	—	—

MILWAUKEE BREWERS

Past 10 Seasons (2013-2022)

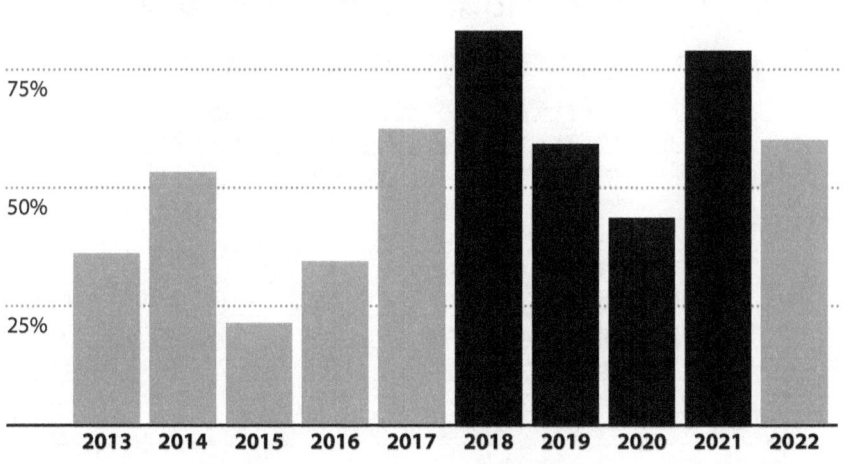

Year	Team	W	L	Pct.	Post	TS	ME%
2013	Milwaukee Brewers	74	88	.457	—	39.507	36.1%
2014	Milwaukee Brewers	82	80	.506	—	47.887	53.3%
2015	Milwaukee Brewers	68	94	.420	—	31.853	21.4%
2016	Milwaukee Brewers	73	89	.451	—	38.609	34.4%
2017	Milwaukee Brewers	86	76	.531	—	51.884	62.4%
2018	Milwaukee Brewers	96	67	.589	P	62.382	83.1%
2019	Milwaukee Brewers	89	73	.549	P	50.908	59.2%
2020	Milwaukee Brewers	29	31	.483	P	42.825	43.6%
2021	Milwaukee Brewers	95	67	.586	P	60.272	78.9%
2022	Milwaukee Brewers	86	76	.531	—	51.203	60.1%

Best Seasons of Modern Era (1969-2022)

Year	Team	W	L	Pct.	Post	TS	ME%
1982	Milwaukee Brewers	95	67	.586	LP	74.675	94.3%
1992	Milwaukee Brewers	92	70	.568	—	67.284	88.9%
2011	Milwaukee Brewers	96	66	.593	P	66.346	88.0%
1978	Milwaukee Brewers	93	69	.574	—	64.905	86.8%
2018	Milwaukee Brewers	96	67	.589	P	62.382	83.1%
1979	Milwaukee Brewers	95	66	.590	—	60.796	79.5%
2021	Milwaukee Brewers	95	67	.586	P	60.272	78.9%
1980	Milwaukee Brewers	86	76	.531	—	59.597	77.9%
2008	Milwaukee Brewers	90	72	.556	P	59.283	77.2%
1987	Milwaukee Brewers	91	71	.562	—	58.723	76.5%

Worst Seasons of Modern Era (1969-2022)

Year	Team	W	L	Pct.	Post	TS	ME%
2002	Milwaukee Brewers	56	106	.346	—	15.584	2.2%
1984	Milwaukee Brewers	67	94	.416	—	23.864	9.1%
2003	Milwaukee Brewers	68	94	.420	—	25.058	9.8%
1969	Seattle Pilots	64	98	.395	—	25.510	10.8%
1976	Milwaukee Brewers	66	95	.410	—	25.517	10.8%
1972	Milwaukee Brewers	65	91	.417	—	27.472	14.1%
1993	Milwaukee Brewers	69	93	.426	—	27.915	14.8%
2001	Milwaukee Brewers	68	94	.420	—	28.450	15.5%
1970	Milwaukee Brewers	65	97	.401	—	28.466	15.6%
1985	Milwaukee Brewers	71	90	.441	—	28.961	16.6%

Season Breakdown (2022)

Category	W	L	Pct.	R	RA	R/G	RA/G
Overall record in 2022	86	76	.531	725	688	4.48	4.25
Home games	46	35	.568	362	322	4.47	3.98
Away games	40	41	.494	363	366	4.48	4.52
First half of 2022 season	46	35	.568	374	337	4.62	4.16
Second half of 2022 season	40	41	.494	351	351	4.33	4.33
Against first-place teams	17	18	.486	126	152	3.60	4.34
Against playoff teams	30	31	.492	221	259	3.62	4.25
Against non-playoff teams	56	45	.554	504	429	4.99	4.25

Season as Nine-Inning Game (2022)

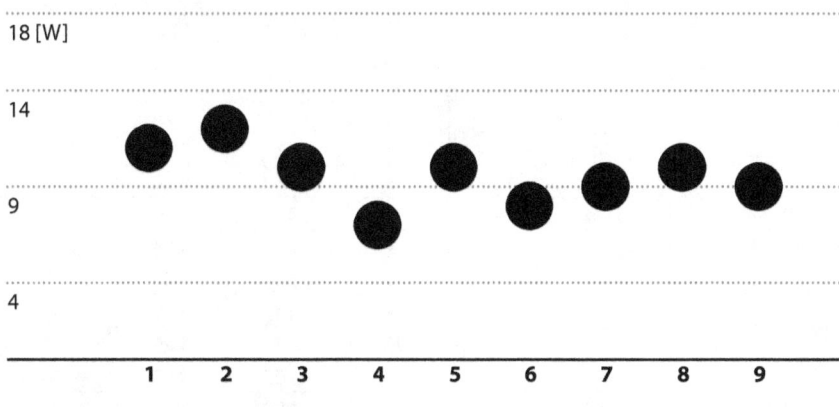

Result	1	2	3	4	5	6	7	8	9	Total
Wins	11	12	10	7	10	8	9	10	9	86
Losses	7	6	8	11	8	10	9	8	9	76

Scoring by Game (2022)

Runs Scored	G	W	L	Pct.	R/G	RA/G
Overall record	162	86	76	.531	4.48	4.25
0	11	0	11	.000	0.00	4.73
1	15	3	12	.200	1.00	3.20
2	22	5	17	.227	2.00	4.14
3	17	6	11	.353	3.00	4.24
4	19	11	8	.579	4.00	3.63
5	29	22	7	.759	5.00	4.00
6	15	12	3	.800	6.00	4.33
7	15	10	5	.667	7.00	5.53
8	4	3	1	.750	8.00	5.50
9	4	4	0	1.000	9.00	4.00
10 or more	11	10	1	.909	11.91	4.91

Scoring Allowed by Game (2022)

Runs Allowed	G	W	L	Pct.	R/G	RA/G
Overall record	162	86	76	.531	4.48	4.25
0	11	11	0	1.000	3.82	0.00
1	19	19	0	1.000	4.74	1.00
2	21	12	9	.571	3.86	2.00
3	21	16	5	.762	4.62	3.00
4	31	14	17	.452	4.26	4.00
5	12	5	7	.417	4.58	5.00
6	11	6	5	.545	5.36	6.00
7	7	1	6	.143	3.86	7.00
8	14	1	13	.071	5.29	8.00
9	6	1	5	.167	4.00	9.00
10 or more	9	0	9	.000	4.89	11.00

Margins (2022)

Category	Margin	G	W	L	Pct.	GShr	WShr
Overall record	—	162	86	76	.531	—	—
Close	1 or 2 runs	86	46	40	.535	53.1%	53.5%
Medium	3 or 4 runs	40	23	17	.575	24.7%	26.7%
Distant	5 or more runs	36	17	19	.472	22.2%	19.8%

Individual Scoring Leaders (2022)

Team Rank	Batter	R	(+) RBI	(-) HR	(=) SC
1	Willy Adames	83	98	31	150
2	Christian Yelich	99	57	14	142
3	Rowdy Tellez	67	89	35	121
4	Andrew McCutchen	66	69	17	118
5	Hunter Renfroe	62	72	29	105
6	Kolten Wong	65	47	15	97
7	Luis Urias	54	47	16	85
8	Tyrone Taylor	49	51	17	83
9	Jace Peterson	44	34	8	70
10	Keston Hiura	34	32	14	52

Team Ratings (2022)

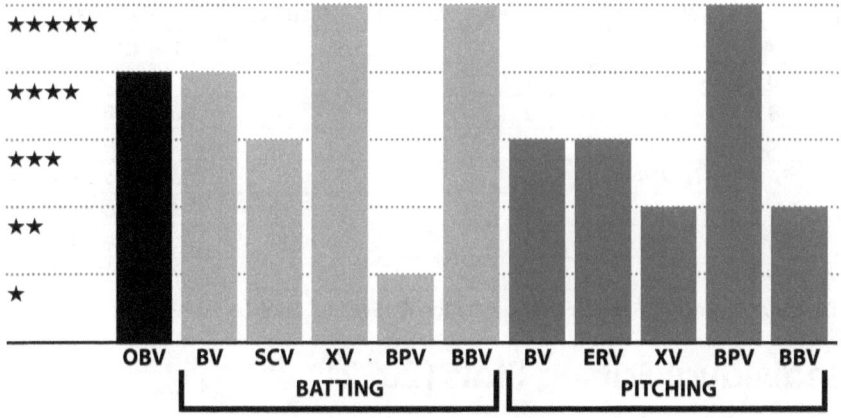

Quality	Type	Indicator	Value	Rating
Overall performance	Overall	OBV	199	★★★★
Base production	Batting	BV	149	★★★★
Run production	Batting	SCV	16	★★★
Power hitting	Batting	XV	118	★★★★★
Contact hitting	Batting	BPV	-112	★
Batting eye	Batting	BBV	69	★★★★★
Base prevention	Pitching	BV	-50	★★★
Run prevention	Pitching	ERV	-22	★★★
Power prevention	Pitching	XV	39	★★
Strikeout pitching	Pitching	BPV	-180	★★★★★
Control pitching	Pitching	BBV	30	★★

Team Batting Stats (2022)

Stat	Number	Div Rank	Lg Rank	MLB Rank	MLB Best
R	725	2	6	10	847 (Dodgers)
H	1,271	3	10	21	1,464 (Blue Jays)
HR	219	1	2	3	254 (Yankees)
BPO	.694	2	6	9	.764 (Dodgers)
BA	.235	4	11	22	.264 (Blue Jays)
OBP	.315	2	7	13	.333 (Dodgers)
SA	.409	2	6	10	.443 (Braves)

Division: NL Central, 5 teams. **League:** National, 15 teams. **MLB:** 30 teams.

Team Pitching Stats (2022)

Stat	Number	Div Rank	Lg Rank	MLB Rank	MLB Best
ERA	3.83	2	6	12	2.80 (Dodgers)
SO	1,530	1	3	3	1,565 (Mets)
BB	521	2	10	20	384 (Rays)
BPO	.649	2	8	14	.551 (Astros)
BA	.229	1	3	5	.209 (Dodgers)
OBP	.302	1	5	10	.273 (Dodgers)
SA	.388	2	6	12	.332 (Astros)

Division: NL Central, 5 teams. **League:** National, 15 teams. **MLB:** 30 teams.

Individual Batting Stats (2022)

Batter	PA	BPO	BA	OBP	SA	ISO	CT	EY
Willy Adames	617	.716	.238	.298	.458	.220	.705	.075
Andrew McCutchen	580	.656	.237	.316	.384	.148	.759	.097
Jace Peterson	328	.692	.236	.316	.382	.146	.705	.095
Hunter Renfroe	522	.762	.255	.315	.492	.236	.745	.073
Tyrone Taylor	405	.662	.233	.286	.442	.209	.727	.054
Rowdy Tellez	599	.723	.219	.306	.461	.242	.771	.090
Luis Urias	472	.711	.239	.335	.404	.165	.756	.106
Kolten Wong	497	.791	.251	.339	.430	.179	.795	.089
Christian Yelich	671	.753	.252	.355	.383	.130	.718	.125

Individual Pitching Stats for Starters (2022)

Pitcher	IP	BPO	ERA	BA	SA	ISO	CT	EY
Aaron Ashby	107.1	.730	4.44	.254	.416	.163	.699	.099
Corbin Burnes	202.0	.526	2.94	.197	.341	.144	.668	.064
Adrian Houser	102.2	.691	4.73	.258	.388	.130	.828	.101
Eric Lauer	158.2	.665	3.69	.228	.410	.182	.735	.089
Brandon Woodruff	153.1	.579	3.05	.215	.366	.151	.665	.068

Individual Pitching Stats for Relievers (2022)

Pitcher	GR	BPO	ERA	BA	SA	ISO	CT	EY
Brad Boxberger	70	.639	2.95	.223	.343	.120	.708	.097
Trevor Gott	45	.626	4.14	.205	.392	.187	.743	.065
Hoby Milner	67	.624	3.76	.250	.377	.127	.738	.055
Brent Suter	54	.655	3.78	.236	.407	.171	.785	.081
Devin Williams	65	.456	1.93	.151	.205	.054	.532	.121

Best Stats on Team (2022)

Stat	Batter	Number
2B	Willy Adames	31
3B	Christian Yelich, Kolten Wong	4
BA	Hunter Renfroe	.255
BB	Christian Yelich	88
BBV	Christian Yelich	30
BPO	Kolten Wong	.791
BPV	Kolten Wong	19
BV	Kolten Wong	45
CT	Kolten Wong	.795
EY	Christian Yelich	.125
H	Christian Yelich	145
HR	Rowdy Tellez	35
ISO	Rowdy Tellez	.242
OBP	Christian Yelich	.355
R	Christian Yelich	99
RBI	Willy Adames	98
SA	Hunter Renfroe	.492
SB	Christian Yelich	19
SC	Willy Adames	150
SCV	Willy Adames	30
SE	Willy Adames	.243
XV	Rowdy Tellez	48

Stat	Pitcher	Number
BA	Corbin Burnes	.197
BBV	Corbin Burnes	-12
BPO-R	Devin Williams	.456
BPO-S	Corbin Burnes	.526
BPV	Corbin Burnes	-60
BV	Corbin Burnes	-81
CT	Brandon Woodruff	.665
ERA-R	Devin Williams	1.93
ERA-S	Corbin Burnes	2.94
ERV	Corbin Burnes	-23
EY	Corbin Burnes	.064
GR	Brad Boxberger	70
GS	Corbin Burnes	33
IP	Corbin Burnes	202.0
ISO	Adrian Houser	.130
OBP	Corbin Burnes	.261
SA	Corbin Burnes	.341
SO	Corbin Burnes	243
SV	Josh Hader	29
W	Brandon Woodruff	13
XV	Devin Williams	-20

Worst Stats on Team (2022)

Stat	Batter	Number
BA	Rowdy Tellez	.219
BBV	Tyrone Taylor	-10
BPO	Andrew McCutchen	.656
BPV	Keston Hiura	-53
BV	Lorenzo Cain	-36
CT	Jace Peterson	.705
EY	Tyrone Taylor	.054
ISO	Christian Yelich	.130
OBP	Tyrone Taylor	.286
SA	Jace Peterson	.382
SCV	Omar Narvaez	-18
SE	Luis Urias	.180
SO	Willy Adames	166
XV	Lorenzo Cain, Omar Narvaez	-14

Stat	Pitcher	Number
BA	Adrian Houser	.258
BB	Eric Lauer	59
BBV	Adrian Houser, Devin Williams	10
BPO-R	Brent Suter	.655
BPO-S	Aaron Ashby	.730
BPV	Adrian Houser	31
BV	Jason Alexander	45
CT	Adrian Houser	.828
ERA-R	Trevor Gott	4.14
ERA-S	Adrian Houser	4.73
ERV	Jason Alexander	11
EY	Adrian Houser	.101
ISO	Eric Lauer	.182
L	Adrian Houser, Aaron Ashby	10
OBP	Aaron Ashby	.335
SA	Aaron Ashby	.416
XV	Eric Lauer	18

Overall Base Value Leaders (2022)

Team Rank	Player	BV [bat]	(-) BV [pitch]	(=) OBV
1	Corbin Burnes	0	-81	81
2	Kolten Wong	45	0	45
3	Christian Yelich	41	0	41
4	Hunter Renfroe	38	0	38
5	Devin Williams	0	-37	37
5	Brandon Woodruff	0	-37	37
7	Freddy Peralta	0	-33	33
8	Rowdy Tellez	28	0	28
9	Willy Adames	25	0	25
10	Keston Hiura	19	0	19

Fan Support in Past 10 Seasons (2013-2022)

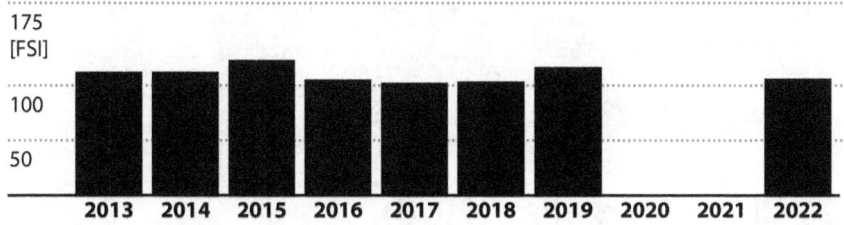

Year	Team	Attendance	W	Att:W	FSI
2013	Milwaukee Brewers	2,531,105	74	34,204	112.3
2014	Milwaukee Brewers	2,797,384	82	34,114	112.4
2015	Milwaukee Brewers	2,542,558	68	37,391	123.1
2016	Milwaukee Brewers	2,314,614	73	31,707	105.2
2017	Milwaukee Brewers	2,627,705	86	30,555	102.2
2018	Milwaukee Brewers	2,850,875	96	29,697	103.6
2019	Milwaukee Brewers	2,923,333	89	32,846	116.5
2022	Milwaukee Brewers	2,422,420	86	28,168	106.0

Extreme Games for Batters (2022)

Stat	Team Total	Individual Leader	G
3+ H	50	Hunter Renfroe, Willy Adames	9
2+ HR	15	Rowdy Tellez	5
5+ RBI	6	Rowdy Tellez	3
0 H in 5+ AB	45	Rowdy Tellez	12
4+ SO	5	Christian Yelich	2

Extreme Games for Pitchers (2022)

Stat	Team Total	Individual Leader	G
0-2 ER in 7+ IP	21	Corbin Burnes	11
10+ SO	20	Corbin Burnes	9
0 BR in SV	28	Josh Hader	12
10+ BR	27	Jason Alexander	6
1+ ER in SV	4	Josh Hader	3

Predictions for Coming Season (2023)

Group	Next W	Next L	Next Pct.	WS	LC	PQ
10 closest matches (avg. W-L)	76.6	75.1	.505	0	0	4
25 closest matches (avg. W-L)	80.1	77.8	.507	0	0	7
50 closest matches (avg. W-L)	82.9	72.9	.532	1	4	22

25 Closest Matches (2023)

Rank	Team	Next	W	L	Pct.	WS	LC	PQ
1	Red Sox (1987-1989)	1990	88	74	.543	—	—	X
2	Reds (1998-2000)	2001	66	96	.407	—	—	—
3	Astros (2000-2002)	2003	87	75	.537	—	—	—
4	Dodgers (1999-2001)	2002	92	70	.568	—	—	—
5	Orioles (1993-1995)	1996	88	74	.543	—	—	X
6	Brewers (2017-2019)	2020	29	31	.483	—	—	X
7	Twins (2007-2009)	2010	94	68	.580	—	—	X
8	Diamondbacks (2006-2008)	2009	70	92	.432	—	—	—
9	Brewers (2010-2012)	2013	74	88	.457	—	—	—
10	Expos (1981-1983)	1984	78	83	.484	—	—	—
11	Phillies (2002-2004)	2005	88	74	.543	—	—	—
12	Rockies (2008-2010)	2011	73	89	.451	—	—	—
13	Rangers (1976-1978)	1979	83	79	.512	—	—	—
14	Diamondbacks (2010-2012)	2013	81	81	.500	—	—	—
15	Giants (1997-1999)	2000	97	65	.599	—	—	X
16	Brewers (1986-1988)	1989	81	81	.500	—	—	—
17	Expos (1986-1988)	1989	81	81	.500	—	—	—
18	Dodgers (2005-2007)	2008	84	78	.519	—	—	X
19	Indians (2004-2006)	2007	96	66	.593	—	—	X
20	Red Sox (1989-1991)	1992	73	89	.451	—	—	—
21	Indians (2006-2008)	2009	65	97	.401	—	—	—
22	Blue Jays (1997-1999)	2000	83	79	.512	—	—	—
23	Blue Jays (2005-2007)	2008	86	76	.531	—	—	—
24	Twins (1975-1977)	1978	73	89	.451	—	—	—
25	Tigers (1980-1982)	1983	92	70	.568	—	—	—

MINNESOTA TWINS

Past 10 Seasons (2013-2022)

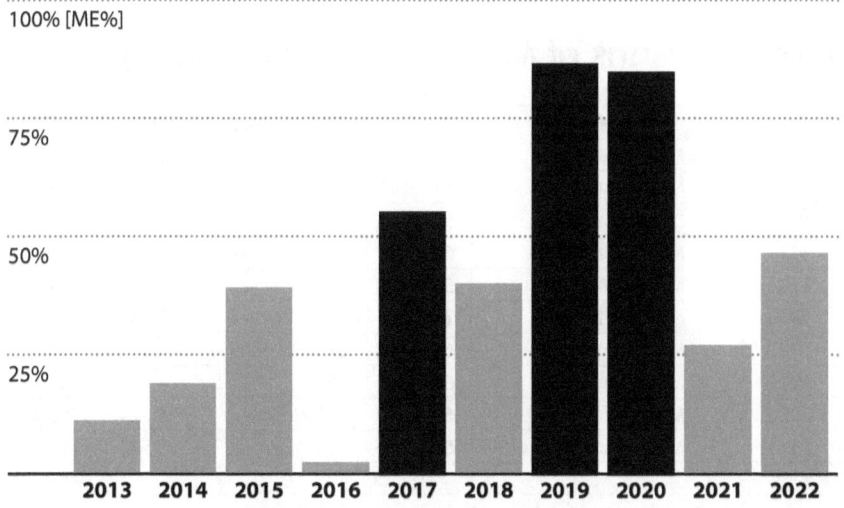

Year	Team	W	L	Pct.	Post	TS	ME%
2013	Minnesota Twins	66	96	.407	—	25.589	11.1%
2014	Minnesota Twins	70	92	.432	—	30.177	19.0%
2015	Minnesota Twins	83	79	.512	—	40.877	39.2%
2016	Minnesota Twins	59	103	.364	—	15.628	2.2%
2017	Minnesota Twins	85	77	.525	P	48.628	55.2%
2018	Minnesota Twins	78	84	.481	—	41.223	40.1%
2019	Minnesota Twins	101	61	.623	P	64.878	86.6%
2020	Minnesota Twins	36	24	.600	P	63.663	84.8%
2021	Minnesota Twins	73	89	.451	—	35.010	27.0%
2022	Minnesota Twins	78	84	.481	—	44.243	46.5%

Best Seasons of Modern Era (1961-2022)

Year	Team	W	L	Pct.	Post	TS	ME%
1991	Minnesota Twins	95	67	.586	WLP	82.261	98.0%
1965	Minnesota Twins	102	60	.630	LP	78.002	96.4%
1969	Minnesota Twins	97	65	.599	P	66.735	88.3%
2019	Minnesota Twins	101	61	.623	P	64.878	86.6%
1963	Minnesota Twins	91	70	.565	—	64.600	86.2%
1970	Minnesota Twins	98	64	.605	P	63.997	85.1%
2020	Minnesota Twins	36	24	.600	P	63.663	84.8%
1962	Minnesota Twins	91	71	.562	—	62.387	83.2%
1966	Minnesota Twins	89	73	.549	—	62.142	82.4%
1967	Minnesota Twins	91	71	.562	—	61.032	80.1%

Worst Seasons of Modern Era (1961-2022)

Year	Team	W	L	Pct.	Post	TS	ME%
2016	Minnesota Twins	59	103	.364	—	15.628	2.2%
1981	Minnesota Twins	41	68	.376	—	16.267	2.6%
1982	Minnesota Twins	60	102	.370	—	17.191	3.2%
2011	Minnesota Twins	63	99	.389	—	18.200	3.9%
1995	Minnesota Twins	56	88	.389	—	21.344	6.4%
1993	Minnesota Twins	71	91	.438	—	21.567	6.6%
1999	Minnesota Twins	63	97	.394	—	22.942	7.8%
2012	Minnesota Twins	66	96	.407	—	24.040	9.3%
2000	Minnesota Twins	69	93	.426	—	24.224	9.5%
2013	Minnesota Twins	66	96	.407	—	25.589	11.1%

Season Breakdown (2022)

Category	W	L	Pct.	R	RA	R/G	RA/G
Overall record in 2022	78	84	.481	696	684	4.30	4.22
Home games	46	35	.568	343	316	4.23	3.90
Away games	32	49	.395	353	368	4.36	4.54
First half of 2022 season	45	36	.556	363	317	4.48	3.91
Second half of 2022 season	33	48	.407	333	367	4.11	4.53
Against first-place teams	8	28	.222	140	198	3.89	5.50
Against playoff teams	21	38	.356	248	298	4.20	5.05
Against non-playoff teams	57	46	.553	448	386	4.35	3.75

Season as Nine-Inning Game (2022)

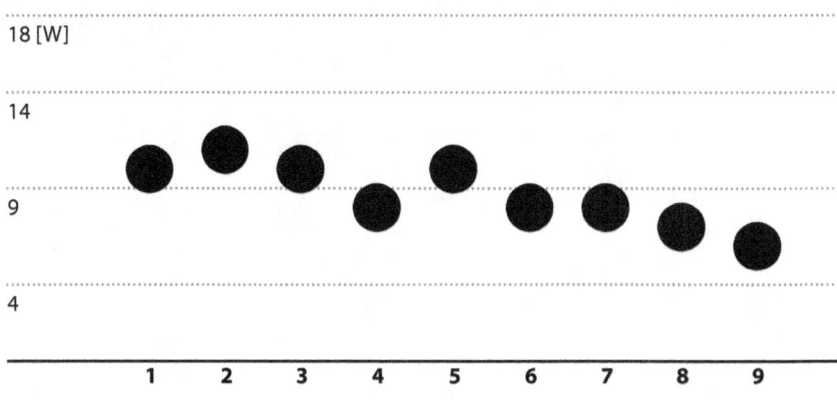

Result	1	2	3	4	5	6	7	8	9	Total
Wins	10	11	10	8	10	8	8	7	6	78
Losses	8	7	8	10	8	10	10	11	12	84

Scoring by Game (2022)

Runs Scored	G	W	L	Pct.	R/G	RA/G
Overall record	162	78	84	.481	4.30	4.22
0	13	0	13	.000	0.00	5.77
1	14	3	11	.214	1.00	4.14
2	25	5	20	.200	2.00	3.84
3	27	7	20	.259	3.00	5.11
4	19	12	7	.632	4.00	3.74
5	11	6	5	.545	5.00	4.09
6	15	11	4	.733	6.00	4.20
7	9	7	2	.778	7.00	4.22
8	11	10	1	.909	8.00	3.82
9	9	9	0	1.000	9.00	1.78
10 or more	9	8	1	.889	10.89	4.67

Scoring Allowed by Game (2022)

Runs Allowed	G	W	L	Pct.	R/G	RA/G
Overall record	162	78	84	.481	4.30	4.22
0	17	17	0	1.000	4.41	0.00
1	17	16	1	.941	5.41	1.00
2	14	11	3	.786	4.50	2.00
3	23	14	9	.609	4.61	3.00
4	26	12	14	.462	4.69	4.00
5	20	4	16	.200	3.00	5.00
6	11	2	9	.182	3.91	6.00
7	13	1	12	.077	3.69	7.00
8	4	1	3	.250	5.25	8.00
9	4	0	4	.000	5.50	9.00
10 or more	13	0	13	.000	3.38	10.85

Margins (2022)

Category	Margin	G	W	L	Pct.	GShr	WShr
Overall record	—	162	78	84	.481	—	—
Close	1 or 2 runs	71	29	42	.408	43.8%	37.2%
Medium	3 or 4 runs	37	22	15	.595	22.8%	28.2%
Distant	5 or more runs	54	27	27	.500	33.3%	34.6%

Individual Scoring Leaders (2022)

Team Rank	Batter	R	(+) RBI	(-) HR	(=) SC
1	Luis Arraez	88	49	8	129
2	Carlos Correa	70	64	22	112
2	Gio Urshela	61	64	13	112
4	Jose Miranda	45	66	15	96
5	Jorge Polanco	54	56	16	94
6	Max Kepler	54	43	9	88
7	Gary Sanchez	42	61	16	87
8	Nick Gordon	45	50	9	86
9	Byron Buxton	61	51	28	84
10	Gilberto Celestino	30	24	2	52

Team Ratings (2022)

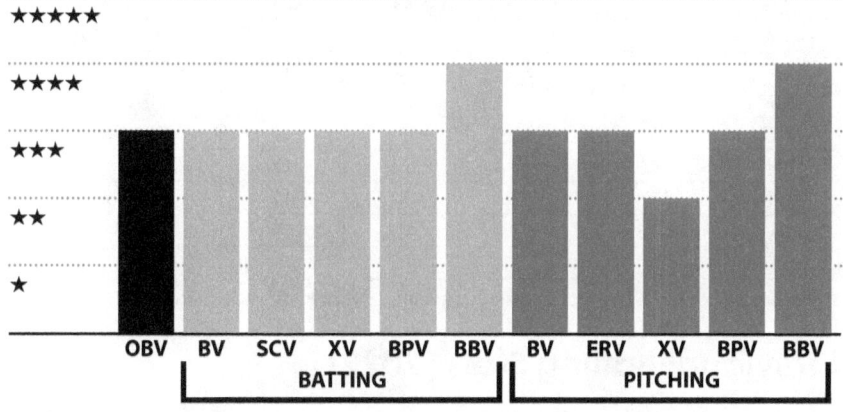

Quality	Type	Indicator	Value	Rating
Overall performance	Overall	OBV	6	★★★
Base production	Batting	BV	13	★★★
Run production	Batting	SCV	-6	★★★
Power hitting	Batting	XV	6	★★★
Contact hitting	Batting	BPV	14	★★★
Batting eye	Batting	BBV	24	★★★★
Base prevention	Pitching	BV	7	★★★
Run prevention	Pitching	ERV	3	★★★
Power prevention	Pitching	XV	32	★★
Strikeout pitching	Pitching	BPV	27	★★★
Control pitching	Pitching	BBV	-28	★★★★

Team Batting Stats (2022)

Stat	Number	Div Rank	Lg Rank	MLB Rank	MLB Best
R	696	2	7	17	847 (Dodgers)
H	1,356	3	5	11	1,464 (Blue Jays)
HR	178	1	7	13	254 (Yankees)
BPO	.663	1	6	13	.764 (Dodgers)
BA	.248	3	6	13	.264 (Blue Jays)
OBP	.317	1	5	10	.333 (Dodgers)
SA	.401	1	5	11	.443 (Braves)

Division: AL Central, 5 teams. **League:** American, 15 teams. **MLB:** 30 teams.

Team Pitching Stats (2022)

Stat	Number	Div Rank	Lg Rank	MLB Rank	MLB Best
ERA	3.98	3	10	19	2.80 (Dodgers)
SO	1,336	3	10	20	1,565 (Mets)
BB	468	2	8	12	384 (Rays)
BPO	.662	3	9	17	.551 (Astros)
BA	.242	2	7	13	.209 (Dodgers)
OBP	.307	2	7	12	.273 (Dodgers)
SA	.400	4	11	19	.332 (Astros)

Division: AL Central, 5 teams. **League:** American, 15 teams. **MLB:** 30 teams.

Individual Batting Stats (2022)

Batter	PA	BPO	BA	OBP	SA	ISO	CT	EY
Luis Arraez	603	.749	.316	.375	.420	.104	.921	.080
Byron Buxton	382	.857	.224	.306	.526	.303	.659	.089
Gilberto Celestino	347	.530	.238	.313	.302	.064	.752	.092
Carlos Correa	590	.794	.291	.366	.467	.176	.768	.100
Nick Gordon	443	.687	.272	.316	.427	.156	.741	.041
Max Kepler	446	.626	.227	.318	.348	.121	.830	.108
Jose Miranda	483	.662	.268	.325	.426	.158	.795	.058
Jorge Polanco	445	.755	.235	.346	.405	.171	.747	.142
Gary Sanchez	471	.606	.205	.282	.377	.172	.675	.085
Gio Urshela	551	.689	.285	.338	.429	.144	.808	.071

Individual Pitching Stats for Starters (2022)

Pitcher	IP	BPO	ERA	BA	SA	ISO	CT	EY
Chris Archer	102.2	.670	4.56	.228	.391	.163	.780	.110
Dylan Bundy	140.0	.721	4.89	.271	.459	.188	.832	.047
Sonny Gray	119.2	.585	3.08	.224	.349	.125	.735	.074
Joe Ryan	147.0	.623	3.55	.211	.379	.168	.723	.078

Individual Pitching Stats for Relievers (2022)

Pitcher	GR	BPO	ERA	BA	SA	ISO	CT	EY
Jhoan Duran	57	.495	1.86	.207	.306	.099	.632	.049
Griffin Jax	65	.541	3.36	.212	.333	.121	.705	.059
Emilio Pagan	59	.747	4.43	.245	.457	.212	.657	.088
Caleb Thielbar	67	.545	3.49	.226	.332	.106	.646	.070

Best Stats on Team (2022)

Stat	Batter	Number
2B	Luis Arraez	31
3B	Nick Gordon	4
BA	Luis Arraez	.316
BB	Jorge Polanco	64
BBV	Jorge Polanco	28
BPO	Byron Buxton	.857
BPV	Luis Arraez	94
BV	Carlos Correa	53
CT	Luis Arraez	.921
EY	Jorge Polanco	.142
H	Luis Arraez	173
HR	Byron Buxton	28
ISO	Byron Buxton	.303
OBP	Luis Arraez	.375
R	Luis Arraez	88
RBI	Jose Miranda	66
SA	Byron Buxton	.526
SB	Byron Buxton, Nick Gordon	6
SC	Luis Arraez	129
SCV	Luis Arraez	11
SE	Byron Buxton	.220
XV	Byron Buxton	51

Stat	Pitcher	Number
BA	Joe Ryan	.211
BBV	Dylan Bundy	-19
BPO-R	Jhoan Duran	.495
BPO-S	Sonny Gray	.585
BPV	Jhoan Duran	-29
BV	Jhoan Duran	-34
CT	Joe Ryan	.723
ERA-R	Jhoan Duran	1.86
ERA-S	Sonny Gray	3.08
ERV	Jhoan Duran	-16
EY	Dylan Bundy	.047
GR	Caleb Thielbar	67
GS	Dylan Bundy	29
IP	Joe Ryan	147.0
ISO	Sonny Gray	.125
OBP	Joe Ryan	.285
SA	Sonny Gray	.349
SO	Joe Ryan	151
SV	Emilio Pagan	9
W	Joe Ryan	13
XV	Jovani Moran	-14

Worst Stats on Team (2022)

Stat	Batter	Number
BA	Gary Sanchez	.205
BBV	Nick Gordon	-17
BPO	Gilberto Celestino	.530
BPV	Gary Sanchez, Byron Buxton	-31
BV	Gilberto Celestino	-33
CT	Byron Buxton	.659
EY	Nick Gordon	.041
ISO	Gilberto Celestino	.064
OBP	Gary Sanchez	.282
SA	Gilberto Celestino	.302
SCV	Gilberto Celestino	-16
SE	Gilberto Celestino	.150
SO	Gary Sanchez	136
XV	Gilberto Celestino	-27

Stat	Pitcher	Number
BA	Dylan Bundy	.271
BB	Chris Archer	48
BBV	Chris Archer	13
BPO-R	Emilio Pagan	.747
BPO-S	Dylan Bundy	.721
BPV	Dylan Bundy	45
BV	Dylan Bundy	25
CT	Dylan Bundy	.832
ERA-R	Emilio Pagan	4.43
ERA-S	Dylan Bundy	4.89
ERV	Dylan Bundy	14
EY	Chris Archer	.110
ISO	Dylan Bundy	.188
L	Joe Ryan, Dylan Bundy, Chris Archer	8
OBP	Chris Archer	.317
SA	Dylan Bundy	.459
XV	Dylan Bundy	20

Overall Base Value Leaders (2022)

Team Rank	Player	BV [bat]	(-) BV [pitch]	(=) OBV
1	Carlos Correa	53	0	53
2	Byron Buxton	52	0	52
3	Luis Arraez	35	0	35
4	Jhoan Duran	0	-34	34
5	Jorge Polanco	28	0	28
6	Sonny Gray	0	-27	27
7	Griffin Jax	0	-26	26
8	Jovani Moran	0	-24	24
9	Bailey Ober	0	-21	21
10	Caleb Thielbar	0	-20	20

Fan Support in Past 10 Seasons (2013-2022)

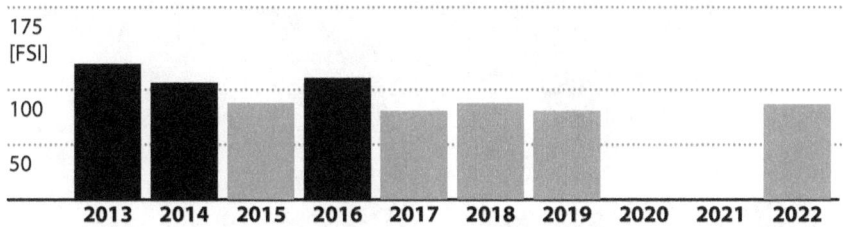

Year	Team	Attendance	W	Att:W	FSI
2013	Minnesota Twins	2,477,644	66	37,540	123.3
2014	Minnesota Twins	2,250,606	70	32,152	106.0
2015	Minnesota Twins	2,220,054	83	26,748	88.1
2016	Minnesota Twins	1,963,912	59	33,287	110.4
2017	Minnesota Twins	2,051,279	85	24,133	80.7
2018	Minnesota Twins	1,959,197	78	25,118	87.6
2019	Minnesota Twins	2,303,299	101	22,805	80.9
2022	Minnesota Twins	1,801,128	78	23,091	86.9

Extreme Games for Batters (2022)

Stat	Team Total	Individual Leader	G
3+ H	81	Luis Arraez	17
2+ HR	11	Byron Buxton	4
5+ RBI	3	Byron Buxton, Gary Sanchez, Nick Gordon	1
0 H in 5+ AB	39	Luis Arraez	7
4+ SO	8	Jake Cave	2

Extreme Games for Pitchers (2022)

Stat	Team Total	Individual Leader	G
0-2 ER in 7+ IP	10	Joe Ryan	4
10+ SO	3	Sonny Gray	2
0 BR in SV	7	Jhoan Duran	3
10+ BR	16	Dylan Bundy, Joe Ryan	5
1+ ER in SV	1	Emilio Pagan	1

Predictions for Coming Season (2023)

Group	Next W	Next L	Next Pct.	WS	LC	PQ
10 closest matches (avg. W-L)	78.5	78.6	.500	0	0	2
25 closest matches (avg. W-L)	79.3	78.9	.501	1	1	5
50 closest matches (avg. W-L)	77.9	80.1	.493	1	2	8

25 Closest Matches (2023)

Rank	Team	Next	W	L	Pct.	WS	LC	PQ
1	Astros (1986-1988)	1989	86	76	.531	—	—	—
2	Angels (1982-1984)	1985	90	72	.556	—	—	—
3	Mets (2008-2010)	2011	77	85	.475	—	—	—
4	Rangers (1993-1995)	1996	90	72	.556	—	—	X
5	Tigers (2007-2009)	2010	81	81	.500	—	—	—
6	White Sox (1983-1985)	1986	72	90	.444	—	—	—
7	Cubs (1989-1991)	1992	78	84	.481	—	—	—
8	Red Sox (1991-1993)	1994	54	61	.470	—	—	—
9	Yankees (2012-2014)	2015	87	75	.537	—	—	X
10	White Sox (1977-1979)	1980	70	90	.438	—	—	—
11	Royals (1991-1993)	1994	64	51	.557	—	—	—
12	Padres (2010-2012)	2013	76	86	.469	—	—	—
13	Padres (1989-1991)	1992	82	80	.506	—	—	—
14	Angels (2015-2017)	2018	80	82	.494	—	—	—
15	Angels (1979-1981)	1982	93	69	.574	—	—	X
16	Rays (2013-2015)	2016	68	94	.420	—	—	—
17	Cardinals (1989-1991)	1992	83	79	.512	—	—	—
18	Giants (2004-2006)	2007	71	91	.438	—	—	—
19	Reds (1996-1998)	1999	96	67	.589	—	—	—
20	Rays (2015-2017)	2018	90	72	.556	—	—	—
21	Royals (1989-1991)	1992	72	90	.444	—	—	—
22	Pirates (1997-1999)	2000	69	93	.426	—	—	—
23	Angels (1989-1991)	1992	72	90	.444	—	—	—
24	Royals (1982-1984)	1985	91	71	.562	X	X	X
25	Mariners (1997-1999)	2000	91	71	.562	—	—	X

NEW YORK METS

Past 10 Seasons (2013-2022)

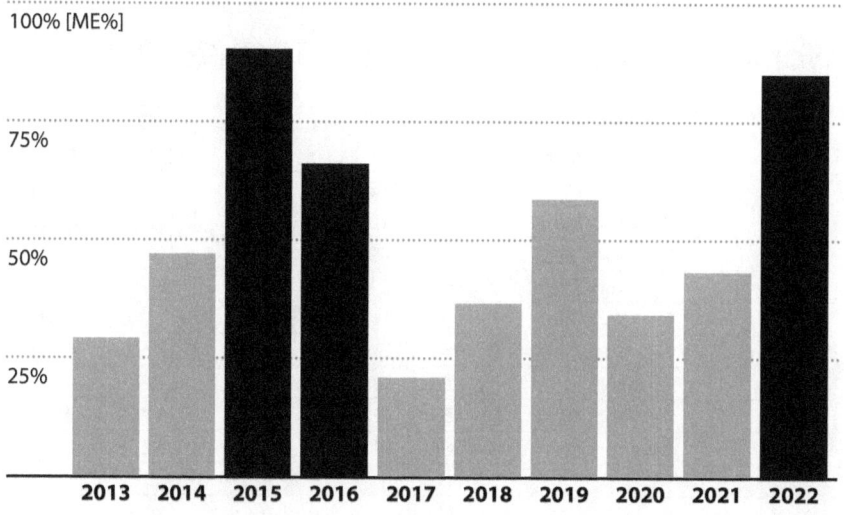

Year	Team	W	L	Pct.	Post	TS	ME%
2013	New York Mets	74	88	.457	—	36.107	29.1%
2014	New York Mets	79	83	.488	—	44.502	47.0%
2015	New York Mets	90	72	.556	LP	68.509	90.2%
2016	New York Mets	87	75	.537	P	53.717	66.0%
2017	New York Mets	70	92	.432	—	31.513	20.9%
2018	New York Mets	77	85	.475	—	39.758	36.6%
2019	New York Mets	86	76	.531	—	50.595	58.6%
2020	New York Mets	26	34	.433	—	38.523	34.2%
2021	New York Mets	77	85	.475	—	42.744	43.3%
2022	New York Mets	101	61	.623	P	63.991	85.0%

Best Seasons of Modern Era (1962-2022)

Year	Team	W	L	Pct.	Post	TS	ME%
1986	New York Mets	108	54	.667	WLP	94.962	99.9%
1988	New York Mets	100	60	.625	P	74.761	94.5%
2006	New York Mets	97	65	.599	P	74.757	94.4%
1969	New York Mets	100	62	.617	WLP	72.856	93.2%
1987	New York Mets	92	70	.568	—	71.263	91.8%
2000	New York Mets	94	68	.580	LP	70.288	91.1%
2015	New York Mets	90	72	.556	LP	68.509	90.2%
1990	New York Mets	91	71	.562	—	67.119	88.6%
1985	New York Mets	98	64	.605	—	65.210	87.1%
2022	New York Mets	101	61	.623	P	63.991	85.0%

Worst Seasons of Modern Era (1962-2022)

Year	Team	W	L	Pct.	Post	TS	ME%
1963	New York Mets	51	111	.315	—	8.162	0.2%
1965	New York Mets	50	112	.309	—	9.282	0.4%
1962	New York Mets	40	120	.250	—	10.038	0.5%
1964	New York Mets	53	109	.327	—	10.277	0.7%
1967	New York Mets	61	101	.377	—	14.743	1.7%
1983	New York Mets	68	94	.420	—	17.063	3.0%
1982	New York Mets	65	97	.401	—	18.665	4.2%
1966	New York Mets	66	95	.410	—	19.679	4.7%
1979	New York Mets	63	99	.389	—	21.352	6.5%
2003	New York Mets	66	95	.410	—	23.508	8.6%

Season Breakdown (2022)

Category	W	L	Pct.	R	RA	R/G	RA/G
Overall record in 2022	101	61	.623	772	606	4.77	3.74
Home games	54	27	.667	376	266	4.64	3.28
Away games	47	34	.580	396	340	4.89	4.20
First half of 2022 season	50	31	.617	384	325	4.74	4.01
Second half of 2022 season	51	30	.630	388	281	4.79	3.47
Against first-place teams	20	21	.488	155	178	3.78	4.34
Against playoff teams	37	32	.536	291	291	4.22	4.22
Against non-playoff teams	64	29	.688	481	315	5.17	3.39

Season as Nine-Inning Game (2022)

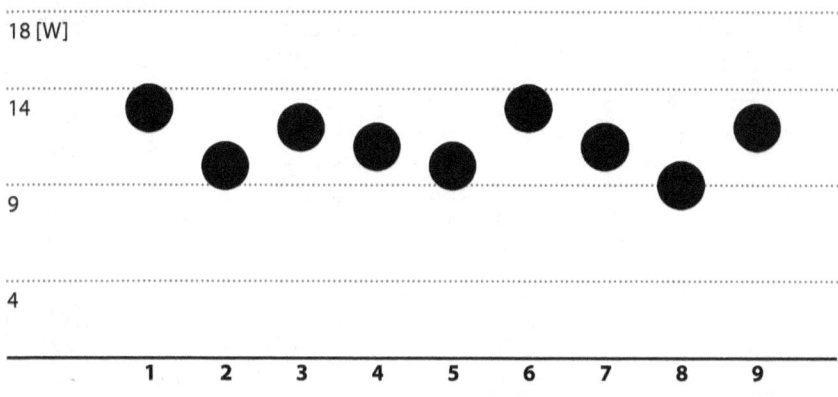

Result	1	2	3	4	5	6	7	8	9	Total
Wins	13	10	12	11	10	13	11	9	12	101
Losses	5	8	6	7	8	5	7	9	6	61

Scoring by Game (2022)

Runs Scored	G	W	L	Pct.	R/G	RA/G
Overall record	162	101	61	.623	4.77	3.74
0	8	0	8	.000	0.00	3.25
1	15	1	14	.067	1.00	4.87
2	25	4	21	.160	2.00	4.68
3	19	9	10	.474	3.00	3.79
4	14	11	3	.786	4.00	2.71
5	22	21	1	.955	5.00	2.73
6	13	11	2	.846	6.00	3.46
7	14	13	1	.929	7.00	3.71
8	9	9	0	1.000	8.00	3.33
9	8	8	0	1.000	9.00	4.00
10 or more	15	14	1	.933	10.93	4.07

Scoring Allowed by Game (2022)

Runs Allowed	G	W	L	Pct.	R/G	RA/G
Overall record	162	101	61	.623	4.77	3.74
0	19	19	0	1.000	5.16	0.00
1	18	16	2	.889	3.72	1.00
2	23	17	6	.739	4.74	2.00
3	24	19	5	.792	6.04	3.00
4	26	15	11	.577	4.65	4.00
5	18	7	11	.389	4.72	5.00
6	11	5	6	.455	4.91	6.00
7	6	2	4	.333	3.67	7.00
8	4	0	4	.000	3.50	8.00
9	5	1	4	.200	4.40	9.00
10 or more	8	0	8	.000	4.38	11.38

Margins (2022)

Category	Margin	G	W	L	Pct.	GShr	WShr
Overall record	—	162	101	61	.623	—	—
Close	1 or 2 runs	61	36	25	.590	37.7%	35.6%
Medium	3 or 4 runs	51	34	17	.667	31.5%	33.7%
Distant	5 or more runs	50	31	19	.620	30.9%	30.7%

Individual Scoring Leaders (2022)

Team Rank	Batter	R	(+) RBI	(-) HR	(=) SC
1	Pete Alonso	95	131	40	186
2	Francisco Lindor	98	107	26	179
3	Brandon Nimmo	102	64	16	150
4	Jeff McNeil	73	62	9	126
5	Starling Marte	76	63	16	123
6	Mark Canha	71	61	13	119
7	Eduardo Escobar	58	69	20	107
8	Tomas Nido	31	28	3	56
9	Luis Guillorme	33	17	2	48
10	J.D. Davis	26	21	4	43

Team Ratings (2022)

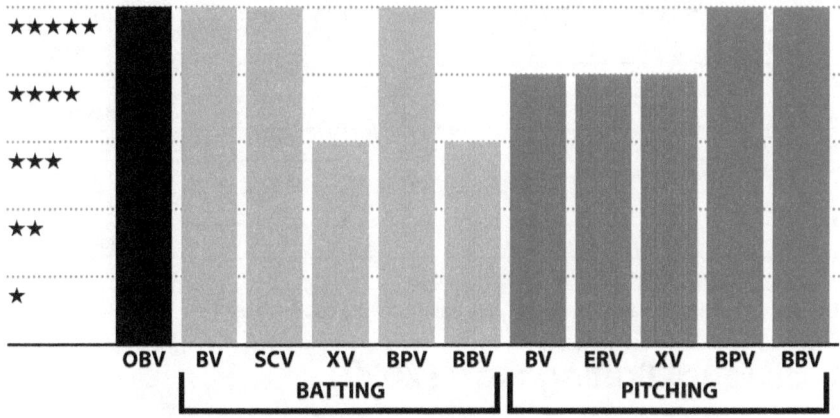

Quality	Type	Indicator	Value	Rating
Overall performance	Overall	OBV	376	★★★★★
Base production	Batting	BV	187	★★★★★
Run production	Batting	SCV	132	★★★★★
Power hitting	Batting	XV	4	★★★
Contact hitting	Batting	BPV	153	★★★★★
Batting eye	Batting	BBV	-2	★★★
Base prevention	Pitching	BV	-189	★★★★
Run prevention	Pitching	ERV	-63	★★★★
Power prevention	Pitching	XV	-60	★★★★
Strikeout pitching	Pitching	BPV	-215	★★★★★
Control pitching	Pitching	BBV	-55	★★★★★

Team Batting Stats (2022)

Stat	Number	Div Rank	Lg Rank	MLB Rank	MLB Best
R	772	2	3	5	847 (Dodgers)
H	1,422	1	1	4	1,464 (Blue Jays)
HR	171	3	8	15	254 (Yankees)
BPO	.704	2	4	7	.764 (Dodgers)
BA	.259	1	1	2	.264 (Blue Jays)
OBP	.332	1	2	2	.333 (Dodgers)
SA	.412	3	5	8	.443 (Braves)

Division: NL East, 5 teams. **League:** National, 15 teams. **MLB:** 30 teams.

Team Pitching Stats (2022)

Stat	Number	Div Rank	Lg Rank	MLB Rank	MLB Best
ERA	3.57	2	3	7	2.80 (Dodgers)
SO	1,565	1	1	1	1,565 (Mets)
BB	428	1	2	4	384 (Rays)
BPO	.616	2	3	7	.551 (Astros)
BA	.236	2	5	11	.209 (Dodgers)
OBP	.299	2	3	8	.273 (Dodgers)
SA	.377	2	3	6	.332 (Astros)

Division: NL East, 5 teams. **League:** National, 15 teams. **MLB:** 30 teams.

Individual Batting Stats (2022)

Batter	PA	BPO	BA	OBP	SA	ISO	CT	EY
Pete Alonso	685	.870	.271	.352	.518	.246	.786	.076
Mark Canha	542	.775	.266	.367	.403	.136	.790	.087
Eduardo Escobar	542	.670	.240	.295	.430	.190	.739	.069
Luis Guillorme	335	.601	.273	.351	.340	.067	.845	.099
Francisco Lindor	706	.775	.270	.339	.449	.179	.789	.081
Starling Marte	505	.770	.292	.347	.468	.176	.792	.051
Jeff McNeil	589	.816	.326	.382	.454	.128	.886	.066
Brandon Nimmo	673	.792	.274	.367	.433	.159	.800	.105

Individual Pitching Stats for Starters (2022)

Pitcher	IP	BPO	ERA	BA	SA	ISO	CT	EY
Chris Bassitt	181.2	.575	3.42	.234	.359	.125	.754	.066
Carlos Carrasco	152.0	.687	3.97	.272	.425	.153	.744	.061
David Peterson	105.2	.665	3.83	.236	.378	.142	.680	.104
Max Scherzer	145.1	.489	2.29	.207	.319	.113	.669	.042
Taijuan Walker	157.1	.591	3.49	.240	.364	.124	.779	.068

Individual Pitching Stats for Relievers (2022)

Pitcher	GR	BPO	ERA	BA	SA	ISO	CT	EY
Edwin Diaz	61	.414	1.31	.160	.216	.056	.446	.073
Seth Lugo	62	.607	3.60	.233	.378	.145	.723	.063
Adam Ottavino	66	.590	2.06	.204	.323	.119	.664	.055
Joely Rodriguez	55	.599	4.47	.226	.312	.086	.694	.116
Drew Smith	44	.620	3.33	.222	.404	.181	.690	.080

Best Stats on Team (2022)

Stat	Batter	Number
2B	Jeff McNeil	39
3B	Brandon Nimmo	7
BA	Jeff McNeil	.326
BB	Brandon Nimmo	71
BBV	Brandon Nimmo, Daniel Vogelbach	18
BPO	Pete Alonso	.870
BPV	Jeff McNeil	72
BV	Pete Alonso	97
CT	Jeff McNeil	.886
EY	Brandon Nimmo	.105
H	Jeff McNeil	174
HR	Pete Alonso	40
ISO	Pete Alonso	.246
OBP	Jeff McNeil	.382
R	Brandon Nimmo	102
RBI	Pete Alonso	131
SA	Pete Alonso	.518
SB	Starling Marte	18
SC	Pete Alonso	186
SCV	Pete Alonso	52
SE	Pete Alonso	.272
XV	Pete Alonso	56

Stat	Pitcher	Number
BA	Max Scherzer	.207
BBV	Max Scherzer	-21
BPO-R	Edwin Diaz	.414
BPO-S	Max Scherzer	.489
BPV	Edwin Diaz	-65
BV	Max Scherzer	-75
CT	Max Scherzer	.669
ERA-R	Edwin Diaz	1.31
ERA-S	Max Scherzer	2.29
ERV	Max Scherzer	-27
EY	Max Scherzer	.042
GR	Adam Ottavino	66
GS	Chris Bassitt	30
IP	Chris Bassitt	181.2
ISO	Max Scherzer	.113
OBP	Max Scherzer	.254
SA	Max Scherzer	.319
SO	Max Scherzer	173
SV	Edwin Diaz	32
W	Chris Bassitt, Carlos Carrasco	15
XV	Max Scherzer	-21

Worst Stats on Team (2022)

Stat	Batter	Number
BA	Eduardo Escobar	.240
BBV	Starling Marte	-14
BPO	Luis Guillorme	.601
BPV	J.D. Davis	-21
BV	Tomas Nido	-40
CT	Eduardo Escobar	.739
EY	Starling Marte	.051
ISO	Luis Guillorme	.067
OBP	Eduardo Escobar	.295
SA	Luis Guillorme	.340
SCV	Luis Guillorme	-17
SE	Luis Guillorme	.143
SO	Francisco Lindor	133
XV	Luis Guillorme	-25

Stat	Pitcher	Number
BA	Carlos Carrasco	.272
BB	Chris Bassitt	49
BBV	David Peterson	11
BPO-R	Drew Smith	.620
BPO-S	Carlos Carrasco	.687
BPV	Taijuan Walker	17
BV	Thomas Szapucki	22
CT	Taijuan Walker	.779
ERA-R	Joely Rodriguez	4.47
ERA-S	Carlos Carrasco	3.97
ERV	Thomas Szapucki	8
EY	David Peterson	.104
ISO	Carlos Carrasco	.153
L	Chris Bassitt	9
OBP	David Peterson	.327
SA	Carlos Carrasco	.425
XV	Thomas Szapucki	13

Overall Base Value Leaders (2022)

Team Rank	Player	BV [bat]	(-) BV [pitch]	(=) OBV
1	Pete Alonso	97	0	97
2	Max Scherzer	0	-75	75
3	Jeff McNeil	58	0	58
3	Brandon Nimmo	58	0	58
5	Francisco Lindor	56	0	56
6	Chris Bassitt	0	-47	47
7	Edwin Diaz	0	-46	46
8	Mark Canha	40	0	40
8	Jacob deGrom	0	-40	40
10	Starling Marte	39	0	39

Fan Support in Past 10 Seasons (2013-2022)

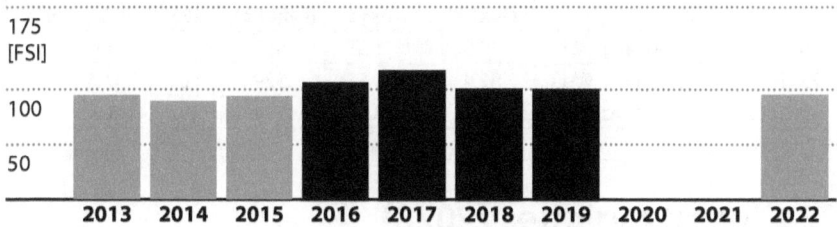

Year	Team	Attendance	W	Att:W	FSI
2013	New York Mets	2,135,657	74	28,860	94.8
2014	New York Mets	2,148,808	79	27,200	89.6
2015	New York Mets	2,569,753	90	28,553	94.0
2016	New York Mets	2,789,602	87	32,064	106.4
2017	New York Mets	2,460,622	70	35,152	117.5
2018	New York Mets	2,224,995	77	28,896	100.8
2019	New York Mets	2,442,532	86	28,402	100.7
2022	New York Mets	2,564,737	101	25,393	95.6

Extreme Games for Batters (2022)

Stat	Team Total	Individual Leader	G
3+ H	84	Jeff McNeil	16
2+ HR	7	Pete Alonso	3
5+ RBI	9	Pete Alonso	4
0 H in 5+ AB	22	Francisco Lindor	5
4+ SO	2	Pete Alonso, Tyler Naquin	1

Extreme Games for Pitchers (2022)

Stat	Team Total	Individual Leader	G
0-2 ER in 7+ IP	28	Max Scherzer	8
10+ SO	19	Max Scherzer	6
0 BR in SV	17	Edwin Diaz	13
10+ BR	23	Chris Bassitt	7
1+ ER in SV	2	Edwin Diaz	2

Predictions for Coming Season (2023)

Group	Next W	Next L	Next Pct.	WS	LC	PQ
10 closest matches (avg. W-L)	80.8	71.0	.532	0	0	3
25 closest matches (avg. W-L)	82.4	73.5	.529	0	0	9
50 closest matches (avg. W-L)	84.4	73.8	.534	3	6	21

25 Closest Matches (2023)

Rank	Team	Next	W	L	Pct.	WS	LC	PQ
1	Padres (1994-1996)	1997	76	86	.469	—	—	—
2	Mariners (1998-2000)	2001	116	46	.716	—	—	X
3	Reds (1997-1999)	2000	85	77	.525	—	—	—
4	Expos (1977-1979)	1980	90	72	.556	—	—	—
5	Indians (2003-2005)	2006	78	84	.481	—	—	—
6	Cubs (1987-1989)	1990	77	85	.475	—	—	—
7	Brewers (2009-2011)	2012	83	79	.512	—	—	—
8	Twins (2017-2019)	2020	36	24	.600	—	—	X
9	Reds (2008-2010)	2011	79	83	.488	—	—	—
10	Pirates (2011-2013)	2014	88	74	.543	—	—	X
11	Red Sox (1996-1998)	1999	94	68	.580	—	—	X
12	Rangers (1994-1996)	1997	77	85	.475	—	—	—
13	Mets (2013-2015)	2016	87	75	.537	—	—	X
14	Red Sox (1993-1995)	1996	85	77	.525	—	—	—
15	Cardinals (1998-2000)	2001	93	69	.574	—	—	X
16	Nationals (2010-2012)	2013	86	76	.531	—	—	—
17	Astros (1984-1986)	1987	76	86	.469	—	—	—
18	Padres (1982-1984)	1985	83	79	.512	—	—	—
19	Brewers (2016-2018)	2019	89	73	.549	—	—	X
20	Angels (1980-1982)	1983	70	92	.432	—	—	—
21	Rangers (1975-1977)	1978	87	75	.537	—	—	—
22	White Sox (1998-2000)	2001	83	79	.512	—	—	—
23	Astros (1978-1980)	1981	61	49	.555	—	—	X
24	Yankees (2015-2017)	2018	100	62	.617	—	—	X
25	Braves (1981-1983)	1984	80	82	.494	—	—	—

NEW YORK YANKEES

Past 10 Seasons (2013-2022)

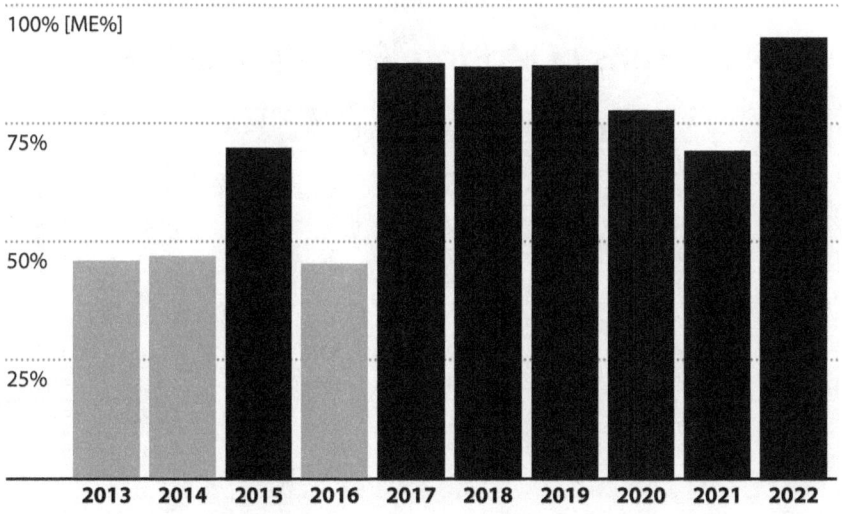

Year	Team	W	L	Pct.	Post	TS	ME%
2013	New York Yankees	85	77	.525	—	43.844	45.9%
2014	New York Yankees	84	78	.519	—	44.471	46.9%
2015	New York Yankees	87	75	.537	P	55.222	69.8%
2016	New York Yankees	84	78	.519	—	43.581	45.3%
2017	New York Yankees	91	71	.562	P	66.019	87.7%
2018	New York Yankees	100	62	.617	P	64.936	86.9%
2019	New York Yankees	103	59	.636	P	65.290	87.2%
2020	New York Yankees	33	27	.550	P	59.553	77.7%
2021	New York Yankees	92	70	.568	P	55.083	69.1%
2022	New York Yankees	99	63	.611	P	72.714	93.1%

Best Seasons of Modern Era (1961-2022)

Year	Team	W	L	Pct.	Post	TS	ME%
1998	New York Yankees	114	48	.704	WLP	96.123	99.9%
2009	New York Yankees	103	59	.636	WLP	87.433	99.4%
1961	New York Yankees	109	53	.673	WLP	85.319	98.9%
1962	New York Yankees	96	66	.593	WLP	85.088	98.8%
1999	New York Yankees	98	64	.605	WLP	83.564	98.4%
1976	New York Yankees	97	62	.610	LP	81.368	97.6%
1977	New York Yankees	100	62	.617	WLP	80.125	97.0%
1978	New York Yankees	100	63	.613	WLP	77.438	96.0%
1963	New York Yankees	104	57	.646	LP	77.023	95.8%
2003	New York Yankees	101	61	.623	LP	75.850	95.3%

Worst Seasons of Modern Era (1961-2022)

Year	Team	W	L	Pct.	Post	TS	ME%
1990	New York Yankees	67	95	.414	—	17.305	3.4%
1991	New York Yankees	71	91	.438	—	26.296	12.4%
1967	New York Yankees	72	90	.444	—	27.641	14.4%
1989	New York Yankees	74	87	.460	—	31.965	21.5%
1966	New York Yankees	70	89	.440	—	38.125	33.4%
1992	New York Yankees	76	86	.469	—	39.488	36.0%
1965	New York Yankees	77	85	.475	—	41.574	40.8%
2016	New York Yankees	84	78	.519	—	43.581	45.3%
2013	New York Yankees	85	77	.525	—	43.844	45.9%
2014	New York Yankees	84	78	.519	—	44.471	46.9%

Season Breakdown (2022)

Category	W	L	Pct.	R	RA	R/G	RA/G
Overall record in 2022	99	63	.611	807	567	4.98	3.50
Home games	57	24	.704	419	265	5.17	3.27
Away games	42	39	.519	388	302	4.79	3.73
First half of 2022 season	58	23	.716	405	246	5.00	3.04
Second half of 2022 season	41	40	.506	402	321	4.96	3.96
Against first-place teams	7	9	.438	72	58	4.50	3.63
Against playoff teams	33	31	.516	263	221	4.11	3.45
Against non-playoff teams	66	32	.673	544	346	5.55	3.53

Season as Nine-Inning Game (2022)

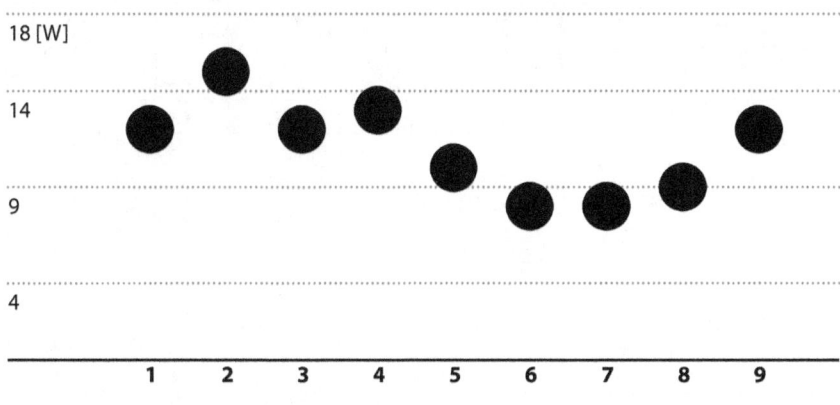

Result	1	2	3	4	5	6	7	8	9	Total
Wins	12	15	12	13	10	8	8	9	12	99
Losses	6	3	6	5	8	10	10	9	6	63

Scoring by Game (2022)

Runs Scored	G	W	L	Pct.	R/G	RA/G
Overall record	162	99	63	.611	4.98	3.50
0	12	0	12	.000	0.00	3.58
1	15	2	13	.133	1.00	2.73
2	25	10	15	.400	2.00	2.60
3	17	8	9	.471	3.00	3.06
4	14	10	4	.714	4.00	2.71
5	19	17	2	.895	5.00	3.47
6	15	9	6	.600	6.00	5.07
7	11	11	0	1.000	7.00	4.45
8	5	5	0	1.000	8.00	2.40
9	7	5	2	.714	9.00	5.86
10 or more	22	22	0	1.000	12.27	3.82

Scoring Allowed by Game (2022)

Runs Allowed	G	W	L	Pct.	R/G	RA/G
Overall record	162	99	63	.611	4.98	3.50
0	16	16	0	1.000	4.88	0.00
1	17	15	2	.882	4.41	1.00
2	28	22	6	.786	4.93	2.00
3	26	9	17	.346	3.12	3.00
4	31	17	14	.548	5.29	4.00
5	15	9	6	.600	5.73	5.00
6	10	5	5	.500	5.40	6.00
7	7	3	4	.429	7.57	7.00
8	6	3	3	.500	7.67	8.00
9	3	0	3	.000	2.67	9.00
10 or more	3	0	3	.000	8.00	11.00

Margins (2022)

Category	Margin	G	W	L	Pct.	GShr	WShr
Overall record	—	162	99	63	.611	—	—
Close	1 or 2 runs	91	49	42	.538	56.2%	49.5%
Medium	3 or 4 runs	33	18	15	.545	20.4%	18.2%
Distant	5 or more runs	38	32	6	.842	23.5%	32.3%

Individual Scoring Leaders (2022)

Team Rank	Batter	R	(+) RBI	(-) HR	(=) SC
1	Aaron Judge	133	131	62	202
2	Gleyber Torres	73	76	24	125
3	Anthony Rizzo	77	75	32	120
4	Isiah Kiner-Falefa	66	48	4	110
5	DJ LeMahieu	74	46	12	108
6	Josh Donaldson	59	62	15	106
7	Giancarlo Stanton	53	78	31	100
8	Aaron Hicks	54	40	8	86
9	Jose Trevino	39	43	11	71
10	Matt Carpenter	28	37	15	50

Team Ratings (2022)

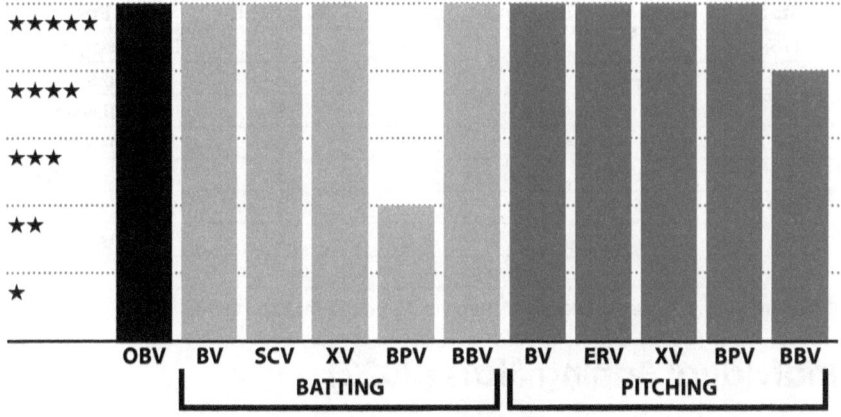

Quality	Type	Indicator	Value	Rating
Overall performance	Overall	OBV	674	★★★★★
Base production	Batting	BV	304	★★★★★
Run production	Batting	SCV	114	★★★★★
Power hitting	Batting	XV	178	★★★★★
Contact hitting	Batting	BPV	-37	★★
Batting eye	Batting	BBV	98	★★★★★
Base prevention	Pitching	BV	-370	★★★★★
Run prevention	Pitching	ERV	-107	★★★★★
Power prevention	Pitching	XV	-85	★★★★★
Strikeout pitching	Pitching	BPV	-116	★★★★★
Control pitching	Pitching	BBV	-35	★★★★

Team Batting Stats (2022)

Stat	Number	Div Rank	Lg Rank	MLB Rank	MLB Best
R	807	1	1	2	847 (Dodgers)
H	1,308	3	8	16	1,464 (Blue Jays)
HR	254	1	1	1	254 (Yankees)
BPO	.731	1	1	2	.764 (Dodgers)
BA	.241	3	8	15	.264 (Blue Jays)
OBP	.325	2	2	5	.333 (Dodgers)
SA	.426	2	2	4	.443 (Braves)

Division: AL East, 5 teams. **League:** American, 15 teams. **MLB:** 30 teams.

Team Pitching Stats (2022)

Stat	Number	Div Rank	Lg Rank	MLB Rank	MLB Best
ERA	3.30	1	2	3	2.80 (Dodgers)
SO	1,459	1	2	6	1,565 (Mets)
BB	444	4	5	8	384 (Rays)
BPO	.575	1	2	3	.551 (Astros)
BA	.219	1	2	3	.209 (Dodgers)
OBP	.285	1	2	3	.273 (Dodgers)
SA	.355	1	2	4	.332 (Astros)

Division: AL East, 5 teams. **League:** American, 15 teams. **MLB:** 30 teams.

Individual Batting Stats (2022)

Batter	PA	BPO	BA	OBP	SA	ISO	CT	EY
Josh Donaldson	546	.634	.222	.308	.374	.153	.690	.097
Aaron Hicks	453	.628	.216	.330	.313	.096	.716	.131
Aaron Judge	696	1.275	.311	.425	.686	.375	.693	.136
Isiah Kiner-Falefa	531	.597	.261	.314	.327	.066	.851	.062
DJ LeMahieu	541	.700	.261	.357	.377	.116	.848	.124
Anthony Rizzo	548	.819	.224	.338	.480	.256	.783	.096
Giancarlo Stanton	452	.729	.211	.297	.462	.251	.656	.107
Gleyber Torres	572	.711	.257	.310	.451	.194	.755	.065
Jose Trevino	353	.579	.248	.283	.388	.140	.815	.042

Individual Pitching Stats for Starters (2022)

Pitcher	IP	BPO	ERA	BA	SA	ISO	CT	EY
Gerrit Cole	200.2	.585	3.50	.209	.390	.182	.652	.063
Nestor Cortes	158.1	.474	2.44	.189	.313	.124	.715	.062
Jordan Montgomery	114.2	.595	3.69	.236	.385	.149	.778	.049
Luis Severino	102.0	.545	3.18	.196	.353	.158	.696	.074
Jameson Taillon	177.1	.645	3.91	.246	.430	.184	.779	.044

Individual Pitching Stats for Relievers (2022)

Pitcher	GR	BPO	ERA	BA	SA	ISO	CT	EY
Aroldis Chapman	43	.673	4.46	.188	.320	.133	.664	.175
Clay Holmes	62	.476	2.54	.196	.261	.065	.717	.070
Jonathan Loaisiga	50	.517	4.13	.234	.293	.060	.799	.089
Lucas Luetge	50	.657	2.67	.276	.386	.110	.737	.064
Wandy Peralta	56	.433	2.72	.208	.262	.054	.767	.072

Best Stats on Team (2022)

Stat	Batter	Number
2B	Aaron Judge, Gleyber Torres, Josh Donaldson	28
3B	Aaron Hicks	2
BA	Aaron Judge	.311
BB	Aaron Judge	111
BBV	Aaron Judge	38
BPO	Aaron Judge	1.275
BPV	Isiah Kiner-Falefa	49
BV	Aaron Judge	255
CT	Isiah Kiner-Falefa	.851
EY	Aaron Judge	.136
H	Aaron Judge	177
HR	Aaron Judge	62
ISO	Aaron Judge	.375
OBP	Aaron Judge	.425
R	Aaron Judge	133
RBI	Aaron Judge	131
SA	Aaron Judge	.686
SB	Isiah Kiner-Falefa	22
SC	Aaron Judge	202
SCV	Aaron Judge	66
SE	Aaron Judge	.290
XV	Aaron Judge	127

Stat	Pitcher	Number
BA	Nestor Cortes	.189
BBV	Jameson Taillon	-26
BPO-R	Wandy Peralta	.433
BPO-S	Nestor Cortes	.474
BPV	Gerrit Cole	-73
BV	Nestor Cortes	-89
CT	Gerrit Cole	.652
ERA-R	Clay Holmes	2.54
ERA-S	Nestor Cortes	2.44
ERV	Nestor Cortes	-27
EY	Jameson Taillon	.044
GR	Clay Holmes	62
GS	Gerrit Cole	33
IP	Gerrit Cole	200.2
ISO	Nestor Cortes	.124
OBP	Nestor Cortes	.241
SA	Nestor Cortes	.313
SO	Gerrit Cole	257
SV	Clay Holmes	20
W	Jameson Taillon	14
XV	Clay Holmes, Wandy Peralta	-20

Worst Stats on Team (2022)

Stat	Batter	Number
BA	Giancarlo Stanton	.211
BBV	Jose Trevino	-13
BPO	Jose Trevino	.579
BPV	Joey Gallo	-48
BV	Isiah Kiner-Falefa	-24
CT	Giancarlo Stanton	.656
EY	Jose Trevino	.042
ISO	Isiah Kiner-Falefa	.066
OBP	Jose Trevino	.283
SA	Aaron Hicks	.313
SCV	Joey Gallo	-9
SE	Aaron Hicks	.190
SO	Aaron Judge	175
XV	Isiah Kiner-Falefa	-41

Stat	Pitcher	Number
BA	Jameson Taillon	.246
BB	Gerrit Cole	50
BBV	Aroldis Chapman	15
BPO-R	Aroldis Chapman	.673
BPO-S	Jameson Taillon	.645
BPV	Jameson Taillon	20
BV	Frankie Montas	21
CT	Jameson Taillon	.779
ERA-R	Aroldis Chapman	4.46
ERA-S	Jameson Taillon	3.91
ERV	Frankie Montas	11
EY	Luis Severino	.074
ISO	Jameson Taillon	.184
L	Gerrit Cole	8
OBP	Jordan Montgomery	.285
SA	Jameson Taillon	.430
XV	Gerrit Cole, Jameson Taillon	22

Overall Base Value Leaders (2022)

Team Rank	Player	BV [bat]	(-) BV [pitch]	(=) OBV
1	Aaron Judge	255	0	255
2	Nestor Cortes	0	-89	89
3	Anthony Rizzo	61	0	61
4	Matt Carpenter	58	0	58
5	Gerrit Cole	0	-45	45
6	Wandy Peralta	0	-39	39
7	Clay Holmes	0	-35	35
7	Luis Severino	0	-35	35
9	Michael King	0	-30	30
10	Jordan Montgomery	0	-22	22
10	Giancarlo Stanton	22	0	22

Fan Support in Past 10 Seasons (2013-2022)

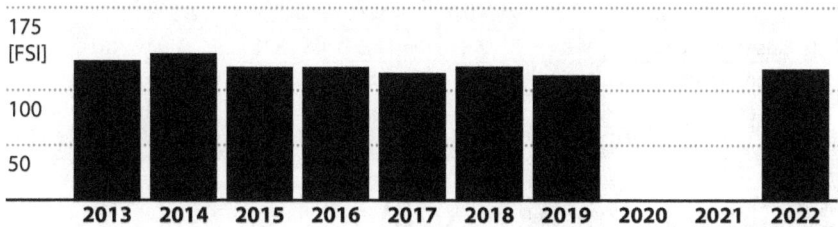

Year	Team	Attendance	W	Att:W	FSI
2013	New York Yankees	3,279,589	85	38,583	126.7
2014	New York Yankees	3,401,624	84	40,496	133.4
2015	New York Yankees	3,193,795	87	36,710	120.9
2016	New York Yankees	3,063,405	84	36,469	121.0
2017	New York Yankees	3,154,938	91	34,670	115.9
2018	New York Yankees	3,482,855	100	34,829	121.5
2019	New York Yankees	3,304,404	103	32,082	113.7
2022	New York Yankees	3,136,207	99	31,679	119.2

Extreme Games for Batters (2022)

Stat	Team Total	Individual Leader	G
3+ H	69	Aaron Judge	13
2+ HR	22	Aaron Judge	11
5+ RBI	8	Gleyber Torres, Matt Carpenter	2
0 H in 5+ AB	38	DJ LeMahieu	7
4+ SO	8	Giancarlo Stanton	5

Extreme Games for Pitchers (2022)

Stat	Team Total	Individual Leader	G
0-2 ER in 7+ IP	25	Gerrit Cole	9
10+ SO	15	Gerrit Cole	9
0 BR in SV	16	Clay Holmes	10
10+ BR	10	Jameson Taillon	4
1+ ER in SV	6	Aroldis Chapman, Clay Holmes	2

Predictions for Coming Season (2023)

Group	Next W	Next L	Next Pct.	WS	LC	PQ
10 closest matches (avg. W-L)	77.8	71.6	.521	0	0	2
25 closest matches (avg. W-L)	82.6	70.3	.540	0	1	7
50 closest matches (avg. W-L)	84.3	70.5	.545	2	5	21

25 Closest Matches (2023)

Rank	Team	Next	W	L	Pct.	WS	LC	PQ
1	Brewers (1980-1982)	1983	87	75	.537	—	—	—
2	Royals (1978-1980)	1981	50	53	.485	—	—	X
3	Astros (2003-2005)	2006	82	80	.506	—	—	—
4	Yankees (1983-1985)	1986	90	72	.556	—	—	—
5	Giants (1998-2000)	2001	90	72	.556	—	—	—
6	Expos (1992-1994)	1995	66	78	.458	—	—	—
7	Dodgers (2007-2009)	2010	80	82	.494	—	—	—
8	Cardinals (2009-2011)	2012	88	74	.543	—	—	X
9	Red Sox (1984-1986)	1987	78	84	.481	—	—	—
10	White Sox (1991-1993)	1994	67	46	.593	—	—	—
11	Phillies (1981-1983)	1984	81	81	.500	—	—	—
12	Dodgers (1975-1977)	1978	95	67	.586	—	X	X
13	Blue Jays (1983-1985)	1986	86	76	.531	—	—	—
14	Yankees (1994-1996)	1997	96	66	.593	—	—	X
15	Orioles (1977-1979)	1980	100	62	.617	—	—	—
16	Tigers (1985-1987)	1988	88	74	.543	—	—	—
17	White Sox (1981-1983)	1984	74	88	.457	—	—	—
18	Nationals (2012-2014)	2015	83	79	.512	—	—	—
19	Giants (1987-1989)	1990	85	77	.525	—	—	—
20	Blue Jays (1985-1987)	1988	87	75	.537	—	—	—
21	Nationals (2017-2019)	2020	26	34	.433	—	—	—
22	Indians (1997-1999)	2000	90	72	.556	—	—	—
23	Braves (2000-2002)	2003	101	61	.623	—	—	X
24	Indians (2014-2016)	2017	102	60	.630	—	—	X
25	Royals (1975-1977)	1978	92	70	.568	—	—	X

OAKLAND ATHLETICS

Past 10 Seasons (2013-2022)

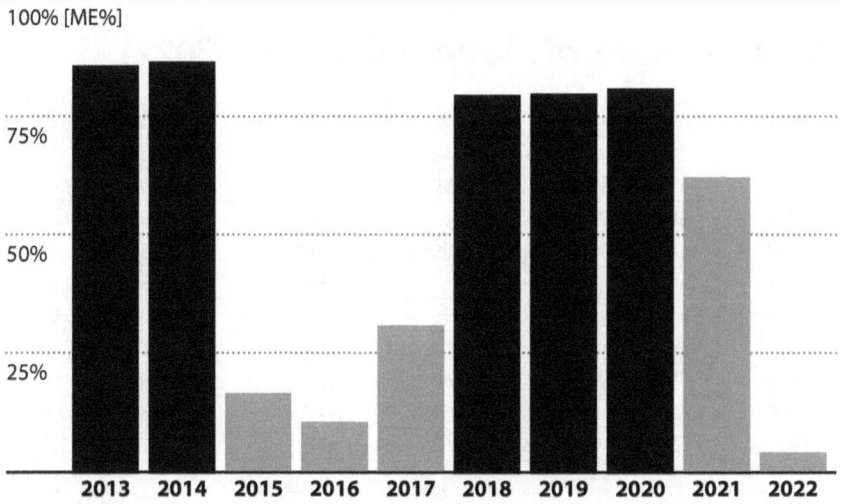

Year	Team	W	L	Pct.	Post	TS	ME%
2013	Oakland Athletics	96	66	.593	P	64.237	85.7%
2014	Oakland Athletics	88	74	.543	P	64.760	86.5%
2015	Oakland Athletics	68	94	.420	—	28.945	16.5%
2016	Oakland Athletics	69	93	.426	—	25.326	10.5%
2017	Oakland Athletics	75	87	.463	—	36.892	30.8%
2018	Oakland Athletics	97	65	.599	P	60.810	79.5%
2019	Oakland Athletics	97	65	.599	P	60.881	79.8%
2020	Oakland Athletics	36	24	.600	P	61.371	80.9%
2021	Oakland Athletics	86	76	.531	—	51.818	62.1%
2022	Oakland Athletics	60	102	.370	—	18.351	4.0%

Best Seasons of Modern Era (1961-2022)

Year	Team	W	L	Pct.	Post	TS	ME%
1990	Oakland Athletics	103	59	.636	LP	89.366	99.6%
1974	Oakland Athletics	90	72	.556	WLP	86.731	99.1%
1989	Oakland Athletics	99	63	.611	WLP	85.486	98.9%
1972	Oakland Athletics	93	62	.600	WLP	84.430	98.5%
1988	Oakland Athletics	104	58	.642	LP	80.527	97.3%
1973	Oakland Athletics	94	68	.580	WLP	79.826	97.0%
2001	Oakland Athletics	102	60	.630	P	70.213	91.0%
1975	Oakland Athletics	98	64	.605	P	70.016	90.9%
1971	Oakland Athletics	101	60	.627	P	66.960	88.5%
2014	Oakland Athletics	88	74	.543	P	64.760	86.5%

Worst Seasons of Modern Era (1961-2022)

Year	Team	W	L	Pct.	Post	TS	ME%
1979	Oakland Athletics	54	108	.333	—	11.385	1.1%
1964	Kansas City Athletics	57	105	.352	—	16.031	2.4%
1997	Oakland Athletics	65	97	.401	—	16.589	2.8%
2022	Oakland Athletics	60	102	.370	—	18.351	4.0%
1967	Kansas City Athletics	62	99	.385	—	19.836	4.8%
1965	Kansas City Athletics	59	103	.364	—	20.043	5.0%
1961	Kansas City Athletics	61	100	.379	—	22.027	7.1%
1993	Oakland Athletics	68	94	.420	—	22.975	7.9%
2016	Oakland Athletics	69	93	.426	—	25.326	10.5%
1982	Oakland Athletics	68	94	.420	—	26.689	13.0%

Season Breakdown (2022)

Category	W	L	Pct.	R	RA	R/G	RA/G
Overall record in 2022	60	102	.370	568	770	3.51	4.75
Home games	29	51	.363	251	396	3.14	4.95
Away games	31	51	.378	317	374	3.87	4.56
First half of 2022 season	26	55	.321	255	371	3.15	4.58
Second half of 2022 season	34	47	.420	313	399	3.86	4.93
Against first-place teams	10	27	.270	127	204	3.43	5.51
Against playoff teams	26	49	.347	280	381	3.73	5.08
Against non-playoff teams	34	53	.391	288	389	3.31	4.47

Season as Nine-Inning Game (2022)

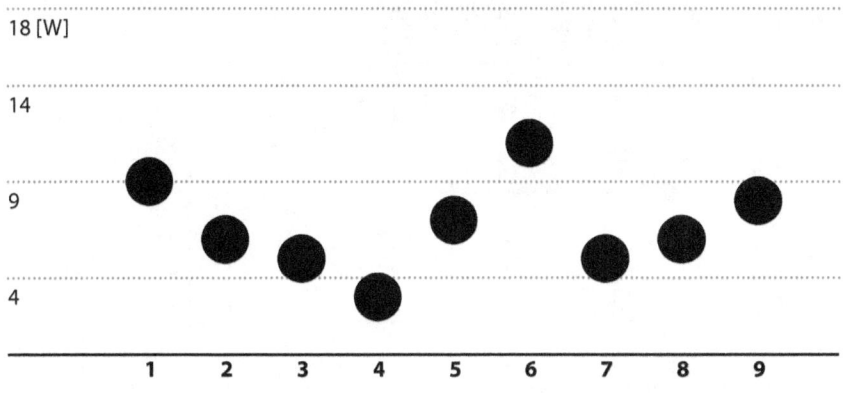

Result	1	2	3	4	5	6	7	8	9	Total
Wins	9	6	5	3	7	11	5	6	8	60
Losses	9	12	13	15	11	7	13	12	10	102

Scoring by Game (2022)

Runs Scored	G	W	L	Pct.	R/G	RA/G
Overall record	162	60	102	.370	3.51	4.75
0	14	0	14	.000	0.00	4.00
1	32	1	31	.031	1.00	4.16
2	25	5	20	.200	2.00	5.60
3	21	7	14	.333	3.00	4.48
4	21	13	8	.619	4.00	4.71
5	20	14	6	.700	5.00	3.90
6	5	3	2	.600	6.00	5.40
7	7	5	2	.714	7.00	5.43
8	7	3	4	.429	8.00	8.29
9	3	2	1	.667	9.00	5.67
10 or more	7	7	0	1.000	11.00	4.29

Scoring Allowed by Game (2022)

Runs Allowed	G	W	L	Pct.	R/G	RA/G
Overall record	162	60	102	.370	3.51	4.75
0	7	7	0	1.000	4.00	0.00
1	17	14	3	.824	3.00	1.00
2	22	11	11	.500	2.77	2.00
3	24	13	11	.542	3.63	3.00
4	15	4	11	.267	3.00	4.00
5	23	6	17	.261	3.39	5.00
6	8	1	7	.125	2.88	6.00
7	12	4	8	.333	5.67	7.00
8	11	0	11	.000	2.82	8.00
9	8	0	8	.000	4.25	9.00
10 or more	15	0	15	.000	4.13	11.33

Margins (2022)

Category	Margin	G	W	L	Pct.	GShr	WShr
Overall record	—	162	60	102	.370	—	—
Close	1 or 2 runs	80	36	44	.450	49.4%	60.0%
Medium	3 or 4 runs	43	14	29	.326	26.5%	23.3%
Distant	5 or more runs	39	10	29	.256	24.1%	16.7%

Individual Scoring Leaders (2022)

Team Rank	Batter	R	(+) RBI	(-) HR	(=) SC
1	Sean Murphy	67	66	18	115
2	Seth Brown	55	73	25	103
3	Tony Kemp	61	46	7	100
4	Ramon Laureano	49	34	13	70
5	Chad Pinder	38	42	12	68
6	Elvis Andrus	41	30	8	63
7	Sheldon Neuse	25	26	4	47
8	Nick Allen	31	19	4	46
9	Christian Bethancourt	23	19	4	38
9	Vimael Machin	26	13	1	38

Team Ratings (2022)

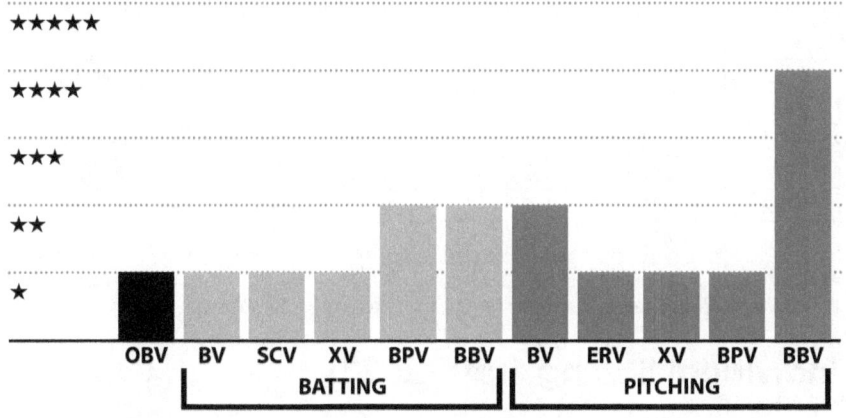

Quality	Type	Indicator	Value	Rating
Overall performance	Overall	OBV	-629	★
Base production	Batting	BV	-412	★
Run production	Batting	SCV	-175	★
Power hitting	Batting	XV	-119	★
Contact hitting	Batting	BPV	-62	★★
Batting eye	Batting	BBV	-38	★★
Base prevention	Pitching	BV	217	★★
Run prevention	Pitching	ERV	89	★
Power prevention	Pitching	XV	118	★
Strikeout pitching	Pitching	BPV	168	★
Control pitching	Pitching	BBV	-16	★★★★

Team Batting Stats (2022)

Stat	Number	Div Rank	Lg Rank	MLB Rank	MLB Best
R	568	5	14	29	847 (Dodgers)
H	1,147	5	15	30	1,464 (Blue Jays)
HR	137	5	13	27	254 (Yankees)
BPO	.565	5	14	29	.764 (Dodgers)
BA	.216	5	15	30	.264 (Blue Jays)
OBP	.281	5	15	30	.333 (Dodgers)
SA	.346	5	14	29	.443 (Braves)

Division: AL West, 5 teams. **League:** American, 15 teams. **MLB:** 30 teams.

Team Pitching Stats (2022)

Stat	Number	Div Rank	Lg Rank	MLB Rank	MLB Best
ERA	4.52	5	13	24	2.80 (Dodgers)
SO	1,203	5	13	26	1,565 (Mets)
BB	503	3	9	16	384 (Rays)
BPO	.710	5	13	24	.551 (Astros)
BA	.254	5	12	24	.209 (Dodgers)
OBP	.323	4	12	23	.273 (Dodgers)
SA	.428	5	15	27	.332 (Astros)

Division: AL West, 5 teams. **League:** American, 15 teams. **MLB:** 30 teams.

Individual Batting Stats (2022)

Batter	PA	BPO	BA	OBP	SA	ISO	CT	EY
Nick Allen	326	.466	.207	.256	.291	.084	.786	.058
Elvis Andrus	386	.602	.237	.301	.373	.136	.825	.078
Seth Brown	555	.729	.230	.305	.444	.214	.708	.087
Tony Kemp	558	.604	.235	.307	.334	.099	.861	.081
Ramon Laureano	383	.625	.211	.287	.376	.165	.699	.065
Sean Murphy	612	.720	.250	.332	.426	.177	.769	.089
Chad Pinder	379	.547	.235	.263	.385	.150	.673	.037

Individual Pitching Stats for Starters (2022)

Pitcher	IP	BPO	ERA	BA	SA	ISO	CT	EY
Paul Blackburn	111.1	.720	4.28	.255	.441	.186	.794	.060
Cole Irvin	181.0	.620	3.98	.251	.416	.165	.815	.045
James Kaprielian	134.0	.705	4.23	.239	.414	.176	.807	.102
Frankie Montas	104.2	.568	3.18	.233	.372	.138	.721	.060

Individual Pitching Stats for Relievers (2022)

Pitcher	GR	BPO	ERA	BA	SA	ISO	CT	EY
Domingo Acevedo	70	.576	3.33	.206	.370	.165	.761	.050
Zach Jackson	54	.552	3.00	.171	.232	.061	.591	.151
Sam Moll	53	.612	2.91	.205	.335	.130	.714	.088
A.J. Puk	62	.653	3.12	.217	.357	.139	.689	.072
Kirby Snead	46	.897	5.84	.308	.478	.170	.808	.092

Best Stats on Team (2022)

Stat	Batter	Number
2B	Sean Murphy	37
3B	Seth Brown	3
BA	Sean Murphy	.250
BB	Sean Murphy	56
BBV	Sean Murphy	6
BPO	Seth Brown	.729
BPV	Tony Kemp	55
BV	Seth Brown	27
CT	Tony Kemp	.861
EY	Sean Murphy	.089
H	Sean Murphy	134
HR	Seth Brown	25
ISO	Seth Brown	.214
OBP	Sean Murphy	.332
R	Sean Murphy	67
RBI	Seth Brown	73
SA	Seth Brown	.444
SB	Seth Brown, Tony Kemp, Ramon Laureano	11
SC	Sean Murphy	115
SCV	Conner Capel	5
SE	Sean Murphy	.188
XV	Seth Brown	31

Stat	Pitcher	Number
BA	Frankie Montas	.233
BBV	Cole Irvin	-25
BPO-R	Zach Jackson	.552
BPO-S	Frankie Montas	.568
BPV	Zach Jackson	-26
BV	Frankie Montas	-29
CT	Frankie Montas	.721
ERA-R	Sam Moll	2.91
ERA-S	Frankie Montas	3.18
ERV	Frankie Montas	-9
EY	Cole Irvin	.045
GR	Domingo Acevedo	70
GS	Cole Irvin	30
IP	Cole Irvin	181.0
ISO	Frankie Montas	.138
OBP	Frankie Montas	.284
SA	Frankie Montas	.372
SO	Cole Irvin	128
SV	Dany Jimenez	11
W	Cole Irvin	9
XV	Zach Jackson	-15

Worst Stats on Team (2022)

Stat	Batter	Number
BA	Nick Allen	.207
BBV	Chad Pinder	-16
BPO	Nick Allen	.466
BPV	Chad Pinder	-28
BV	Cristian Pache	-60
CT	Chad Pinder	.673
EY	Chad Pinder	.037
ISO	Nick Allen	.084
OBP	Nick Allen	.256
SA	Nick Allen	.291
SCV	Nick Allen, Cristian Pache	-18
SE	Nick Allen	.141
SO	Seth Brown	146
XV	Tony Kemp	-27

Stat	Pitcher	Number
BA	Paul Blackburn	.255
BB	James Kaprielian	59
BBV	Zach Jackson	14
BPO-R	Kirby Snead	.897
BPO-S	Paul Blackburn	.720
BPV	Cole Irvin	45
BV	Adam Oller	59
CT	Cole Irvin	.815
ERA-R	Kirby Snead	5.84
ERA-S	Paul Blackburn	4.28
ERV	Adam Oller	19
EY	James Kaprielian	.102
ISO	Paul Blackburn	.186
L	Cole Irvin	13
OBP	James Kaprielian	.321
SA	Paul Blackburn	.441
XV	Adam Oller	34

Overall Base Value Leaders (2022)

Team Rank	Player	BV [bat]	(-) BV [pitch]	(=) OBV
1	Frankie Montas	0	-29	29
2	Seth Brown	27	0	27
3	Sean Murphy	25	0	25
4	Cole Irvin	0	-22	22
5	Domingo Acevedo	0	-17	17
6	Zach Jackson	0	-15	15
7	Conner Capel	10	0	10
8	Dany Jimenez	0	-9	9
9	Tyler Cyr	0	-6	6
9	Sam Moll	0	-6	6

Fan Support in Past 10 Seasons (2013-2022)

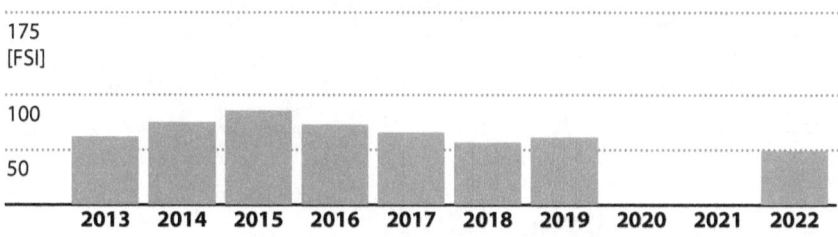

Year	Team	Attendance	W	Att:W	FSI
2013	Oakland Athletics	1,809,302	96	18,847	61.9
2014	Oakland Athletics	2,003,628	88	22,769	75.0
2015	Oakland Athletics	1,768,175	68	26,003	85.6
2016	Oakland Athletics	1,521,506	69	22,051	73.2
2017	Oakland Athletics	1,475,721	75	19,676	65.8
2018	Oakland Athletics	1,573,616	97	16,223	56.6
2019	Oakland Athletics	1,670,734	97	17,224	61.1
2022	Oakland Athletics	787,902	60	13,132	49.4

Extreme Games for Batters (2022)

Stat	Team Total	Individual Leader	G
3+ H	43	Sean Murphy, Tony Kemp	7
2+ HR	5	Seth Brown	2
5+ RBI	1	Sean Murphy	1
0 H in 5+ AB	22	Sean Murphy	4
4+ SO	5	Chad Pinder, Cody Thomas, Ramon Laureano, Sean Murphy, Seth Brown	1

Extreme Games for Pitchers (2022)

Stat	Team Total	Individual Leader	G
0-2 ER in 7+ IP	16	Cole Irvin	6
10+ SO	3	Frankie Montas	2
0 BR in SV	14	Dany Jimenez	6
10+ BR	29	Cole Irvin	5
1+ ER in SV	1	Lou Trivino	1

Predictions for Coming Season (2023)

Group	Next W	Next L	Next Pct.	WS	LC	PQ
10 closest matches (avg. W-L)	76.4	85.5	.472	0	0	2
25 closest matches (avg. W-L)	72.2	87.3	.453	0	0	2
50 closest matches (avg. W-L)	71.1	84.6	.457	0	0	3

25 Closest Matches (2023)

Rank	Team	Next	W	L	Pct.	WS	LC	PQ
1	Rangers (2012-2014)	2015	88	74	.543	—	—	X
2	Cubs (2004-2006)	2007	85	77	.525	—	—	X
3	Reds (1980-1982)	1983	74	88	.457	—	—	—
4	Reds (1999-2001)	2002	78	84	.481	—	—	—
5	Twins (2009-2011)	2012	66	96	.407	—	—	—
6	Diamondbacks (2012-2014)	2015	79	83	.488	—	—	—
7	Diamondbacks (2002-2004)	2005	77	85	.475	—	—	—
8	Brewers (1982-1984)	1985	71	90	.441	—	—	—
9	Indians (2007-2009)	2010	69	93	.426	—	—	—
10	Rangers (1980-1982)	1983	77	85	.475	—	—	—
11	Giants (1982-1984)	1985	62	100	.383	—	—	—
12	Mariners (1990-1992)	1993	82	80	.506	—	—	—
13	Giants (2015-2017)	2018	73	89	.451	—	—	—
14	Braves (1983-1985)	1986	72	89	.447	—	—	—
15	Pirates (1983-1985)	1986	64	98	.395	—	—	—
16	Padres (2006-2008)	2009	75	87	.463	—	—	—
17	Tigers (1987-1989)	1990	79	83	.488	—	—	—
18	Tigers (2013-2015)	2016	86	75	.534	—	—	—
19	Cubs (1978-1980)	1981	38	65	.369	—	—	—
20	Mariners (2002-2004)	2005	69	93	.426	—	—	—
21	Braves (2013-2015)	2016	68	93	.422	—	—	—
22	Astros (2005-2007)	2008	86	75	.534	—	—	—
23	Twins (1979-1981)	1982	60	102	.370	—	—	—
24	Tigers (1993-1995)	1996	53	109	.327	—	—	—
25	White Sox (2011-2013)	2014	73	89	.451	—	—	—

PHILADELPHIA PHILLIES

Past 10 Seasons (2013-2022)

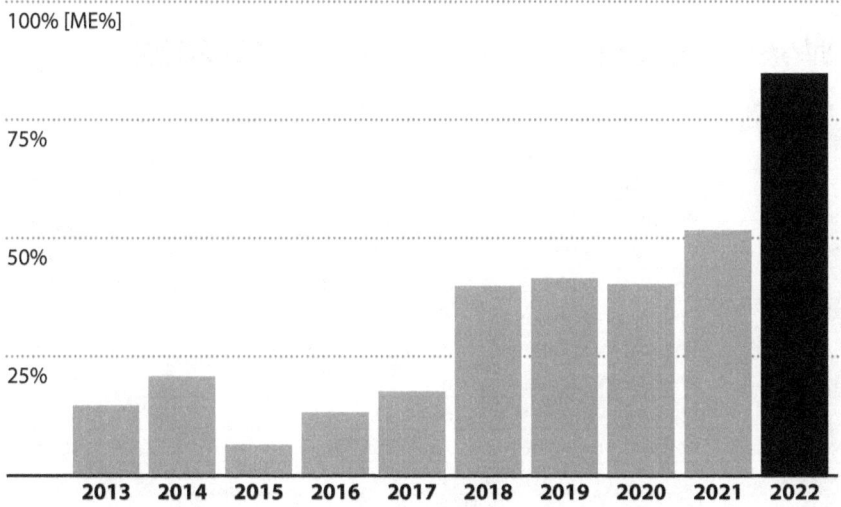

Year	Team	W	L	Pct.	Post	TS	ME%
2013	Philadelphia Phillies	73	89	.451	—	27.696	14.6%
2014	Philadelphia Phillies	73	89	.451	—	31.358	20.8%
2015	Philadelphia Phillies	63	99	.389	—	21.197	6.3%
2016	Philadelphia Phillies	71	91	.438	—	26.933	13.2%
2017	Philadelphia Phillies	66	96	.407	—	29.373	17.6%
2018	Philadelphia Phillies	80	82	.494	—	41.200	39.9%
2019	Philadelphia Phillies	81	81	.500	—	41.788	41.5%
2020	Philadelphia Phillies	28	32	.467	—	41.279	40.3%
2021	Philadelphia Phillies	82	80	.506	—	46.864	51.6%
2022	Philadelphia Phillies	87	75	.537	LP	63.652	84.7%

Best Seasons of Modern Era (1961-2022)

Year	Team	W	L	Pct.	Post	TS	ME%
2008	Philadelphia Phillies	92	70	.568	WLP	78.344	96.6%
1980	Philadelphia Phillies	91	71	.562	WLP	75.971	95.3%
2011	Philadelphia Phillies	102	60	.630	P	75.484	94.9%
1993	Philadelphia Phillies	97	65	.599	LP	74.189	94.0%
2009	Philadelphia Phillies	93	69	.574	LP	72.790	93.1%
1983	Philadelphia Phillies	90	72	.556	LP	71.305	91.9%
1976	Philadelphia Phillies	101	61	.623	P	69.638	90.7%
1977	Philadelphia Phillies	101	61	.623	P	69.438	90.5%
2010	Philadelphia Phillies	97	65	.599	P	65.952	87.6%
2022	Philadelphia Phillies	87	75	.537	LP	63.652	84.7%

Worst Seasons of Modern Era (1961-2022)

Year	Team	W	L	Pct.	Post	TS	ME%
1961	Philadelphia Phillies	47	107	.305	—	8.887	0.3%
1989	Philadelphia Phillies	67	95	.414	—	20.184	5.2%
1997	Philadelphia Phillies	68	94	.420	—	20.921	5.9%
2015	Philadelphia Phillies	63	99	.389	—	21.197	6.3%
1988	Philadelphia Phillies	65	96	.404	—	21.740	6.7%
1996	Philadelphia Phillies	67	95	.414	—	22.649	7.7%
1972	Philadelphia Phillies	59	97	.378	—	23.253	8.3%
1971	Philadelphia Phillies	67	95	.414	—	23.805	9.1%
2000	Philadelphia Phillies	65	97	.401	—	24.967	9.8%
1970	Philadelphia Phillies	73	88	.453	—	25.097	10.1%

Season Breakdown (2022)

Category	W	L	Pct.	R	RA	R/G	RA/G
Overall record in 2022	87	75	.537	747	685	4.61	4.23
Home games	47	34	.580	396	336	4.89	4.15
Away games	40	41	.494	351	349	4.33	4.31
First half of 2022 season	43	38	.531	396	340	4.89	4.20
Second half of 2022 season	44	37	.543	351	345	4.33	4.26
Against first-place teams	17	19	.472	154	160	4.28	4.44
Against playoff teams	29	40	.420	275	315	3.99	4.57
Against non-playoff teams	58	35	.624	472	370	5.08	3.98

Season as Nine-Inning Game (2022)

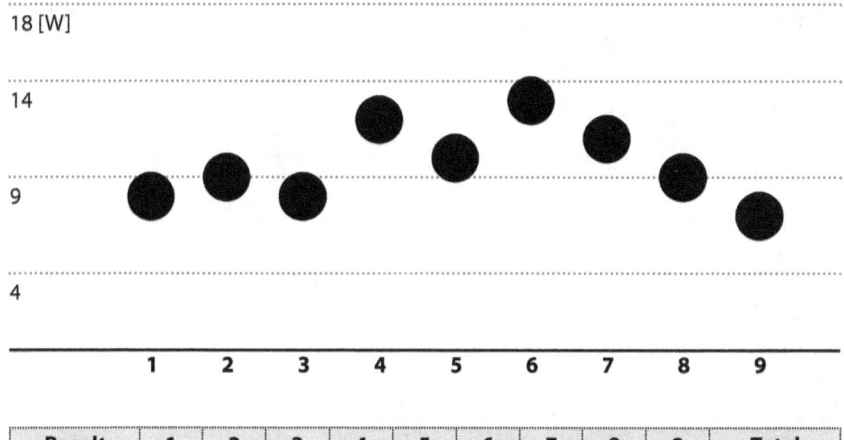

Result	1	2	3	4	5	6	7	8	9	Total
Wins	8	9	8	12	10	13	11	9	7	87
Losses	10	9	10	6	8	5	7	9	11	75

Scoring by Game (2022)

Runs Scored	G	W	L	Pct.	R/G	RA/G
Overall record	162	87	75	.537	4.61	4.23
0	14	0	14	.000	0.00	3.36
1	14	2	12	.143	1.00	5.57
2	18	6	12	.333	2.00	4.61
3	22	8	14	.364	3.00	4.27
4	29	19	10	.655	4.00	3.31
5	10	7	3	.700	5.00	3.90
6	9	5	4	.556	6.00	5.11
7	14	11	3	.786	7.00	4.79
8	10	10	0	1.000	8.00	3.70
9	8	6	2	.750	9.00	5.88
10 or more	14	13	1	.929	11.50	3.64

Scoring Allowed by Game (2022)

Runs Allowed	G	W	L	Pct.	R/G	RA/G
Overall record	162	87	75	.537	4.61	4.23
0	15	15	0	1.000	5.47	0.00
1	23	19	4	.826	4.09	1.00
2	22	17	5	.773	4.68	2.00
3	20	15	5	.750	4.70	3.00
4	17	6	11	.353	4.18	4.00
5	19	8	11	.421	5.11	5.00
6	12	2	10	.167	3.75	6.00
7	11	4	7	.364	4.82	7.00
8	7	0	7	.000	4.29	8.00
9	2	0	2	.000	4.50	9.00
10 or more	14	1	13	.071	4.93	12.29

Margins (2022)

Category	Margin	G	W	L	Pct.	GShr	WShr
Overall record	—	162	87	75	.537	—	—
Close	1 or 2 runs	78	41	37	.526	48.1%	47.1%
Medium	3 or 4 runs	36	20	16	.556	22.2%	23.0%
Distant	5 or more runs	48	26	22	.542	29.6%	29.9%

Individual Scoring Leaders (2022)

Team Rank	Batter	R	(+) RBI	(-) HR	(=) SC
1	Kyle Schwarber	100	94	46	148
2	Alec Bohm	79	72	13	138
3	J.T. Realmuto	75	84	22	137
4	Rhys Hoskins	81	79	30	130
5	Bryce Harper	63	65	18	110
6	Nick Castellanos	56	62	13	105
7	Bryson Stott	58	49	10	97
8	Jean Segura	45	33	10	68
9	Matt Vierling	41	32	6	67
10	Odubel Herrera	23	21	5	39

Team Ratings (2022)

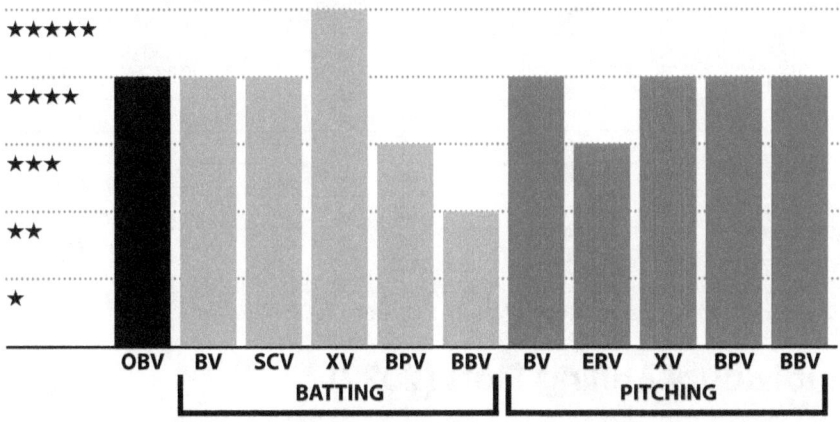

Quality	Type	Indicator	Value	Rating
Overall performance	Overall	OBV	244	★★★★
Base production	Batting	BV	168	★★★★
Run production	Batting	SCV	76	★★★★
Power hitting	Batting	XV	92	★★★★★
Contact hitting	Batting	BPV	9	★★★
Batting eye	Batting	BBV	-17	★★
Base prevention	Pitching	BV	-76	★★★★
Run prevention	Pitching	ERV	1	★★★
Power prevention	Pitching	XV	-34	★★★★
Strikeout pitching	Pitching	BPV	-67	★★★★
Control pitching	Pitching	BBV	-27	★★★★

Team Batting Stats (2022)

Stat	Number	Div Rank	Lg Rank	MLB Rank	MLB Best
R	747	3	5	7	847 (Dodgers)
H	1,392	3	5	9	1,464 (Blue Jays)
HR	205	2	4	6	254 (Yankees)
BPO	.699	3	5	8	.764 (Dodgers)
BA	.253	2	4	8	.264 (Blue Jays)
OBP	.317	3	6	11	.333 (Dodgers)
SA	.422	2	3	6	.443 (Braves)

Division: NL East, 5 teams. **League:** National, 15 teams. **MLB:** 30 teams.

Team Pitching Stats (2022)

Stat	Number	Div Rank	Lg Rank	MLB Rank	MLB Best
ERA	3.97	4	9	18	2.80 (Dodgers)
SO	1,423	4	7	10	1,565 (Mets)
BB	463	2	4	11	384 (Rays)
BPO	.642	3	6	11	.551 (Astros)
BA	.245	4	8	16	.209 (Dodgers)
OBP	.310	3	6	14	.273 (Dodgers)
SA	.391	3	8	15	.332 (Astros)

Division: NL East, 5 teams. **League:** National, 15 teams. **MLB:** 30 teams.

Individual Batting Stats (2022)

Batter	PA	BPO	BA	OBP	SA	ISO	CT	EY
Alec Bohm	631	.618	.280	.315	.398	.118	.812	.048
Nick Castellanos	558	.606	.263	.305	.389	.126	.752	.052
Bryce Harper	426	.892	.286	.364	.514	.227	.765	.089
Rhys Hoskins	672	.772	.246	.332	.462	.216	.713	.107
J.T. Realmuto	562	.847	.276	.342	.478	.202	.764	.071
Kyle Schwarber	669	.847	.218	.323	.504	.286	.653	.125
Jean Segura	387	.656	.277	.336	.387	.110	.836	.062
Bryson Stott	466	.607	.234	.295	.358	.124	.792	.077
Matt Vierling	357	.584	.246	.297	.351	.105	.785	.064

Individual Pitching Stats for Starters (2022)

Pitcher	IP	BPO	ERA	BA	SA	ISO	CT	EY
Kyle Gibson	167.2	.694	5.05	.268	.434	.166	.780	.067
Aaron Nola	205.0	.515	3.25	.219	.347	.128	.693	.035
Ranger Suarez	155.1	.640	3.65	.249	.396	.147	.784	.088
Zack Wheeler	153.0	.541	2.82	.221	.352	.131	.712	.054

Individual Pitching Stats for Relievers (2022)

Pitcher	GR	BPO	ERA	BA	SA	ISO	CT	EY
Jose Alvarado	59	.558	3.18	.203	.289	.086	.567	.095
Andrew Bellatti	58	.686	3.31	.234	.383	.149	.612	.105
Connor Brogdon	47	.662	3.27	.253	.414	.161	.713	.059
Seranthony Dominguez	54	.545	3.00	.197	.311	.115	.667	.102
Brad Hand	55	.652	2.80	.223	.319	.096	.771	.112
Corey Knebel	46	.672	3.43	.202	.337	.135	.748	.131
Nick Nelson	45	.698	4.85	.257	.350	.093	.732	.118

Best Stats on Team (2022)

Stat	Batter	Number
2B	Rhys Hoskins	33
3B	J.T. Realmuto	5
BA	Bryce Harper	.286
BB	Kyle Schwarber	86
BBV	Kyle Schwarber	30
BPO	Bryce Harper	.892
BPV	Alec Bohm	36
BV	Kyle Schwarber	87
CT	Jean Segura	.836
EY	Kyle Schwarber	.125
H	Alec Bohm	164
HR	Kyle Schwarber	46
ISO	Kyle Schwarber	.286
OBP	Bryce Harper	.364
R	Kyle Schwarber	100
RBI	Kyle Schwarber	94
SA	Bryce Harper	.514
SB	J.T. Realmuto	21
SC	Kyle Schwarber	148
SCV	J.T. Realmuto, Bryce Harper	27
SE	Bryce Harper	.258
XV	Kyle Schwarber	77

Stat	Pitcher	Number
BA	Aaron Nola	.219
BBV	Aaron Nola	-36
BPO-R	Seranthony Dominguez	.545
BPO-S	Aaron Nola	.515
BPV	Aaron Nola	-44
BV	Aaron Nola	-90
CT	Aaron Nola	.693
ERA-R	Brad Hand	2.80
ERA-S	Zack Wheeler	2.82
ERV	Zack Wheeler	-19
EY	Aaron Nola	.035
GR	Jose Alvarado	59
GS	Aaron Nola	32
IP	Aaron Nola	205.0
ISO	Aaron Nola	.128
OBP	Aaron Nola	.256
SA	Aaron Nola	.347
SO	Aaron Nola	235
SV	Corey Knebel	12
W	Zack Wheeler	12
XV	Aaron Nola	-19

Worst Stats on Team (2022)

Stat	Batter	Number
BA	Kyle Schwarber	.218
BBV	Alec Bohm	-20
BPO	Matt Vierling	.584
BPV	Kyle Schwarber	-56
BV	Didi Gregorius	-29
CT	Kyle Schwarber	.653
EY	Alec Bohm	.048
ISO	Matt Vierling	.105
OBP	Bryson Stott	.295
SA	Matt Vierling	.351
SCV	Johan Camargo	-12
SE	Jean Segura	.176
SO	Kyle Schwarber	200
XV	Alec Bohm	-20

Stat	Pitcher	Number
BA	Kyle Gibson	.268
BB	Ranger Suarez	58
BBV	Nick Nelson	12
BPO-R	Nick Nelson	.698
BPO-S	Kyle Gibson	.694
BPV	Noah Syndergaard	23
BV	Jeurys Familia	24
CT	Ranger Suarez	.784
ERA-R	Nick Nelson	4.85
ERA-S	Kyle Gibson	5.05
ERV	Kyle Gibson	20
EY	Ranger Suarez	.088
ISO	Kyle Gibson	.166
L	Aaron Nola	13
OBP	Kyle Gibson	.325
SA	Kyle Gibson	.434
XV	Bailey Falter	20

Overall Base Value Leaders (2022)

Team Rank	Player	BV [bat]	(-) BV [pitch]	(=) OBV
1	Aaron Nola	0	-90	90
2	Kyle Schwarber	87	0	87
3	J.T. Realmuto	70	0	70
4	Bryce Harper	67	0	67
5	Zack Wheeler	0	-54	54
6	Rhys Hoskins	52	0	52
7	Seranthony Dominguez	0	-18	18
8	Jose Alvarado	-1	-16	15
9	Edmundo Sosa	12	0	12
10	Zach Eflin	0	-11	11
10	Nick Maton	13	2	11

Fan Support in Past 10 Seasons (2013-2022)

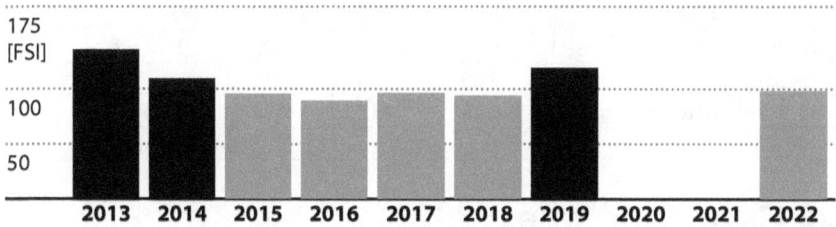

Year	Team	Attendance	W	Att:W	FSI
2013	Philadelphia Phillies	3,012,403	73	41,266	135.5
2014	Philadelphia Phillies	2,423,852	73	33,203	109.4
2015	Philadelphia Phillies	1,831,080	63	29,065	95.7
2016	Philadelphia Phillies	1,915,144	71	26,974	89.5
2017	Philadelphia Phillies	1,905,354	66	28,869	96.5
2018	Philadelphia Phillies	2,158,124	80	26,977	94.1
2019	Philadelphia Phillies	2,727,421	81	33,672	119.4
2022	Philadelphia Phillies	2,276,736	87	26,169	98.5

Extreme Games for Batters (2022)

Stat	Team Total	Individual Leader	G
3+ H	80	Bryce Harper, J.T. Realmuto, Rhys Hoskins	11
2+ HR	18	Kyle Schwarber	8
5+ RBI	4	Rhys Hoskins	2
0 H in 5+ AB	33	J.T. Realmuto, Kyle Schwarber	6
4+ SO	9	Kyle Schwarber	4

Extreme Games for Pitchers (2022)

Stat	Team Total	Individual Leader	G
0-2 ER in 7+ IP	31	Aaron Nola	11
10+ SO	9	Aaron Nola	5
0 BR in SV	23	Corey Knebel, Seranthony Dominguez	6
10+ BR	18	Kyle Gibson	6
1+ ER in SV	2	Connor Brogdon, Cristopher Sanchez	1

Predictions for Coming Season (2023)

Group	Next W	Next L	Next Pct.	WS	LC	PQ
10 closest matches (avg. W-L)	87.3	74.7	.539	0	1	5
25 closest matches (avg. W-L)	81.6	73.5	.526	1	3	10
50 closest matches (avg. W-L)	82.8	75.7	.522	3	6	19

25 Closest Matches (2023)

Rank	Team	Next	W	L	Pct.	WS	LC	PQ
1	Astros (1984-1986)	1987	76	86	.469	—	—	—
2	Red Sox (1996-1998)	1999	94	68	.580	—	—	X
3	Mariners (1998-2000)	2001	116	46	.716	—	—	X
4	Indians (2003-2005)	2006	78	84	.481	—	—	—
5	Red Sox (2000-2002)	2003	95	67	.586	—	—	X
6	Brewers (2016-2018)	2019	89	73	.549	—	—	X
7	Padres (1994-1996)	1997	76	86	.469	—	—	—
8	Orioles (2012-2014)	2015	81	81	.500	—	—	—
9	Tigers (2009-2011)	2012	88	74	.543	—	X	X
10	Braves (1981-1983)	1984	80	82	.494	—	—	—
11	Astros (1978-1980)	1981	61	49	.555	—	—	X
12	Rangers (1997-1999)	2000	71	91	.438	—	—	—
13	Dodgers (1989-1991)	1992	63	99	.389	—	—	—
14	Royals (2012-2014)	2015	95	67	.586	X	X	X
15	Reds (1997-1999)	2000	85	77	.525	—	—	—
16	Rangers (1994-1996)	1997	77	85	.475	—	—	—
17	Padres (2004-2006)	2007	89	74	.546	—	—	—
18	Astros (1992-1994)	1995	76	68	.528	—	—	—
19	Brewers (1990-1992)	1993	69	93	.426	—	—	—
20	Brewers (2009-2011)	2012	83	79	.512	—	—	—
21	Twins (2017-2019)	2020	36	24	.600	—	—	X
22	Athletics (1998-2000)	2001	102	60	.630	—	—	X
23	Cubs (1987-1989)	1990	77	85	.475	—	—	—
24	Mets (1997-1999)	2000	94	68	.580	—	X	X
25	Expos (1977-1979)	1980	90	72	.556	—	—	—

PITTSBURGH PIRATES

Past 10 Seasons (2013-2022)

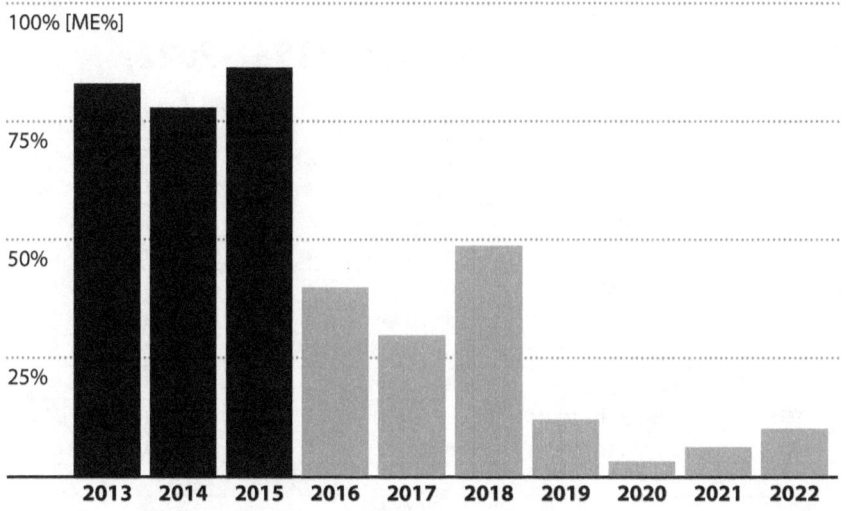

Year	Team	W	L	Pct.	Post	TS	ME%
2013	Pittsburgh Pirates	94	68	.580	P	62.354	82.9%
2014	Pittsburgh Pirates	88	74	.543	P	59.584	77.8%
2015	Pittsburgh Pirates	98	64	.605	P	64.640	86.3%
2016	Pittsburgh Pirates	78	83	.484	—	41.195	39.9%
2017	Pittsburgh Pirates	75	87	.463	—	36.451	29.7%
2018	Pittsburgh Pirates	82	79	.509	—	45.315	48.7%
2019	Pittsburgh Pirates	69	93	.426	—	26.069	12.0%
2020	Pittsburgh Pirates	19	41	.317	—	17.177	3.1%
2021	Pittsburgh Pirates	61	101	.377	—	21.054	6.1%
2022	Pittsburgh Pirates	62	100	.383	—	25.094	10.0%

Best Seasons of Modern Era (1961-2022)

Year	Team	W	L	Pct.	Post	TS	ME%
1971	Pittsburgh Pirates	97	65	.599	WLP	87.094	99.2%
1979	Pittsburgh Pirates	98	64	.605	WLP	83.113	98.2%
1991	Pittsburgh Pirates	98	64	.605	P	73.933	93.9%
1972	Pittsburgh Pirates	96	59	.619	P	70.056	90.9%
1990	Pittsburgh Pirates	95	67	.586	P	68.780	90.3%
1992	Pittsburgh Pirates	96	66	.593	P	67.165	88.8%
2015	Pittsburgh Pirates	98	64	.605	P	64.640	86.3%
2013	Pittsburgh Pirates	94	68	.580	P	62.354	82.9%
1975	Pittsburgh Pirates	92	69	.571	P	62.292	82.7%
1966	Pittsburgh Pirates	92	70	.568	—	61.980	82.1%

Worst Seasons of Modern Era (1961-2022)

Year	Team	W	L	Pct.	Post	TS	ME%
2010	Pittsburgh Pirates	57	105	.352	—	7.550	0.1%
2001	Pittsburgh Pirates	62	100	.383	—	16.421	2.7%
2020	Pittsburgh Pirates	19	41	.317	—	17.177	3.1%
2006	Pittsburgh Pirates	67	95	.414	—	20.254	5.3%
2009	Pittsburgh Pirates	62	99	.385	—	20.632	5.7%
1995	Pittsburgh Pirates	58	86	.403	—	20.970	5.9%
2021	Pittsburgh Pirates	61	101	.377	—	21.054	6.1%
2007	Pittsburgh Pirates	68	94	.420	—	21.338	6.3%
1985	Pittsburgh Pirates	57	104	.354	—	22.334	7.3%
2008	Pittsburgh Pirates	67	95	.414	—	23.421	8.6%

Season Breakdown (2022)

Category	W	L	Pct.	R	RA	R/G	RA/G
Overall record in 2022	62	100	.383	591	817	3.65	5.04
Home games	34	47	.420	313	413	3.86	5.10
Away games	28	53	.346	278	404	3.43	4.99
First half of 2022 season	33	48	.407	296	425	3.65	5.25
Second half of 2022 season	29	52	.358	295	392	3.64	4.84
Against first-place teams	12	24	.333	136	228	3.78	6.33
Against playoff teams	16	46	.258	209	357	3.37	5.76
Against non-playoff teams	46	54	.460	382	460	3.82	4.60

Season as Nine-Inning Game (2022)

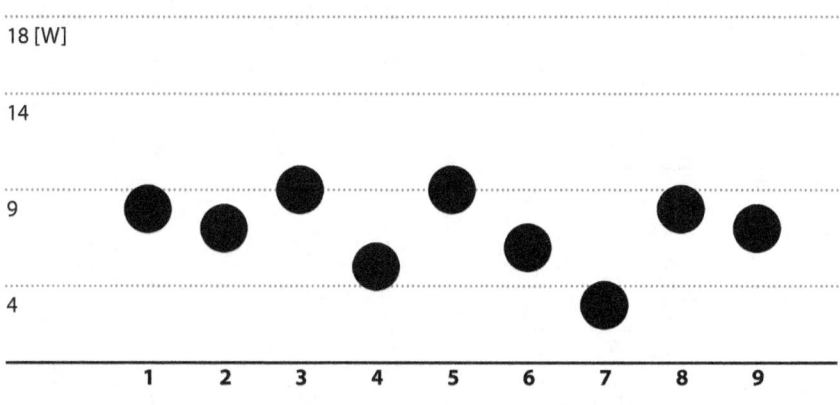

Result	1	2	3	4	5	6	7	8	9	Total
Wins	8	7	9	5	9	6	3	8	7	62
Losses	10	11	9	13	9	12	15	10	11	100

Scoring by Game (2022)

Runs Scored	G	W	L	Pct.	R/G	RA/G
Overall record	162	62	100	.383	3.65	5.04
0	15	0	15	.000	0.00	6.53
1	25	3	22	.120	1.00	4.28
2	25	2	23	.080	2.00	6.08
3	24	5	19	.208	3.00	5.04
4	16	10	6	.625	4.00	4.69
5	20	11	9	.550	5.00	4.80
6	9	8	1	.889	6.00	3.44
7	8	5	3	.625	7.00	5.25
8	15	13	2	.867	8.00	5.13
9	2	2	0	1.000	9.00	4.00
10 or more	3	3	0	1.000	10.67	3.33

Scoring Allowed by Game (2022)

Runs Allowed	G	W	L	Pct.	R/G	RA/G
Overall record	162	62	100	.383	3.65	5.04
0	6	6	0	1.000	2.83	0.00
1	11	10	1	.909	4.91	1.00
2	22	13	9	.591	3.27	2.00
3	25	13	12	.520	3.36	3.00
4	25	10	15	.400	4.08	4.00
5	16	4	12	.250	3.81	5.00
6	12	2	10	.167	3.50	6.00
7	15	4	11	.267	4.53	7.00
8	9	0	9	.000	4.22	8.00
9	7	0	7	.000	2.71	9.00
10 or more	14	0	14	.000	2.43	13.93

Margins (2022)

Category	Margin	G	W	L	Pct.	GShr	WShr
Overall record	—	162	62	100	.383	—	—
Close	1 or 2 runs	89	36	53	.404	54.9%	58.1%
Medium	3 or 4 runs	27	10	17	.370	16.7%	16.1%
Distant	5 or more runs	46	16	30	.348	28.4%	25.8%

Individual Scoring Leaders (2022)

Team Rank	Batter	R	(+) RBI	(-) HR	(=) SC
1	Bryan Reynolds	74	62	27	109
2	Ke'Bryan Hayes	55	41	7	89
3	Oneil Cruz	45	54	17	82
4	Ben Gamel	42	46	9	79
5	Michael Chavis	39	49	14	74
6	Jack Suwinski	45	38	19	64
7	Kevin Newman	31	24	2	53
8	Daniel Vogelbach	29	34	12	51
9	Diego Castillo	28	29	11	46
10	Rodolfo Castro	25	27	11	41

Team Ratings (2022)

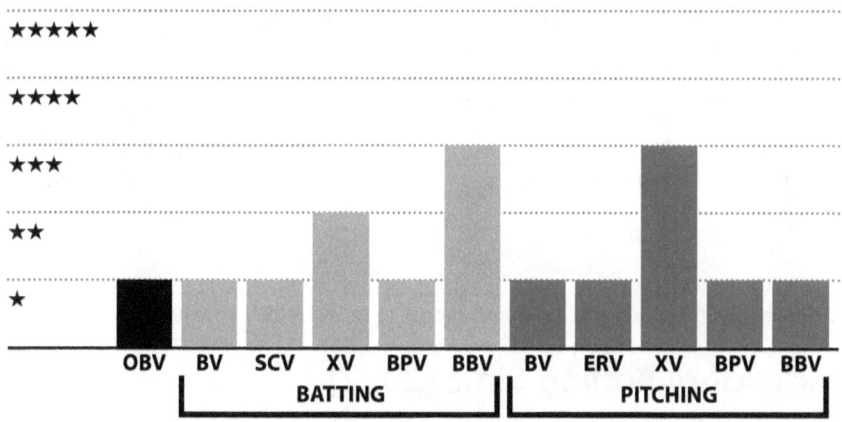

Quality	Type	Indicator	Value	Rating
Overall performance	Overall	OBV	-484	★
Base production	Batting	BV	-244	★
Run production	Batting	SCV	-165	★
Power hitting	Batting	XV	-58	★★
Contact hitting	Batting	BPV	-166	★
Batting eye	Batting	BBV	-5	★★★
Base prevention	Pitching	BV	240	★
Run prevention	Pitching	ERV	109	★
Power prevention	Pitching	XV	1	★★★
Strikeout pitching	Pitching	BPV	133	★
Control pitching	Pitching	BBV	69	★

Team Batting Stats (2022)

Stat	Number	Div Rank	Lg Rank	MLB Rank	MLB Best
R	591	5	14	27	847 (Dodgers)
H	1,186	5	15	29	1,464 (Blue Jays)
HR	158	4	10	18	254 (Yankees)
BPO	.604	5	15	28	.764 (Dodgers)
BA	.222	5	15	29	.264 (Blue Jays)
OBP	.291	5	15	28	.333 (Dodgers)
SA	.364	5	14	27	.443 (Braves)

Division: NL Central, 5 teams. **League:** National, 15 teams. **MLB:** 30 teams.

Team Pitching Stats (2022)

Stat	Number	Div Rank	Lg Rank	MLB Rank	MLB Best
ERA	4.66	4	12	26	2.80 (Dodgers)
SO	1,250	4	11	22	1,565 (Mets)
BB	586	4	14	28	384 (Rays)
BPO	.716	4	12	26	.551 (Astros)
BA	.259	5	13	27	.209 (Dodgers)
OBP	.337	5	13	27	.273 (Dodgers)
SA	.411	3	10	22	.332 (Astros)

Division: NL Central, 5 teams. **League:** National, 15 teams. **MLB:** 30 teams.

Individual Batting Stats (2022)

Batter	PA	BPO	BA	OBP	SA	ISO	CT	EY
Michael Chavis	426	.572	.229	.265	.389	.160	.686	.042
Oneil Cruz	361	.725	.233	.294	.450	.218	.619	.075
Ben Gamel	423	.664	.232	.324	.369	.137	.736	.109
Ke'Bryan Hayes	560	.621	.244	.314	.345	.101	.758	.086
Bryan Reynolds	614	.787	.262	.345	.461	.199	.740	.082
Jack Suwinski	372	.687	.202	.298	.411	.209	.650	.108

Individual Pitching Stats for Starters (2022)

Pitcher	IP	BPO	ERA	BA	SA	ISO	CT	EY
JT Brubaker	144.0	.727	4.69	.271	.433	.162	.747	.084
Mitch Keller	159.0	.692	3.91	.266	.388	.122	.773	.086
Jose Quintana	103.0	.591	3.50	.251	.371	.120	.777	.070
Zach Thompson	121.2	.755	5.18	.280	.446	.166	.817	.085
Bryse Wilson	115.2	.787	5.52	.287	.485	.198	.828	.061

Individual Pitching Stats for Relievers (2022)

Pitcher	GR	BPO	ERA	BA	SA	ISO	CT	EY
David Bednar	45	.562	2.61	.218	.337	.119	.642	.067
Wil Crowe	59	.627	4.38	.235	.356	.121	.765	.114
Chase De Jong	42	.640	2.64	.204	.380	.176	.769	.099
Duane Underwood Jr.	50	.614	4.40	.254	.320	.066	.750	.093

Best Stats on Team (2022)

Stat	Batter	Number
2B	Ke'Bryan Hayes	24
3B	Bryan Reynolds, Oneil Cruz, Rodolfo Castro	4
BA	Bryan Reynolds	.262
BB	Bryan Reynolds	56
BBV	Daniel Vogelbach	17
BPO	Bryan Reynolds	.787
BPV	Kevin Newman	24
BV	Bryan Reynolds	53
CT	Ke'Bryan Hayes	.758
EY	Ben Gamel	.109
H	Bryan Reynolds	142
HR	Bryan Reynolds	27
ISO	Oneil Cruz	.218
OBP	Bryan Reynolds	.345
R	Bryan Reynolds	74
RBI	Bryan Reynolds	62
SA	Bryan Reynolds	.461
SB	Ke'Bryan Hayes	20
SC	Bryan Reynolds	109
SCV	Oneil Cruz	12
SE	Oneil Cruz	.227
XV	Bryan Reynolds	26

Stat	Pitcher	Number
BA	Jose Quintana	.251
BBV	Bryse Wilson	-9
BPO-R	David Bednar	.562
BPO-S	Jose Quintana	.591
BPV	David Bednar	-21
BV	Jose Quintana	-22
CT	JT Brubaker	.747
ERA-R	David Bednar	2.61
ERA-S	Jose Quintana	3.50
ERV	Chase De Jong	-11
EY	Bryse Wilson	.061
GR	Wil Crowe	59
GS	Mitch Keller	29
IP	Mitch Keller	159.0
ISO	Jose Quintana	.120
OBP	Jose Quintana	.308
SA	Jose Quintana	.371
SO	JT Brubaker	147
SV	David Bednar	19
W	Wil Crowe, Chase De Jong	6
XV	Duane Underwood Jr.	-20

Worst Stats on Team (2022)

Stat	Batter	Number
BA	Jack Suwinski	.202
BBV	Michael Chavis	-16
BPO	Michael Chavis	.572
BPV	Oneil Cruz	-43
BV	Yoshi Tsutsugo	-36
CT	Oneil Cruz	.619
EY	Michael Chavis	.042
ISO	Ke'Bryan Hayes	.101
OBP	Michael Chavis	.265
SA	Ke'Bryan Hayes	.345
SCV	Ke'Bryan Hayes	-20
SE	Ke'Bryan Hayes	.159
SO	Bryan Reynolds	141
XV	Ke'Bryan Hayes	-26

Stat	Pitcher	Number
BA	Bryse Wilson	.287
BB	Mitch Keller	60
BBV	Wil Crowe	12
BPO-R	Chase De Jong	.640
BPO-S	Bryse Wilson	.787
BPV	Bryse Wilson	36
BV	Bryse Wilson	45
CT	Bryse Wilson	.828
ERA-R	Duane Underwood Jr.	4.40
ERA-S	Bryse Wilson	5.52
ERV	Bryse Wilson	20
EY	Mitch Keller	.086
ISO	Bryse Wilson	.198
L	Mitch Keller, JT Brubaker	12
OBP	Zach Thompson	.344
SA	Bryse Wilson	.485
XV	Bryse Wilson	21

Overall Base Value Leaders (2022)

Team Rank	Player	BV [bat]	(-) BV [pitch]	(=) OBV
1	Bryan Reynolds	53	0	53
2	Jose Quintana	0	-22	22
3	Oneil Cruz	17	0	17
4	Daniel Vogelbach	16	0	16
5	David Bednar	0	-15	15
5	Johan Oviedo	0	-15	15
7	Luis Ortiz	0	-11	11
8	Wil Crowe	0	-8	8
8	Duane Underwood Jr.	0	-8	8
10	Jack Suwinski	7	0	7

Fan Support in Past 10 Seasons (2013-2022)

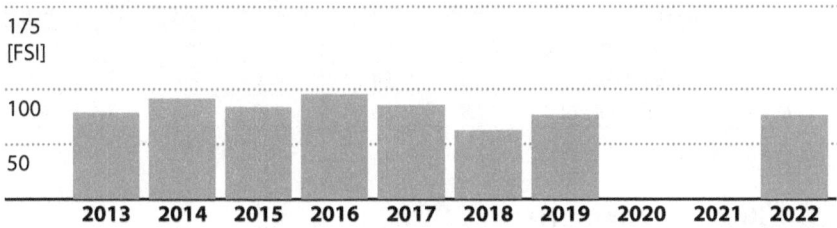

Year	Team	Attendance	W	Att:W	FSI
2013	Pittsburgh Pirates	2,256,862	94	24,009	78.8
2014	Pittsburgh Pirates	2,442,564	88	27,756	91.5
2015	Pittsburgh Pirates	2,498,596	98	25,496	84.0
2016	Pittsburgh Pirates	2,249,201	78	28,836	95.7
2017	Pittsburgh Pirates	1,919,447	75	25,593	85.6
2018	Pittsburgh Pirates	1,465,316	82	17,870	62.4
2019	Pittsburgh Pirates	1,491,439	69	21,615	76.6
2022	Pittsburgh Pirates	1,257,458	62	20,282	76.3

Extreme Games for Batters (2022)

Stat	Team Total	Individual Leader	G
3+ H	55	Bryan Reynolds, Ke'Bryan Hayes	9
2+ HR	5	Bryan Reynolds	2
5+ RBI	3	Bryan Reynolds	2
0 H in 5+ AB	28	Bryan Reynolds, Ke'Bryan Hayes	5
4+ SO	12	Oneil Cruz	4

Extreme Games for Pitchers (2022)

Stat	Team Total	Individual Leader	G
0-2 ER in 7+ IP	9	Jose Quintana, JT Brubaker, Mitch Keller	2
10+ SO	3	JT Brubaker, Mitch Keller, Roansy Contreras	1
0 BR in SV	11	David Bednar	8
10+ BR	29	JT Brubaker	9
1+ ER in SV	1	Miguel Yajure	1

Predictions for Coming Season (2023)

Group	Next W	Next L	Next Pct.	WS	LC	PQ
10 closest matches (avg. W-L)	69.7	80.5	.464	0	1	2
25 closest matches (avg. W-L)	72.3	84.9	.460	0	2	3
50 closest matches (avg. W-L)	70.8	86.4	.450	0	2	3

25 Closest Matches (2023)

Rank	Team	Next	W	L	Pct.	WS	LC	PQ
1	Orioles (2009-2011)	2012	93	69	.574	—	—	X
2	Braves (1977-1979)	1980	81	80	.503	—	—	—
3	Twins (2011-2013)	2014	70	92	.432	—	—	—
4	Pirates (2006-2008)	2009	62	99	.385	—	—	—
5	Twins (1981-1983)	1984	81	81	.500	—	—	—
6	Mets (1979-1981)	1982	65	97	.401	—	—	—
7	Mets (1978-1980)	1981	41	62	.398	—	—	—
8	Devil Rays (2005-2007)	2008	97	65	.599	—	X	X
9	Devil Rays (2001-2003)	2004	70	91	.435	—	—	—
10	Blue Jays (1978-1980)	1981	37	69	.349	—	—	—
11	Royals (2008-2010)	2011	71	91	.438	—	—	—
12	Reds (1982-1984)	1985	89	72	.553	—	—	—
13	Twins (1998-2000)	2001	85	77	.525	—	—	—
14	Phillies (2014-2016)	2017	66	96	.407	—	—	—
15	Devil Rays (1998-2000)	2001	62	100	.383	—	—	—
16	Pirates (2007-2009)	2010	57	105	.352	—	—	—
17	Brewers (2001-2003)	2004	67	94	.416	—	—	—
18	Pirates (2005-2007)	2008	67	95	.414	—	—	—
19	Mariners (1979-1981)	1982	76	86	.469	—	—	—
20	Expos (1999-2001)	2002	83	79	.512	—	—	—
21	Braves (1988-1990)	1991	94	68	.580	—	X	X
22	Orioles (2008-2010)	2011	69	93	.426	—	—	—
23	Cubs (2011-2013)	2014	73	89	.451	—	—	—
24	Royals (2005-2007)	2008	75	87	.463	—	—	—
25	Yankees (1989-1991)	1992	76	86	.469	—	—	—

ST. LOUIS CARDINALS

Past 10 Seasons (2013-2022)

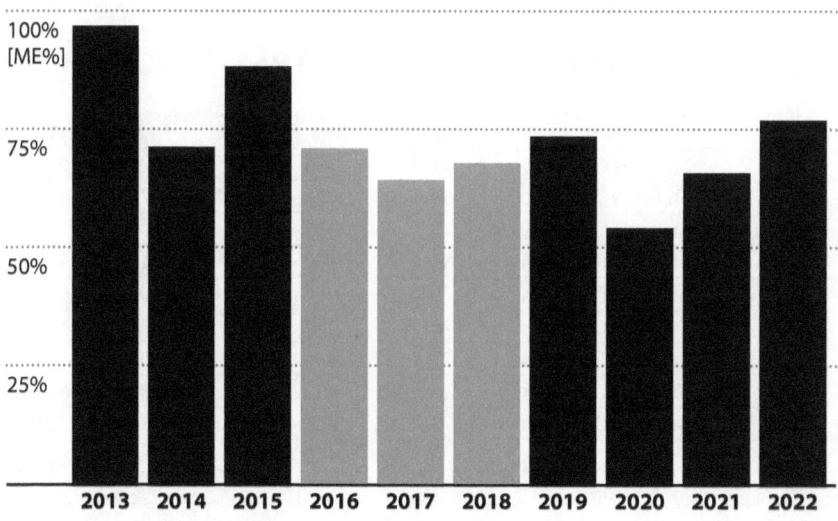

Year	Team	W	L	Pct.	Post	TS	ME%
2013	St. Louis Cardinals	97	65	.599	LP	78.949	96.8%
2014	St. Louis Cardinals	90	72	.556	P	55.739	71.2%
2015	St. Louis Cardinals	100	62	.617	P	66.634	88.2%
2016	St. Louis Cardinals	86	76	.531	—	55.595	70.9%
2017	St. Louis Cardinals	83	79	.512	—	52.679	64.2%
2018	St. Louis Cardinals	88	74	.543	—	54.488	67.9%
2019	St. Louis Cardinals	91	71	.562	P	56.847	73.5%
2020	St. Louis Cardinals	30	28	.517	P	48.121	54.1%
2021	St. Louis Cardinals	90	72	.556	P	53.496	65.7%
2022	St. Louis Cardinals	93	69	.574	P	59.061	76.9%

Best Seasons of Modern Era (1961-2022)

Year	Team	W	L	Pct.	Post	TS	ME%
1967	St. Louis Cardinals	101	60	.627	WLP	84.556	98.6%
1968	St. Louis Cardinals	97	65	.599	LP	83.157	98.2%
2004	St. Louis Cardinals	105	57	.648	LP	81.249	97.5%
1985	St. Louis Cardinals	101	61	.623	LP	80.680	97.3%
2013	St. Louis Cardinals	97	65	.599	LP	78.949	96.8%
2005	St. Louis Cardinals	100	62	.617	P	76.624	95.6%
2011	St. Louis Cardinals	90	72	.556	WLP	75.595	95.0%
1982	St. Louis Cardinals	92	70	.568	WLP	75.018	94.7%
1987	St. Louis Cardinals	95	67	.586	LP	73.602	93.7%
1964	St. Louis Cardinals	93	69	.574	WLP	72.585	92.9%

Worst Seasons of Modern Era (1961-2022)

Year	Team	W	L	Pct.	Post	TS	ME%
1995	St. Louis Cardinals	62	81	.434	—	25.262	10.3%
1978	St. Louis Cardinals	69	93	.426	—	29.702	18.1%
1990	St. Louis Cardinals	70	92	.432	—	32.020	21.5%
1994	St. Louis Cardinals	53	61	.465	—	33.454	25.1%
2007	St. Louis Cardinals	78	84	.481	—	34.938	26.9%
1988	St. Louis Cardinals	76	86	.469	—	38.800	34.7%
1976	St. Louis Cardinals	72	90	.444	—	39.041	35.2%
1997	St. Louis Cardinals	73	89	.451	—	39.805	36.8%
1999	St. Louis Cardinals	75	86	.466	—	40.119	37.5%
1970	St. Louis Cardinals	76	86	.469	—	41.648	41.0%

Season Breakdown (2022)

Category	W	L	Pct.	R	RA	R/G	RA/G
Overall record in 2022	93	69	.574	772	637	4.77	3.93
Home games	53	28	.654	392	283	4.84	3.49
Away games	40	41	.494	380	354	4.69	4.37
First half of 2022 season	44	37	.543	383	318	4.73	3.93
Second half of 2022 season	49	32	.605	389	319	4.80	3.94
Against first-place teams	8	8	.500	67	76	4.19	4.75
Against playoff teams	19	24	.442	156	191	3.63	4.44
Against non-playoff teams	74	45	.622	616	446	5.18	3.75

Season as Nine-Inning Game (2022)

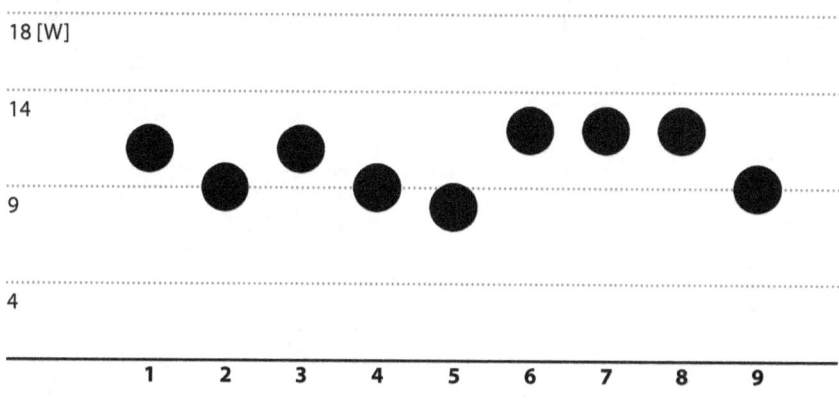

Result	1	2	3	4	5	6	7	8	9	Total
Wins	11	9	11	9	8	12	12	12	9	93
Losses	7	9	7	9	10	6	6	6	9	69

Scoring by Game (2022)

Runs Scored	G	W	L	Pct.	R/G	RA/G
Overall record	162	93	69	.574	4.77	3.93
0	16	0	16	.000	0.00	3.38
1	16	4	12	.250	1.00	3.94
2	15	5	10	.333	2.00	3.40
3	15	5	10	.333	3.00	4.53
4	17	10	7	.588	4.00	4.59
5	24	17	7	.708	5.00	4.08
6	22	16	6	.727	6.00	4.23
7	11	10	1	.909	7.00	4.82
8	6	6	0	1.000	8.00	3.33
9	4	4	0	1.000	9.00	1.50
10 or more	16	16	0	1.000	12.50	3.31

Scoring Allowed by Game (2022)

Runs Allowed	G	W	L	Pct.	R/G	RA/G
Overall record	162	93	69	.574	4.77	3.93
0	17	17	0	1.000	5.29	0.00
1	18	16	2	.889	4.78	1.00
2	17	12	5	.706	3.82	2.00
3	31	22	9	.710	4.94	3.00
4	18	10	8	.556	5.00	4.00
5	19	10	9	.526	4.84	5.00
6	15	3	12	.200	4.47	6.00
7	11	2	9	.182	5.55	7.00
8	6	0	6	.000	2.50	8.00
9	3	1	2	.333	7.00	9.00
10 or more	7	0	7	.000	4.57	11.86

Margins (2022)

Category	Margin	G	W	L	Pct.	GShr	WShr
Overall record	—	162	93	69	.574	—	—
Close	1 or 2 runs	74	42	32	.568	45.7%	45.2%
Medium	3 or 4 runs	40	22	18	.550	24.7%	23.7%
Distant	5 or more runs	48	29	19	.604	29.6%	31.2%

Individual Scoring Leaders (2022)

Team Rank	Batter	R	(+) RBI	(-) HR	(=) SC
1	Paul Goldschmidt	106	115	35	186
2	Nolan Arenado	73	103	30	146
3	Tommy Edman	95	57	13	139
4	Brendan Donovan	64	45	5	104
5	Tyler O'Neill	56	58	14	100
6	Dylan Carlson	56	42	8	90
7	Albert Pujols	42	68	24	86
8	Lars Nootbaar	53	40	14	79
9	Nolan Gorman	44	35	14	65
10	Corey Dickerson	28	36	6	58

Team Ratings (2022)

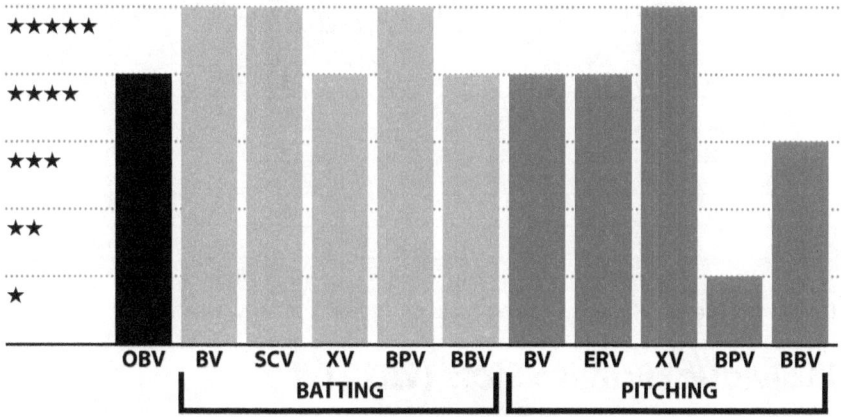

Quality	Type	Indicator	Value	Rating
Overall performance	Overall	OBV	360	★★★★
Base production	Batting	BV	235	★★★★★
Run production	Batting	SCV	112	★★★★★
Power hitting	Batting	XV	87	★★★★
Contact hitting	Batting	BPV	146	★★★★★
Batting eye	Batting	BBV	39	★★★★
Base prevention	Pitching	BV	-125	★★★★
Run prevention	Pitching	ERV	-27	★★★★
Power prevention	Pitching	XV	-94	★★★★★
Strikeout pitching	Pitching	BPV	173	★
Control pitching	Pitching	BBV	3	★★★

Team Batting Stats (2022)

Stat	Number	Div Rank	Lg Rank	MLB Rank	MLB Best
R	772	1	3	5	847 (Dodgers)
H	1,386	1	6	10	1,464 (Blue Jays)
HR	197	2	5	9	254 (Yankees)
BPO	.715	1	3	4	.764 (Dodgers)
BA	.252	1	6	10	.264 (Blue Jays)
OBP	.325	1	3	4	.333 (Dodgers)
SA	.420	1	4	7	.443 (Braves)

Division: NL Central, 5 teams. **League:** National, 15 teams. **MLB:** 30 teams.

Team Pitching Stats (2022)

Stat	Number	Div Rank	Lg Rank	MLB Rank	MLB Best
ERA	3.79	1	4	10	2.80 (Dodgers)
SO	1,177	5	15	30	1,565 (Mets)
BB	489	1	6	14	384 (Rays)
BPO	.631	1	4	8	.551 (Astros)
BA	.247	3	9	18	.209 (Dodgers)
OBP	.314	2	9	18	.273 (Dodgers)
SA	.382	1	5	10	.332 (Astros)

Division: NL Central, 5 teams. **League:** National, 15 teams. **MLB:** 30 teams.

Individual Batting Stats (2022)

Batter	PA	BPO	BA	OBP	SA	ISO	CT	EY
Nolan Arenado	620	.877	.293	.358	.533	.241	.871	.079
Dylan Carlson	488	.658	.236	.316	.380	.144	.782	.090
Brendan Donovan	468	.769	.281	.394	.379	.097	.821	.126
Tommy Edman	630	.720	.265	.324	.400	.135	.808	.070
Paul Goldschmidt	651	1.063	.317	.404	.578	.260	.749	.120
Lars Nootbaar	347	.820	.228	.340	.448	.221	.755	.145
Tyler O'Neill	383	.698	.228	.308	.392	.165	.692	.099
Albert Pujols	351	.873	.270	.345	.550	.280	.821	.077

Individual Pitching Stats for Starters (2022)

Pitcher	IP	BPO	ERA	BA	SA	ISO	CT	EY
Dakota Hudson	139.2	.676	4.45	.273	.375	.103	.849	.102
Miles Mikolas	202.1	.554	3.29	.226	.373	.146	.796	.048
Andre Pallante	108.0	.649	3.17	.274	.387	.114	.823	.084
Adam Wainwright	191.2	.623	3.71	.261	.382	.121	.806	.066

Individual Pitching Stats for Relievers (2022)

Pitcher	GR	BPO	ERA	BA	SA	ISO	CT	EY
Giovanny Gallegos	57	.545	3.05	.197	.338	.141	.657	.073
Ryan Helsley	54	.376	1.25	.128	.237	.110	.571	.080

Best Stats on Team (2022)

Stat	Batter	Number
2B	Nolan Arenado	42
3B	Tommy Edman, Dylan Carlson	4
BA	Paul Goldschmidt	.317
BB	Paul Goldschmidt	79
BBV	Paul Goldschmidt	27
BPO	Paul Goldschmidt	1.063
BPV	Nolan Arenado	67
BV	Paul Goldschmidt	159
CT	Nolan Arenado	.871
EY	Lars Nootbaar	.145
H	Paul Goldschmidt	178
HR	Paul Goldschmidt	35
ISO	Albert Pujols	.280
OBP	Paul Goldschmidt	.404
R	Paul Goldschmidt	106
RBI	Paul Goldschmidt	115
SA	Paul Goldschmidt	.578
SB	Tommy Edman	32
SC	Paul Goldschmidt	186
SCV	Paul Goldschmidt	59
SE	Paul Goldschmidt	.286
XV	Paul Goldschmidt	61

Stat	Pitcher	Number
BA	Miles Mikolas	.226
BBV	Miles Mikolas	-25
BPO-R	Ryan Helsley	.376
BPO-S	Miles Mikolas	.554
BPV	Ryan Helsley	-39
BV	Miles Mikolas	-65
CT	Miles Mikolas	.796
ERA-R	Ryan Helsley	1.25
ERA-S	Andre Pallante	3.17
ERV	Ryan Helsley	-19
EY	Miles Mikolas	.048
GR	Giovanny Gallegos	57
GS	Adam Wainwright, Miles Mikolas	32
IP	Miles Mikolas	202.1
ISO	Dakota Hudson	.103
OBP	Miles Mikolas	.267
SA	Miles Mikolas	.373
SO	Miles Mikolas	153
SV	Ryan Helsley	19
W	Miles Mikolas	12
XV	Dakota Hudson	-26

Worst Stats on Team (2022)

Stat	Batter	Number
BA	Tyler O'Neill	.228
BBV	Yadier Molina	-16
BPO	Dylan Carlson	.658
BPV	Nolan Gorman	-32
BV	Yadier Molina	-54
CT	Tyler O'Neill	.692
EY	Tommy Edman	.070
ISO	Brendan Donovan	.097
OBP	Tyler O'Neill	.308
SA	Brendan Donovan	.379
SCV	Yadier Molina	-15
SE	Dylan Carlson	.184
SO	Paul Goldschmidt	141
XV	Brendan Donovan	-21

Stat	Pitcher	Number
BA	Andre Pallante	.274
BB	Dakota Hudson	61
BBV	Dakota Hudson, Jordan Hicks	14
BPO-R	Giovanny Gallegos	.545
BPO-S	Dakota Hudson	.676
BPV	Dakota Hudson	51
BV	Matthew Liberatore	28
CT	Dakota Hudson	.849
ERA-R	Giovanny Gallegos	3.05
ERA-S	Dakota Hudson	4.45
ERV	T.J. McFarland	10
EY	Dakota Hudson	.102
ISO	Miles Mikolas	.146
L	Miles Mikolas	13
OBP	Dakota Hudson	.356
SA	Andre Pallante	.387
XV	Matthew Liberatore	10

Overall Base Value Leaders (2022)

Team Rank	Player	BV [bat]	(-) BV [pitch]	(=) OBV
1	Paul Goldschmidt	159	0	159
2	Nolan Arenado	90	0	90
3	Miles Mikolas	0	-65	65
4	Ryan Helsley	0	-55	55
5	Albert Pujols	52	8	44
6	Lars Nootbaar	37	0	37
7	Jose Quintana	0	-36	36
8	Brendan Donovan	32	0	32
9	Tommy Edman	26	0	26
10	Jake Woodford	0	-23	23

Fan Support in Past 10 Seasons (2013-2022)

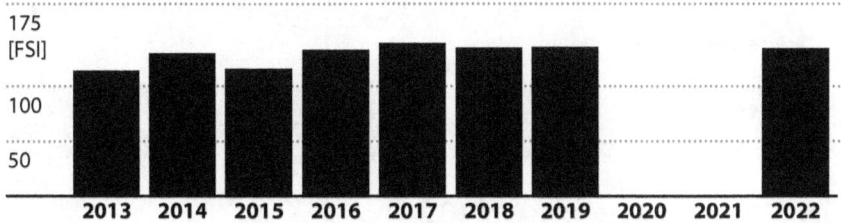

Year	Team	Attendance	W	Att:W	FSI
2013	St. Louis Cardinals	3,369,769	97	34,740	114.1
2014	St. Louis Cardinals	3,540,649	90	39,341	129.6
2015	St. Louis Cardinals	3,520,889	100	35,209	115.9
2016	St. Louis Cardinals	3,444,490	86	40,052	132.9
2017	St. Louis Cardinals	3,448,337	83	41,546	138.9
2018	St. Louis Cardinals	3,403,587	88	38,677	135.0
2019	St. Louis Cardinals	3,480,393	91	38,246	135.6
2022	St. Louis Cardinals	3,320,551	93	35,705	134.4

Extreme Games for Batters (2022)

Stat	Team Total	Individual Leader	G
3+ H	81	Paul Goldschmidt	15
2+ HR	13	Albert Pujols	4
5+ RBI	7	Albert Pujols, Paul Goldschmidt	2
0 H in 5+ AB	38	Dylan Carlson	8
4+ SO	6	Edmundo Sosa	2

Extreme Games for Pitchers (2022)

Stat	Team Total	Individual Leader	G
0-2 ER in 7+ IP	29	Miles Mikolas	11
10+ SO	1	Adam Wainwright	1
0 BR in SV	14	Ryan Helsley	8
10+ BR	33	Adam Wainwright	11
1+ ER in SV	6	Ryan Helsley	3

Predictions for Coming Season (2023)

Group	Next W	Next L	Next Pct.	WS	LC	PQ
10 closest matches (avg. W-L)	73.0	66.5	.523	0	2	5
25 closest matches (avg. W-L)	79.5	73.4	.520	0	3	9
50 closest matches (avg. W-L)	83.0	74.4	.527	1	6	21

25 Closest Matches (2023)

Rank	Team	Next	W	L	Pct.	WS	LC	PQ
1	Royals (1987-1989)	1990	75	86	.466	—	—	—
2	Twins (2002-2004)	2005	83	79	.512	—	—	—
3	Rays (2017-2019)	2020	40	20	.667	—	X	X
4	Astros (2002-2004)	2005	89	73	.549	—	X	X
5	Twins (2008-2010)	2011	63	99	.389	—	—	—
6	Cardinals (2017-2019)	2020	30	28	.517	—	—	X
7	Angels (2005-2007)	2008	100	62	.617	—	—	X
8	Dodgers (2011-2013)	2014	94	68	.580	—	—	X
9	Orioles (1992-1994)	1995	71	73	.493	—	—	—
10	Phillies (2003-2005)	2006	85	77	.525	—	—	—
11	Cubs (2002-2004)	2005	79	83	.488	—	—	—
12	Dodgers (1994-1996)	1997	88	74	.543	—	—	—
13	Angels (2003-2005)	2006	89	73	.549	—	—	—
14	Reds (1979-1981)	1982	61	101	.377	—	—	—
15	Brewers (2006-2008)	2009	80	82	.494	—	—	—
16	Blue Jays (1982-1984)	1985	99	62	.615	—	—	X
17	Reds (1977-1979)	1980	89	73	.549	—	—	—
18	Dodgers (1995-1997)	1998	83	79	.512	—	—	—
19	Tigers (1979-1981)	1982	83	79	.512	—	—	—
20	Rangers (1997-1999)	2000	71	91	.438	—	—	—
21	Yankees (1982-1984)	1985	97	64	.602	—	—	—
22	Angels (2006-2008)	2009	97	65	.599	—	—	X
23	Tigers (2009-2011)	2012	88	74	.543	—	X	X
24	Dodgers (1989-1991)	1992	63	99	.389	—	—	—
25	Dodgers (1993-1995)	1996	90	72	.556	—	—	X

SAN DIEGO PADRES

Past 10 Seasons (2013-2022)

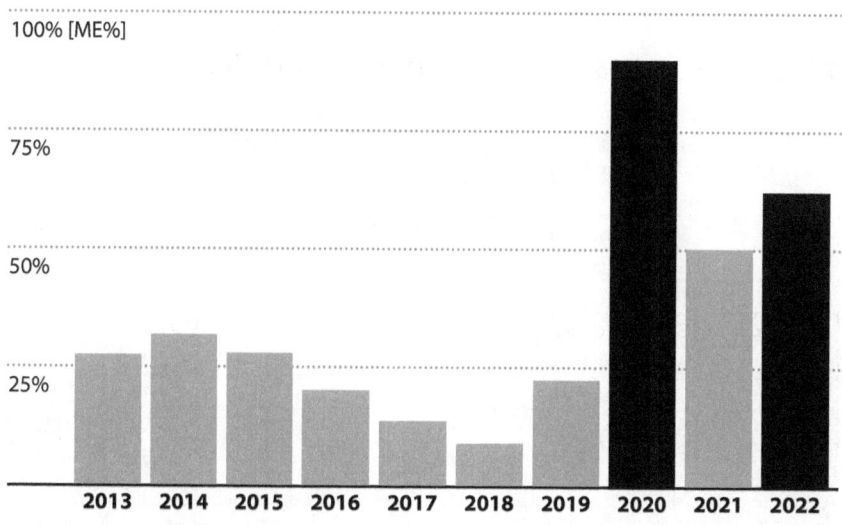

Year	Team	W	L	Pct.	Post	TS	ME%
2013	San Diego Padres	76	86	.469	—	35.281	27.5%
2014	San Diego Padres	77	85	.475	—	37.441	31.8%
2015	San Diego Padres	74	88	.457	—	35.395	27.9%
2016	San Diego Padres	68	94	.420	—	30.933	20.1%
2017	San Diego Padres	71	91	.438	—	27.203	13.7%
2018	San Diego Padres	66	96	.407	—	23.626	8.9%
2019	San Diego Padres	70	92	.432	—	32.488	22.3%
2020	San Diego Padres	37	23	.617	P	68.422	90.0%
2021	San Diego Padres	79	83	.488	—	46.026	50.2%
2022	San Diego Padres	89	73	.549	P	51.860	62.2%

Best Seasons of Modern Era (1969-2022)

Year	Team	W	L	Pct.	Post	TS	ME%
1998	San Diego Padres	98	64	.605	LP	70.298	91.2%
2020	San Diego Padres	37	23	.617	P	68.422	90.0%
1984	San Diego Padres	92	70	.568	LP	67.737	89.3%
1996	San Diego Padres	91	71	.562	P	64.199	85.6%
2006	San Diego Padres	88	74	.543	P	61.246	80.8%
2007	San Diego Padres	89	74	.546	—	60.913	79.8%
2010	San Diego Padres	90	72	.556	—	57.864	75.2%
1989	San Diego Padres	89	73	.549	—	54.892	68.7%
2004	San Diego Padres	87	75	.537	—	52.461	63.6%
2022	San Diego Padres	89	73	.549	P	51.860	62.2%

Worst Seasons of Modern Era (1969-2022)

Year	Team	W	L	Pct.	Post	TS	ME%
1973	San Diego Padres	60	102	.370	—	10.185	0.6%
1969	San Diego Padres	52	110	.321	—	10.456	0.8%
1974	San Diego Padres	60	102	.370	—	13.763	1.6%
1972	San Diego Padres	58	95	.379	—	18.969	4.4%
1971	San Diego Padres	61	100	.379	—	20.541	5.6%
1970	San Diego Padres	63	99	.389	—	21.769	6.8%
1981	San Diego Padres	41	69	.373	—	22.232	7.2%
2003	San Diego Padres	64	98	.395	—	22.436	7.5%
2002	San Diego Padres	66	96	.407	—	23.540	8.8%
2018	San Diego Padres	66	96	.407	—	23.626	8.9%

Season Breakdown (2022)

Category	W	L	Pct.	R	RA	R/G	RA/G
Overall record in 2022	89	73	.549	705	660	4.35	4.07
Home games	44	37	.543	301	301	3.72	3.72
Away games	45	36	.556	404	359	4.99	4.43
First half of 2022 season	47	34	.580	365	307	4.51	3.79
Second half of 2022 season	42	39	.519	340	353	4.20	4.36
Against first-place teams	12	24	.333	116	175	3.22	4.86
Against playoff teams	20	33	.377	174	239	3.28	4.51
Against non-playoff teams	69	40	.633	531	421	4.87	3.86

Season as Nine-Inning Game (2022)

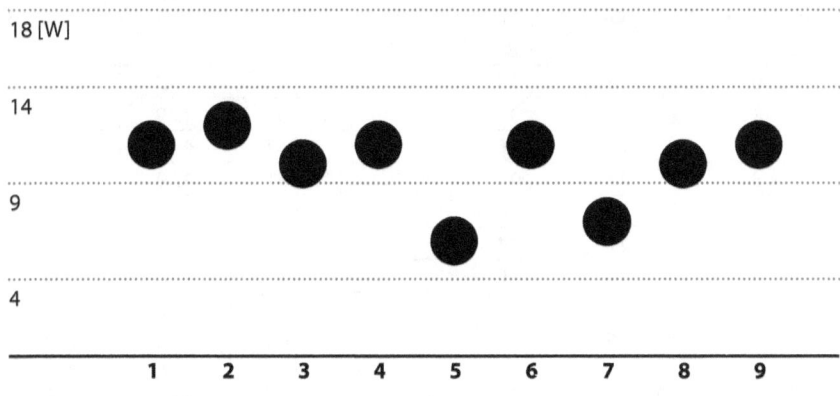

Result	1	2	3	4	5	6	7	8	9	Total
Wins	11	12	10	11	6	11	7	10	11	89
Losses	7	6	8	7	12	7	11	8	7	73

Scoring by Game (2022)

Runs Scored	G	W	L	Pct.	R/G	RA/G
Overall record	162	89	73	.549	4.35	4.07
0	11	0	11	.000	0.00	4.91
1	18	2	16	.111	1.00	4.06
2	28	11	17	.393	2.00	4.07
3	19	9	10	.474	3.00	3.68
4	23	15	8	.652	4.00	3.78
5	16	9	7	.563	5.00	4.94
6	16	13	3	.813	6.00	3.88
7	9	8	1	.889	7.00	3.89
8	2	2	0	1.000	8.00	6.00
9	4	4	0	1.000	9.00	2.50
10 or more	16	16	0	1.000	11.94	4.00

Scoring Allowed by Game (2022)

Runs Allowed	G	W	L	Pct.	R/G	RA/G
Overall record	162	89	73	.549	4.35	4.07
0	15	15	0	1.000	4.13	0.00
1	21	19	2	.905	4.29	1.00
2	19	16	3	.842	4.00	2.00
3	22	13	9	.591	4.09	3.00
4	21	10	11	.476	3.95	4.00
5	21	11	10	.524	6.38	5.00
6	13	3	10	.231	4.38	6.00
7	9	2	7	.222	5.22	7.00
8	10	0	10	.000	2.90	8.00
9	1	0	1	.000	4.00	9.00
10 or more	10	0	10	.000	3.30	11.60

Margins (2022)

Category	Margin	G	W	L	Pct.	GShr	WShr
Overall record	—	162	89	73	.549	—	—
Close	1 or 2 runs	70	41	29	.586	43.2%	46.1%
Medium	3 or 4 runs	44	22	22	.500	27.2%	24.7%
Distant	5 or more runs	48	26	22	.542	29.6%	29.2%

Individual Scoring Leaders (2022)

Team Rank	Batter	R	(+) RBI	(-) HR	(=) SC
1	Manny Machado	100	102	32	170
2	Jake Cronenworth	88	88	17	159
3	Jurickson Profar	82	58	15	125
4	Ha-Seong Kim	58	59	11	106
5	Trent Grisham	58	53	17	94
6	Austin Nola	40	40	4	76
7	Luke Voit	38	48	13	73
8	Eric Hosmer	32	40	8	64
9	Wil Myers	29	41	7	63
10	Jorge Alfaro	25	40	7	58

Team Ratings (2022)

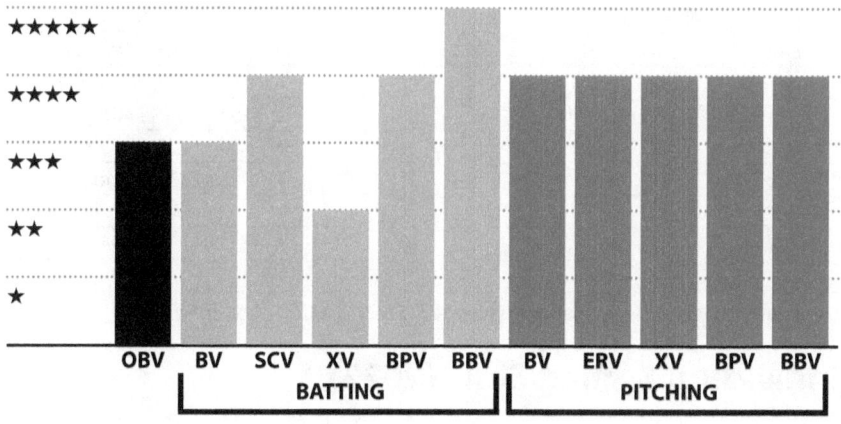

Quality	Type	Indicator	Value	Rating
Overall performance	Overall	OBV	98	★★★
Base production	Batting	BV	-18	★★★
Run production	Batting	SCV	30	★★★★
Power hitting	Batting	XV	-61	★★
Contact hitting	Batting	BPV	38	★★★★
Batting eye	Batting	BBV	63	★★★★★
Base prevention	Pitching	BV	-116	★★★★
Run prevention	Pitching	ERV	-24	★★★★
Power prevention	Pitching	XV	-40	★★★★
Strikeout pitching	Pitching	BPV	-95	★★★★
Control pitching	Pitching	BBV	-16	★★★★

Team Batting Stats (2022)

Stat	Number	Div Rank	Lg Rank	MLB Rank	MLB Best
R	705	3	8	13	847 (Dodgers)
H	1,318	3	8	15	1,464 (Blue Jays)
HR	153	4	12	21	254 (Yankees)
BPO	.656	3	8	14	.764 (Dodgers)
BA	.241	3	8	16	.264 (Blue Jays)
OBP	.318	2	4	8	.333 (Dodgers)
SA	.382	5	11	22	.443 (Braves)

Division: NL West, 5 teams. **League:** National, 15 teams. **MLB:** 30 teams.

Team Pitching Stats (2022)

Stat	Number	Div Rank	Lg Rank	MLB Rank	MLB Best
ERA	3.81	2	5	11	2.80 (Dodgers)
SO	1,451	2	5	7	1,565 (Mets)
BB	468	3	5	12	384 (Rays)
BPO	.633	2	5	9	.551 (Astros)
BA	.232	2	4	9	.209 (Dodgers)
OBP	.301	2	4	9	.273 (Dodgers)
SA	.377	2	4	7	.332 (Astros)

Division: NL West, 5 teams. **League:** National, 15 teams. **MLB:** 30 teams.

Individual Batting Stats (2022)

Batter	PA	BPO	BA	OBP	SA	ISO	CT	EY
Jake Cronenworth	684	.719	.240	.333	.394	.153	.777	.098
Trent Grisham	524	.614	.184	.284	.341	.157	.667	.107
Eric Hosmer	369	.647	.272	.336	.391	.119	.836	.077
Ha-Seong Kim	582	.679	.251	.325	.383	.132	.807	.088
Manny Machado	644	.907	.298	.366	.531	.234	.770	.084
Austin Nola	397	.601	.251	.321	.329	.078	.827	.083
Jurickson Profar	658	.689	.243	.331	.391	.148	.821	.111
Luke Voit	344	.710	.225	.317	.416	.191	.631	.111

Individual Pitching Stats for Starters (2022)

Pitcher	IP	BPO	ERA	BA	SA	ISO	CT	EY
Mike Clevinger	114.1	.703	4.33	.233	.412	.178	.792	.072
Yu Darvish	194.2	.524	3.10	.207	.331	.124	.724	.048
Sean Manaea	158.0	.724	4.96	.254	.455	.201	.745	.073
Nick Martinez	106.1	.660	3.47	.239	.398	.159	.764	.092
Joe Musgrove	181.0	.603	2.93	.227	.383	.156	.729	.055
Blake Snell	128.0	.599	3.38	.216	.342	.126	.641	.095

Individual Pitching Stats for Relievers (2022)

Pitcher	GR	BPO	ERA	BA	SA	ISO	CT	EY
Nabil Crismatt	49	.621	2.94	.226	.361	.135	.742	.075
Luis Garcia	64	.551	3.39	.243	.311	.068	.711	.066
Tim Hill	55	.538	3.56	.251	.313	.061	.860	.066
Taylor Rogers	42	.608	4.35	.239	.348	.110	.690	.046
Robert Suarez	45	.525	2.27	.176	.285	.109	.630	.110
Steven Wilson	49	.592	3.06	.191	.346	.154	.718	.093

Best Stats on Team (2022)

Stat	Batter	Number
2B	Manny Machado	37
3B	Jake Cronenworth	4
BA	Manny Machado	.298
BB	Jurickson Profar	73
BBV	Juan Soto	24
BPO	Manny Machado	.907
BPV	Jurickson Profar	41
BV	Manny Machado	104
CT	Eric Hosmer	.836
EY	Jurickson Profar	.111
H	Manny Machado	172
HR	Manny Machado	32
ISO	Manny Machado	.234
OBP	Manny Machado	.366
R	Manny Machado	100
RBI	Manny Machado	102
SA	Manny Machado	.531
SB	Ha-Seong Kim	12
SC	Manny Machado	170
SCV	Manny Machado	44
SE	Manny Machado	.264
XV	Manny Machado	47

Stat	Pitcher	Number
BA	Yu Darvish	.207
BBV	Yu Darvish	-24
BPO-R	Robert Suarez	.525
BPO-S	Yu Darvish	.524
BPV	Blake Snell	-52
BV	Yu Darvish	-80
CT	Blake Snell	.641
ERA-R	Robert Suarez	2.27
ERA-S	Joe Musgrove	2.93
ERV	Joe Musgrove	-21
EY	Yu Darvish	.048
GR	Luis Garcia	64
GS	Yu Darvish, Joe Musgrove	30
IP	Yu Darvish	194.2
ISO	Yu Darvish	.124
OBP	Yu Darvish	.256
SA	Yu Darvish	.331
SO	Yu Darvish	197
SV	Taylor Rogers	28
W	Yu Darvish	16
XV	Yu Darvish, Luis Garcia	-20

Worst Stats on Team (2022)

Stat	Batter	Number
BA	Trent Grisham	.184
BBV	Jorge Alfaro	-11
BPO	Austin Nola	.601
BPV	Trent Grisham	-37
BV	Jose Azocar	-22
CT	Luke Voit	.631
EY	Eric Hosmer	.077
ISO	Austin Nola	.078
OBP	Trent Grisham	.284
SA	Austin Nola	.329
SCV	Jose Azocar, Eric Hosmer, Trent Grisham	-8
SE	Eric Hosmer	.173
SO	Trent Grisham	150
XV	Austin Nola	-26

Stat	Pitcher	Number
BA	Sean Manaea	.254
BB	Blake Snell	51
BBV	MacKenzie Gore	13
BPO-R	Nabil Crismatt	.621
BPO-S	Sean Manaea	.724
BPV	Tim Hill	20
BV	Sean Manaea	30
CT	Mike Clevinger	.792
ERA-R	Taylor Rogers	4.35
ERA-S	Sean Manaea	4.96
ERV	Sean Manaea	17
EY	Blake Snell	.095
ISO	Sean Manaea	.201
L	Blake Snell	10
OBP	Nick Martinez	.315
SA	Sean Manaea	.455
XV	Sean Manaea	30

Overall Base Value Leaders (2022)

Team Rank	Player	BV [bat]	(-) BV [pitch]	(=) OBV
1	Manny Machado	104	0	104
2	Yu Darvish	0	-80	80
3	Joe Musgrove	0	-31	31
4	Jake Cronenworth	27	0	27
5	Blake Snell	0	-24	24
5	Juan Soto	24	0	24
7	Luis Garcia	0	-20	20
8	Robert Suarez	0	-19	19
9	Tim Hill	0	-17	17
10	Jurickson Profar	13	0	13

Fan Support in Past 10 Seasons (2013-2022)

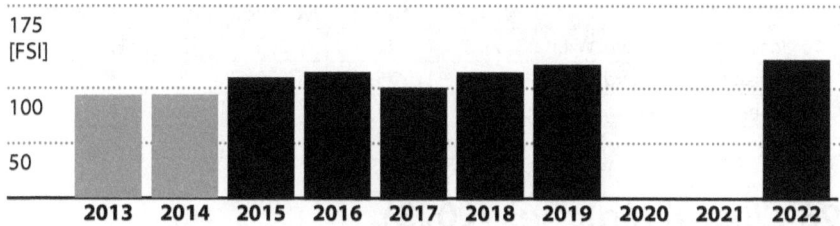

Year	Team	Attendance	W	Att:W	FSI
2013	San Diego Padres	2,166,691	76	28,509	93.6
2014	San Diego Padres	2,195,373	77	28,511	94.0
2015	San Diego Padres	2,459,742	74	33,240	109.5
2016	San Diego Padres	2,351,422	68	34,580	114.7
2017	San Diego Padres	2,138,491	71	30,120	100.7
2018	San Diego Padres	2,168,536	66	32,857	114.6
2019	San Diego Padres	2,396,399	70	34,234	121.4
2022	San Diego Padres	2,987,470	89	33,567	126.3

Extreme Games for Batters (2022)

Stat	Team Total	Individual Leader	G
3+ H	62	Manny Machado	14
2+ HR	5	Manny Machado	3
5+ RBI	3	Ha-Seong Kim, Jake Cronenworth, Luke Voit	1
0 H in 5+ AB	32	Manny Machado	4
4+ SO	6	Luke Voit	3

Extreme Games for Pitchers (2022)

Stat	Team Total	Individual Leader	G
0-2 ER in 7+ IP	26	Yu Darvish	10
10+ SO	12	Blake Snell	5
0 BR in SV	15	Taylor Rogers	11
10+ BR	22	Sean Manaea	5
1+ ER in SV	8	Taylor Rogers	5

Predictions for Coming Season (2023)

Group	Next W	Next L	Next Pct.	WS	LC	PQ
10 closest matches (avg. W-L)	77.3	74.5	.509	0	0	1
25 closest matches (avg. W-L)	82.1	75.7	.520	0	3	7
50 closest matches (avg. W-L)	81.3	77.4	.512	0	4	12

25 Closest Matches (2023)

Rank	Team	Next	W	L	Pct.	WS	LC	PQ
1	Dodgers (2009-2011)	2012	86	76	.531	—	—	—
2	Orioles (2014-2016)	2017	75	87	.463	—	—	—
3	White Sox (2000-2002)	2003	86	76	.531	—	—	—
4	Dodgers (1988-1990)	1991	93	69	.574	—	—	—
5	Diamondbacks (2017-2019)	2020	25	35	.417	—	—	—
6	Red Sox (1979-1981)	1982	89	73	.549	—	—	—
7	Orioles (1997-1999)	2000	74	88	.457	—	—	—
8	Marlins (2003-2005)	2006	78	84	.481	—	—	—
9	White Sox (1994-1996)	1997	80	81	.497	—	—	—
10	Twins (2006-2008)	2009	87	76	.534	—	—	X
11	Royals (1985-1987)	1988	84	77	.522	—	—	—
12	Royals (1980-1982)	1983	79	83	.488	—	—	—
13	Blue Jays (2008-2010)	2011	81	81	.500	—	—	—
14	Orioles (1994-1996)	1997	98	64	.605	—	—	X
15	Phillies (1980-1982)	1983	90	72	.556	—	X	X
16	Indians (2013-2015)	2016	94	67	.584	—	X	X
17	Cardinals (2015-2017)	2018	88	74	.543	—	—	—
18	Cardinals (1982-1984)	1985	101	61	.623	—	X	X
19	Dodgers (2006-2008)	2009	95	67	.586	—	—	X
20	Angels (2009-2011)	2012	89	73	.549	—	—	—
21	Rangers (1996-1998)	1999	95	67	.586	—	—	X
22	White Sox (2010-2012)	2013	63	99	.389	—	—	—
23	Rangers (1989-1991)	1992	77	85	.475	—	—	—
24	Cardinals (1987-1989)	1990	70	92	.432	—	—	—
25	Cardinals (1996-1998)	1999	75	86	.466	—	—	—

SAN FRANCISCO GIANTS

Past 10 Seasons (2013-2022)

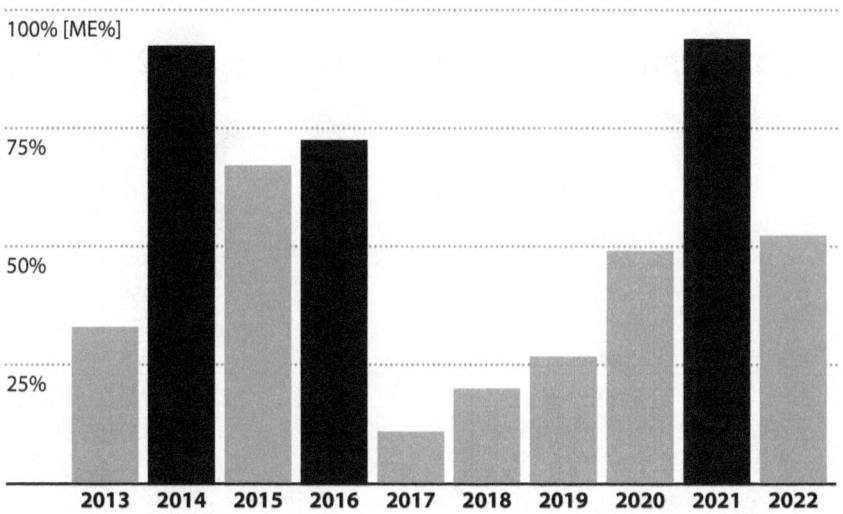

Year	Team	W	L	Pct.	Post	TS	ME%
2013	San Francisco Giants	76	86	.469	—	37.973	32.9%
2014	San Francisco Giants	88	74	.543	WLP	72.008	92.3%
2015	San Francisco Giants	84	78	.519	—	54.269	67.1%
2016	San Francisco Giants	87	75	.537	P	56.381	72.4%
2017	San Francisco Giants	64	98	.395	—	25.547	10.9%
2018	San Francisco Giants	73	89	.451	—	30.930	20.0%
2019	San Francisco Giants	77	85	.475	—	34.710	26.7%
2020	San Francisco Giants	29	31	.483	—	45.582	49.1%
2021	San Francisco Giants	107	55	.660	P	73.634	93.8%
2022	San Francisco Giants	81	81	.500	—	47.298	52.3%

Best Seasons of Modern Era (1961-2022)

Year	Team	W	L	Pct.	Post	TS	ME%
2002	San Francisco Giants	95	66	.590	LP	77.832	96.3%
1989	San Francisco Giants	92	70	.568	LP	76.226	95.5%
2010	San Francisco Giants	92	70	.568	WLP	74.265	94.1%
1962	San Francisco Giants	103	62	.624	LP	74.066	94.0%
2021	San Francisco Giants	107	55	.660	P	73.634	93.8%
2012	San Francisco Giants	94	68	.580	WLP	72.475	92.8%
2000	San Francisco Giants	97	65	.599	P	72.401	92.6%
2014	San Francisco Giants	88	74	.543	WLP	72.008	92.3%
1993	San Francisco Giants	103	59	.636	—	69.504	90.6%
2003	San Francisco Giants	100	61	.621	P	66.748	88.3%

Worst Seasons of Modern Era (1961-2022)

Year	Team	W	L	Pct.	Post	TS	ME%
1984	San Francisco Giants	66	96	.407	—	17.387	3.4%
1996	San Francisco Giants	68	94	.420	—	22.411	7.4%
1985	San Francisco Giants	62	100	.383	—	25.241	10.2%
2017	San Francisco Giants	64	98	.395	—	25.547	10.9%
1979	San Francisco Giants	71	91	.438	—	28.958	16.6%
1995	San Francisco Giants	67	77	.465	—	28.981	16.7%
1992	San Francisco Giants	72	90	.444	—	30.005	18.8%
2018	San Francisco Giants	73	89	.451	—	30.930	20.0%
2008	San Francisco Giants	72	90	.444	—	30.998	20.4%
2005	San Francisco Giants	75	87	.463	—	32.803	23.3%

Season Breakdown (2022)

Category	W	L	Pct.	R	RA	R/G	RA/G
Overall record in 2022	81	81	.500	716	697	4.42	4.30
Home games	44	37	.543	363	332	4.48	4.10
Away games	37	44	.457	353	365	4.36	4.51
First half of 2022 season	41	40	.506	378	358	4.67	4.42
Second half of 2022 season	40	41	.494	338	339	4.17	4.19
Against first-place teams	13	23	.361	135	175	3.75	4.86
Against playoff teams	27	41	.397	295	326	4.34	4.79
Against non-playoff teams	54	40	.574	421	371	4.48	3.95

Season as Nine-Inning Game (2022)

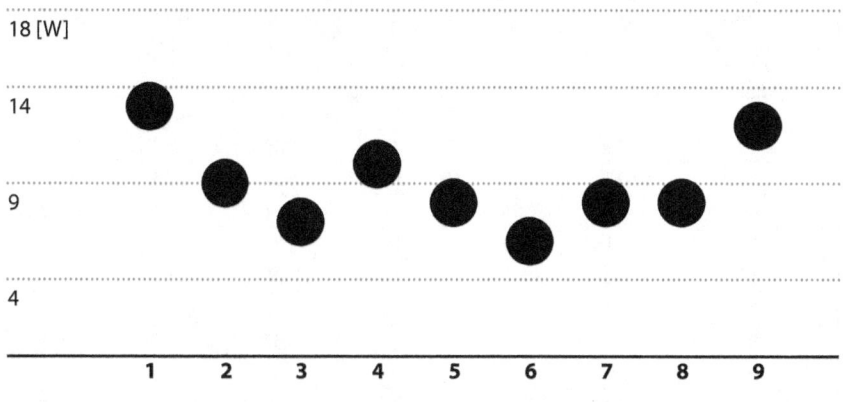

Result	1	2	3	4	5	6	7	8	9	Total
Wins	13	9	7	10	8	6	8	8	12	81
Losses	5	9	11	8	10	12	10	10	6	81

Scoring by Game (2022)

Runs Scored	G	W	L	Pct.	R/G	RA/G
Overall record	162	81	81	.500	4.42	4.30
0	9	0	9	.000	0.00	4.22
1	15	1	14	.067	1.00	4.20
2	27	7	20	.259	2.00	3.37
3	26	7	19	.269	3.00	4.77
4	22	12	10	.545	4.00	4.64
5	14	10	4	.714	5.00	4.21
6	13	10	3	.769	6.00	4.85
7	11	9	2	.818	7.00	4.73
8	7	7	0	1.000	8.00	3.29
9	6	6	0	1.000	9.00	3.83
10 or more	12	12	0	1.000	12.17	4.92

Scoring Allowed by Game (2022)

Runs Allowed	G	W	L	Pct.	R/G	RA/G
Overall record	162	81	81	.500	4.42	4.30
0	8	8	0	1.000	4.88	0.00
1	18	16	2	.889	4.56	1.00
2	25	20	5	.800	4.68	2.00
3	23	12	11	.522	3.96	3.00
4	23	9	14	.391	3.87	4.00
5	21	7	14	.333	3.95	5.00
6	10	2	8	.200	4.50	6.00
7	14	4	10	.286	5.14	7.00
8	6	1	5	.167	4.67	8.00
9	4	0	4	.000	3.00	9.00
10 or more	10	2	8	.200	5.80	12.10

Margins (2022)

Category	Margin	G	W	L	Pct.	GShr	WShr
Overall record	—	162	81	81	.500	—	—
Close	1 or 2 runs	81	40	41	.494	50.0%	49.4%
Medium	3 or 4 runs	41	20	21	.488	25.3%	24.7%
Distant	5 or more runs	40	21	19	.525	24.7%	25.9%

Individual Scoring Leaders (2022)

Team Rank	Batter	R	(+) RBI	(-) HR	(=) SC
1	Wilmer Flores	72	71	19	124
2	Thairo Estrada	71	62	14	119
3	Mike Yastrzemski	73	57	17	113
4	Joc Pederson	57	70	23	104
5	Brandon Crawford	50	52	9	93
6	Austin Slater	49	34	7	76
7	Darin Ruf	46	38	11	73
8	Luis Gonzalez	31	36	4	63
9	Evan Longoria	31	42	14	59
10	Joey Bart	34	25	11	48

Team Ratings (2022)

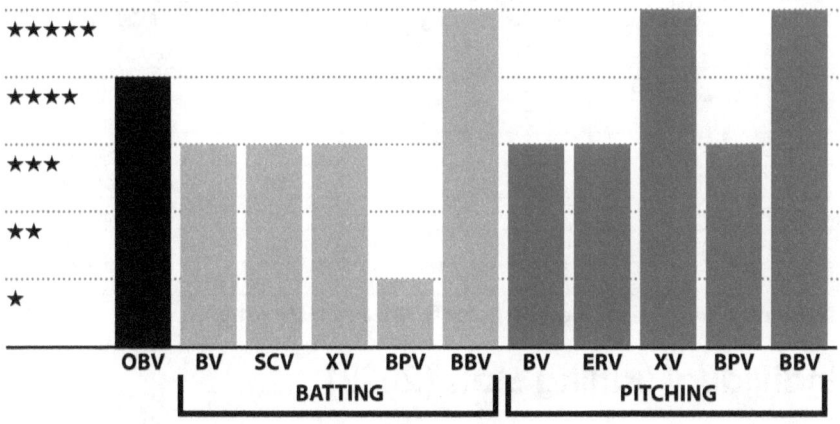

Quality	Type	Indicator	Value	Rating
Overall performance	Overall	OBV	103	★★★★
Base production	Batting	BV	43	★★★
Run production	Batting	SCV	23	★★★
Power hitting	Batting	XV	21	★★★
Contact hitting	Batting	BPV	-116	★
Batting eye	Batting	BBV	74	★★★★★
Base prevention	Pitching	BV	-60	★★★
Run prevention	Pitching	ERV	-18	★★★
Power prevention	Pitching	XV	-86	★★★★★
Strikeout pitching	Pitching	BPV	7	★★★
Control pitching	Pitching	BBV	-54	★★★★★

Team Batting Stats (2022)

Stat	Number	Div Rank	Lg Rank	MLB Rank	MLB Best
R	716	2	7	11	847 (Dodgers)
H	1,261	4	12	24	1,464 (Blue Jays)
HR	183	2	6	12	254 (Yankees)
BPO	.670	2	7	12	.764 (Dodgers)
BA	.234	4	12	23	.264 (Blue Jays)
OBP	.315	4	9	15	.333 (Dodgers)
SA	.390	3	8	16	.443 (Braves)

Division: NL West, 5 teams. **League:** National, 15 teams. **MLB:** 30 teams.

Team Pitching Stats (2022)

Stat	Number	Div Rank	Lg Rank	MLB Rank	MLB Best
ERA	3.85	3	7	13	2.80 (Dodgers)
SO	1,370	3	10	18	1,565 (Mets)
BB	441	2	3	6	384 (Rays)
BPO	.646	3	7	13	.551 (Astros)
BA	.253	4	12	23	.209 (Dodgers)
OBP	.313	3	7	16	.273 (Dodgers)
SA	.390	3	7	14	.332 (Astros)

Division: NL West, 5 teams. **League:** National, 15 teams. **MLB:** 30 teams.

Individual Batting Stats (2022)

Batter	PA	BPO	BA	OBP	SA	ISO	CT	EY
Brandon Crawford	458	.582	.231	.308	.344	.113	.759	.079
Thairo Estrada	541	.705	.260	.322	.402	.141	.818	.061
Wilmer Flores	602	.678	.229	.316	.394	.166	.804	.097
Luis Gonzalez	350	.660	.254	.323	.360	.106	.759	.083
Joc Pederson	433	.885	.274	.353	.521	.247	.737	.091
Austin Slater	325	.801	.264	.366	.408	.144	.679	.123
Mike Yastrzemski	558	.684	.214	.305	.392	.177	.709	.109

Individual Pitching Stats for Starters (2022)

Pitcher	IP	BPO	ERA	BA	SA	ISO	CT	EY
Alex Cobb	149.2	.600	3.73	.262	.350	.088	.740	.068
Jakob Junis	112.0	.719	4.42	.269	.444	.175	.780	.052
Carlos Rodon	178.0	.520	2.88	.202	.308	.106	.635	.073
Logan Webb	192.1	.557	2.90	.240	.346	.106	.775	.062
Alex Wood	130.2	.654	5.10	.262	.407	.145	.740	.052

Individual Pitching Stats for Relievers (2022)

Pitcher	GR	BPO	ERA	BA	SA	ISO	CT	EY
John Brebbia	65	.681	3.18	.268	.423	.155	.796	.056
Camilo Doval	68	.589	2.53	.218	.319	.101	.677	.099
Jarlin Garcia	58	.656	3.74	.242	.415	.173	.774	.063
Dominic Leone	55	.804	4.01	.281	.464	.184	.735	.088
Tyler Rogers	68	.611	3.57	.253	.365	.111	.830	.072

Best Stats on Team (2022)

Stat	Batter	Number
2B	Mike Yastrzemski	31
3B	Joc Pederson	3
BA	Joc Pederson	.274
BB	Mike Yastrzemski	61
BBV	Mike Yastrzemski	17
BPO	Joc Pederson	.885
BPV	Thairo Estrada	33
BV	Joc Pederson	65
CT	Thairo Estrada	.818
EY	Austin Slater	.123
H	Thairo Estrada	127
HR	Joc Pederson	23
ISO	Joc Pederson	.247
OBP	Austin Slater	.366
R	Mike Yastrzemski	73
RBI	Wilmer Flores	71
SA	Joc Pederson	.521
SB	Thairo Estrada	21
SC	Wilmer Flores	124
SCV	Joc Pederson	20
SE	Joc Pederson	.240
XV	Joc Pederson	36

Stat	Pitcher	Number
BA	Carlos Rodon	.202
BBV	Alex Wood	-15
BPO-R	Camilo Doval	.589
BPO-S	Carlos Rodon	.520
BPV	Carlos Rodon	-75
BV	Carlos Rodon	-75
CT	Carlos Rodon	.635
ERA-R	Camilo Doval	2.53
ERA-S	Carlos Rodon	2.88
ERV	Logan Webb	-23
EY	Jakob Junis	.052
GR	Tyler Rogers, Camilo Doval	68
GS	Logan Webb	32
IP	Logan Webb	192.1
ISO	Alex Cobb	.088
OBP	Carlos Rodon	.263
SA	Carlos Rodon	.308
SO	Carlos Rodon	237
SV	Camilo Doval	27
W	Logan Webb	15
XV	Alex Cobb	-37

Worst Stats on Team (2022)

Stat	Batter	Number
BA	Mike Yastrzemski	.214
BBV	Thairo Estrada	-10
BPO	Brandon Crawford	.582
BPV	Joey Bart	-47
BV	Brandon Crawford	-26
CT	Austin Slater	.679
EY	Thairo Estrada	.061
ISO	Luis Gonzalez	.106
OBP	Mike Yastrzemski	.305
SA	Brandon Crawford	.344
SCV	Brandon Belt	-18
SE	Luis Gonzalez	.180
SO	Mike Yastrzemski	141
XV	Brandon Crawford	-16

Stat	Pitcher	Number
BA	Jakob Junis	.269
BB	Carlos Rodon	52
BBV	Camilo Doval	6
BPO-R	Dominic Leone	.804
BPO-S	Jakob Junis	.719
BPV	Tyler Rogers	23
BV	Anthony DeSclafani	27
CT	Jakob Junis	.780
ERA-R	Dominic Leone	4.01
ERA-S	Alex Wood	5.10
ERV	Alex Wood	16
EY	Carlos Rodon	.073
ISO	Jakob Junis	.175
L	Alex Wood	12
OBP	Alex Cobb	.315
SA	Jakob Junis	.444
XV	Sam Long	13

Overall Base Value Leaders (2022)

Team Rank	Player	BV [bat]	(-) BV [pitch]	(=) OBV
1	Carlos Rodon	0	-75	75
2	Joc Pederson	65	0	65
3	Logan Webb	0	-60	60
4	Austin Slater	30	0	30
5	Alex Cobb	0	-27	27
6	J.D. Davis	20	0	20
7	Thairo Estrada	17	0	17
8	Scott Alexander	0	-16	16
9	Camilo Doval	0	-14	14
10	Evan Longoria	13	0	13
10	David Villar	13	0	13

Fan Support in Past 10 Seasons (2013-2022)

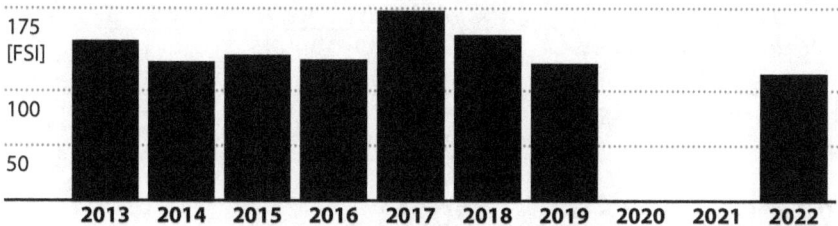

Year	Team	Attendance	W	Att:W	FSI
2013	San Francisco Giants	3,369,106	76	44,330	145.6
2014	San Francisco Giants	3,368,697	88	38,281	126.1
2015	San Francisco Giants	3,375,882	84	40,189	132.3
2016	San Francisco Giants	3,365,256	87	38,681	128.3
2017	San Francisco Giants	3,303,652	64	51,620	172.6
2018	San Francisco Giants	3,156,185	73	43,235	150.9
2019	San Francisco Giants	2,707,760	77	35,166	124.7
2022	San Francisco Giants	2,482,686	81	30,650	115.4

Extreme Games for Batters (2022)

Stat	Team Total	Individual Leader	G
3+ H	48	Wilmer Flores	10
2+ HR	13	Darin Ruf, David Villar, Evan Longoria, Joc Pederson	2
5+ RBI	6	Joc Pederson	2
0 H in 5+ AB	26	Tommy La Stella	4
4+ SO	6	Austin Slater, Curt Casali, Darin Ruf, Joc Pederson, Joey Bart, Mike Yastrzemski	1

Extreme Games for Pitchers (2022)

Stat	Team Total	Individual Leader	G
0-2 ER in 7+ IP	19	Logan Webb	7
10+ SO	14	Carlos Rodon	11
0 BR in SV	12	Camilo Doval	8
10+ BR	21	Alex Cobb	7
1+ ER in SV	3	Camilo Doval, Dominic Leone, Jose Alvarez	1

Predictions for Coming Season (2023)

Group	Next W	Next L	Next Pct.	WS	LC	PQ
10 closest matches (avg. W-L)	85.0	77.0	.525	1	1	3
25 closest matches (avg. W-L)	81.2	80.0	.504	1	1	4
50 closest matches (avg. W-L)	81.2	78.0	.510	4	5	16

25 Closest Matches (2023)

Rank	Team	Next	W	L	Pct.	WS	LC	PQ
1	Marlins (2002-2004)	2005	83	79	.512	—	—	—
2	Giants (2009-2011)	2012	94	68	.580	X	X	X
3	Giants (1988-1990)	1991	75	87	.463	—	—	—
4	Royals (1979-1981)	1982	90	72	.556	—	—	—
5	Phillies (1979-1981)	1982	89	73	.549	—	—	—
6	Padres (1983-1985)	1986	74	88	.457	—	—	—
7	Angels (2013-2015)	2016	74	88	.457	—	—	—
8	Red Sox (1985-1987)	1988	89	73	.549	—	—	X
9	Dodgers (1987-1989)	1990	86	76	.531	—	—	—
10	Indians (2004-2006)	2007	96	66	.593	—	—	X
11	Orioles (1996-1998)	1999	78	84	.481	—	—	—
12	Phillies (1992-1994)	1995	69	75	.479	—	—	—
13	Cubs (2007-2009)	2010	75	87	.463	—	—	—
14	Dodgers (2008-2010)	2011	82	79	.509	—	—	—
15	Angels (2001-2003)	2004	92	70	.568	—	—	X
16	Royals (1984-1986)	1987	83	79	.512	—	—	—
17	Phillies (2010-2012)	2013	73	89	.451	—	—	—
18	Reds (1994-1996)	1997	76	86	.469	—	—	—
19	White Sox (1999-2001)	2002	81	81	.500	—	—	—
20	Brewers (1981-1983)	1984	67	94	.416	—	—	—
21	Indians (2006-2008)	2009	65	97	.401	—	—	—
22	Red Sox (1974-1976)	1977	97	64	.602	—	—	—
23	Cardinals (1986-1988)	1989	86	76	.531	—	—	—
24	White Sox (2004-2006)	2007	72	90	.444	—	—	—
25	Cardinals (1981-1983)	1984	84	78	.519	—	—	—

SEATTLE MARINERS

Past 10 Seasons (2013-2022)

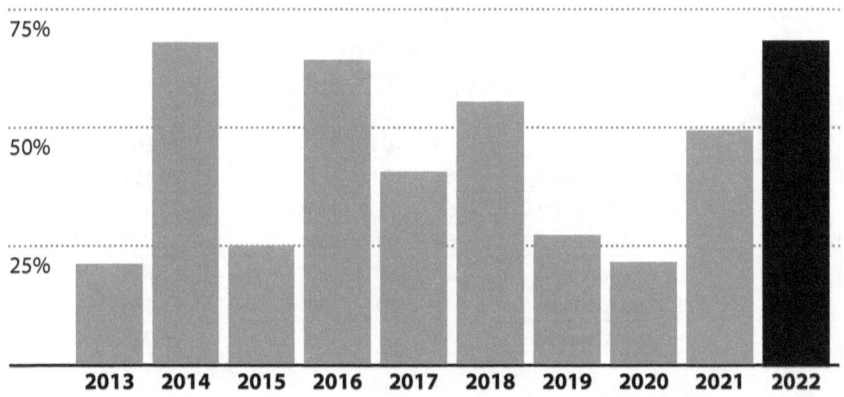

Year	Team	W	L	Pct.	Post	TS	ME%
2013	Seattle Mariners	71	91	.438	—	31.740	21.2%
2014	Seattle Mariners	87	75	.537	—	54.608	68.0%
2015	Seattle Mariners	76	86	.469	—	33.493	25.1%
2016	Seattle Mariners	86	76	.531	—	52.729	64.3%
2017	Seattle Mariners	78	84	.481	—	41.486	40.7%
2018	Seattle Mariners	89	73	.549	—	48.761	55.5%
2019	Seattle Mariners	68	94	.420	—	35.241	27.3%
2020	Seattle Mariners	27	33	.450	—	32.025	21.6%
2021	Seattle Mariners	90	72	.556	—	45.671	49.4%
2022	Seattle Mariners	90	72	.556	P	54.850	68.3%

Best Seasons of Modern Era (1977-2022)

Year	Team	W	L	Pct.	Post	TS	ME%
2001	Seattle Mariners	116	46	.716	P	81.959	97.9%
2000	Seattle Mariners	91	71	.562	P	64.047	85.3%
1997	Seattle Mariners	90	72	.556	P	63.106	83.9%
2003	Seattle Mariners	93	69	.574	—	61.134	80.4%
2002	Seattle Mariners	93	69	.574	—	58.523	76.2%
1996	Seattle Mariners	85	76	.528	—	55.530	70.7%
2022	Seattle Mariners	90	72	.556	P	54.850	68.3%
2014	Seattle Mariners	87	75	.537	—	54.608	68.0%
1995	Seattle Mariners	79	66	.545	P	54.377	67.4%
2016	Seattle Mariners	86	76	.531	—	52.729	64.3%

Worst Seasons of Modern Era (1977-2022)

Year	Team	W	L	Pct.	Post	TS	ME%
2008	Seattle Mariners	61	101	.377	—	14.853	1.9%
1983	Seattle Mariners	60	102	.370	—	17.114	3.1%
1978	Seattle Mariners	56	104	.350	—	17.225	3.3%
1980	Seattle Mariners	59	103	.364	—	17.863	3.7%
2010	Seattle Mariners	61	101	.377	—	20.157	5.1%
1986	Seattle Mariners	67	95	.414	—	20.577	5.7%
1977	Seattle Mariners	64	98	.395	—	21.837	6.9%
1992	Seattle Mariners	64	98	.395	—	21.894	7.0%
2004	Seattle Mariners	63	99	.389	—	25.068	9.9%
1981	Seattle Mariners	44	65	.404	—	26.020	11.8%

Season Breakdown (2022)

Category	W	L	Pct.	R	RA	R/G	RA/G
Overall record in 2022	90	72	.556	690	623	4.26	3.85
Home games	46	35	.568	318	299	3.93	3.69
Away games	44	37	.543	372	324	4.59	4.00
First half of 2022 season	39	42	.481	319	317	3.94	3.91
Second half of 2022 season	51	30	.630	371	306	4.58	3.78
Against first-place teams	19	16	.543	135	126	3.86	3.60
Against playoff teams	32	27	.542	229	214	3.88	3.63
Against non-playoff teams	58	45	.563	461	409	4.48	3.97

Season as Nine-Inning Game (2022)

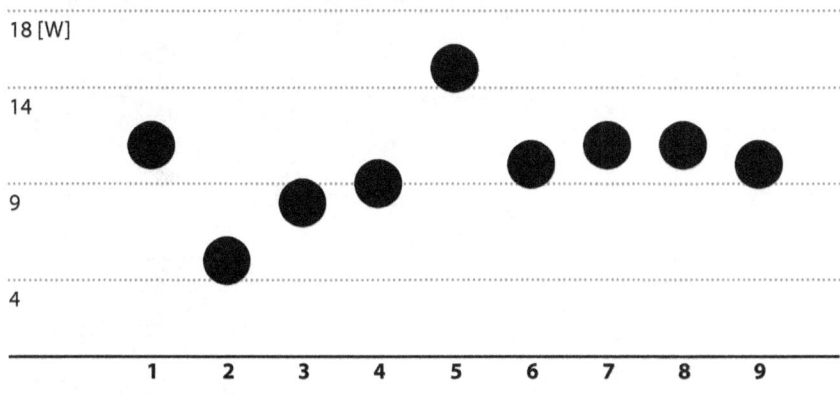

Result	1	2	3	4	5	6	7	8	9	Total
Wins	11	5	8	9	15	10	11	11	10	90
Losses	7	13	10	9	3	8	7	7	8	72

Scoring by Game (2022)

Runs Scored	G	W	L	Pct.	R/G	RA/G
Overall record	162	90	72	.556	4.26	3.85
0	12	0	12	.000	0.00	4.00
1	17	1	16	.059	1.00	3.65
2	28	11	17	.393	2.00	3.39
3	16	6	10	.375	3.00	3.63
4	18	11	7	.611	4.00	4.06
5	15	12	3	.800	5.00	3.47
6	21	17	4	.810	6.00	3.95
7	11	9	2	.818	7.00	4.73
8	11	11	0	1.000	8.00	3.91
9	6	6	0	1.000	9.00	3.00
10 or more	7	6	1	.857	11.00	5.57

Scoring Allowed by Game (2022)

Runs Allowed	G	W	L	Pct.	R/G	RA/G
Overall record	162	90	72	.556	4.26	3.85
0	10	10	0	1.000	5.10	0.00
1	23	23	0	1.000	4.09	1.00
2	23	16	7	.696	4.30	2.00
3	29	16	13	.552	3.86	3.00
4	25	8	17	.320	3.00	4.00
5	13	5	8	.385	3.62	5.00
6	11	7	4	.636	6.18	6.00
7	10	4	6	.400	5.70	7.00
8	7	0	7	.000	5.29	8.00
9	6	1	5	.167	4.00	9.00
10 or more	5	0	5	.000	5.20	11.20

Margins (2022)

Category	Margin	G	W	L	Pct.	GShr	WShr
Overall record	—	162	90	72	.556	—	—
Close	1 or 2 runs	85	46	39	.541	52.5%	51.1%
Medium	3 or 4 runs	42	23	19	.548	25.9%	25.6%
Distant	5 or more runs	35	21	14	.600	21.6%	23.3%

Individual Scoring Leaders (2022)

Team Rank	Batter	R	(+) RBI	(-) HR	(=) SC
1	Eugenio Suarez	76	87	31	132
2	Julio Rodriguez	84	75	28	131
3	Ty France	65	84	20	129
4	Adam Frazier	61	42	3	100
5	J.P. Crawford	57	42	6	93
6	Jesse Winker	51	53	14	90
7	Cal Raleigh	46	63	27	82
8	Abraham Toro	36	35	10	61
9	Dylan Moore	41	24	6	59
9	Carlos Santana	35	39	15	59

Team Ratings (2022)

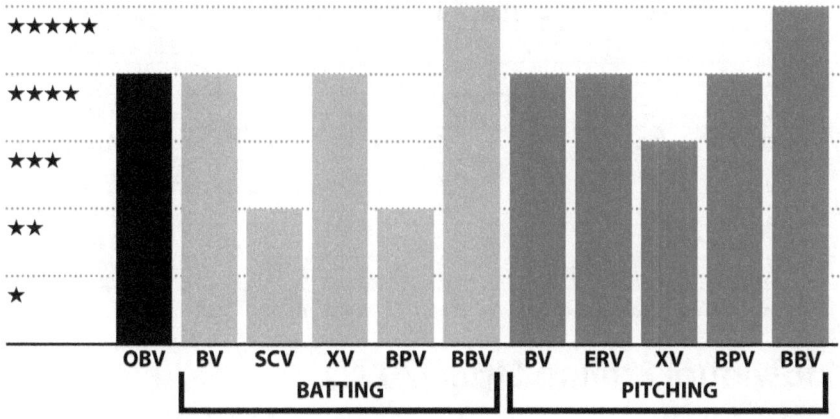

Quality	Type	Indicator	Value	Rating
Overall performance	Overall	OBV	160	★★★★
Base production	Batting	BV	53	★★★★
Run production	Batting	SCV	-36	★★
Power hitting	Batting	XV	40	★★★★
Contact hitting	Batting	BPV	-55	★★
Batting eye	Batting	BBV	96	★★★★★
Base prevention	Pitching	BV	-107	★★★★
Run prevention	Pitching	ERV	-60	★★★★
Power prevention	Pitching	XV	10	★★★
Strikeout pitching	Pitching	BPV	-36	★★★★
Control pitching	Pitching	BBV	-49	★★★★★

Team Batting Stats (2022)

Stat	Number	Div Rank	Lg Rank	MLB Rank	MLB Best
R	690	3	8	18	847 (Dodgers)
H	1,237	4	14	27	1,464 (Blue Jays)
HR	197	3	5	9	254 (Yankees)
BPO	.672	2	5	11	.764 (Dodgers)
BA	.230	4	14	27	.264 (Blue Jays)
OBP	.315	2	7	16	.333 (Dodgers)
SA	.390	4	9	17	.443 (Braves)

Division: AL West, 5 teams. **League:** American, 15 teams. **MLB:** 30 teams.

Team Pitching Stats (2022)

Stat	Number	Div Rank	Lg Rank	MLB Rank	MLB Best
ERA	3.59	2	5	8	2.80 (Dodgers)
SO	1,391	2	4	12	1,565 (Mets)
BB	447	1	6	9	384 (Rays)
BPO	.635	2	5	10	.551 (Astros)
BA	.235	3	6	10	.209 (Dodgers)
OBP	.298	2	5	7	.273 (Dodgers)
SA	.389	3	7	13	.332 (Astros)

Division: AL West, 5 teams. **League:** American, 15 teams. **MLB:** 30 teams.

Individual Batting Stats (2022)

Batter	PA	BPO	BA	OBP	SA	ISO	CT	EY
J.P. Crawford	603	.636	.243	.339	.336	.093	.846	.113
Ty France	613	.716	.276	.340	.437	.162	.829	.052
Adam Frazier	602	.542	.238	.301	.311	.072	.865	.075
Cal Raleigh	415	.752	.211	.284	.489	.278	.670	.092
Julio Rodriguez	560	.877	.284	.345	.509	.225	.716	.065
Eugenio Suarez	629	.775	.236	.332	.459	.223	.639	.116
Abraham Toro	352	.496	.185	.239	.324	.139	.799	.060
Jesse Winker	547	.676	.219	.344	.344	.125	.774	.152

Individual Pitching Stats for Starters (2022)

Pitcher	IP	BPO	ERA	BA	SA	ISO	CT	EY
Chris Flexen	137.2	.689	3.73	.250	.408	.159	.820	.082
Logan Gilbert	185.2	.618	3.20	.242	.390	.148	.752	.062
Marco Gonzales	183.0	.731	4.13	.271	.457	.187	.856	.063
George Kirby	130.0	.614	3.39	.264	.393	.129	.740	.041
Robbie Ray	189.0	.680	3.71	.231	.423	.191	.699	.080

Individual Pitching Stats for Relievers (2022)

Pitcher	GR	BPO	ERA	BA	SA	ISO	CT	EY
Diego Castillo	59	.573	3.64	.203	.299	.096	.731	.083
Matthew Festa	53	.689	4.17	.218	.426	.208	.675	.082
Andres Munoz	64	.458	2.49	.189	.273	.084	.577	.049
Penn Murfee	63	.505	2.99	.192	.320	.128	.696	.063
Paul Sewald	65	.487	2.67	.146	.301	.155	.671	.055
Erik Swanson	56	.453	1.68	.202	.290	.088	.637	.044

Best Stats on Team (2022)

Stat	Batter	Number
2B	Ty France	27
3B	Adam Frazier	4
BA	Julio Rodriguez	.284
BB	Jesse Winker	84
BBV	Jesse Winker	40
BPO	Julio Rodriguez	.877
BPV	Adam Frazier	62
BV	Julio Rodriguez	83
CT	Adam Frazier	.865
EY	Jesse Winker	.152
H	Ty France	152
HR	Eugenio Suarez	31
ISO	Cal Raleigh	.278
OBP	Julio Rodriguez	.345
R	Julio Rodriguez	84
RBI	Eugenio Suarez	87
SA	Julio Rodriguez	.509
SB	Julio Rodriguez	25
SC	Eugenio Suarez	132
SCV	Julio Rodriguez	22
SE	Julio Rodriguez	.234
XV	Cal Raleigh	47

Stat	Pitcher	Number
BA	Robbie Ray	.231
BBV	George Kirby	-21
BPO-R	Erik Swanson	.453
BPO-S	George Kirby	.614
BPV	Andres Munoz	-39
BV	Andres Munoz	-39
CT	Robbie Ray	.699
ERA-R	Erik Swanson	1.68
ERA-S	Logan Gilbert	3.20
ERV	Logan Gilbert	-16
EY	George Kirby	.041
GR	Paul Sewald	65
GS	Marco Gonzales, Robbie Ray, Logan Gilbert	32
IP	Robbie Ray	189.0
ISO	George Kirby	.129
OBP	Logan Gilbert	.295
SA	Logan Gilbert	.390
SO	Robbie Ray	212
SV	Paul Sewald	20
W	Logan Gilbert	13
XV	Andres Munoz	-16

Worst Stats on Team (2022)

Stat	Batter	Number
BA	Abraham Toro	.185
BBV	Ty France	-16
BPO	Abraham Toro	.496
BPV	Eugenio Suarez	-60
BV	Adam Frazier	-52
CT	Eugenio Suarez	.639
EY	Ty France	.052
ISO	Adam Frazier	.072
OBP	Abraham Toro	.239
SA	Adam Frazier	.311
SCV	J.P. Crawford	-25
SE	J.P. Crawford	.154
SO	Eugenio Suarez	196
XV	Adam Frazier	-43

Stat	Pitcher	Number
BA	Marco Gonzales	.271
BB	Robbie Ray	62
BBV	Matt Brash	15
BPO-R	Matthew Festa	.689
BPO-S	Marco Gonzales	.731
BPV	Marco Gonzales	76
BV	Marco Gonzales	39
CT	Marco Gonzales	.856
ERA-R	Matthew Festa	4.17
ERA-S	Marco Gonzales	4.13
ERV	Sergio Romo	7
EY	Chris Flexen	.082
ISO	Robbie Ray	.191
L	Marco Gonzales	15
OBP	Marco Gonzales	.322
SA	Marco Gonzales	.457
XV	Robbie Ray	28

Overall Base Value Leaders (2022)

Team Rank	Player	BV [bat]	(-) BV [pitch]	(=) OBV
1	Julio Rodriguez	83	0	83
2	Eugenio Suarez	50	0	50
3	Andres Munoz	0	-39	39
4	Dylan Moore	34	0	34
5	Paul Sewald	0	-33	33
5	Erik Swanson	0	-33	33
7	Penn Murfee	0	-32	32
8	Cal Raleigh	28	0	28
9	Logan Gilbert	0	-24	24
10	Ty France	23	0	23

Fan Support in Past 10 Seasons (2013-2022)

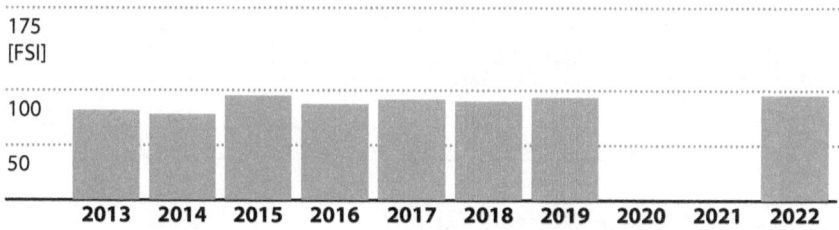

Year	Team	Attendance	W	Att:W	FSI
2013	Seattle Mariners	1,761,546	71	24,811	81.5
2014	Seattle Mariners	2,064,334	87	23,728	78.2
2015	Seattle Mariners	2,193,581	76	28,863	95.1
2016	Seattle Mariners	2,267,928	86	26,371	87.5
2017	Seattle Mariners	2,135,445	78	27,378	91.5
2018	Seattle Mariners	2,299,489	89	25,837	90.2
2019	Seattle Mariners	1,791,109	68	26,340	93.4
2022	Seattle Mariners	2,287,267	90	25,414	95.7

Extreme Games for Batters (2022)

Stat	Team Total	Individual Leader	G
3+ H	55	Julio Rodriguez	14
2+ HR	13	Carlos Santana, Eugenio Suarez	4
5+ RBI	4	Carlos Santana, Eugenio Suarez, Julio Rodriguez, Ty France	1
0 H in 5+ AB	39	Adam Frazier	7
4+ SO	10	Eugenio Suarez	3

Extreme Games for Pitchers (2022)

Stat	Team Total	Individual Leader	G
0-2 ER in 7+ IP	17	Robbie Ray	6
10+ SO	9	Robbie Ray	7
0 BR in SV	19	Paul Sewald	11
10+ BR	30	Marco Gonzales	11
1+ ER in SV	5	Paul Sewald	4

Predictions for Coming Season (2023)

Group	Next W	Next L	Next Pct.	WS	LC	PQ
10 closest matches (avg. W-L)	80.6	79.4	.504	0	0	3
25 closest matches (avg. W-L)	82.0	79.2	.509	0	0	6
50 closest matches (avg. W-L)	80.8	75.8	.516	0	3	14

25 Closest Matches (2023)

Rank	Team	Next	W	L	Pct.	WS	LC	PQ
1	Rays (2016-2018)	2019	96	66	.593	—	—	X
2	Royals (1992-1994)	1995	70	74	.486	—	—	—
3	Mets (1974-1976)	1977	64	98	.395	—	—	—
4	Cardinals (1990-1992)	1993	87	75	.537	—	—	—
5	Blue Jays (2004-2006)	2007	83	79	.512	—	—	—
6	Angels (1983-1985)	1986	92	70	.568	—	—	X
7	Padres (1987-1989)	1990	75	87	.463	—	—	—
8	Twins (2000-2002)	2003	90	72	.556	—	—	X
9	Yankees (2013-2015)	2016	84	78	.519	—	—	—
10	Angels (1977-1979)	1980	65	95	.406	—	—	—
11	Diamondbacks (2005-2007)	2008	82	80	.506	—	—	—
12	Pirates (1986-1988)	1989	74	88	.457	—	—	—
13	Rockies (2015-2017)	2018	91	72	.558	—	—	X
14	Giants (1976-1978)	1979	71	91	.438	—	—	—
15	Expos (1988-1990)	1991	71	90	.441	—	—	—
16	Tigers (1976-1978)	1979	85	76	.528	—	—	—
17	Rangers (1994-1996)	1997	77	85	.475	—	—	—
18	Dodgers (1998-2000)	2001	86	76	.531	—	—	—
19	Angels (2010-2012)	2013	78	84	.481	—	—	—
20	Giants (1980-1982)	1983	79	83	.488	—	—	—
21	Braves (1980-1982)	1983	88	74	.543	—	—	—
22	Blue Jays (1996-1998)	1999	84	78	.519	—	—	—
23	Mariners (1994-1996)	1997	90	72	.556	—	—	X
24	Brewers (2015-2017)	2018	96	67	.589	—	—	X
25	Royals (1986-1988)	1989	92	70	.568	—	—	—

TAMPA BAY RAYS

Past 10 Seasons (2013-2022)

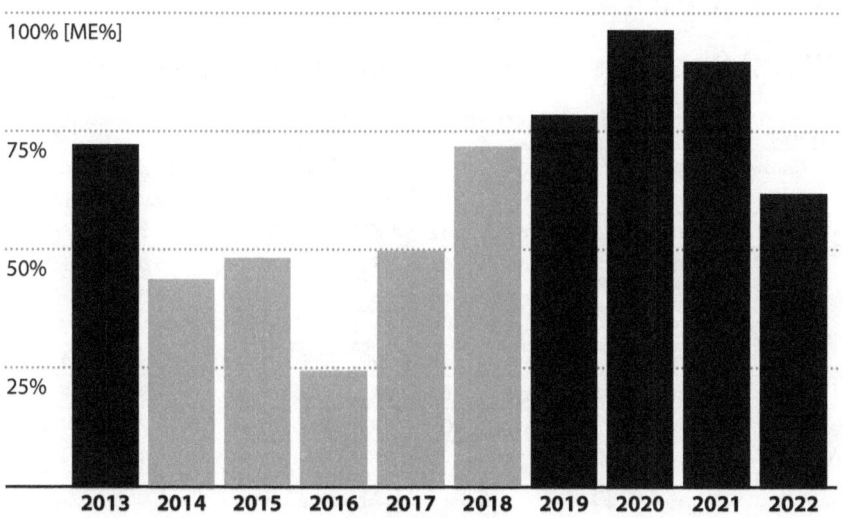

Year	Team	W	L	Pct.	Post	TS	ME%
2013	Tampa Bay Rays	92	71	.564	P	56.180	72.1%
2014	Tampa Bay Rays	77	85	.475	—	42.842	43.7%
2015	Tampa Bay Rays	80	82	.494	—	45.003	48.2%
2016	Tampa Bay Rays	68	94	.420	—	33.259	24.4%
2017	Tampa Bay Rays	80	82	.494	—	45.857	49.8%
2018	Tampa Bay Rays	90	72	.556	—	56.087	71.8%
2019	Tampa Bay Rays	96	66	.593	P	60.049	78.4%
2020	Tampa Bay Rays	40	20	.667	LP	77.699	96.3%
2021	Tampa Bay Rays	100	62	.617	P	68.089	89.7%
2022	Tampa Bay Rays	86	76	.531	P	51.731	61.8%

Best Seasons of Modern Era (1998-2022)

Year	Team	W	L	Pct.	Post	TS	ME%
2020	Tampa Bay Rays	40	20	.667	LP	77.699	96.3%
2008	Tampa Bay Rays	97	65	.599	LP	73.410	93.5%
2021	Tampa Bay Rays	100	62	.617	P	68.089	89.7%
2010	Tampa Bay Rays	96	66	.593	P	65.174	87.1%
2012	Tampa Bay Rays	90	72	.556	—	62.548	83.4%
2019	Tampa Bay Rays	96	66	.593	P	60.049	78.4%
2011	Tampa Bay Rays	91	71	.562	P	58.431	76.0%
2013	Tampa Bay Rays	92	71	.564	P	56.180	72.1%
2018	Tampa Bay Rays	90	72	.556	—	56.087	71.8%
2009	Tampa Bay Rays	84	78	.519	—	54.852	68.4%

Worst Seasons of Modern Era (1998-2022)

Year	Team	W	L	Pct.	Post	TS	ME%
2006	Tampa Bay Devil Rays	61	101	.377	—	18.251	3.9%
2002	Tampa Bay Devil Rays	55	106	.342	—	19.054	4.4%
2001	Tampa Bay Devil Rays	62	100	.383	—	22.360	7.4%
2005	Tampa Bay Devil Rays	67	95	.414	—	23.637	8.9%
2007	Tampa Bay Devil Rays	66	96	.407	—	24.089	9.4%
2000	Tampa Bay Devil Rays	69	92	.429	—	25.349	10.5%
1998	Tampa Bay Devil Rays	63	99	.389	—	25.582	11.1%
1999	Tampa Bay Devil Rays	69	93	.426	—	27.389	14.0%
2003	Tampa Bay Devil Rays	63	99	.389	—	27.743	14.6%
2004	Tampa Bay Devil Rays	70	91	.435	—	29.348	17.5%

Season Breakdown (2022)

Category	W	L	Pct.	R	RA	R/G	RA/G
Overall record in 2022	86	76	.531	666	614	4.11	3.79
Home games	51	30	.630	336	279	4.15	3.44
Away games	35	46	.432	330	335	4.07	4.14
First half of 2022 season	44	37	.543	333	314	4.11	3.88
Second half of 2022 season	42	39	.519	333	300	4.11	3.70
Against first-place teams	14	20	.412	107	117	3.15	3.44
Against playoff teams	29	31	.483	219	215	3.65	3.58
Against non-playoff teams	57	45	.559	447	399	4.38	3.91

Season as Nine-Inning Game (2022)

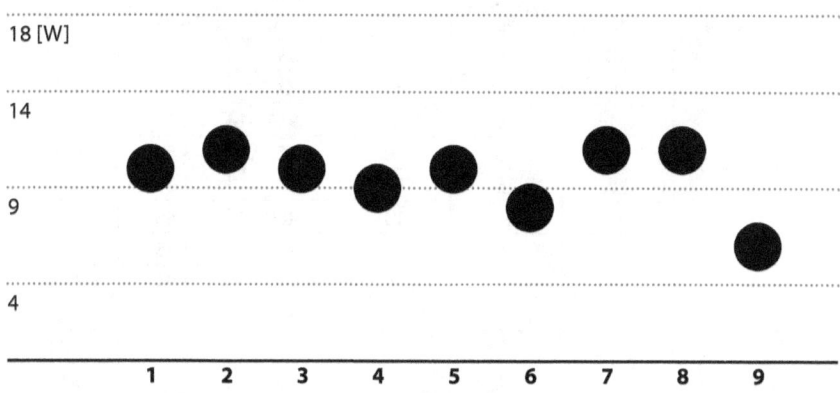

Result	1	2	3	4	5	6	7	8	9	Total
Wins	10	11	10	9	10	8	11	11	6	86
Losses	8	7	8	9	8	10	7	7	12	76

Scoring by Game (2022)

Runs Scored	G	W	L	Pct.	R/G	RA/G
Overall record	162	86	76	.531	4.11	3.79
0	10	0	10	.000	0.00	4.20
1	21	1	20	.048	1.00	3.71
2	21	6	15	.286	2.00	3.86
3	27	10	17	.370	3.00	4.30
4	21	15	6	.714	4.00	3.43
5	15	11	4	.733	5.00	4.20
6	15	13	2	.867	6.00	3.27
7	10	9	1	.900	7.00	3.20
8	10	9	1	.900	8.00	3.40
9	3	3	0	1.000	9.00	3.67
10 or more	9	9	0	1.000	10.67	4.00

Scoring Allowed by Game (2022)

Runs Allowed	G	W	L	Pct.	R/G	RA/G
Overall record	162	86	76	.531	4.11	3.79
0	10	10	0	1.000	5.60	0.00
1	21	20	1	.952	4.33	1.00
2	30	20	10	.667	3.50	2.00
3	26	15	11	.577	4.04	3.00
4	22	9	13	.409	3.86	4.00
5	20	7	13	.350	4.25	5.00
6	9	2	7	.222	4.44	6.00
7	6	2	4	.333	4.83	7.00
8	4	1	3	.250	6.50	8.00
9	7	0	7	.000	3.43	9.00
10 or more	7	0	7	.000	2.86	10.86

Margins (2022)

Category	Margin	G	W	L	Pct.	GShr	WShr
Overall record	—	162	86	76	.531	—	—
Close	1 or 2 runs	85	42	43	.494	52.5%	48.8%
Medium	3 or 4 runs	36	20	16	.556	22.2%	23.3%
Distant	5 or more runs	41	24	17	.585	25.3%	27.9%

Individual Scoring Leaders (2022)

Team Rank	Batter	R	(+) RBI	(-) HR	(=) SC
1	Randy Arozarena	72	89	20	141
2	Yandy Diaz	71	57	9	119
3	Harold Ramirez	46	58	6	98
4	Manuel Margot	36	47	4	79
5	Taylor Walls	53	33	8	78
6	Ji-Man Choi	36	52	11	77
7	Wander Franco	46	33	6	73
7	Isaac Paredes	48	45	20	73
9	Francisco Mejia	32	31	6	57
10	Brandon Lowe	31	25	8	48

Team Ratings (2022)

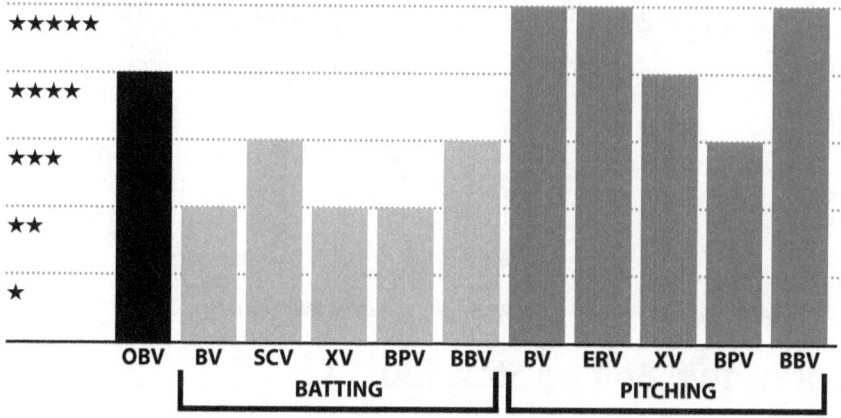

Quality	Type	Indicator	Value	Rating
Overall performance	Overall	OBV	133	★★★★
Base production	Batting	BV	-98	★★
Run production	Batting	SCV	-10	★★★
Power hitting	Batting	XV	-76	★★
Contact hitting	Batting	BPV	-44	★★
Batting eye	Batting	BBV	12	★★★
Base prevention	Pitching	BV	-231	★★★★★
Run prevention	Pitching	ERV	-88	★★★★★
Power prevention	Pitching	XV	-28	★★★★
Strikeout pitching	Pitching	BPV	-30	★★★
Control pitching	Pitching	BBV	-99	★★★★★

Team Batting Stats (2022)

Stat	Number	Div Rank	Lg Rank	MLB Rank	MLB Best
R	666	5	11	21	847 (Dodgers)
H	1,294	4	10	18	1,464 (Blue Jays)
HR	139	5	11	25	254 (Yankees)
BPO	.637	5	10	21	.764 (Dodgers)
BA	.239	4	9	17	.264 (Blue Jays)
OBP	.309	4	9	20	.333 (Dodgers)
SA	.377	5	13	25	.443 (Braves)

Division: AL East, 5 teams. **League:** American, 15 teams. **MLB:** 30 teams.

Team Pitching Stats (2022)

Stat	Number	Div Rank	Lg Rank	MLB Rank	MLB Best
ERA	3.41	2	3	4	2.80 (Dodgers)
SO	1,384	3	7	15	1,565 (Mets)
BB	384	1	1	1	384 (Rays)
BPO	.607	2	3	5	.551 (Astros)
BA	.232	2	5	8	.209 (Dodgers)
OBP	.289	2	3	4	.273 (Dodgers)
SA	.379	2	5	9	.332 (Astros)

Division: AL East, 5 teams. **League:** American, 15 teams. **MLB:** 30 teams.

Individual Batting Stats (2022)

Batter	PA	BPO	BA	OBP	SA	ISO	CT	EY
Randy Arozarena	645	.760	.263	.327	.445	.183	.734	.068
Ji-Man Choi	419	.720	.233	.341	.388	.154	.654	.132
Yandy Diaz	558	.830	.296	.401	.423	.127	.873	.137
Wander Franco	344	.716	.277	.328	.417	.140	.895	.073
Manuel Margot	363	.627	.274	.325	.375	.101	.798	.064
Isaac Paredes	381	.698	.205	.304	.435	.230	.798	.115
Harold Ramirez	435	.669	.300	.343	.404	.104	.821	.041
Taylor Walls	466	.526	.172	.268	.285	.113	.705	.112

Individual Pitching Stats for Starters (2022)

Pitcher	IP	BPO	ERA	BA	SA	ISO	CT	EY
Corey Kluber	164.0	.650	4.34	.274	.425	.151	.786	.030
Shane McClanahan	166.1	.477	2.54	.194	.317	.122	.675	.058
Drew Rasmussen	146.0	.532	2.84	.222	.347	.125	.771	.053
Jeffrey Springs	135.1	.530	2.46	.222	.353	.131	.719	.056

Individual Pitching Stats for Relievers (2022)

Pitcher	GR	BPO	ERA	BA	SA	ISO	CT	EY
Jason Adam	67	.463	1.56	.147	.242	.095	.645	.064
Colin Poche	65	.667	3.99	.211	.408	.197	.706	.090
Brooks Raley	60	.470	2.68	.189	.276	.087	.689	.068
Ryan Thompson	47	.595	3.80	.234	.359	.126	.766	.050

Best Stats on Team (2022)

Stat	Batter	Number
2B	Randy Arozarena	41
3B	Randy Arozarena, Wander Franco	3
BA	Harold Ramirez	.300
BB	Yandy Diaz	78
BBV	Yandy Diaz	32
BPO	Yandy Diaz	.830
BPV	Yandy Diaz	58
BV	Yandy Diaz	59
CT	Wander Franco	.895
EY	Yandy Diaz	.137
H	Randy Arozarena	154
HR	Randy Arozarena, Isaac Paredes	20
ISO	Isaac Paredes	.230
OBP	Yandy Diaz	.401
R	Randy Arozarena	72
RBI	Randy Arozarena	89
SA	Randy Arozarena	.445
SB	Randy Arozarena	32
SC	Randy Arozarena	141
SCV	Randy Arozarena	15
SE	Harold Ramirez	.225
XV	Isaac Paredes	26

Stat	Pitcher	Number
BA	Shane McClanahan	.194
BBV	Corey Kluber	-34
BPO-R	Jason Adam	.463
BPO-S	Shane McClanahan	.477
BPV	Shane McClanahan	-45
BV	Shane McClanahan	-91
CT	Shane McClanahan	.675
ERA-R	Jason Adam	1.56
ERA-S	Jeffrey Springs	2.46
ERV	Shane McClanahan	-26
EY	Corey Kluber	.030
GR	Jason Adam	67
GS	Corey Kluber	31
IP	Shane McClanahan	166.1
ISO	Shane McClanahan	.122
OBP	Shane McClanahan	.246
SA	Shane McClanahan	.317
SO	Shane McClanahan	194
SV	Jason Adam, Pete Fairbanks	8
W	Shane McClanahan	12
XV	Shane McClanahan	-18

Worst Stats on Team (2022)

Stat	Batter	Number
BA	Taylor Walls	.172
BBV	Francisco Mejia	-17
BPO	Taylor Walls	.526
BPV	Brett Phillips	-39
BV	Taylor Walls	-47
CT	Ji-Man Choi	.654
EY	Harold Ramirez	.041
ISO	Manuel Margot	.101
OBP	Taylor Walls	.268
SA	Taylor Walls	.285
SCV	Taylor Walls	-13
SE	Taylor Walls	.167
SO	Randy Arozarena	156
XV	Harold Ramirez	-19

Stat	Pitcher	Number
BA	Corey Kluber	.274
BB	Shane McClanahan	38
BBV	Luis Patino	4
BPO-R	Colin Poche	.667
BPO-S	Corey Kluber	.650
BPV	Corey Kluber	23
BV	Josh Fleming, Luis Patino	27
CT	Corey Kluber	.786
ERA-R	Colin Poche	3.99
ERA-S	Corey Kluber	4.34
ERV	Josh Fleming	10
EY	Shane McClanahan	.058
ISO	Corey Kluber	.151
L	Corey Kluber	10
OBP	Corey Kluber	.304
SA	Corey Kluber	.425
XV	Luis Patino	11

Overall Base Value Leaders (2022)

Team Rank	Player	BV [bat]	(-) BV [pitch]	(=) OBV
1	Shane McClanahan	0	-91	91
2	Yandy Diaz	59	0	59
3	Drew Rasmussen	0	-56	56
4	Jeffrey Springs	0	-54	54
5	Randy Arozarena	46	0	46
6	J.P. Feyereisen	0	-38	38
7	Jason Adam	0	-37	37
8	Brooks Raley	0	-31	31
9	Pete Fairbanks	0	-23	23
10	Garrett Cleavinger	0	-19	19

Fan Support in Past 10 Seasons (2013-2022)

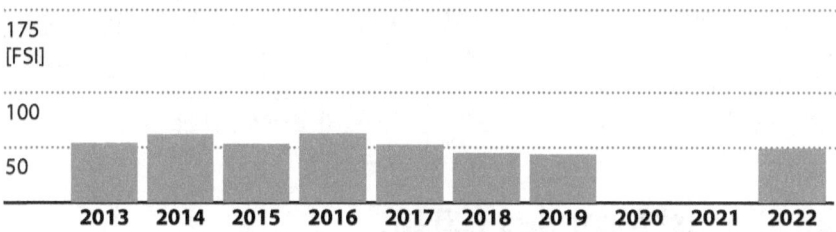

Year	Team	Attendance	W	Att:W	FSI
2013	Tampa Bay Rays	1,510,300	92	16,416	53.9
2014	Tampa Bay Rays	1,446,464	77	18,785	61.9
2015	Tampa Bay Rays	1,287,054	80	16,088	53.0
2016	Tampa Bay Rays	1,286,163	68	18,914	62.7
2017	Tampa Bay Rays	1,253,619	80	15,670	52.4
2018	Tampa Bay Rays	1,154,973	90	12,833	44.8
2019	Tampa Bay Rays	1,178,735	96	12,278	43.5
2022	Tampa Bay Rays	1,128,127	86	13,118	49.4

Extreme Games for Batters (2022)

Stat	Team Total	Individual Leader	G
3+ H	72	Randy Arozarena	14
2+ HR	7	Isaac Paredes	3
5+ RBI	1	Randy Arozarena	1
0 H in 5+ AB	30	Randy Arozarena, Wander Franco	4
4+ SO	5	Brett Phillips, Manuel Margot, Roman Quinn, Taylor Walls, Yu Chang	1

Extreme Games for Pitchers (2022)

Stat	Team Total	Individual Leader	G
0-2 ER in 7+ IP	13	Shane McClanahan	8
10+ SO	6	Shane McClanahan	4
0 BR in SV	20	Jason Adam, Pete Fairbanks	4
10+ BR	10	Corey Kluber	4
1+ ER in SV	5	Andrew Kittredge	2

Predictions for Coming Season (2023)

Group	Next W	Next L	Next Pct.	WS	LC	PQ
10 closest matches (avg. W-L)	88.4	73.2	.547	2	2	5
25 closest matches (avg. W-L)	85.4	72.4	.541	4	7	11
50 closest matches (avg. W-L)	82.6	73.1	.531	5	11	21

25 Closest Matches (2023)

Rank	Team	Next	W	L	Pct.	WS	LC	PQ
1	Orioles (1979-1981)	1982	94	68	.580	—	—	—
2	Diamondbacks (2001-2003)	2004	51	111	.315	—	—	—
3	Nationals (2016-2018)	2019	93	69	.574	X	X	X
4	Indians (1996-1998)	1999	97	65	.599	—	—	X
5	Yankees (1985-1987)	1988	85	76	.528	—	—	—
6	Yankees (2006-2008)	2009	103	59	.636	X	X	X
7	Giants (2002-2004)	2005	75	87	.463	—	—	—
8	Braves (1999-2001)	2002	101	59	.631	—	—	X
9	Red Sox (1998-2000)	2001	82	79	.509	—	—	—
10	Yankees (1977-1979)	1980	103	59	.636	—	—	X
11	Royals (1977-1979)	1980	97	65	.599	—	X	X
12	Cardinals (2001-2003)	2004	105	57	.648	—	X	X
13	Dodgers (1974-1976)	1977	98	64	.605	—	X	X
14	Tigers (1986-1988)	1989	59	103	.364	—	—	—
15	Orioles (1974-1976)	1977	97	64	.602	—	—	—
16	Rangers (2011-2013)	2014	67	95	.414	—	—	—
17	Astros (2004-2006)	2007	73	89	.451	—	—	—
18	Indians (1999-2001)	2002	74	88	.457	—	—	—
19	Cubs (2017-2019)	2020	34	26	.567	—	—	X
20	Yankees (1993-1995)	1996	92	70	.568	X	X	X
21	Red Sox (2008-2010)	2011	90	72	.556	—	—	—
22	Phillies (1977-1979)	1980	91	71	.562	X	X	X
23	Red Sox (1974-1976)	1977	97	64	.602	—	—	—
24	Braves (2004-2006)	2007	84	78	.519	—	—	—
25	Dodgers (1977-1979)	1980	92	71	.564	—	—	—

TEXAS RANGERS

Past 10 Seasons (2013-2022)

100% [ME%]

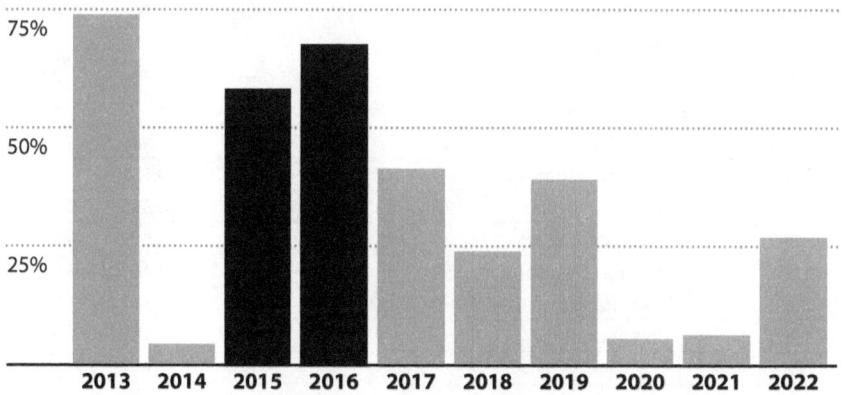

Year	Team	W	L	Pct.	Post	TS	ME%
2013	Texas Rangers	91	72	.558	—	57.120	73.9%
2014	Texas Rangers	67	95	.414	—	18.535	4.2%
2015	Texas Rangers	88	74	.543	P	50.348	58.2%
2016	Texas Rangers	95	67	.586	P	54.453	67.7%
2017	Texas Rangers	78	84	.481	—	41.771	41.4%
2018	Texas Rangers	67	95	.414	—	32.994	23.9%
2019	Texas Rangers	78	84	.481	—	40.863	39.1%
2020	Texas Rangers	22	38	.367	—	20.335	5.4%
2021	Texas Rangers	60	102	.370	—	21.157	6.2%
2022	Texas Rangers	68	94	.420	—	34.910	26.9%

Best Seasons of Modern Era (1961-2022)

Year	Team	W	L	Pct.	Post	TS	ME%
2011	Texas Rangers	96	66	.593	LP	78.226	96.4%
2010	Texas Rangers	90	72	.556	LP	67.736	89.2%
1999	Texas Rangers	95	67	.586	P	62.355	83.0%
2012	Texas Rangers	93	69	.574	P	62.186	82.5%
1977	Texas Rangers	94	68	.580	—	60.866	79.7%
1996	Texas Rangers	90	72	.556	P	60.383	79.0%
2013	Texas Rangers	91	72	.558	—	57.120	73.9%
1981	Texas Rangers	57	48	.543	—	56.719	73.1%
1993	Texas Rangers	86	76	.531	—	56.107	71.9%
1978	Texas Rangers	87	75	.537	—	55.433	70.5%

Worst Seasons of Modern Era (1961-2022)

Year	Team	W	L	Pct.	Post	TS	ME%
1972	Texas Rangers	54	100	.351	—	11.812	1.1%
1973	Texas Rangers	57	105	.352	—	12.786	1.2%
1963	Washington Senators	56	106	.346	—	14.790	1.8%
2014	Texas Rangers	67	95	.414	—	18.535	4.2%
1962	Washington Senators	60	101	.373	—	20.181	5.1%
2020	Texas Rangers	22	38	.367	—	20.335	5.4%
1982	Texas Rangers	64	98	.395	—	20.462	5.4%
1968	Washington Senators	65	96	.404	—	20.463	5.5%
2021	Texas Rangers	60	102	.370	—	21.157	6.2%
1985	Texas Rangers	62	99	.385	—	22.350	7.3%

Season Breakdown (2022)

Category	W	L	Pct.	R	RA	R/G	RA/G
Overall record in 2022	68	94	.420	707	743	4.36	4.59
Home games	34	47	.420	342	396	4.22	4.89
Away games	34	47	.420	365	347	4.51	4.28
First half of 2022 season	38	43	.469	358	347	4.42	4.28
Second half of 2022 season	30	51	.370	349	396	4.31	4.89
Against first-place teams	11	24	.314	105	137	3.00	3.91
Against playoff teams	26	48	.351	269	306	3.64	4.14
Against non-playoff teams	42	46	.477	438	437	4.98	4.97

Season as Nine-Inning Game (2022)

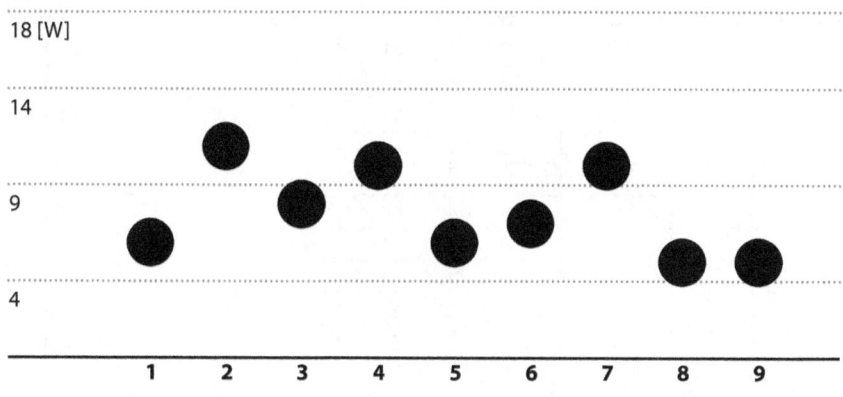

Result	1	2	3	4	5	6	7	8	9	Total
Wins	6	11	8	10	6	7	10	5	5	68
Losses	12	7	10	8	12	11	8	13	13	94

Scoring by Game (2022)

Runs Scored	G	W	L	Pct.	R/G	RA/G
Overall record	162	68	94	.420	4.36	4.59
0	4	0	4	.000	0.00	2.00
1	20	0	20	.000	1.00	3.70
2	26	5	21	.192	2.00	4.85
3	34	10	24	.294	3.00	4.41
4	14	8	6	.571	4.00	3.86
5	11	6	5	.545	5.00	4.00
6	10	6	4	.600	6.00	5.60
7	17	12	5	.706	7.00	4.88
8	12	9	3	.750	8.00	5.00
9	4	2	2	.500	9.00	8.00
10 or more	10	10	0	1.000	11.10	5.60

Scoring Allowed by Game (2022)

Runs Allowed	G	W	L	Pct.	R/G	RA/G
Overall record	162	68	94	.420	4.36	4.59
0	10	10	0	1.000	5.20	0.00
1	12	10	2	.833	3.17	1.00
2	22	14	8	.636	3.23	2.00
3	18	11	7	.611	4.17	3.00
4	25	8	17	.320	4.36	4.00
5	20	6	14	.300	4.15	5.00
6	17	4	13	.235	4.76	6.00
7	11	2	9	.182	4.27	7.00
8	10	2	8	.200	4.60	8.00
9	7	1	6	.143	6.14	9.00
10 or more	10	0	10	.000	6.20	11.10

Margins (2022)

Category	Margin	G	W	L	Pct.	GShr	WShr
Overall record	—	162	68	94	.420	—	—
Close	1 or 2 runs	86	33	53	.384	53.1%	48.5%
Medium	3 or 4 runs	39	16	23	.410	24.1%	23.5%
Distant	5 or more runs	37	19	18	.514	22.8%	27.9%

Individual Scoring Leaders (2022)

Team Rank	Batter	R	(+) RBI	(-) HR	(=) SC
1	Adolis Garcia	88	101	27	162
2	Marcus Semien	101	83	26	158
3	Corey Seager	91	83	33	141
4	Nathaniel Lowe	74	76	27	123
5	Jonah Heim	51	48	16	83
6	Kole Calhoun	36	49	12	73
7	Leody Taveras	39	34	5	68
8	Ezequiel Duran	25	25	5	45
8	Brad Miller	20	32	7	45
10	Mitch Garver	23	24	10	37
10	Josh Smith	23	16	2	37

Team Ratings (2022)

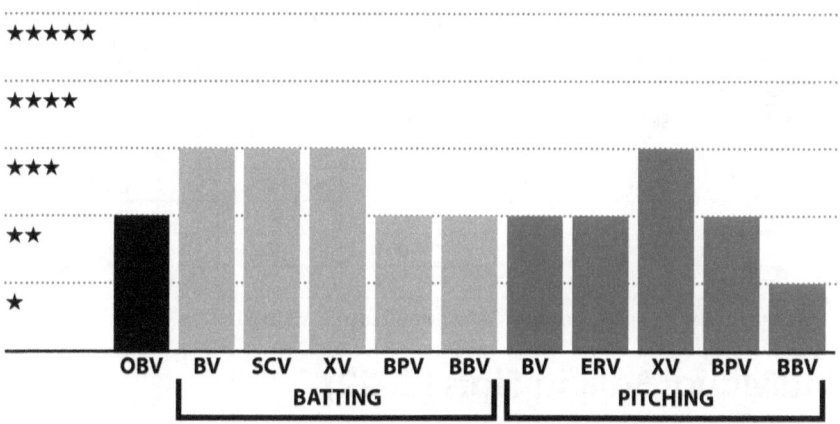

Quality	Type	Indicator	Value	Rating
Overall performance	Overall	OBV	-153	★★
Base production	Batting	BV	-20	★★★
Run production	Batting	SCV	4	★★★
Power hitting	Batting	XV	24	★★★
Contact hitting	Batting	BPV	-78	★★
Batting eye	Batting	BBV	-32	★★
Base prevention	Pitching	BV	133	★★
Run prevention	Pitching	ERV	41	★★
Power prevention	Pitching	XV	-8	★★★
Strikeout pitching	Pitching	BPV	47	★★
Control pitching	Pitching	BBV	78	★

Team Batting Stats (2022)

Stat	Number	Div Rank	Lg Rank	MLB Rank	MLB Best
R	707	2	5	12	847 (Dodgers)
H	1,308	2	8	16	1,464 (Blue Jays)
HR	198	2	4	8	254 (Yankees)
BPO	.655	3	7	17	.764 (Dodgers)
BA	.239	2	10	18	.264 (Blue Jays)
OBP	.301	3	12	25	.333 (Dodgers)
SA	.395	2	6	13	.443 (Braves)

Division: AL West, 5 teams. **League:** American, 15 teams. **MLB:** 30 teams.

Team Pitching Stats (2022)

Stat	Number	Div Rank	Lg Rank	MLB Rank	MLB Best
ERA	4.22	4	12	22	2.80 (Dodgers)
SO	1,314	4	11	21	1,565 (Mets)
BB	581	5	14	27	384 (Rays)
BPO	.691	4	12	23	.551 (Astros)
BA	.247	4	9	17	.209 (Dodgers)
OBP	.325	5	13	24	.273 (Dodgers)
SA	.397	4	9	17	.332 (Astros)

Division: AL West, 5 teams. **League:** American, 15 teams. **MLB:** 30 teams.

Individual Batting Stats (2022)

Batter	PA	BPO	BA	OBP	SA	ISO	CT	EY
Kole Calhoun	424	.517	.196	.257	.330	.134	.649	.064
Adolis Garcia	657	.743	.250	.300	.456	.207	.698	.058
Jonah Heim	450	.638	.227	.298	.399	.172	.786	.091
Nathaniel Lowe	645	.812	.302	.358	.492	.191	.752	.072
Corey Seager	663	.734	.245	.317	.455	.211	.826	.078
Marcus Semien	724	.721	.248	.304	.429	.181	.817	.073
Leody Taveras	341	.630	.261	.309	.366	.105	.720	.062

Individual Pitching Stats for Starters (2022)

Pitcher	IP	BPO	ERA	BA	SA	ISO	CT	EY
Dane Dunning	153.1	.764	4.46	.268	.443	.175	.767	.092
Jon Gray	127.1	.628	3.96	.222	.375	.153	.716	.075
Taylor Hearn	100.0	.741	5.13	.268	.428	.160	.758	.096
Glenn Otto	135.2	.739	4.64	.236	.402	.166	.788	.106
Martin Perez	196.1	.578	2.89	.241	.336	.095	.771	.084

Individual Pitching Stats for Relievers (2022)

Pitcher	GR	BPO	ERA	BA	SA	ISO	CT	EY
Brock Burke	52	.556	1.97	.211	.356	.144	.698	.070
Brett Martin	54	.656	4.14	.260	.396	.135	.792	.072
Matt Moore	63	.545	1.95	.187	.275	.088	.683	.119
Dennis Santana	62	.600	5.22	.228	.315	.087	.753	.106

Best Stats on Team (2022)

Stat	Batter	Number
2B	Adolis Garcia	34
3B	Adolis Garcia, Marcus Semien	5
BA	Nathaniel Lowe	.302
BB	Corey Seager	58
BBV	Josh Smith	8
BPO	Nathaniel Lowe	.812
BPV	Corey Seager	45
BV	Nathaniel Lowe	65
CT	Corey Seager	.826
EY	Jonah Heim	.091
H	Nathaniel Lowe	179
HR	Corey Seager	33
ISO	Corey Seager	.211
OBP	Nathaniel Lowe	.358
R	Marcus Semien	101
RBI	Adolis Garcia	101
SA	Nathaniel Lowe	.492
SB	Adolis Garcia, Marcus Semien	25
SC	Adolis Garcia	162
SCV	Adolis Garcia	34
SE	Adolis Garcia	.247
XV	Corey Seager	35

Stat	Pitcher	Number
BA	Jon Gray	.222
BBV	John King	-6
BPO-R	Matt Moore	.545
BPO-S	Martin Perez	.578
BPV	Matt Moore	-18
BV	Martin Perez	-48
CT	Jon Gray	.716
ERA-R	Matt Moore	1.95
ERA-S	Martin Perez	2.89
ERV	Martin Perez	-23
EY	Jon Gray	.075
GR	Matt Moore	63
GS	Martin Perez	32
IP	Martin Perez	196.1
ISO	Martin Perez	.095
OBP	Jon Gray	.288
SA	Martin Perez	.336
SO	Martin Perez	169
SV	Joe Barlow	13
W	Martin Perez	12
XV	Martin Perez	-42

Worst Stats on Team (2022)

Stat	Batter	Number
BA	Kole Calhoun	.196
BBV	Adolis Garcia	-14
BPO	Kole Calhoun	.517
BPV	Kole Calhoun	-39
BV	Kole Calhoun	-46
CT	Kole Calhoun	.649
EY	Adolis Garcia	.058
ISO	Leody Taveras	.105
OBP	Kole Calhoun	.257
SA	Kole Calhoun	.330
SCV	Josh Smith	-12
SE	Kole Calhoun	.172
SO	Adolis Garcia	183
XV	Josh Smith	-21

Stat	Pitcher	Number
BA	Dane Dunning	.268
BB	Martin Perez	69
BBV	Glenn Otto	16
BPO-R	Brett Martin	.656
BPO-S	Dane Dunning	.764
BPV	John King	21
BV	Dane Dunning	47
CT	Glenn Otto	.788
ERA-R	Dennis Santana	5.22
ERA-S	Taylor Hearn	5.13
ERV	Spencer Howard	14
EY	Glenn Otto	.106
ISO	Dane Dunning	.175
L	Glenn Otto	10
OBP	Dane Dunning	.345
SA	Dane Dunning	.443
XV	Spencer Howard	25

Overall Base Value Leaders (2022)

Team Rank	Player	BV [bat]	(-) BV [pitch]	(=) OBV
1	Nathaniel Lowe	65	0	65
2	Martin Perez	0	-48	48
3	Adolis Garcia	39	0	39
4	Corey Seager	35	0	35
5	Marcus Semien	31	0	31
6	Brock Burke	0	-26	26
6	Matt Moore	0	-26	26
8	Mark Mathias	16	0	16
9	Matt Bush	0	-12	12
9	Jon Gray	0	-12	12

Fan Support in Past 10 Seasons (2013-2022)

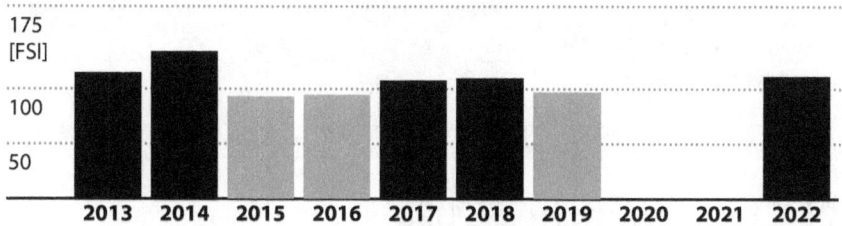

Year	Team	Attendance	W	Att:W	FSI
2013	Texas Rangers	3,178,273	91	34,926	114.7
2014	Texas Rangers	2,718,733	67	40,578	133.7
2015	Texas Rangers	2,491,875	88	28,317	93.3
2016	Texas Rangers	2,710,402	95	28,531	94.6
2017	Texas Rangers	2,507,760	78	32,151	107.5
2018	Texas Rangers	2,107,107	67	31,449	109.7
2019	Texas Rangers	2,132,994	78	27,346	97.0
2022	Texas Rangers	2,011,381	68	29,579	111.3

Extreme Games for Batters (2022)

Stat	Team Total	Individual Leader	G
3+ H	58	Marcus Semien	13
2+ HR	9	Corey Seager, Kole Calhoun, Marcus Semien	2
5+ RBI	7	Adolis Garcia	2
0 H in 5+ AB	33	Marcus Semien	10
4+ SO	13	Eli White, Josh Jung, Kole Calhoun, Nathaniel Lowe	2

Extreme Games for Pitchers (2022)

Stat	Team Total	Individual Leader	G
0-2 ER in 7+ IP	16	Martin Perez	9
10+ SO	2	Jon Gray	2
0 BR in SV	21	Joe Barlow	7
10+ BR	33	Dane Dunning	8
1+ ER in SV	1	Jose Leclerc	1

Predictions for Coming Season (2023)

Group	Next W	Next L	Next Pct.	WS	LC	PQ
10 closest matches (avg. W-L)	66.2	75.3	.468	0	0	2
25 closest matches (avg. W-L)	73.3	76.4	.490	0	0	5
50 closest matches (avg. W-L)	73.4	81.3	.474	0	0	7

25 Closest Matches (2023)

Rank	Team	Next	W	L	Pct.	WS	LC	PQ
1	Phillies (1988-1990)	1991	78	84	.481	—	—	—
2	Phillies (1996-1998)	1999	77	85	.475	—	—	—
3	Royals (2009-2011)	2012	72	90	.444	—	—	—
4	Nationals (2008-2010)	2011	80	81	.497	—	—	—
5	Cubs (1980-1982)	1983	71	91	.438	—	—	—
6	Mariners (1980-1982)	1983	60	102	.370	—	—	—
7	Mariners (2010-2012)	2013	71	91	.438	—	—	—
8	Brewers (2002-2004)	2005	81	81	.500	—	—	—
9	Padres (2017-2019)	2020	37	23	.617	—	—	X
10	White Sox (2017-2019)	2020	35	25	.583	—	—	X
11	Cubs (2012-2014)	2015	97	65	.599	—	—	X
12	Astros (1990-1992)	1993	85	77	.525	—	—	—
13	Mariners (1977-1979)	1980	59	103	.364	—	—	—
14	Marlins (1998-2000)	2001	76	86	.469	—	—	—
15	Braves (2015-2017)	2018	90	72	.556	—	—	X
16	Athletics (2015-2017)	2018	97	65	.599	—	—	X
17	Mariners (1983-1985)	1986	67	95	.414	—	—	—
18	Pirates (1994-1996)	1997	79	83	.488	—	—	—
19	Brewers (1984-1986)	1987	91	71	.562	—	—	—
20	Giants (2017-2019)	2020	29	31	.483	—	—	—
21	Pirates (2000-2002)	2003	75	87	.463	—	—	—
22	Tigers (1974-1976)	1977	74	88	.457	—	—	—
23	Reds (2003-2005)	2006	80	82	.494	—	—	—
24	Twins (2012-2014)	2015	83	79	.512	—	—	—
25	Yankees (1990-1992)	1993	88	74	.543	—	—	—

TORONTO BLUE JAYS

Past 10 Seasons (2013-2022)

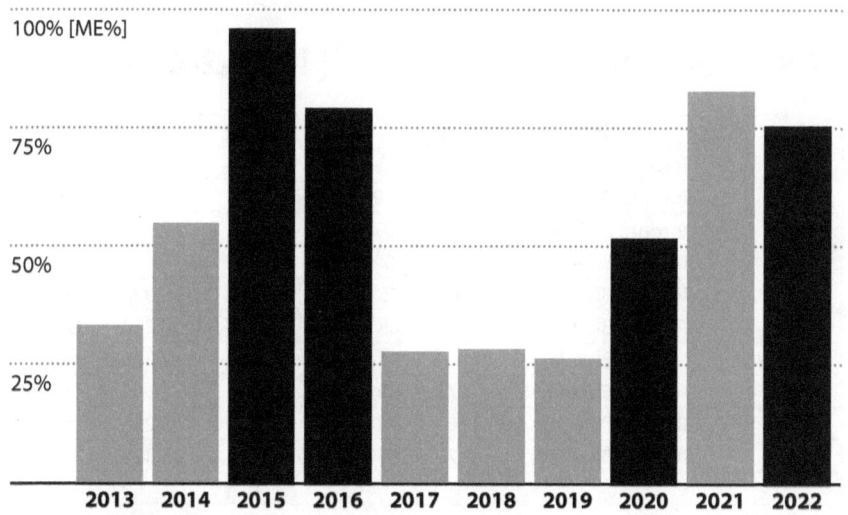

Year	Team	W	L	Pct.	Post	TS	ME%
2013	Toronto Blue Jays	74	88	.457	—	38.112	33.2%
2014	Toronto Blue Jays	83	79	.512	—	48.496	54.8%
2015	Toronto Blue Jays	93	69	.574	P	77.296	96.0%
2016	Toronto Blue Jays	89	73	.549	P	60.489	79.1%
2017	Toronto Blue Jays	76	86	.469	—	35.329	27.7%
2018	Toronto Blue Jays	73	89	.451	—	35.537	28.2%
2019	Toronto Blue Jays	67	95	.414	—	34.294	26.3%
2020	Toronto Blue Jays	32	28	.533	P	46.890	51.7%
2021	Toronto Blue Jays	91	71	.562	—	62.303	82.8%
2022	Toronto Blue Jays	92	70	.568	P	58.043	75.5%

Best Seasons of Modern Era (1977-2022)

Year	Team	W	L	Pct.	Post	TS	ME%
1993	Toronto Blue Jays	95	67	.586	WLP	82.767	98.1%
1992	Toronto Blue Jays	96	66	.593	WLP	81.049	97.4%
2015	Toronto Blue Jays	93	69	.574	P	77.296	96.0%
1985	Toronto Blue Jays	99	62	.615	P	71.062	91.7%
1987	Toronto Blue Jays	96	66	.593	—	70.746	91.4%
1991	Toronto Blue Jays	91	71	.562	P	64.362	85.9%
2021	Toronto Blue Jays	91	71	.562	—	62.303	82.8%
1990	Toronto Blue Jays	86	76	.531	—	60.794	79.4%
2016	Toronto Blue Jays	89	73	.549	P	60.489	79.1%
1984	Toronto Blue Jays	89	73	.549	—	59.809	78.1%

Worst Seasons of Modern Era (1977-2022)

Year	Team	W	L	Pct.	Post	TS	ME%
1981	Toronto Blue Jays	37	69	.349	—	13.370	1.5%
1979	Toronto Blue Jays	53	109	.327	—	13.628	1.6%
1977	Toronto Blue Jays	54	107	.335	—	17.412	3.5%
1978	Toronto Blue Jays	59	102	.366	—	17.817	3.6%
1980	Toronto Blue Jays	67	95	.414	—	25.922	11.8%
1995	Toronto Blue Jays	56	88	.389	—	26.272	12.3%
2004	Toronto Blue Jays	67	94	.416	—	27.576	14.4%
2012	Toronto Blue Jays	73	89	.451	—	31.560	21.0%
2019	Toronto Blue Jays	67	95	.414	—	34.294	26.3%
2017	Toronto Blue Jays	76	86	.469	—	35.329	27.7%

Season Breakdown (2022)

Category	W	L	Pct.	R	RA	R/G	RA/G
Overall record in 2022	92	70	.568	775	679	4.78	4.19
Home games	47	34	.580	359	355	4.43	4.38
Away games	45	36	.556	416	324	5.14	4.00
First half of 2022 season	44	37	.543	381	361	4.70	4.46
Second half of 2022 season	48	33	.593	394	318	4.86	3.93
Against first-place teams	16	20	.444	133	164	3.69	4.56
Against playoff teams	30	36	.455	260	294	3.94	4.45
Against non-playoff teams	62	34	.646	515	385	5.36	4.01

Season as Nine-Inning Game (2022)

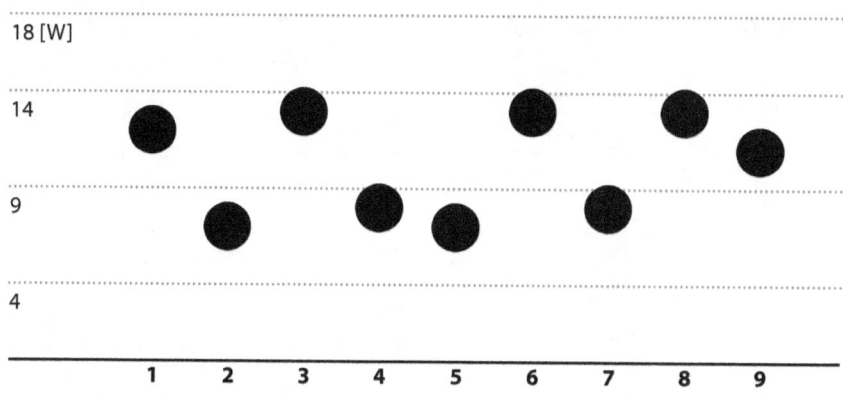

Result	1	2	3	4	5	6	7	8	9	Total
Wins	12	7	13	8	7	13	8	13	11	92
Losses	6	11	5	10	11	5	10	5	7	70

Scoring by Game (2022)

Runs Scored	G	W	L	Pct.	R/G	RA/G
Overall record	162	92	70	.568	4.78	4.19
0	8	0	8	.000	0.00	5.88
1	11	1	10	.091	1.00	4.18
2	19	5	14	.263	2.00	4.00
3	26	12	14	.462	3.00	4.54
4	21	16	5	.762	4.00	2.81
5	20	9	11	.450	5.00	4.80
6	21	16	5	.762	6.00	4.67
7	10	7	3	.700	7.00	4.40
8	8	8	0	1.000	8.00	2.25
9	7	7	0	1.000	9.00	2.71
10 or more	11	11	0	1.000	12.82	5.27

Scoring Allowed by Game (2022)

Runs Allowed	G	W	L	Pct.	R/G	RA/G
Overall record	162	92	70	.568	4.78	4.19
0	10	10	0	1.000	5.50	0.00
1	25	25	0	1.000	4.76	1.00
2	19	16	3	.842	4.42	2.00
3	29	22	7	.759	5.00	3.00
4	14	5	9	.357	3.64	4.00
5	18	8	10	.444	5.50	5.00
6	10	1	9	.100	4.50	6.00
7	11	1	10	.091	4.18	7.00
8	10	1	9	.100	4.50	8.00
9	4	1	3	.250	5.00	9.00
10 or more	12	2	10	.167	5.50	10.83

Margins (2022)

Category	Margin	G	W	L	Pct.	GShr	WShr
Overall record	—	162	92	70	.568	—	—
Close	1 or 2 runs	71	39	32	.549	43.8%	42.4%
Medium	3 or 4 runs	47	27	20	.574	29.0%	29.3%
Distant	5 or more runs	44	26	18	.591	27.2%	28.3%

Individual Scoring Leaders (2022)

Team Rank	Batter	R	(+) RBI	(-) HR	(=) SC
1	Bo Bichette	91	93	24	160
2	Vladimir Guerrero Jr.	90	97	32	155
3	George Springer	89	76	25	140
4	Matt Chapman	83	76	27	132
5	Teoscar Hernandez	71	77	25	123
6	Alejandro Kirk	59	63	14	108
7	Lourdes Gurriel Jr.	52	52	5	99
8	Santiago Espinal	51	51	7	95
9	Raimel Tapia	47	52	7	92
10	Danny Jansen	34	44	15	63

Team Ratings (2022)

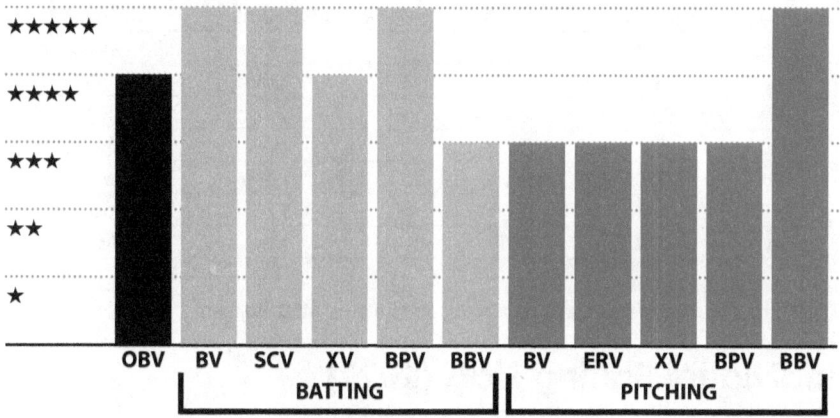

Quality	Type	Indicator	Value	Rating
Overall performance	Overall	OBV	239	★★★★
Base production	Batting	BV	218	★★★★★
Run production	Batting	SCV	130	★★★★★
Power hitting	Batting	XV	86	★★★★
Contact hitting	Batting	BPV	145	★★★★★
Batting eye	Batting	BBV	0	★★★
Base prevention	Pitching	BV	-21	★★★
Run prevention	Pitching	ERV	-15	★★★
Power prevention	Pitching	XV	2	★★★
Strikeout pitching	Pitching	BPV	-19	★★★
Control pitching	Pitching	BBV	-69	★★★★★

Team Batting Stats (2022)

Stat	Number	Div Rank	Lg Rank	MLB Rank	MLB Best
R	775	2	2	4	847 (Dodgers)
H	1,464	1	1	1	1,464 (Blue Jays)
HR	200	2	3	7	254 (Yankees)
BPO	.711	2	2	5	.764 (Dodgers)
BA	.264	1	1	1	.264 (Blue Jays)
OBP	.329	1	1	3	.333 (Dodgers)
SA	.431	1	1	3	.443 (Braves)

Division: AL East, 5 teams. **League:** American, 15 teams. **MLB:** 30 teams.

Team Pitching Stats (2022)

Stat	Number	Div Rank	Lg Rank	MLB Rank	MLB Best
ERA	3.87	3	7	15	2.80 (Dodgers)
SO	1,390	2	5	13	1,565 (Mets)
BB	424	2	2	3	384 (Rays)
BPO	.655	3	7	15	.551 (Astros)
BA	.247	3	10	19	.209 (Dodgers)
OBP	.308	3	8	13	.273 (Dodgers)
SA	.399	3	10	18	.332 (Astros)

Division: AL East, 5 teams. **League:** American, 15 teams. **MLB:** 30 teams.

Individual Batting Stats (2022)

Batter	PA	BPO	BA	OBP	SA	ISO	CT	EY
Bo Bichette	697	.737	.290	.333	.469	.179	.762	.059
Matt Chapman	621	.741	.229	.324	.433	.204	.684	.108
Santiago Espinal	491	.610	.267	.322	.370	.102	.849	.071
Vladimir Guerrero Jr.	706	.770	.274	.339	.480	.205	.818	.074
Lourdes Gurriel Jr.	493	.660	.291	.343	.400	.108	.817	.061
Teoscar Hernandez	535	.742	.267	.316	.491	.224	.695	.064
Alejandro Kirk	541	.758	.285	.372	.415	.130	.877	.113
George Springer	583	.826	.267	.342	.472	.205	.805	.091
Raimel Tapia	433	.575	.265	.292	.380	.114	.803	.037

Individual Pitching Stats for Starters (2022)

Pitcher	IP	BPO	ERA	BA	SA	ISO	CT	EY
Jose Berrios	172.0	.756	5.23	.288	.465	.178	.785	.060
Kevin Gausman	174.2	.631	3.35	.272	.400	.128	.703	.039
Yusei Kikuchi	100.2	.859	5.19	.243	.493	.251	.676	.128
Alek Manoah	196.2	.514	2.24	.202	.314	.112	.748	.065
Ross Stripling	134.1	.525	3.01	.229	.354	.125	.783	.037

Individual Pitching Stats for Relievers (2022)

Pitcher	GR	BPO	ERA	BA	SA	ISO	CT	EY
Adam Cimber	77	.629	2.80	.248	.368	.120	.782	.041
Yimi Garcia	61	.576	3.10	.215	.345	.130	.740	.053
Tim Mayza	63	.618	3.14	.237	.401	.164	.751	.052
David Phelps	64	.571	2.83	.220	.301	.081	.729	.114
Trevor Richards	58	.727	5.34	.238	.396	.158	.658	.121
Jordan Romano	63	.477	2.11	.190	.263	.073	.685	.067

Best Stats on Team (2022)

Stat	Batter	Number
2B	Bo Bichette	43
3B	George Springer	4
BA	Lourdes Gurriel Jr.	.291
BB	Matt Chapman	68
BBV	Alejandro Kirk, Matt Chapman	18
BPO	George Springer	.826
BPV	Alejandro Kirk	59
BV	George Springer	65
CT	Alejandro Kirk	.877
EY	Alejandro Kirk	.113
H	Bo Bichette	189
HR	Vladimir Guerrero Jr.	32
ISO	Teoscar Hernandez	.224
OBP	Alejandro Kirk	.372
R	Bo Bichette	91
RBI	Vladimir Guerrero Jr.	97
SA	Teoscar Hernandez	.491
SB	George Springer	14
SC	Bo Bichette	160
SCV	George Springer	26
SE	George Springer	.240
XV	Teoscar Hernandez	36

Stat	Pitcher	Number
BA	Alek Manoah	.202
BBV	Kevin Gausman	-29
BPO-R	Jordan Romano	.477
BPO-S	Alek Manoah	.514
BPV	Kevin Gausman	-33
BV	Alek Manoah	-87
CT	Yusei Kikuchi	.676
ERA-R	Jordan Romano	2.11
ERA-S	Alek Manoah	2.24
ERV	Alek Manoah	-38
EY	Ross Stripling	.037
GR	Adam Cimber	77
GS	Jose Berrios	32
IP	Alek Manoah	196.2
ISO	Alek Manoah	.112
OBP	Ross Stripling	.259
SA	Alek Manoah	.314
SO	Kevin Gausman	205
SV	Jordan Romano	36
W	Alek Manoah	16
XV	Alek Manoah	-28

Worst Stats on Team (2022)

Stat	Batter	Number
BA	Matt Chapman	.229
BBV	Raimel Tapia	-18
BPO	Raimel Tapia	.575
BPV	Matt Chapman	-36
BV	Raimel Tapia	-27
CT	Matt Chapman	.684
EY	Raimel Tapia	.037
ISO	Santiago Espinal	.102
OBP	Raimel Tapia	.292
SA	Santiago Espinal	.370
SCV	Bradley Zimmer	-3
SE	Santiago Espinal	.193
SO	Matt Chapman	170
XV	Santiago Espinal	-22

Stat	Pitcher	Number
BA	Jose Berrios	.288
BB	Yusei Kikuchi	58
BBV	Yusei Kikuchi	22
BPO-R	Trevor Richards	.727
BPO-S	Yusei Kikuchi	.859
BPV	Jose Berrios	24
BV	Yusei Kikuchi	60
CT	Jose Berrios	.785
ERA-R	Trevor Richards	5.34
ERA-S	Jose Berrios	5.23
ERV	Jose Berrios	24
EY	Yusei Kikuchi	.128
ISO	Yusei Kikuchi	.251
L	Kevin Gausman	10
OBP	Yusei Kikuchi	.353
SA	Yusei Kikuchi	.493
XV	Yusei Kikuchi	38

Overall Base Value Leaders (2022)

Team Rank	Player	BV [bat]	(-) BV [pitch]	(=) OBV
1	Alek Manoah	0	-87	87
2	George Springer	65	0	65
3	Vladimir Guerrero Jr.	55	0	55
3	Ross Stripling	0	-55	55
5	Bo Bichette	38	0	38
6	Danny Jansen	36	0	36
7	Matt Chapman	35	0	35
7	Jordan Romano	0	-35	35
9	Alejandro Kirk	34	0	34
10	Teoscar Hernandez	32	0	32

Fan Support in Past 10 Seasons (2013-2022)

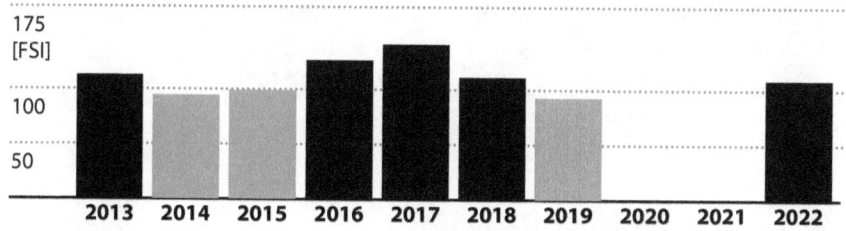

Year	Team	Attendance	W	Att:W	FSI
2013	Toronto Blue Jays	2,536,562	74	34,278	112.6
2014	Toronto Blue Jays	2,375,525	83	28,621	94.3
2015	Toronto Blue Jays	2,794,891	93	30,053	99.0
2016	Toronto Blue Jays	3,392,099	89	38,113	126.4
2017	Toronto Blue Jays	3,203,886	76	42,156	140.9
2018	Toronto Blue Jays	2,325,281	73	31,853	111.1
2019	Toronto Blue Jays	1,750,144	67	26,122	92.6
2022	Toronto Blue Jays	2,653,830	92	28,846	108.6

Extreme Games for Batters (2022)

Stat	Team Total	Individual Leader	G
3+ H	88	Bo Bichette	12
2+ HR	14	Bo Bichette	3
5+ RBI	6	Danny Jansen, Lourdes Gurriel Jr.	2
0 H in 5+ AB	38	Bo Bichette	8
4+ SO	8	Matt Chapman, Vladimir Guerrero Jr.	2

Extreme Games for Pitchers (2022)

Stat	Team Total	Individual Leader	G
0-2 ER in 7+ IP	20	Alek Manoah	9
10+ SO	6	Kevin Gausman	4
0 BR in SV	20	Jordan Romano	15
10+ BR	16	Jose Berrios	10
1+ ER in SV	2	Jordan Romano	2

Predictions for Coming Season (2023)

Group	Next W	Next L	Next Pct.	WS	LC	PQ
10 closest matches (avg. W-L)	87.0	74.9	.537	1	2	4
25 closest matches (avg. W-L)	83.9	69.8	.546	3	5	11
50 closest matches (avg. W-L)	81.4	69.0	.541	3	7	23

25 Closest Matches (2023)

Rank	Team	Next	W	L	Pct.	WS	LC	PQ
1	Pirates (2012-2014)	2015	98	64	.605	—	—	X
2	Pirates (1974-1976)	1977	96	66	.593	—	—	—
3	Yankees (1982-1984)	1985	97	64	.602	—	—	—
4	Reds (2011-2013)	2014	76	86	.469	—	—	—
5	Padres (2005-2007)	2008	63	99	.389	—	—	—
6	Cardinals (2008-2010)	2011	90	72	.556	X	X	X
7	Astros (1993-1995)	1996	82	80	.506	—	—	—
8	Astros (2002-2004)	2005	89	73	.549	—	X	X
9	Phillies (2004-2006)	2007	89	73	.549	—	—	X
10	Rays (2009-2011)	2012	90	72	.556	—	—	—
11	Angels (2003-2005)	2006	89	73	.549	—	—	—
12	Pirates (1976-1978)	1979	98	64	.605	X	X	X
13	Rays (2011-2013)	2014	77	85	.475	—	—	—
14	Astros (1979-1981)	1982	77	85	.475	—	—	—
15	Rays (2017-2019)	2020	40	20	.667	—	X	X
16	Dodgers (1994-1996)	1997	88	74	.543	—	—	—
17	Rangers (1976-1978)	1979	83	79	.512	—	—	—
18	Angels (2006-2008)	2009	97	65	.599	—	—	X
19	Royals (1974-1976)	1977	102	60	.630	—	—	X
20	White Sox (1989-1991)	1992	86	76	.531	—	—	—
21	Athletics (2017-2019)	2020	36	24	.600	—	—	X
22	Rockies (2008-2010)	2011	73	89	.451	—	—	—
23	Blue Jays (1982-1984)	1985	99	62	.615	—	—	X
24	Red Sox (2001-2003)	2004	98	64	.605	X	X	X
25	Red Sox (1997-1999)	2000	85	77	.525	—	—	—

WASHINGTON NATIONALS

Past 10 Seasons (2013-2022)

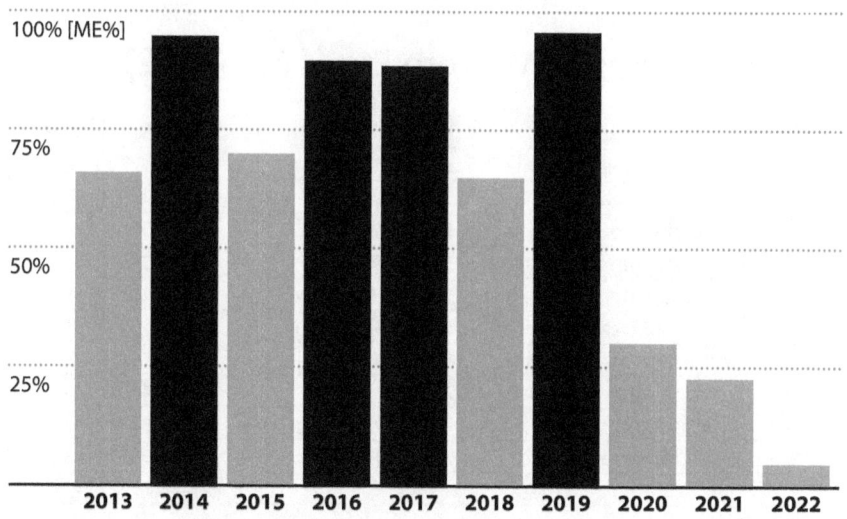

Year	Team	W	L	Pct.	Post	TS	ME%
2013	Washington Nationals	86	76	.531	—	53.619	65.9%
2014	Washington Nationals	96	66	.593	P	75.183	94.7%
2015	Washington Nationals	83	79	.512	—	55.244	69.9%
2016	Washington Nationals	95	67	.586	P	67.777	89.5%
2017	Washington Nationals	97	65	.599	P	66.906	88.4%
2018	Washington Nationals	82	80	.506	—	53.050	64.8%
2019	Washington Nationals	93	69	.574	WLP	76.595	95.6%
2020	Washington Nationals	26	34	.433	—	36.489	30.0%
2021	Washington Nationals	65	97	.401	—	32.604	22.5%
2022	Washington Nationals	55	107	.340	—	19.213	4.5%

Best Seasons of Modern Era (1969-2022)

Year	Team	W	L	Pct.	Post	TS	ME%
2019	Washington Nationals	93	69	.574	WLP	76.595	95.6%
1994	Montreal Expos	74	40	.649	—	75.628	95.1%
2014	Washington Nationals	96	66	.593	P	75.183	94.7%
2012	Washington Nationals	98	64	.605	P	67.836	89.5%
2016	Washington Nationals	95	67	.586	P	67.777	89.5%
2017	Washington Nationals	97	65	.599	P	66.906	88.4%
1979	Montreal Expos	95	65	.594	—	66.653	88.2%
1980	Montreal Expos	90	72	.556	—	61.171	80.5%
1982	Montreal Expos	86	76	.531	—	60.371	79.0%
1981	Montreal Expos	60	48	.556	P	59.895	78.2%

Worst Seasons of Modern Era (1969-2022)

Year	Team	W	L	Pct.	Post	TS	ME%
1969	Montreal Expos	52	110	.321	—	15.677	2.4%
1976	Montreal Expos	55	107	.340	—	16.785	2.8%
2008	Washington Nationals	59	102	.366	—	17.664	3.6%
2022	Washington Nationals	55	107	.340	—	19.213	4.5%
2009	Washington Nationals	59	103	.364	—	19.467	4.7%
2001	Montreal Expos	68	94	.420	—	23.109	8.1%
2000	Montreal Expos	67	95	.414	—	23.592	8.8%
2006	Washington Nationals	71	91	.438	—	26.483	12.6%
2007	Washington Nationals	73	89	.451	—	26.828	13.1%
1971	Montreal Expos	71	90	.441	—	26.965	13.3%

Season Breakdown (2022)

Category	W	L	Pct.	R	RA	R/G	RA/G
Overall record in 2022	55	107	.340	603	855	3.72	5.28
Home games	26	55	.321	297	430	3.67	5.31
Away games	29	52	.358	306	425	3.78	5.25
First half of 2022 season	29	52	.358	325	442	4.01	5.46
Second half of 2022 season	26	55	.321	278	413	3.43	5.10
Against first-place teams	12	23	.343	132	199	3.77	5.69
Against playoff teams	24	60	.286	289	471	3.44	5.61
Against non-playoff teams	31	47	.397	314	384	4.03	4.92

Season as Nine-Inning Game (2022)

Result	1	2	3	4	5	6	7	8	9	Total
Wins	6	6	7	6	5	6	6	8	5	55
Losses	12	12	11	12	13	12	12	10	13	107

Scoring by Game (2022)

Runs Scored	G	W	L	Pct.	R/G	RA/G
Overall record	162	55	107	.340	3.72	5.28
0	12	0	12	.000	0.00	6.92
1	26	2	24	.077	1.00	5.00
2	29	1	28	.034	2.00	5.79
3	28	10	18	.357	3.00	4.36
4	16	4	12	.250	4.00	6.38
5	16	7	9	.438	5.00	6.31
6	8	7	1	.875	6.00	3.63
7	11	8	3	.727	7.00	4.45
8	5	5	0	1.000	8.00	3.80
9	1	1	0	1.000	9.00	3.00
10 or more	10	10	0	1.000	11.70	4.90

Scoring Allowed by Game (2022)

Runs Allowed	G	W	L	Pct.	R/G	RA/G
Overall record	162	55	107	.340	3.72	5.28
0	4	4	0	1.000	2.75	0.00
1	12	12	0	1.000	4.50	1.00
2	16	10	6	.625	3.81	2.00
3	18	10	8	.556	4.33	3.00
4	19	7	12	.368	4.05	4.00
5	26	6	20	.231	3.46	5.00
6	15	4	11	.267	4.53	6.00
7	15	1	14	.067	3.27	7.00
8	14	1	13	.071	3.07	8.00
9	7	0	7	.000	4.29	9.00
10 or more	16	0	16	.000	2.63	11.31

Margins (2022)

Category	Margin	G	W	L	Pct.	GShr	WShr
Overall record	—	162	55	107	.340	—	—
Close	1 or 2 runs	64	27	37	.422	39.5%	49.1%
Medium	3 or 4 runs	40	9	31	.225	24.7%	16.4%
Distant	5 or more runs	58	19	39	.328	35.8%	34.5%

Individual Scoring Leaders (2022)

Team Rank	Batter	R	(+) RBI	(-) HR	(=) SC
1	Nelson Cruz	50	64	10	104
2	Cesar Hernandez	64	34	1	97
2	Lane Thomas	62	52	17	97
4	Josh Bell	52	57	14	95
5	Juan Soto	62	46	21	87
6	Victor Robles	42	33	6	69
7	Luis Garcia	29	45	7	67
8	Yadiel Hernandez	30	41	9	62
8	Keibert Ruiz	33	36	7	62
10	Maikel Franco	31	39	9	61

Team Ratings (2022)

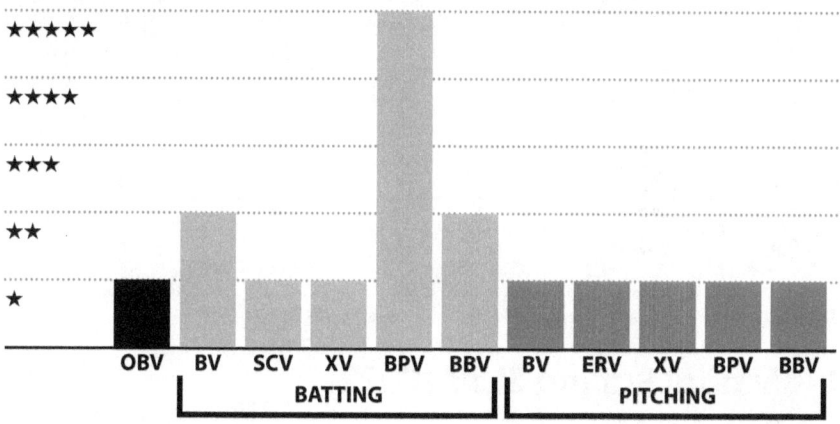

Quality	Type	Indicator	Value	Rating
Overall performance	Overall	OBV	-647	★
Base production	Batting	BV	-161	★★
Run production	Batting	SCV	-123	★
Power hitting	Batting	XV	-127	★
Contact hitting	Batting	BPV	136	★★★★★
Batting eye	Batting	BBV	-44	★★
Base prevention	Pitching	BV	486	★
Run prevention	Pitching	ERV	163	★
Power prevention	Pitching	XV	189	★
Strikeout pitching	Pitching	BPV	159	★
Control pitching	Pitching	BBV	54	★

Team Batting Stats (2022)

Stat	Number	Div Rank	Lg Rank	MLB Rank	MLB Best
R	603	4	13	26	847 (Dodgers)
H	1,351	4	7	12	1,464 (Blue Jays)
HR	136	5	15	28	254 (Yankees)
BPO	.623	4	12	25	.764 (Dodgers)
BA	.249	4	7	11	.264 (Blue Jays)
OBP	.310	4	11	19	.333 (Dodgers)
SA	.377	4	12	24	.443 (Braves)

Division: NL East, 5 teams. **League:** National, 15 teams. **MLB:** 30 teams.

Team Pitching Stats (2022)

Stat	Number	Div Rank	Lg Rank	MLB Rank	MLB Best
ERA	5.00	5	14	29	2.80 (Dodgers)
SO	1,220	5	12	23	1,565 (Mets)
BB	558	5	13	26	384 (Rays)
BPO	.774	5	15	30	.551 (Astros)
BA	.266	5	14	28	.209 (Dodgers)
OBP	.339	5	14	28	.273 (Dodgers)
SA	.452	5	15	30	.332 (Astros)

Division: NL East, 5 teams. **League:** National, 15 teams. **MLB:** 30 teams.

Individual Batting Stats (2022)

Batter	PA	BPO	BA	OBP	SA	ISO	CT	EY
Josh Bell	437	.851	.301	.384	.493	.192	.837	.104
Nelson Cruz	507	.583	.234	.313	.337	.103	.734	.095
Maikel Franco	388	.472	.229	.255	.342	.113	.798	.031
Luis Garcia	377	.607	.275	.295	.408	.133	.767	.027
Cesar Hernandez	617	.558	.248	.311	.318	.070	.796	.073
Yadiel Hernandez	327	.634	.269	.312	.410	.141	.757	.058
Victor Robles	407	.556	.224	.273	.311	.087	.716	.042
Keibert Ruiz	433	.607	.251	.313	.360	.109	.873	.069
Juan Soto	436	.982	.246	.408	.485	.240	.819	.201
Lane Thomas	548	.656	.241	.301	.404	.163	.735	.075

Individual Pitching Stats for Starters (2022)

Pitcher	IP	BPO	ERA	BA	SA	ISO	CT	EY
Patrick Corbin	152.2	.876	6.31	.321	.513	.192	.805	.067
Paolo Espino	113.1	.765	4.84	.287	.493	.206	.798	.049
Erick Fedde	127.0	.843	5.81	.293	.470	.177	.815	.101
Josiah Gray	148.2	.821	5.02	.239	.489	.250	.729	.100

Individual Pitching Stats for Relievers (2022)

Pitcher	GR	BPO	ERA	BA	SA	ISO	CT	EY
Victor Arano	43	.702	4.50	.278	.408	.130	.740	.064
Steve Cishek	69	.707	4.21	.223	.380	.157	.694	.091
Carl Edwards Jr.	57	.592	2.76	.224	.351	.127	.754	.098
Kyle Finnegan	66	.611	3.51	.221	.381	.160	.713	.075
Andres Machado	51	.735	3.34	.241	.404	.162	.798	.100
Erasmo Ramirez	58	.579	2.92	.245	.390	.146	.811	.038

Best Stats on Team (2022)

Stat	Batter	Number
2B	Cesar Hernandez	28
3B	Cesar Hernandez	4
BA	Josh Bell	.301
BB	Juan Soto	91
BBV	Juan Soto	53
BPO	Juan Soto	.982
BPV	Keibert Ruiz	48
BV	Juan Soto	87
CT	Keibert Ruiz	.873
EY	Juan Soto	.201
H	Cesar Hernandez	139
HR	Juan Soto	21
ISO	Juan Soto	.240
OBP	Juan Soto	.408
R	Cesar Hernandez	64
RBI	Nelson Cruz	64
SA	Josh Bell	.493
SB	Victor Robles	15
SC	Nelson Cruz	104
SCV	Josh Bell	10
SE	Josh Bell	.217
XV	Juan Soto	30

Stat	Pitcher	Number
BA	Josiah Gray	.239
BBV	Paolo Espino	-15
BPO-R	Erasmo Ramirez	.579
BPO-S	Paolo Espino	.765
BPV	Steve Cishek	-14
BV	Erasmo Ramirez	-21
CT	Josiah Gray	.729
ERA-R	Carl Edwards Jr.	2.76
ERA-S	Paolo Espino	4.84
ERV	Erasmo Ramirez	-10
EY	Paolo Espino	.049
GR	Steve Cishek	69
GS	Patrick Corbin	31
IP	Patrick Corbin	152.2
ISO	Erick Fedde	.177
OBP	Paolo Espino	.322
SA	Erick Fedde	.470
SO	Josiah Gray	154
SV	Tanner Rainey	12
W	Josiah Gray	7
XV	Hunter Harvey	-7

Worst Stats on Team (2022)

Stat	Batter	Number
BA	Victor Robles	.224
BBV	Luis Garcia	-20
BPO	Maikel Franco	.472
BPV	Luke Voit	-19
BV	Maikel Franco	-58
CT	Victor Robles	.716
EY	Luis Garcia	.027
ISO	Cesar Hernandez	.070
OBP	Maikel Franco	.255
SA	Victor Robles	.311
SCV	Cesar Hernandez	-23
SE	Keibert Ruiz	.143
SO	Lane Thomas	132
XV	Cesar Hernandez	-46

Stat	Pitcher	Number
BA	Patrick Corbin	.321
BB	Josiah Gray	66
BBV	Joan Adon, Josiah Gray	14
BPO-R	Andres Machado	.735
BPO-S	Patrick Corbin	.876
BPV	Patrick Corbin	36
BV	Patrick Corbin	100
CT	Erick Fedde	.815
ERA-R	Victor Arano	4.50
ERA-S	Patrick Corbin	6.31
ERV	Patrick Corbin	40
EY	Erick Fedde	.101
ISO	Josiah Gray	.250
L	Patrick Corbin	19
OBP	Patrick Corbin	.374
SA	Patrick Corbin	.513
XV	Josiah Gray	55

Overall Base Value Leaders (2022)

Team Rank	Player	BV [bat]	(-) BV [pitch]	(=) OBV
1	Juan Soto	87	0	87
2	Josh Bell	55	0	55
3	Joey Meneses	35	0	35
4	Erasmo Ramirez	0	-21	21
5	Carl Edwards Jr.	0	-12	12
6	Kyle Finnegan	0	-10	10
7	Sean Doolittle	0	-9	9
7	Hunter Harvey	0	-9	9
9	Mason Thompson	0	-8	8
10	Alex Call	7	0	7

Fan Support in Past 10 Seasons (2013-2022)

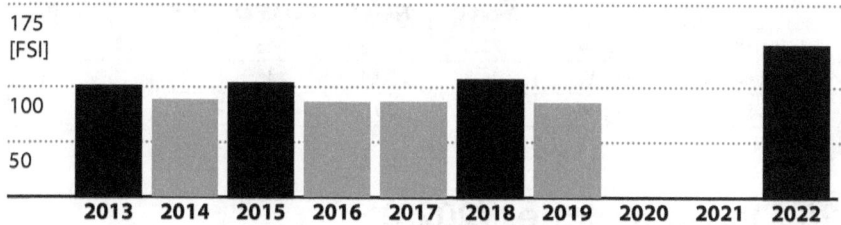

Year	Team	Attendance	W	Att:W	FSI
2013	Washington Nationals	2,652,422	86	30,842	101.3
2014	Washington Nationals	2,579,389	96	26,869	88.5
2015	Washington Nationals	2,619,843	83	31,564	103.9
2016	Washington Nationals	2,481,938	95	26,126	86.7
2017	Washington Nationals	2,524,980	97	26,031	87.0
2018	Washington Nationals	2,529,604	82	30,849	107.6
2019	Washington Nationals	2,259,781	93	24,299	86.2
2022	Washington Nationals	2,026,401	55	36,844	138.7

Extreme Games for Batters (2022)

Stat	Team Total	Individual Leader	G
3+ H	70	Cesar Hernandez, Josh Bell	8
2+ HR	4	Josh Bell, Juan Soto, Keibert Ruiz, Lane Thomas	1
5+ RBI	5	Alex Call, Luis Garcia, Maikel Franco, Victor Robles, Yadiel Hernandez	1
0 H in 5+ AB	27	Cesar Hernandez	7
4+ SO	7	Lane Thomas	4

Extreme Games for Pitchers (2022)

Stat	Team Total	Individual Leader	G
0-2 ER in 7+ IP	7	Patrick Corbin	3
10+ SO	4	Josiah Gray	3
0 BR in SV	10	Kyle Finnegan	7
10+ BR	40	Patrick Corbin	12
1+ ER in SV	1	Tanner Rainey	1

Predictions for Coming Season (2023)

Group	Next W	Next L	Next Pct.	WS	LC	PQ
10 closest matches (avg. W-L)	72.5	89.4	.448	0	0	0
25 closest matches (avg. W-L)	71.2	88.4	.446	0	0	1
50 closest matches (avg. W-L)	69.5	89.8	.436	0	0	2

25 Closest Matches (2023)

Rank	Team	Next	W	L	Pct.	WS	LC	PQ
1	Marlins (2011-2013)	2014	77	85	.475	—	—	—
2	Cubs (2010-2012)	2013	66	96	.407	—	—	—
3	Rockies (2003-2005)	2006	76	86	.469	—	—	—
4	Astros (1989-1991)	1992	81	81	.500	—	—	—
5	Pirates (1993-1995)	1996	73	89	.451	—	—	—
6	Mariners (1984-1986)	1987	78	84	.481	—	—	—
7	Pirates (2004-2006)	2007	68	94	.420	—	—	—
8	Padres (1979-1981)	1982	81	81	.500	—	—	—
9	Phillies (2013-2015)	2016	71	91	.438	—	—	—
10	Orioles (1985-1987)	1988	54	107	.335	—	—	—
11	Indians (1983-1985)	1986	84	78	.519	—	—	—
12	White Sox (1974-1976)	1977	90	72	.556	—	—	—
13	Pirates (1999-2001)	2002	72	89	.447	—	—	—
14	Yankees (1988-1990)	1991	71	91	.438	—	—	—
15	Royals (2007-2009)	2010	67	95	.414	—	—	—
16	Tigers (2000-2002)	2003	43	119	.265	—	—	—
17	Braves (1975-1977)	1978	69	93	.426	—	—	—
18	Orioles (2007-2009)	2010	66	96	.407	—	—	—
19	Twins (1997-1999)	2000	69	93	.426	—	—	—
20	Giants (1994-1996)	1997	90	72	.556	—	—	X
21	Brewers (2000-2002)	2003	68	94	.420	—	—	—
22	Expos (1974-1976)	1977	75	87	.463	—	—	—
23	Mariners (1981-1983)	1984	74	88	.457	—	—	—
24	Cubs (1978-1980)	1981	38	65	.369	—	—	—
25	Twins (1993-1995)	1996	78	84	.481	—	—	—

www.ingramcontent.com/pod-product-compliance
Lightning Source LLC
Chambersburg PA
CBHW020937180426
43194CB00038B/210